FOURTH EDITION

Elementary Classroom Management

C. M. Charles

(Emeritus) San Diego State University

Gail W. Senter

California State University San Marcos

PEARSON

Boston ■ New York ■ San Francisco
Mexico City ■ Montreal ■ Toronto ■ London ■ Madrid ■ Munich ■ Paris
Hong Kong ■ Singapore ■ Tokyo ■ Cape Town ■ Sydney

Senior Editor: *Arnis E. Burvikovs*
Editorial Assistant: *Megan Smallidge*
Marketing Manager: *Tara Whorf*
Production Administrator: *Michael Granger*
Editorial-Production Service: *Omegatype Typography, Inc.*
Composition Buyer: *Linda Cox*
Manufacturing Buyer: *Andrew Turso*
Cover Administrator: *Joel Gendron*
Electronic Composition: *Omegatype Typography, Inc.*

For related titles and support materials, visit our online catalog at www.ablongman.com.

Between the time Website information is gathered and published, some sites may have closed. Also, the transcription of URLs can result in typographical errors. The publisher would appreciate notification where these errors occur so that they may be corrected in subsequent editions.

Library of Congress Cataloging-in-Publication Data

Charles, C. M.
    Elementary classroom management / C. M. Charles, Gail W. Senter.—4th ed.
      p. cm.
    Senter's name appears first on previous ed.
    Includes bibliographical references and index.
    ISBN 0-205-41266-1 (alk. paper)
      1. Classroom management. 2. Education, Elementary. I. Senter, Gail W. II. Title.

  LB3013.C465 2005
  371.102'4—dc22

                                           2003070683

Printed in the United States of America

10 9 8 7 6 5 4 3 2 1   09 08 07 06 05 04

CONTENTS

8 Managing Special Groups   136

P R E F A C E

The Purpose of This Book

This fourth edition of *Elementary Classroom Management* once again focuses on the improvement of instruction and learning through good classroom management. Classroom management, when done well, helps establish learning environments and instructional programs that are well organized and efficient, in which communication is good, and in which teachers, students, and others are considerate of each other and dedicated to learning. As teachers improve their skills in classroom management, they find that students also become more cooperative, make responsible choices, and happily engage in learning activities.

Relating This Book to Standards for Teachers

In recent years, new standards of teacher preparation and performance have been set forth by a number of agencies. The purpose of these standards is to help guide the development of new teachers, help in-service teachers improve their performance, and assess both teacher preparation and teacher performance. This book discusses the many subjects—complete with examples, recommendations for additional sources, and quotations from highly experienced teachers—that apply to these standards. Notable efforts include the Interstate New Teacher Assessment and Support Consortium standards (INTASC), the Praxis series of tests, the National Board for Professional Teaching Standards (NBPTS), and the National Council for Accreditation of Teacher Education (NCATE). They are described briefly in the paragraphs that follow. A list of the standards and their chapter coverages appears on pages xviii–xx.

INTASC Standards

The Interstate New Teacher Assessment and Support Consortium (INTASC) has worked diligently to set forth standards teachers should meet in order to be licensed to teach in public schools. The consortium is composed of more than thirty states that have developed standards and assessment processes for initial teacher certification. The INTASC core standards are based on ten principles of effective teaching, for all subjects and grade levels. The principles focus on effective integration of content knowledge and pedagogical understanding—knowledge of how to teach (Interstate New Teacher Assesssment and Support Consortium, 2003).

Praxis Series

The Praxis Series is a series of assessments for beginning teachers. Developed and disseminated by the Educational Testing Service (ETS), the Praxis Series assesses academic skills, subject knowledge, and classroom performance during the early stages of a beginning teacher's career, from entry into teacher education to the first year of teaching. Praxis I measures basic skills in reading, writing, and mathematics and may be used as an admission tool for teacher education programs. Praxis II measures prospective teachers' knowledge of the subjects they will teach as well as pedagogical skills and knowledge. It includes tests on principles of learning and teaching, specific subject assessments, and multiple subject assessments. Praxis III measures the classroom performance of beginning teachers. It includes instructional planning and teaching, classroom management, and student assessment, and may be used as a licensure tool.

Several states have worked to align the INTASC principles and the Praxis criteria. One such example was developed by the Utah State Department of Education (2003).

NBPTS Standards

The National Board for Professional Teaching Standards (NBPTS) is an organization that has established standards for highly accomplished teaching, as seen in the National Board's central policy statement, *What Teachers Should Know and Be Able to Do*. NBPTS has developed five core propositions on which voluntary national teacher certification is based (National Board for Professional Teaching Standards, 2003).

NBPTS issues professional certificates to teachers who possess extensive professional knowledge and the ability to perform at a high level. Certification candidates submit a portfolio including videotapes of classroom interactions, samples of student work, and the teacher's reflective comments. Trained NBPTS evaluators who teach in the same field as the candidate judge all elements of the assessments.

NCATE Standards

The National Council for Accreditation of Teacher Education (NCATE) is an accrediting agency that serves many institutions with programs in teacher education. The Council has set six criteria of prospective teacher performance in a context of professional and liberal arts studies. Although NCATE standards apply to teacher preparation programs, not to teacher education students per se, NCATE believes that the new professional teachers who graduate from accredited schools, colleges, or departments of education should be able to meet the criteria (National Council for Accreditation of Teacher Education, 2002).

Chapter Topics and Contents

This fourth edition of *Elementary Classroom Management* retains most of the chapters from previous editions and **adds a new section on how teachers (and others) can manage the emotions of stress caused by unexpected or traumatic events.** In addition, it emphasizes matters such as curriculum standards and testing, curriculum mapping, backward design planning, differentiated instruction for teaching all learners, classbuilding and teambuilding, multi-age and looped classes, cooperative learning, authentic assessment, student-led conferences, and the use of technology, including adaptive technology for children with special needs.

The chapter topics have been sequenced in an order that the authors believe best corresponds to the development of good management skills. It is not essential that the skills be learned in the order listed. Discussions are embedded in each chapter for a variety of management concerns, and commentary and suggestions from a number of expert teachers are included to illustrate how those teachers have implemented certain management techniques.

Chapter 1 deals with the nature of classroom management.

Chapter 2 shows how to plan out instructional days and the entire school year.

Chapter 3 describes how to organize and manage the physical environment of the classroom.

Chapter 4 explains how to establish and maintain a positive psychosocial environment in the classroom.

Chapter 5 explores human motivation and motivation management.

Chapter 6 describes effective ways of organizing, differentiating, and presenting instruction.

Chapter 7 provides suggestions for managing students during work time.

Chapter 8 describes the natures and special needs of diverse groups of students.

Chapter 9 explains how to prevent and deal with disruptive student behavior.

Chapter 10 provides detailed suggestions concerning assessment, record keeping, and reporting.

Chapter 11 explains how to establish and maintain good communication with students, caregivers, and others.

Chapter 12 suggests procedures for managing the work of paraprofessionals, substitutes, and student teachers.

Chapter 13 suggests how to deal with emotions of stress that result from unexpected or disastrous events, and stress that is related to work.

Chapter 14 presents a resource guide for expanding horizons and opportunities for teachers.

Management Knowledge
from Research and Experience

A strong body of academic material related to classroom management provides the basis for many of the observations and suggestions presented in this book. In addition, experience from highly qualified teachers is included to provide the professional practitioner's perspective. Works of special importance in classroom management are cited within chapters and presented at the ends of chapters.

Help to Readers

The text is written in an informal, inviting tone to make information accessible for readers. Each chapter begins with an Anticipation–Reaction Guide. By responding in the column labeled Anticipation before reading the chapter, readers are able to record what they know, don't know, think they know, or assume about the chapter topics. After reading the chapter they can reflect on their earlier responses by responding to the same statements in the Reaction column. Reflective discussions can be organized for use in class, based on these statements and reader responses. Examples and contributions from highly qualified teachers are used throughout the chapters for clarification or illustration. To help readers strengthen their learning and acquire a sense of progressive accomplishments, checklists, practice applications, and discussion questions are included at the ends of chapters.

Help to Instructors

Included in the Instructor's Manual that accompanies the text are the following to help instructors manage the course or topics effectively and efficiently: suggestions for introducing the textbook to students; course organization options, including both goals and calendar suggestions; additional end-of-chapter activities; and evaluation procedures and expectations. The manual also includes a number of templates you can use to make overhead transparencies for use in class presentations and discussions. They have been reduced to the size of this manual and presented on single pages to facilitate duplication on copy machines. Permission is granted to reproduce the templates for classroom use.

In light of current reform efforts to teacher preparation and performance and the No Child Left Behind Act, both the text and the Instructor's Manual include a quick guide to the chapters in the text where you will find reference to these current standards: the Interstate New Teacher Assessment and Support Consortium (INTASC) standards, the Praxis series of tests, The National Board for Professional Teaching Standards (NBPTS), and The National Council for Accreditation of Teacher Education (NCATE).

Additionally, a new classroom management video, with classroom vignettes that can be used as visual prompts for discussion of the text, is available to adopters by contacting their local Allyn and Bacon representatives.

Acknowledgments

Teacher Contributors

The fine teachers whose contributions are featured in various chapters include Gloria Anderson, Kim Anderson, Eileen Andreoli, Jearine Bacon, Kay Ballantyne, Frank Barnes, Janet Beyea, Scott Boyens, Mary Brewer, Dyanna Burak, Bernardo Campos, Della Casteñeda, Ruth Charles, Tim Charles, Sherry Coburn, Debbie Comer, Keith Correll, Marilyn Cox, Rebecca Cumming, Elizabeth Davies, Ginger DeNigro, Hollie Foster, Stacy Ganzer, Devora Garrison, Jennifer George, Jan Gretlein, Lynne Harvey, Carolyn Haslett, Ellen Hodgers, Beth Johnson, Lisa Johnston, Rose Mary Johnston, Pam Klevesahl, Kathryn Krainock, Ginny Lorenz, Cathy McCloud, Cynthia McDermott, Carol Mercer, Janet Mulder, Karen O'Connor, Patti Petersen, Roberta Revetta, Charlotte Rodzach, Ronda Royal, Jamie Ruben, Karen Runyon, Nancy Rutherford, Rebecca Santibanez, Ted Saulino, David Sisk, and Candace Young.

Professional Analysts

The quality of any textbook is heavily dependent on critical analyses and suggestions made by knowledgeable experts. Among the professionals whose suggestions have helped improve this book are the following, to whom the authors express their sincere gratitude: Margaret Cochran; Gregory Childs; Leslie Fadem; Bruce Frazee, Trinity University; Dr. C. Bobbi Hansen, University of San Diego; Dr. Spencer Kagan; Dr. Robin Kellogg, Chapman University; Marvin Lynn, University of Maryland; Dr. Donald Mass, California Polytechnic State University; Juanita Moore, University of Portland; Gabriela Sonntag; Dr. Jacqueline Thousand, California State University San Marcos; Joyce A. Van Pelt, Somerset Community College; Dr. Kimberly Woo, California State University San Marcos.

The authors also gratefully acknowledge the assistance provided by Arnis Burvikovs, Editor at Allyn and Bacon, and Christine Lyons, Editorial Assistant at Allyn and Bacon.

On this journey
You will encounter all different paths;
paths of hardships,
paths of beauty,
paths of trial,
and paths of error.
You may get lost,
but if you give up,
you will not reach your destination.
If you did not want to reach your destination,
why did you begin the journey?
Be strong.
Keep faith.
The journey,
you know in your heart,
is worth it.

Written by Dyanna Burak during teacher training.
Dyanna is now a second-grade teacher.

INTASC Standards

INTASC stands for Interstate New Teacher Assessment and Support Consortium (see www.ccsso.org/Projects/interstate_new_teacher_assessment_and_support_consortium/780.cfm). This consortium, which consists of more than thirty states that have developed standards and assessment procedures for initial teacher certification, has issued licensing standards that should be met in order to teach in public schools. The INTASC core standards are based on ten principles of effective teaching, which focus on integration of content knowledge and pedagogical understanding.

INTASC Standards	Chapter Coverage
1. **Knowledge of Subject Matter** The teacher understands the central concepts, tools of inquiry, and structures of the subject being taught and can create learning experiences that make these aspects of subject matter meaningful for students.	2, 6, 8
2. **Knowledge of Human Development and Learning** The teacher understands how children learn and develop, and can provide learning opportunities that support their intellectual, social, and personal development.	4, 5, 8, 9
3. **Adapting Instruction for Individual Needs** The teacher understands how students differ in their approaches to learning and creates instructional opportunities that are adapted to diverse learners.	3, 6, 8
4. **Multiple Instructional Strategies** The teacher uses various instructional strategies to encourage students' development of critical thinking, problem solving, and performance skills.	6, 8
5. **Classroom Motivation and Management** The teacher uses an understanding of individual and group motivation and behavior to create a learning environment that encourages positive social interaction, active engagement in learning, and self-motivation.	5, 9
6. **Communication Skills** The teacher uses knowledge of effective verbal, nonverbal, and media communication techniques to foster active inquiry, collaboration, and supportive interaction in the classroom.	4, 11, 12, 13
7. **Instructional Planning Skills** The teacher plans instruction based on knowledge of subject matter, students, the community, and curriculum guides.	2, 6, 7
8. **Assessment of Student Learning** The teacher understands and uses formal and informal assessment strategies to evaluate and ensure the continuous intellectual, social, and physical development of the learner.	10
9. **Professional Commitment** The teacher is a reflective practitioner who continually evaluates the effects of his or her choices and actions on others (students, parents, and other professionals in the learning community) and who actively seeks out opportunities to grow professionally.	11, 12, 13, Appendixes
10. **Partnerships** The teacher fosters relationships with school colleagues, parents, and agencies in the larger community to support students' learning and well being.	11, 12

Praxis Series

The Praxis Series is a series of tests developed and disseminated by the Educational Testing Service (ETS) for assessing skills and knowledge of each stage of a beginning teacher's career, from entry into teacher education to actual classroom performance. It measures basic skills in reading, writing, and mathematics, as well as professional education and subject matter knowledge. Teaching skills measured include instructional planning, teaching, classroom management, and assessment of student learning.

Praxis I assesses reading, writing, and mathematics skills and may be used for admission to a teacher education program.

Praxis II measures prospective teachers' knowledge of the teaching and learning process and the subjects they will teach. It includes tests on Principles of Learning and Teaching, specific subject assessments, and multiple subject assessments.

Praxis III focuses on classroom performance assessment and is usually taken by teachers in their first year of teaching.

Several states have worked to align the INTASC principles and the Praxis criteria. To see one such example from the Utah State Department of Education, consult the following website: www.ed.utah.edu/TandL/NCATE/correlationINTASC-PRAXIS.pdf.

Praxis Standards	Chapter Coverage
1. **Planning and Preparation** ■ Demonstrating knowledge of students ■ Selecting instructional goals ■ Demonstrating knowledge of resources ■ Designing coherent instruction	2, 6, 7
2. **The Classroom Environment** ■ Creating an environment of respect and rapport ■ Establishing a culture for learning ■ Managing classroom procedures ■ Managing student behavior ■ Organizing physical space	3, 4, 9, 13
3. **Instruction** ■ Communicating clearly and accurately ■ Using questioning and discussion techniques ■ Engaging students in learning ■ Providing feedback to students ■ Demonstrating flexibility and responsiveness	5, 6, 7, 8, 13
4. **Professional Responsibilities** ■ Reflecting on teaching ■ Maintaining accurate records ■ Communicating with families ■ Contributing to the school and district ■ Growing and developing professionally	10, 11, 12, Appendixes

NBPTS Standards

The National Board for Professional Teaching Standards (NBPTS) has established standards for highly accomplished teaching, which are outlined in the board's central policy statement, *What Teachers Should Know and Be Able to Do.* NBPTS has based voluntary national certification standards on five core propositions (see http://nbrc.stanford.edu/align/standards.html).

This board issues professional certificates to master teachers—those with vast professional knowledge and highly developed teaching skills. A certification candidate submits a portfolio that includes videotapes of classroom interactions, samples of student work, and the candidate's comments.

NBPTS Standards	Chapter Coverage
1. Teachers are committed to students and their learning.	4, 8, 13
2. Teachers know the subjects they teach and how to teach those subjects to students.	5, 6, 7
3. Teachers are responsible for managing and monitoring student learning.	3, 6, 8, 9
4. Teachers think systematically about their practice and learn from experience.	2, 10
5. Teachers are members of learning communities.	11, 12, Appendixes

NCATE Standards

The National Council for Accreditation of Teacher Education (NCATE) is an accrediting agency that provides guidance to many teacher preparation programs. The Council has set six criteria of prospective teacher performance in professional and liberal arts studies. Although NCATE standards apply to programs, not to individual teacher education students, NCATE believes that the new professional teacher who graduates from an accredited teacher preparation program should be able to meet the criteria (see www.ncate.org/standard/m_stds.htm).

NCATE Standards	Chapter Coverage
Help all pre-kindergarten through twelfth grade (P–12) students learn.	2, 5, 6, 8, 9
Teach to P–12 student standards set by specialized professional associations and the states.	Appendixes
Explain instructional choices based on research-derived knowledge and best practice.	6
Apply effective methods of teaching students who are at different developmental stages, have different learning styles, and come from diverse backgrounds.	3, 4, 5, 7, 8, 9
Reflect on practice, act on feedback, and integrate technology into instruction effectively.	10, 11, 12

1

Classroom Management: Problems and Promises

You make the path when you walk.

—Loosely translated from Spanish poet Antonio Machado

ANTICIPATION–REACTION GUIDE

Before you read the chapter, take a moment to put a check mark in the Anticipation column next to any statement with which you agree.

	Anticipation	Reaction
The main purpose of classroom management is efficiency and effectiveness in teaching.	❏	❏
The *psychosocial environment* refers to class parties and other social events that occur in the classroom.	❏	❏
Feedback is a term used to indicate student responses to a teacher's questions.	❏	❏
When new teachers fail in their jobs, most often it is because their management skills are fine but their content knowledge is weak.	❏	❏
The Cardinal Principles mainly have to do with how teachers should organize and present lessons.	❏	❏
Three fundamental questions in education are: What should students learn? How do they learn? and How should they be taught?	❏	❏
It is suggested that students begin each day with a quiet activity.	❏	❏
The term *monitor* is used to indicate a student who helps with chores in the classroom.	❏	❏
Lesson management, unlike other management chores, requires ongoing attention.	❏	❏
In addition to their classroom responsibilities, teachers are expected to handle extracurricular duties.	❏	❏

This book is about managing the elementary classroom. It explores selected skills of management that lead toward artistry in teaching and pleasure in learning. These skills, among the most important you will encounter in all of teaching, can be taught and learned but rarely occur naturally and thus cannot be taken for granted. Some can be acquired quickly, while others are built up over time. Beginning teachers, in particular, often struggle because their management skills have not yet developed adequately. Such was the case for Janna Smart, a promising new teacher who found that teaching involved considerably more than she had anticipated.

A Modern Parable: The Beginner

Janna Smart decided to follow in the footsteps of her mother, Mercedes Bright, who had taught school when Janna was growing up. Many of Janna's teachers were friends of her mother. While Janna did homework, her mother worked on her own schoolwork—grading papers, planning lessons, and preparing materials. Sometimes Janna followed the directions for a project so Mercedes could check that they were clear enough for her students. Later Janna enjoyed seeing the children's finished work. She often listened when Mercedes spoke with her friends about school, their work, and the children they taught. Thus it was little surprise that when Janna earned her Bachelor of Arts degree, she continued for an additional fifth year to earn her elementary teaching credential.

During the summer following her certification, Janna was called to three interviews. However, it wasn't until mid-September, after school had been in session for two weeks, that Janna was offered a position as a teacher for first and second graders. Because her district supported smaller classes for primary grades, her class had only seventeen students. She accepted the position without hesitation.

Janna knew she was qualified. In addition to all the hours she had volunteered in her mother's classroom, Janna had worked hard and seriously while she was in school. She completed her teacher-training program with honors, and in doing so attracted attention. One professor called her a natural. Both of her cooperating teachers in student teaching ranked her a very strong teacher candidate. Her fellow students often came to her for ideas and support because of her resourcefulness and ability to gather materials for good units. Because she liked children and felt they responded well to her, she felt very comfortable about teaching. For Janna, as for her mother before her, all the pieces seemed to fall into place.

Janna was hired on Thursday morning and would first meet her students the following Monday; she had only three and one half days to prepare! Over the weekend she reviewed the curriculum and standards for both the first and second grades and planned activities that would help everyone get acquainted. Luckily, some of her friends helped with her room. They made attractive bulletin boards and an inviting art exhibit with a related project based on autumn leaves. They made a reading center with large, colorful pillows. They put the several computers in different spots about the room. They created a nature center with some plants, an aquarium of guppies and snails, and a cage with two hamsters, food and water dishes, tunnels, and places for the hamsters to nest.

When her students, along with some parents, arrived on Monday morning, Janna was nervous, but she greeted them all warmly. The students were quite well behaved, although they were a little uneasy and reserved. She taught them how to enter the room in a polite and orderly manner. She told them about herself, and she learned everyone's name by playing a memory game. At the end of the day, Janna felt that she had made a good beginning.

She was confident that the second day would be even better, but to her dismay things did not go perfectly. Some of the students remembered how to enter the room as she had taught them, but most did not. It took her much longer than expected to get them settled. As the day went on, those who had at first been cooperative became slow to follow directions. When she tried to work with the first graders on their curriculum, the second graders fooled around. That made her uneasy, and when some began showing disrespect, it hurt her feelings.

By the third morning, Janna was struggling. She had several confrontations with students who talked, called out, wandered out of their seats, would not pay attention, sharpened pencils needlessly, and asked repeatedly to go to the restroom. When dismissed for recess, three boys raced out the room and down the corridor. As the day progressed, almost every child had splashed in the aquarium, and it seemed they simply could not leave the hamsters alone.

The fourth day moved toward chaos. Every boy seemed bent on snatching another's paper, and every girl on tattling. No one seemed at all willing to listen to Janna or do as she requested. When Janna worked with the second graders, the first graders played or wandered around the room. When assigned seatwork had been completed (or not completed, or completed incorrectly, or messed up impossibly), students shouted, waved their arms, and annoyed the few who still were trying to work. Many seemed never to have heard of standards of human decency, much less of classroom behavior. Janna's efforts to plan for two grades and the curricular expectations for each only added to her struggles.

By the fifth day, Janna began to despair. Students now blatantly broke rules and seemed unaffected by her kindest, most sincere counseling. It was not so much that they were cruel or hostile toward her—they simply disregarded her, and clowned, giggled, fussed, fought, and shouted. She was frustrated with the double curricula and the broad ranges of age and maturity within the two grades.

Other surprises caught Janna off-guard as well. On Wednesday, two mothers stayed to help in the room, but because Janna didn't know what to have them do, they spent the day watching her sweat and struggle. On Thursday, a child with learning disabilities was brought in to be included in her room. The student called out incessantly and made noises, which the other students found bizarre and delightedly mimicked. Two new girls arrived on Friday; one spoke little English, and the other spoke none at all. One of them vomited during the math lesson, which made everyone laugh. Unable to get the class back into the lesson, Janna shouted at the students about being cruel and inconsiderate and made them put their heads down on their desks.

These events almost obscured the fact that, by Friday, a third of the scissors had disappeared; the computers were making distracting noises; all of the guppies were dead, evidently killed by something put in the water; and no one knew where to find one of the hamsters that was missing from its cage. That afternoon a parent confronted her, swearing and complaining that her son was being bullied on the playground and demanding that Janna put a stop to it. Two boys got in a fight and ruined a new shirt, and Janna was called to the phone after school and was reprimanded by another parent about the cost of shirts and her lack of control. She also received a note in her mailbox informing her that her support provider, an experienced teacher assigned by the district's Beginning Teacher Support Assistance program to work with Janna during her first year, intended to visit her classroom the following week.

Janna dragged herself home, her spirits crushed and her mind in turmoil. She now doubted that she would ever get those six-, seven-, and eight-year-olds to learn, much less behave like civilized boys and girls. She cried for two hours and seriously contemplated moving to Australia, before she called a friend. They went out to a coffeehouse, and Janna talked and cried some more. That took her mind off escaping to Australia, however, and by the next morning she found a trace of determination returning.

During the night she had faced the fact that most of the problems had to do with three things: her own instruction, her curriculum planning and organization, and her ability to manage the class.

Previously she had been confident with her own ability to instruct. Now she knew her lessons were not running smoothly. Some were too long, some too short, and most too difficult. Though interesting to Janna, some were obviously boring the students. She could see why they might lose interest and look for something more stimulating. In addition, the two grade levels of curricula and standards only added to her challenge.

She realized, too, that she was having trouble monitoring seatwork while she worked with one grade or the other and with small groups. Students, often several at a time, were forever coming up to her with questions, usually about what she had carefully explained only minutes before. Also, she noticed that most anything would take the students off-task, and she could hardly get them back.

While at her university, she remembered hearing about using technology in the classroom, about curriculum standards, and about teacher and student rights. She realized now how little she knew about technology. While she was aware of the standards in general, she was not overly familiar with the specific standards for first and second grades. She also realized that she knew little about the rights and responsibilities that applied to her situation and her students. She knew that English language learners and students with special needs had rights that would affect her decisions and ability to include them in her class and instruct them so they could be successful.

On Saturday morning she made three phone calls—one to her mother, one to a teacher who had been at the school a few years, and the third to her support provider. With all three she swallowed her pride and confessed her difficulties. She learned that her experiences were hardly unusual and she accepted a number of suggestions for redoing the operation of her classroom. She went to school that afternoon and there, in the calm solitude, began her new arrangements.

When students returned on Monday, Janna seated them farther apart and separated those who had been encouraging each other's disruptive behavior. She had moved all the computers to a separate area in the room, moved her desk to the back of the room, and repositioned the small-group area so she would be closer to the rest of the class. She found she was better able to quickly reach all her students with this new arrangement. She set up a signal system using colored cups and kinesthetic signs that students could use to ask for help. This allowed her to go to them, not vice-versa, and gave the students fewer opportunities to get into trouble. She also planned several classbuilding and teambuilding activities to bring everyone together, and was prepared with quick brain energizers for when students showed signs of needing a break.

She installed a new system of distributing and collecting materials, with students assigned to help. In fact, she assigned special responsibilities to every student in the class. She added more structure to her lessons and organized them so students were quickly and actively involved. She printed simple directions on the board, using separate areas and different colors for each grade, and referred students to them. She resolutely began to follow through on insisting that students complete their work and fulfill their obligations, and she set up record-keeping and parent-communication systems to ensure that they did so. She also put into place a system of incentives and activities for students when they worked and behaved appropriately. Although she initially hated such a system because it seemed to her that she was bribing students, Janna soon discovered the value of it. By using activities for learning and for incentive, she encouraged the students to save time by working hard and behaving well, and she allowed them to do fun learning activities that she wanted to include anyway, if time permitted. Most of her changes worked, and by the end of the second week Janna was almost back to where she had started, which she considered a grand achievement.

The Lesson: The Weight of Minor Details

Janna's trials point to one of the most significant realities in teaching, one that is especially important to beginning teachers. The reality is, no matter how much you know of philosophy, child psychology, and the subject matter you teach, teaching will inevitably dump in your lap an enormity of minor details that can, if not dealt with quickly, overwhelm everything else you are trying to do.

Fortunately Janna had the determination to withstand defeat. She was also helped in that effort by a story that had inspired her mother and by some readings in her university courses. Her mother often repeated a story that she had read in *Teacher and Child* (1972), a book by Haim Ginott. The story was about a river boatman who was ferrying a passenger across the river. The passenger, a scholar, asked the boatman, "Do you know philosophy?" "I can't say I do," answered the boatman. "Then you have lost a third of your life," declared the scholar. After a time the scholar asked, "Do you know literature?" "I can't say I do," answered the boatman. "Then you have lost another third of your life," said the philosopher. A bit farther along the boat was seized by the current and dashed against a boulder, whereupon it split and began to sink. The boatman asked the scholar, "Do you know how to swim?" "No," cried the scholar. "Then," concluded the boatman, "you have lost all your life." Janna knew the philosophy and the subject matter and was determined that she would also learn how to swim.

In her own classes, Janna had read about Jesse Stuart and Marva Collins. Stuart told his story in *The Thread That Runs So True,* first published in 1949. The book detailed his twenty years of teaching in the mountain region of Kentucky, but seemed to be almost a mini-history of education in the United States. Just a few years older than some of his students, he had only a teaching certificate and three years in high school when he entered his first one-room school. These qualifications did little to prepare him for the ruffian group of older students—boys who delighted in the fact that they had "run off" their previous teachers. Though the boys set out to make the new teacher's life miserable, Stuart was determined to give them the best he had and to never be chased out of the school, no matter what they tried to do to him. Janna decided that she, too, would not be chased away.

In *Marva Collins' Way* (1990), Collins told about how she had turned hopeless, hostile youngsters into eager and ambitious achievers. It was her attitude that made children learn, her constant "You can do it" that convinced students there was nothing they could not achieve. Collins greeted her children daily with endless encouragement: "The first thing we are going to do here, children, is an awful lot of believing in ourselves." Inspired and determined, "I can do it" became Janna's mantra.

Janna knew she could and would succeed, just as Mercedes had done years before. She knew that doing so meant preventing as many problems as possible, and immediately handling those that did arise and threaten to drag her under. She knew (or thought she knew) how to create a class team and how to prepare and present good lessons for one grade level, but not for two grades at the same time. She also realized that she knew very little about the other things that required her attention during the day: collecting lunch money, taking attendance, keeping paper and other supplies available and in good order, distributing and collecting worksheets and other materials, moving students from one place to another, timing the day's activities, correcting student work in helpful ways, ensuring that students kept materials and displays in good order, and generally nipping disruptive behavior in the bud. She realized that somehow or another the plants had to be watered, the fish fed and the water changed, the hamster habitat cleaned, the audiovisual equipment dealt with, the notices sent out, the duplicating done, classroom visitors dealt with in positive ways, and provisions made for students with limited English proficiency and other special needs. She found she was spending enormous amounts of time cajoling students and then waiting exasperatedly for them to follow directions. She added insult to her own injuries by spending evenings, though exhausted, reading papers, preparing materials for the next day, and contacting parents or guardians about a myriad of matters. She hadn't been prepared for all of that. She discovered quickly how heavy the mass of minor details could be.

What Teachers Try to Accomplish, and How

Certainly, lists of specific things teachers try to accomplish during a year would fill the remaining pages of this book. Instead of lists, what you will find here is highly summarized information and examples that are important to your understanding of the linkage between teacher intentions and the managerial tasks that make their accomplishment possible. We'll begin with some very general goals and move toward a few specific examples.

In very broad terms, teachers want to help their students become productive citizens, able to live life fully and well. Teachers everywhere sincerely want their students to make responsible choices and to discriminate between right and wrong. They would like for their students to be healthy and to appreciate life's beauty and joy, but also to be able to deal with adversity. Teachers want all of this for the students they teach. (Of course, teachers also wouldn't mind a bit of appreciation, fond regard, and remembrance, though they don't expect too much of it.)

In more specific terms, teachers aim their efforts toward the goals that have guided modern education for decades. These goals were well articulated in the 1918 *Cardinal Principles of Secondary Education,* though they were certainly evident before that publication. The 1918 goals were (1) health, (2) command of the fundamental processes (communication and math), (3) worthy home membership, (4) vocation, (5) civil education (good citizenship), (6) worthy use of leisure, and (7) ethical character. These goals are not equally emphasized now, if indeed they ever were. While little attention is presently given to worthy home membership or worthy use of leisure, the remaining five goals still figure strongly in the curriculum.

The very specific outcomes of teaching—as well as the procedures designed to bring them about—are published in curriculum guides and statewide frameworks and standards that describe what is to be accomplished at each grade level and in every area of the curriculum. Some states have statewide textbook adoptions (notably California, Texas, New York, and Florida) and select those books that most closely correspond with their curriculum frameworks and standards. As a result, major publishing houses now tailor books and other materials accordingly.

The Instructional Package: Content, Instruction through Experience, and Management

Management is of crucial importance to teaching—in fact, classroom teaching can hardly occur in its absence. As will become evident in later chapters, the management component of teaching varies according to subject, grade level, and method of teaching. A sixth-grade classroom is run quite differently from a kindergarten; multi-age classes are run differently from single-grade rooms. Reading is done differently from art, music differently from math, spelling differently from social studies. Record keeping, activities, groupings, materials, and even work products and expectations for students are likely to differ.

It is difficult, if not impossible, to describe in precise detail exactly what is included and what transpires in the totality of classroom teaching. Identifiable key elements of teaching can be thought of as decision points that call on teachers to decide how they should proceed in the classroom. Let us examine some of teaching's key considerations and decision points by analyzing the following statement:

> Education begins with three fundamental questions that, when considered in light of learner traits and conditions, link to structures called elements of teaching, which have certain identifiable characteristics and certain typical focuses.

Think of it this way—education begins with three fundamental questions that are entwined with learner traits and conditions.

1. *What should learners know?* The answer to this question is determined by deciding what is best for individuals and society. What learners should know—the contents and curricula of education—is a central question in philosophy.

2. *How do learners learn?* The answer to this question is determined by investigating the processes by which individuals acquire, remember, and put knowledge to use. It is a central question in educational psychology. For further enlightenment, this question of how students learn must be considered in light of certain learner traits and conditions known to affect learning. Chief among these are
   - Intelligence and aptitude, which include inborn abilities and proclivities that vary from student to student
   - Individual learning styles and rates
   - Motivation, as indicated by students' willingness to work at the experiences and activities provided them
   - Group behavior, which differs significantly from individual behavior
   - Social and economic realities, which are known to affect individual ability and motivation to learn

3. *How should learners be taught?* The answer to this question is determined by which experiences, instructional strategies, activities, and materials best promote student learning. It is a central question in pedagogy, or methods of teaching.

Consideration of these questions links to structures called elements of teaching, which are the contents to be taught (what learners should learn) and the instruction through experi-

"PRETTY SNEAKY! YOU AGREE TO LEARN
THE ABC'S, AND <u>THEN</u> THEY TELL YOU ABOUT
THE OTHER TWENTY-THREE LETTERS."

ences and activities (how learners learn and how they should be taught). Underlying these elements is yet another element—management—the primary focus of this book. When everything is taken into account, it becomes clear that for a classroom to run smoothly, management techniques must fit the activities and expectations of specific subjects, student ages, and ability levels. In other words, curriculum, instruction, and management must go hand in hand.

In practice, these three elements of teaching are inseparable because of an embedded curriculum in the choice of content (subject matter), instructional strategies, and management systems. Everything we teach and do produces different outcomes and learnings, and so, in effect, delivers a different curriculum. Students learn different things—in fact, sometimes what teachers do not intend—depending on the choices teachers make regarding curriculum, instruction, and management.

The three elements of teaching are judged against the following criteria

- Contents must be worth learning in themselves and further contribute to the overall goals of education.
- Instruction through experiences must be given clearly, must guide and assist learning, must be relevant to both subject matter and students' lives, and must be attractive and enjoyable.
- Management must help teaching run more smoothly and efficiently.

Further, these criteria can be linked as follows: Worthwhile *contents or curricula* are delivered through *instructional strategies,* which include *experiences and activities* that are relevant and attractive, clear and helpful, with the entire process enhanced through *management* that promotes smoothness and efficiency.

Janna Smart Revisited

Mindful of the difficulties Janna Smart experienced, and with the introduction to classroom management now completed, let us see how Janna might have minimized the trouble she encountered. We will give attention to what she could have done before the school year began, or in this case before she first met her students; during the first days and weeks; and as a continual process through the year. This presentation is general for now but will be elaborated in chapters to come.

Before the School Year Begins

Before students are scheduled to arrive, teachers need to take care of several matters, of which the following five are especially important. First, teachers should familiarize themselves with the school facilities and meet as many of the school personnel as possible—administrators, clerical and custodial staff, and other teachers. Janna Smart did this well: As the principal introduced her and showed her around the school on the morning she was hired, she quickly began to establish friendly relationships with him, the staff, and the teachers she met. She learned the locations of the library, playgrounds, restrooms, the cafeteria, the nurse's office, the custodians' station, and the teacher workroom and lounge. She introduced herself to people at school whenever possible.

Second, teachers should familiarize themselves with the curriculum and content standards for their particular grade level, and with textbooks and other materials provided them. Janna did this fairly well. She reviewed curriculum guides and standards for both first and second grades, studied the various textbooks, reviewed and began ordering available media, and familiarized herself with other materials present or typically used in her room.

Third, teachers should lay out a tentative calendar for the year, with specific detailed plans for the first two or three weeks. Janna, who prided herself on attention to detail, had the first month of topics and lessons broadly outlined before her first day with the students. She later found it necessary to modify her plans substantially, but most teachers frequently do.

Fourth, teachers should organize and set up the physical environment of the classroom to include flexible seating; convenient work areas adjacent to needed materials; any special areas in the room such as science corners, computer areas, or reading centers; and storage centers for materials and equipment. Janna thought her well-meaning friends had done a good job of this, though she soon found they had included things that were too distracting (hamsters and an aquarium). She soon realized she had put too much emphasis on classroom appearance and not enough on efficiency of procedures, activities, and student movement.

Fifth, teachers should give thought to the kind of psychosocial climate that they hope to establish and maintain, together with the procedures designed for bringing it about. It was here that Janna made a major mistake. She knew that students needed to feel a sense of belonging, especially because they were moved so abruptly to a new class with a new teacher after the school year had begun. They also needed to experience pleasure in their work. Janna thought she could establish those feelings simply by being kind to students and accepting what they did, believing they would reciprocate in kind. When she found they didn't, she had no effective means for putting an immediate end to disrespect, poor manners, inconsiderate behavior, and irresponsible choices. She had to learn that order and consideration for others must be firmly established and taught before a class can move ahead.

The First Days and the First Weeks

What teachers do in the beginning is crucial in setting tone, expectations, and likelihood of compliance. Good managers make sure the first few days of school are orderly, which calls for tight structure. They explain rules and procedures, introduce materials and various parts of the classroom, monitor students closely, and let them know when they are behaving responsibly and appropriately. They explain and practice routines, a first step in making them habitual. They use a few appropriate classbuilding activities to help create a caring community for the students. The teacher also talks with students about how they must accept responsibility for their own conduct. Janna did not do this well. Of course everything in the program can't be introduced on the first day of school, but by the end of the first week, several issues should be settled.

Attendance and Opening Procedures.   Until students show good self-control, they should begin the day, from the second day onward, with a quiet activity either at their seats or at a designated area in the room. During this time the teacher should take attendance.

Older students should learn at once that they are to go to their assigned seats and begin work immediately. They can be given specific assignments such as five-a-day math problems, journal writing, or reading in library books. Younger students, not yet able to work on their own, are taught to go directly to the circle (kindergarten) or to their seats. Traditionally, on the first morning they are told: "Now we are in school. The first thing we do here is sit down, fold our hands, and close our lips. If we need to say anything, we must raise our hand." The teacher then goes directly into calling the roll, and classbuilding or other opening activities, such as flag salute, calendar counting, song, or sharing. As mentioned, when students show themselves capable of doing other activities with self-control, the opening may be changed. In any case, the beginning tone should be business-like (though it is all right to smile) and should quickly be made routine. Considerable reminding and practice will be necessary at first, but quiet self-control is essential to everything else in the program.

Jones (2001), Kagan (1994), and others encourage teachers to greet students in a manner similar to this: "Welcome everyone. I'm very glad you are with me this year. I know we will have fun and learn a lot, and learning will be fun. There will be time for you to talk and move, and also time to sit. I will use a quiet signal like this when I want your attention on me." Every day teachers should give their students structured activities that allow them to move and talk—two basic human needs.

Seating Arrangements and Orientation to the Classroom. Teachers should explain seating arrangements. Introductions to the uses of the various parts of the classroom, including interest centers and work areas, the materials they contain, and what is to be done there, can be accomplished with teacher demonstration or guided student exploration and discovery.

Class Rules and System of Discipline. On the first day teachers should go over the expected rules of responsible student behavior. There should be no more than four rules for young children and six for older children; greater numbers cannot be remembered. Have in mind what is acceptable to you, but encourage students to give input, ask questions, or discuss the various rules, incentives, and consequences. Make sure students understand the rules, the reasons behind them, and enforcement procedures you will use, and make sure they see the system as fair. If students are old enough, have them sign their names on a sheet of paper containing the rules, to indicate they understand the rules, find them fair, and fully intend to abide by them.

Orientation to the School and School Rules. Most students, unless new to the neighborhood, will already be acquainted with the buildings and grounds. Still, it is advisable to spend time orienting students to restrooms, drinking fountains, playgrounds, the cafeteria, the library, the principal's office, the reception desk, and the nurse's station. Many teachers take their students on a walking tour of these places sometime during the first or second day of school.

Students are expected to follow certain rules that pertain to the school, as distinct from those of the classroom. These rules tell how to behave in common areas such as corridors, on the playground, in the library, in the cafeteria, at bus and parking areas, and at street crossings. It is the teacher's responsibility to thoroughly familiarize students (and aides and visiting parents as well) with these school regulations and procedures.

"I KNOW I CAN TRAIN THEM TO BE THOUGHTFUL, PRODUCTIVE CITIZENS IF I CAN EVER GET PAST SIT."

The Daily Schedule. The daily schedule should be explained in a way that makes clear what activities are to occur during each part of the day and how students are to work and behave for each. Along with a discussion of the schedule and activities, the teacher previews books and materials to be used on a regular basis—where they are located, how they are obtained, how they are cared for, and how they are returned after use.

Monitors (Classroom Helpers). Many teachers use class members to help with the numerous classroom chores. Often called *monitors,* these helpers are selected during the first week of classes and changed several times during the year. Some teachers assign monitors to their duties, while others take applications, ask for volunteers, or make prized assignments (such as feeding a classroom animal) contingent on special accomplishment. A list of duties for which monitors can be particularly helpful may be found in Chapter 7. It is desirable to assign some special job to every student in the class, in order to increase interest and promote a sense of ownership and responsibility.

Miscellaneous Needs. Students continually need help while working independently. They also need to sharpen pencils, get drinks, go to the restroom, and call their parents or guardians. Procedures and routines must be established for all such matters, so students understand how they are to proceed.

Traffic Patterns. Students must be instructed on how to enter the classroom, how to leave when dismissed, what to do during fire drills, and how to move from one area to another. Congestion, prevalent around the teacher's desk and classroom animals, should be eliminated by instructing students on how they are to move about and how many may be out of their seats at a given time.

Paraprofessionals and Volunteers. Many teachers have aides and volunteers working in their rooms, and perhaps even cross-grade partners and cross-age tutors. Some experienced teachers have student teachers assigned to them. The duties of each should be made very clear, as should the extent to which they are to correct and discipline students. When assigned to do clerical work, paraprofessionals should be provided a comfortable workstation with appropriate materials.

Preparing for Substitute Teachers. Every teacher must rely on a substitute from time to time. The class should be able to continue with its normal routines under the direction of a substitute. To make this possible, the teacher must prepare the class to work with, not against, the new teacher. Discussions with the class can clarify students' responsibilities in helping the process. Whenever possible, complete lesson plans should be left for the substitute, and one or two class monitors should be assigned to inform substitutes of routines, locations of materials, and normal work procedures.

Managerial Matters That Require Ongoing Attention

To the extent possible, the matters just described should be discussed with the class and put into place during the first week of school. In addition, several managerial matters require ongoing attention throughout the year. Having regained control of her classroom, Janna placed herself in a position from which she could attend to these matters. Such ongoing matters are mentioned here briefly, and are discussed more fully in later chapters.

Curriculum Management. The curriculum is the program for learners, which is aligned to standards that are described by the state and the school. Its management entails the selection, organization, and presentation of subject matter, plus arrangements for student work and accountability. These matters fluctuate through the year and require continual adjustment.

Lesson Management. Lesson management involves selecting and organizing learning activities, grouping students, giving explanations and directions, providing for student accountability, monitoring and giving feedback, assessing performance, and reteaching as necessary. In such management, teachers find that the pacing of lessons is very important. Pacing means that lessons cover what is intended, with immediate student participation, within the allotted time, with steady momentum but without rush or delay. Also very important are the transitions between lessons, which should be made smoothly and quickly, allowing for no dead time.

Record Keeping, Assessment, and Reporting. Records should be kept that can tell teacher, student, parent, or administrator at a glance a student's achievement levels, work in progress, strengths and weaknesses, and future needs. This requirement is most easily met by keeping records sheets for the entire class plus a separate records folder for each individual student. The folder should include individual progress charts together with samples (good and bad) of student work. As for reporting, each school district has its own system. Most use report cards to show achievement made in different subjects, and may also include effort expended by the student and general behavior or comportment.

Special Groups. Teachers now teach students with diverse abilities and in varied settings. All teachers are expected to welcome, value, and educate all students, including those with special needs. Teachers who teach in inclusive classrooms, multi-age classrooms, or have students with language and cultural diversities, have additional management challenges related to curriculum and lessons, record keeping, and paraprofessionals. Teachers, students, and caregivers all have rights and responsibilities that affect these matters.

Communication.   Teachers are constant communicators. They direct, instruct, and motivate students through lessons. They work with paraprofessionals, support providers, volunteers, and substitute teachers, all of whom have potential to enrich lessons. They communicate with parents and guardians in a variety of ways. They also interact with administrators and colleagues.

Extracurricular Activities.   Teachers' duties range far beyond those of simply organizing and presenting lessons. The following are a few of the important tasks they frequently perform that contribute to children's education but rarely are considered part of teaching.

Plays and Performances.   Teachers are called on to organize, coach, direct, and stage various types of performances, which usually involve organizing help from parents and volunteers.

Field Trips.   When the class is able to leave the school to visit places of special interest, the teacher must oversee transportation, permission slips from parents and guardians, volunteers to help supervise students, and advance preparation to make the trip smooth and beneficial.

Fairs and Carnivals.   Many schools put on fairs, carnivals, and other money-raising activities. Even when such events are under the direction of the parent–teacher organization, teachers are called on for planning, preparation, and work at the events.

Back-to-School and Open House   Almost all schools have one or more evenings during the year in which caregivers and the public are invited to visit the school and classrooms. At these events, teachers describe their programs, activities, and expectations for the year, and samples of student work are displayed.

Assemblies.   Teachers are sometimes put in charge of assemblies for their school, which requires much planning and organization. At other times they are responsible only for the movement of their class to and from the assembly, as well as the behavior of their students while there.

Clubs.   Teachers often assume leadership roles in special clubs or other activities such as student council, safety patrol, cheerleading, athletics, photography, scouts, science groups, after-school recreation, and so forth. Occasionally these extra tasks bring a little extra pay, but typically they are an expected part of the teacher's overall duties.

Here we end our introductory chapter on classroom management, having laid the groundwork for what is to come. The next chapter will deal with how to manage the curriculum and the calendar. Before proceeding to that topic, take a moment to consider this parting thought before reviewing and reflecting on what has been presented so far.

Parting Thought

If you have built castles in the air, your work need not be lost; that is where they should be. Now put foundations under them.

—Thoreau

SUMMARY SELF-CHECK

Check off the following as you either understand or become able to apply them.

❑ Three fundamental questions about education
  ■ What should students know?
  ■ How do learners learn?
  ■ How should learners be taught?

❑ Aspects of classroom management that require attention
  ■ Before the year begins: familiarity with personnel and facilities, curriculum and content standards, calendar; preparation of the classroom; planning for the emotional tone of the class.
  ■ First days and weeks of school: attendance and opening procedures; seating arrangements and classroom orientation; class rules and system of discipline; orientation to the school, classroom, and school rules; the daily class schedule; books and materials; selection of student helpers (monitors); routines for sharpening pencils, getting drinks, and using the restroom; traffic patterns and regulations; use of volunteers and paraprofessionals; preparation for substitute teachers.
  ■ Continual attention throughout the year: curriculum selection and organization; lesson management; special groups; record keeping, assessment, and reporting; extracurricular activities.

ACTIVITIES FOR REFLECTION AND GROWTH

For Thought and Discussion

1. Take a moment to review the statements in the Anticipation–Reaction Guide at the beginning of this chapter. Put a check mark in the Reaction column next to any statement with which you now agree. How have your thoughts changed since reading this chapter?

2. What distinction, if any, can be made between *teaching* and *management*? Describe what you believe each entails. What overlap do you see?

3. From what you have seen or heard, how realistic does the Janna Smart story seem?

4. Have you known teachers who failed, gave up early, or lived through immense frustration? If so, what seemed to be the major difficulties with which they had to contend?

5. The point was made that the instructional program cannot proceed until a semblance of good order is established and maintained in the classroom. Do you agree with that? What if it takes a week or two (or longer) to get the class under control?

6. This first chapter presents a fairly thorough overview of classroom management. Was it worth your time reading it, or did you feel that you more or less knew all these things before you decided to become a teacher?

REFERENCES AND RECOMMENDED READINGS

Arends, R. (1997). *Classroom instruction and management.* New York: McGraw Hill.

Bureau of Education. (1918). *Cardinal principles of secondary education* (Bulletin #35.) Washington, DC: Department of the Interior, Bureau of Education.

Collins, M., & Tamarkin, C. (1990). *Marva Collins' way.* New York: G. P. Putnam's Sons.

Evertson, C., Emmer, E., Clements, B., Sanford, J., & Worsham, M. (2003). *Classroom management for elementary teachers* (6th ed.). Boston: Allyn & Bacon.

Fuery, C. (1996). *Winning year one: A survival guide for first year teachers.* Captiva, FL: Sanibel Sanddollar Publications.

Ginott, H. (1972). *Teacher and child.* New York: Macmillan.

Good, T., & Brophy, J. (2002). *Looking into classrooms* (9th ed.). New York: Pearson Allyn & Bacon.

Jones, F., & Jones, L. (2001). *Comprehensive classroom management: Creating communities of support and solving problems.* (6th ed.). Boston: Allyn & Bacon.

Kagan, S. (1994). *Cooperative learning.* San Clemente, CA: Resources for Teachers.

Lieberman, A., & Miller, L. (1999). *Teachers—Transforming their world and their work.* New York: Teachers College.

Ryan, K., & Cooper, J. (2000). *Those who can, teach* (9th ed.). Boston: Houghton Mifflin.

Sollman, C., Emmons, B., & Paolini, J. (1994). *Through the cracks.* Worcester, MA: Davis Publications.

Stuart, J. (1949). *The threat that runs so true.* New York: Simon & Schuster.

Wong, H., & Wong, R. (2001). *How to be an effective teacher: The first days of school* (17th printing). Mountain View, CA: Harry K. Wong Publications.

CHAPTER

2

Laying Out the School Year

A good plan executed right now is far better than a perfect plan executed next week.

—George S. Patton

ANTICIPATION–REACTION GUIDE

Before you read the chapter, take a moment to put a check mark in the Anticipation column next to any statement with which you agree.

	Anticipation	Reaction
Curriculum is defined as the contents of textbooks and other materials children use.	❏	❏
Teachers are expected to redesign curriculum guides to meet their own specifications.	❏	❏
Ideally, teachers should lay out the yearly calendar before they finalize units of instruction.	❏	❏
Curriculum maps reveal repetitions and gaps in content and skills.	❏	❏
Backward design planning begins with target goals and assessment.	❏	❏
Essential questions are intended to check ongoing student understanding of the fine points of their study.	❏	❏
Authorities recommend that teachers, when planning units, begin by listing the broad objectives they hope to have their students attain.	❏	❏
Thematic plans integrate several subjects into each unit of instruction.	❏	❏
Awareness of what students already know or are able to do provides helpful information to teachers as they plan.	❏	❏
How the curriculum is managed is much more important to education than is the subject matter contained in the curriculum.	❏	❏

One of the first management tasks that awaits teachers—one to be completed at least tentatively before the school year begins—is that of laying out the intended instructional program for the year. This process involves interweaving curriculum with the calendar. Because the reality of schooling is that the curriculum is more flexible than time schedules, the curriculum must be adjusted to the dates and times available for instruction.

This task is more challenging for elementary teachers than for secondary teachers, because elementary classes deal with so many different subject areas on a daily basis—reading, grammar, spelling, composition, listening, speaking, mathematics, history, geography, current events, science, health, safety, physical education, music, art, penmanship, and sometimes others. Elementary teachers are challenged to find ways to deal with, and do justice to, all these subjects for all the children they teach. They accomplish this task in two steps. First, they note what the year's calendar allows in terms of instructional time; then, they organize their instructional programs to fit within time constraints while providing proper emphasis, duration, and continuity over days, weeks, semesters, and the entire year.

How to Lay Out the Year

When you begin considering the curriculum for your grade (or grades, if yours is a multiage class), you should look at what you are supposed to teach (content and standards), available materials, and your students. Having done that, you will find yourself penciling a calendar for the year. Many lesson plan books furnished by schools, or available for purchase, contain spaces to enter your daily plans week by week. These plan books provide a year's calendar formatted as blank boxes for each day of each month.

National holidays will be shown in your plan book, as well as some non-holidays, such as Valentine's Day, Halloween, and Election Day. As you prepare the calendar, you can mark all the holidays, vacation times, teacher in-service days, and days when students will not be present. Your school district calendar, separate from the plan book, will indicate teaching days, in-service days, parent–teacher conference days, and dates when report cards are due. Your school site calendar will include back-to-school and open house nights, and perhaps dates for school assemblies, school carnival, and other school or community events. While these events may seem to interfere with normal teaching, they can also excite and motivate students, and provide themes that you can use to good advantage.

Anticipating Upcoming Events

Once you have marked the yearly calendar in this way, you will have a more accurate view of the blocks of time available for teaching. Now you can make additional notations that offer an even more complete picture of what the months will bring. Assuming a traditional September-to-June schedule, you will find it helpful to anticipate the following realities.

Late August, Early September. School begins, often the week before or after Labor Day, and everyone is excited. These first days tend to be a time of fairly good student behavior. Students are unsure of the new setting, and usually hope they have a teacher who will treat them well. This is a good time for high-interest teaching units; they help get you off to

"ARE YOU SURE THE FOUR SEASONS AREN'T
BASEBALL, FOOTBALL, BASKETBALL, AND HOCKEY?"

a good start with your students. You should expect that the students might try to test you very early in the year, as they did with Janna Smart in Chapter 1. This is also a good time for classbuilding activities that will help create a sense of community among the students, and for teambuilding activities that will encourage cooperation. The first days are usually a time of watchfulness and promise, ideal for establishing routines and expectations.

The Jewish New Year and High Holy Days, from Rosh Hashanah to Yom Kippur, occur in September or October. Check with your building principal regarding the school's policy of drawing attention to religious holidays and discussing their meaning.

October. A back-to-school night is usually scheduled for October (but may be sometime in September). You will be expected to describe your program to those who attend, answer questions, talk with caregivers, and show samples of each student's work. Although your program should already have been communicated to them through a newsletter, this is a good time for reminders.

Parent–teacher conferences are often scheduled close to the back-to-school night. Students are usually dismissed early or do not have school on these days. These conferences call for considerable preparation on your part (as will be explained in Chapter 11). You will need representative samples of each student's work, showing areas of strength and areas for growth. You will also need to plan out what you would like to discuss with each student's parent or guardian.

Columbus Day is observed the second Monday of the month, providing a three-day weekend. Most teachers give some attention to Columbus's efforts through stories and art activities. Halloween is on the last day of the month. Although many schools downplay

"CITY CHILDREN HAVE TROUBLE WITH THE CONCEPT OF HARVEST."

Halloween, students nevertheless will be excited and distracted by it. Many teachers provide stories and writing and art activities on the Halloween theme. Again, check with your principal about district and school policy.

November.   Three events of particular interest occur this month. Election Day, the first Tuesday of the month, is not a school holiday but is usually of interest to older students. Veterans Day, November 11, is a school holiday. It is accompanied by little fanfare in most places, and some school districts move the observance date in order to provide another three-day weekend. In contrast, Thanksgiving, the fourth Thursday of the month, generates much excitement. At least two days of school (in some districts, three days or even the entire week) will be missed. Students will be interested in the origins of Thanksgiving, making this a good time for writing, drama, and art activities on that theme.

December.   The last one-third of the month will be given to vacation, and the early two-thirds will be a time of excited anticipation over Hanukkah, Kwanzaa, and Christmas. Check school policy regarding mention of these celebrations, but recognize that, regardless of policy, the children will be thinking about gifts, travel, special foods and treats, family events, and decorations, and will likely be more excitable and distracted than usual. These weeks are especially good times for activities in art, music, drama, and stories of the season.

January.   Teachers and students return from holiday excitements to the normal school routine with varying degrees of interest, but overall this is a time for everyone to settle back into a productive routine. Martin Luther King Day, celebrating Dr. King's birthday on January 15, is normally scheduled to provide a long weekend in the middle of the month. The days that precede it offer an appropriate time for emphasizing African American history, music, art, and literature. Many students will be interested in the winter Olympic Games and professional football playoffs, with high interest for the Super Bowl at the end of the month. Depending on the locale, wintry weather also will be a topic of interest.

February. This month marks the approximate midpoint of the school year and seems to pass especially quickly because it is short and contains long weekends and dates of interest to children. Children usually enjoy Groundhog Day (February 2) and Valentine's Day (February 14). Lincoln's birthday (February 12) and Washington's birthday (February 20) may also spark student interest and are often observed with one, and sometimes two, long weekends. Also, many schools and teachers enjoy celebrating the 100th day of school with a variety of activities.

March. After the fast pace of February, March may seem rather slow, and student enthusiasm may wane. However, with fewer outside distractions, children can concentrate better on schoolwork, making this a good time to complete longer units of study. Dr. Seuss's birthday is March 2, encouraging many elementary teachers and librarians to plan celebration activities on that day. Also, Saint Patrick's Day receives attention on March 17.

April. Most schools take a weeklong spring break late in March or early April. Students often travel or receive visitors during this time. Also, the month frequently brings commemorations of Passover and Easter. Check with your principal to determine school policy regarding these holidays. Clocks may be moved ahead from standard time to Daylight Saving Time early in the month.

May. At the beginning of this month, schools typically give another invitation for caregivers to visit the schools. This is when teachers and students can display some of their accomplishments of the year, and classrooms are usually decorated accordingly. Mother's Day occurs this month, and students often do art activities in which they make something to give the special women in their lives. Memorial Day falls on May 30, but is usually observed on the last Monday of the month to make a long weekend.

June. The end of the traditional school year is approaching, making the final weeks a time of activity and distraction. Teachers are concerned about report cards. Students' minds are on summer, and a few are concerned about promotion or moving to another school. Flag Day and Father's Day may attract some attention.

Summer. In districts with year-round school calendars, Independence Day, July 4, will affect planning for the first week of July. In some years the summer Olympic Games and the national primaries can provide interesting topics of study, particularly for older students.

The yearly calendar is annotated in this manner not to imply that it is the driving force behind curriculum organization, but to remind teachers of outside forces that can influence instruction. Keep the notations at hand as you use your curriculum guide and textbooks to plot out the selected topics of instruction for your students. Pencil your plans on a separate chart; before finalizing them you will probably make a number of changes. A point to remember: To the extent possible, begin instructional units on Mondays (or the Tuesday following a long weekend) and have them end just before holidays, long weekends, or vacation times, because it is difficult to recapture student enthusiasm after such breaks. You may need to shorten or even bypass some of the units included in your grade and books to fit everything in your schedule.

Laying Out the Day

Once you have the year's calendar blocked out, but before you begin to plan specific lessons and units, it is a good idea to set up the day's schedule as you would like it to be. The school establishes times for recess, lunch, and dismissal, and your grade level team may adjust schedules to create team teaching opportunities. Otherwise, you have considerable discretion in deciding on the schedule of teaching you prefer. However, you should view the daily schedule as more than a matter of convenience. Certain subjects, such as math or language arts, are best studied when students are fresh, alert, and able to concentrate for a long while. Other subjects, such as singing or physical education, are best scheduled to relieve tension from long concentration. Still others that might involve cooperation and talking are good for later in the day when students are getting tired.

Daily Schedules

Stacy Ganzer teaches thirty half-day kindergarten students, many of whom are English language learners. Taking into consideration the short attention spans and the language diversity of her young students, she must plan all her lessons and activities for a far shorter time frame than elementary teachers in other grades.

Stacy's Schedule

7:45–7:50	Students place all their folders in the collection bin; attendance
7:50–8:00	Math problem solving of the day
8:00–8:20	Calendar activities/story
8:20–8:30	Shared writing
8:30–9:30	Reading/math groups (two groups of five children)
9:30–9:55	Snack/PE
9:55–10:10	Story/sharing
10:10–10:20	Daily phonemic awareness activities
10:20–10:50	Language and math centers/English language development groups
10:50–11:00	Free exploration (if time allows)
11:00–11:10	Clean up
11:10–11:12	Line up and dismissal

Reading and math groups alternate days. On Wednesdays, reading and math groups are replaced with a journal writing activity, science lesson, or social studies lesson that the class does as a whole group.

Jan Gretlein is a first-grade teacher. She is with her students all day but follows a schedule that takes into consideration many of the same issues as Stacy's schedule.

Jan's Schedule

8:55	School begins; teacher meets students on the playground and walks with them to the classroom
8:55–9:15	Students read silently; teacher talks to caregivers, takes attendance, and assists individuals or small groups of students, as needed
9:15–9:45	Reading workshop/literacy centers
9:45–10:45	Mini-lessons and guided reading groups that focus on individual and small group reading comprehension activities
10:45–11:00	Recess
11:00–11:45	Writing workshop with varied independent writing activities, such as journal and letter writing, poetry, and fiction and nonfiction stories published in class
11:45–12:45	Math
12:45–1:25	Lunch
1:25–1:45	Reading aloud by teacher
1:45–3:00	Science/social studies/PE
3:00–3:20	Clear up, daily news
3:20	School ends; dismissal

Jan schedules library once a week and computer lab every two weeks. Jan does not begin reading groups in the beginning of the year. First, she establishes routines, sets expectations, and familiarizes children with each of the activities they will use at center time. At the beginning of the year, she plans 30 minutes for literacy centers. Later in the year, this is extended to 45 minutes. For her reading program, Jan uses many of the activities in *Strategies That Work* (Harvey & Goudvis, 2000) and *Mosaic of Thought* (Keene & Zimmermann, 1997).

Marilyn Cox and Bernardo Campos are partners in a fifth-grade team. In their district, fifth graders may participate in several special programs that must be considered as the team plans the daily schedule.

Marilyn and Bernardo's Schedule

8:55	Students gather on the playground with their classmates and enter their classrooms together to begin the day
9:00–11:05	Reader's workshop and writing
11:05–11:20	Recess
11:20–12:45	Math (students are separated by ability groups, and the teaching team rotates to different groups when units change)
12:45–1:00	Homework assignments and explanations
1:00–1:40	Lunch
1:40–2:00	Reading aloud
2:00–2:20	Word study
2:20–3:00	Social studies/science
3:00–3:20	PE/art
3:20	Dismissal

Library is scheduled for one day a week. The school's computer lab is only available by signing up and is often used for project-related work. Marilyn and Bernardo hope to use the portable computer lab, a cart with thirty laptop computers that can be moved from room to room, more often this year and will need to sign up for it accordingly. Many students serve on Student Council, which meets one day a week before school, or on Safety Patrol (in groups of five each day). Because of their responsibilities, these students arrive to class shortly after the bell rings in the morning and leave the classroom five to ten minutes prior to dismissal. Additionally, most of Marilyn and Bernardo's students take band as an elective. Band students are grouped according to the instrument they play and meet with the band teacher one day a week. Also, in anticipation of a school Winter Olympics event, the team has planned for eight rotations over the three-week period before winter break. Students practice eight of the track and field-type events (relay, dash, and so on) in order to participate in Olympics in February or March. The daily schedule will change to allot 2:50–3:20 for these rotations.

Stacy, Jan, and Marilyn and Bernardo teach in schools where they are responsible for the entire curriculum. Some schools, particularly middle schools, also have specialist teachers for physical education, music, art, and occasionally other subjects. These schools may schedule preparation time at the same time for subjects such as social studies and language arts to permit teachers to plan together and do team teaching. Other schools may have a regularly scheduled preparation time that teachers use for planning. In middle schools that include sixth grade, teams of teachers may share two or more groups of students every day. In teams of two, one teacher may teach students language arts and social studies while another teaches math and science. Where there are teams of four, teachers may each have separate subjects.

Sherry Coburn is the social studies teacher for a sixth-grade team at her middle school. Every day she teaches four groups of students for a fifty-six-minute period. The other three teachers on her team teach language arts, math, and science. Sherry has a typical weekly plan for when her students study a chapter in their textbook. On Monday, Sherry assigns eight district geography questions. After some whole-class review, students use their textbooks and other resources to search for the answers. At the start of the year, students need a great deal of help with this but they become more proficient as time goes by. On Tuesday and Wednesday students complete activities using vocabulary from the chapter in the textbook. This work is turned in as homework on Thursday. To help students with their reading, Sherry creates study guides that include questions and missing words. Students use class time on Thursday to search the chapter and complete the study guides. On Friday, after a quiz from their reading, students play review games such as vocabulary concentration and Jeopardy.

Curriculum from the Management Perspective

Our concern here is not with preparing and organizing curriculum, but with managing it. In Chapter 1, classroom management was presented as handling, governing, directing, or controlling so as to bring something about, with prime emphasis on efficiency and effectiveness. In curriculum management, what we intend to bring about is purposeful interaction between students and the information and skills they are intended to learn. We want to accomplish this interaction as effectively and efficiently as possible.

The following account from Keith Correll, a sixth-grade teacher, shows how he manages portions of his curriculum:

> It is important to me for things to run smoothly. I have a daily schedule and expect students to change quickly from one subject to the next. I try to have the first part of a particular period set aside for a whole-class activity. In this way the students all know what is coming and what to do. For example, the first thing in math is always a one-minute timed exercise. The students know that I will quickly say "go," and if they don't have their pencils, scratch paper, and test sheet ready, they are out of luck—they can try again the next day.
>
> The subject matter is also very important to me. Since I teach sixth grade I always have junior high in the back of my mind. Assignments are to be completed. If they are not, a note goes home, filled out by the student, stating what was not completed and why. The work must be made up on his or her own time. I go over all the assignments ahead of time, so students know exactly what is expected. They know the schedule of tests and what they have to do to earn their grades on the report cards. This makes them responsible for their own grades. Occasionally I receive a call from parents whose child has received a failing grade for the first time ever. Their anger quickly subsides when I remind them that the child knew exactly what work was required for a good grade, and I explain how little the child did.
>
> This may sound harsh, but I treat the students with great respect and courtesy. I always say "please" and "thank you" and "excuse me." I admit my mistakes and tell the children I am sorry. They reflect my example. We are courteous, we are considerate, we have an enjoyable time, and best of all, we get our work done.

Teachers usually think of curriculum as the basic material that they are expected to teach or the textbook they use. States now have published standards that describe the specific topics and content for each subject area. Such material is laid out for teachers in the textbooks designed for the students they are teaching. In preparing those textbooks, authors and publishers do their best to interpret and address the published standards, and they work hard to make the books both effective and easy to use. Frequently, textbooks are supplemented with a variety of excellent ancillary materials, such as transparencies or black lines, CDs, DVDs or videos, and test question banks.

However, for the sake of accuracy, it must be noted that textbook contents and curriculum are not synonymous terms. For as long as there have been schools, there has been dispute about what the curriculum ought to be. Even today there is no consensus as to what the term *curriculum* means. Some define it as experiences under the auspices of the school (Rosales-Dordelly & Short, 1985). Some consider it a series of planned events intended to have educational consequence (Eisner, 1985). Goodlad (1984) refers to curriculum as activities, processes, and structural arrangements intended for and used in the school and classroom as a means of accomplishing the educative function. Doll (1992) describes curriculum as formal and informal content and process used to help learners grow in knowledge, understanding, skills, attitudes, appreciations, and values. Ralph Tyler (1949), one of the twentieth century's most influential writers on curriculum, didn't try to define it at all. Instead, he devoted his efforts to describing how curriculum is studied, developed, and evaluated.

Although there is little agreement about definitions of curriculum, there is perhaps even less agreement about the content of curriculum. Philosophers, educators, politicians, critics, individuals with axes to grind, and an infinity of special-interest groups struggle to shape curriculum contents, as each believes proper.

Mapping the Big Picture

"To make sense of our students' experiences over time, we need two lenses: a zoom lens into this year's curriculum for a particular grade and a wide-angle lens to see the K–12 perspective" (Jacobs, 1997, p. 3). Heidi Jacobs describes a procedure she calls curriculum mapping. *Mapping,* used in 1983 by Fenwick English, is "a technique of recording time on task data and then analyzing this data to determine the 'fit' to the officially adopted curriculum and the assessment/testing program" (Jacobs, 1997, p. 7). Curriculum mapping, which involves individual, team, and whole-school input, promotes alignment by revealing gaps and redundancies in content and skills. This process has seven steps.

1. Each teacher independently identifies the major elements that make up the curriculum— the emphasized standards, processes, and skills; the essential content and topics; and the products and performances.
2. In a first read-through, each teacher scans the maps for the entire building (or team), to gather information and identify areas for future examination. Each teacher notes repetitions (of standards, content, and skills), gaps (between standard and goals and what is actually taught), meaningful assessments, matches with content standards and objectives, potential areas for integration, and timeliness (availability of current materials and resources, and knowledge of best current practices).
3. Groups of six or eight teachers who do not teach together then share their individual findings and create a composite list of their observations for large group review.
4. In an all-faculty (or all-team) review, observation findings from all the smaller sessions are charted. Focus is still on the nonjudgmental review of what was observed. When teachers begin to edit, revise, and develop, they may remain together as one large group or move into smaller instructional units.
5. Faculty members begin to sift through the data from the observation findings and determine areas that can immediately and easily be revised by faculty members, teams, and administrators.
6. Faculty members also determine areas that will require more long-range research and development. These areas may require structural decisions, more in-depth investigation, or more consideration of the potential long-range consequences before changes can be made.
7. The steps in the whole curriculum mapping process are then repeated, because curriculum review is active and ongoing.

Backward Design Planning

In an effort to help teachers better plan curriculum and assessments that will result in student *understanding* (as opposed to simple student *knowing*), Wiggins and McTighe (1998) offer another approach to planning. What they call backward design is an alternative to coverage and activity-oriented plans. Teachers plan through three stages. In an intentionally simplified explanation, teachers who use backward design planning first identify the desired results. Then they determine acceptable evidence. Finally, they plan the learning experiences and instruction.

According to Wiggins and McTighe, teachers must reflect on several things when considering the desired results of the teaching and learning. Teachers must identify the understandings students will gain. They must form essential questions that will guide and focus the teaching and learning. They must identify key knowledge and skills students will acquire as a result of the study. Teachers must also consider the evidence, such as performance, quizzes, tests, work samples, and student self-assessment, and determine what evidence they will expect and use to demonstrate student understanding.

Task analyses of performance tasks and assessment greatly help teachers determine acceptable evidence, the second step of backward design. It makes sense in this step to articulate content standards and the desired understandings to be assessed through tasks. It also makes sense to clarify the purpose of the assessment tasks—whether they are diagnostic, formative, or summative. GRASPS is a simple acronym that can help with this: Goals, Role, Audience, Situation, Product or performance, and Standards (Wiggins & McTighe, 1998). Identifying the criteria as well as the scoring tool (rubric, checklist, or other) for evaluating student products and performances is as important to this step as identifying the assessment tool itself.

Only after teachers identify what they want students to understand and be able to do, and consider the evidence they will accept from the students to demonstrate these understandings, are they in a position to plan the learning experiences and instruction. Hence, the process name *backward design planning.*

A Word about Standards

In light of current reform across the nation, such as Goals 2000 and the No Child Left Behind Act of 2001, standards have become a driving force for content and curriculum, performance, opportunities-to-learn, and technology. This is particularly true of literacy, although all individual subject areas are now identifying content standards as well. States and districts are creating or revising learning goals and identifying benchmarks and competencies to define skills, knowledge, and content mastery for students of varying ages and grades.

The Goals of the School Curriculum

The school curriculum is intended to expose students to important subjects and topics, thereby causing them to acquire certain knowledge, attitudes, and values. These goals were partially expressed in the Cardinal Principles mentioned in Chapter 1, especially those of health, good citizenship, and command of the fundamental processes of communication and mathematics. In addition, the curriculum is intended to produce (1) attitudes of openness to ideas, willingness to try, and acceptance of others; (2) knowledge of facts and their application; and (3) growth in thinking skills such as analysis, synthesis, and evaluation.

All of this is to be worked on in school, though, in truth, much of it—especially as concerns attitudes and values—occurs more potently in the home and community. For teachers to best help students acquire attitudes of good character, they must imbed these qualities into the way they teach. They must also provide students with constant opportunities to practice the attributes and attitudes of good character.

Implementing the Curriculum

Activities in teachers' daily schedules are delivered through individual lessons that, in most cases, are episodes within larger units of instruction rather than isolated events. Units consist of closely related lessons that build toward larger understandings, and most are designed to be completed in one to four weeks.

Preorganized units are frequently found in teacher editions of student textbooks, but almost all teachers plan a number of units of their own to better match their students' needs. Unit topics are numerous, and they spread across the spectrum of the curriculum—dinosaurs, weather, the family, pets, poetry, fractions, graphing, physical endurance, landscape drawing, the thirteen colonies, media, and so on. These diverse units are built mostly around concrete concepts. Until they are able to think abstractly, students do not do well in units on intangibles such as prejudice, self-esteem, or feelings. Some attention is given in elementary classes to patriotism, freedom, and equality, though mostly in terms of the beliefs and deeds of heroes and heroines such as George Washington, Abraham Lincoln, Martin Luther King Jr., Harriet Tubman, Clara Barton, and Jade Snow Wong.

The Organization of Units

Authorities in curriculum and instruction believe that, once the topic is selected, units should be planned as follows:

1. Review the local and state standards to determine which may be addressed in this unit of study.
2. Formulate an overall goal that you want your students to achieve, or an essential or guiding question for them to answer. An appropriate overall goal for a unit entitled "Community" might be: "Students will be able to construct a model of a community that includes physical structures as well as evidence of meaningful services." An appropriate essential or guiding question might be: "How does my community affect my life?" For a unit entitled "Maps as Tools," an overall goal might be: "Students will be able to construct a series of maps offering information about a country or region from which some of their ancestors came." An essential or guiding question might be: "In what ways have maps been useful tools for humans?"
3. Formulate several interim subordinate objectives, whose attainment moves learners progressively toward the overall goal. Interim objectives for the unit on community

might call on students to be able to replicate their neighborhood community on a map, list community members and their services, or compare their neighborhood community to one from another time and place in history (ancient Greece or Rome, mid 1800s, early 1900s). The unit on maps might call on students to read latitude and longitude, interpret and use maps in reference books, and make population and climatic maps for a selected country such as Peru.

4. Organize instructional activities that lead to the attainment of each of the interim objectives. For the unit on community, this will result in a number of individual lessons on the nature and meaning of community and neighborhood and on local jobs. The community unit could be integrated with the unit on maps with lessons on map reading; interpreting map legends; pinpointing specific buildings, businesses, and services; creating a map of the area where one lives; and learning how different types of maps convey the information intended. A variety of materials will be needed for the lessons, as well as appropriate space and arrangements for engaging in the activities. All of this will have to be planned and managed carefully if you are to keeps students productively on track.

5. Provide assessment activities that will give the students opportunities to demonstrate what and how they reached the objective or were able to provide the answer to the essential or guiding question.

Note that this approach to unit planning emphasizes the curriculum standards, essential or guiding questions, or the objectives—what you hope your students will know or will be able to do as a result of their working through the unit.

The Way Many Teachers Organize Units

Although curriculum standards remain a key consideration, many teachers do not organize units from the basis of objectives or essential questions, but rather from a consideration of desirable experiences. In planning, those teachers follow a process of self-questioning somewhat like the following:

1. What topics do the textbook, curriculum guide, achievement tests, and my personal beliefs and experiences suggest that I ought to cover this year?
2. What beneficial experiences can I provide for my students within each of these topics? What will students find enjoyable and worthwhile? What books, pictures, videotapes, and other materials and objects (and maybe even guests) can I use?
3. Which district, state, and federal standards will be addressed through these activities?
4. How can I organize these activities to fit into the time allotments I have available?
5. How will I evaluate my students' work, and how can I let them show their parents and others how much they have learned?

You can see that this procedure for organizing instructional units proceeds from a list of experiences that teachers believe good for their students, not from a list of objectives. The teachers still have objectives, or outcomes, in mind, but they think first about quality experiences.

For Lisa Johnston, who teaches a multi-age class, it is important that all her students receive adequate instruction in the appropriate fourth- and fifth-grade content areas.

> At the beginning of the year I decide on the themes that will organize my teaching and provide frameworks for my students to make meaningful connections throughout the year. I plan my curriculum after I review the state and local standards for the two grade levels. To engage and help all my students be successful, I mentally divide them into three categories based on their readiness, interest, and learning profile for this topic or concept: advanced, average, and struggling learners. Then I plan different ways to approach the topic for each of the three groups. For example, I might provide different reading materials to differentiate the content. I might vary the process by which students make sense out of their study. Or I might suggest different ways for students to extend their learning and demonstrate their understanding.

It is important to note here that teachers can use the backward design process to develop unit plans and apply it to their planning for the entire year. The process is the same: First, identify the desired results for the unit of study. Then, determine acceptable evidence to demonstrate student understanding. Finally, plan the learning experiences and instruction.

Organizing Thematic Units of Instruction

Thematic units of instruction that integrate teaching from several different subject areas are strongly popular. To show how thematic units are planned, let's consider a unit entitled "Lands and People of South America." For this unit we want to integrate social studies, art, music, math, science, reading, and language arts, all having to do with the regions being studied—and all contributing to a greater breadth of understanding of South American people and geography.

We begin by selecting the broad central theme, "Lands and People of South America." That theme can be visualized as the hub of a wheel, whose spokes are composed of the various subjects to be integrated, such as social studies, art, music, math, science, reading, and language arts.

First, list separate regions of South America on the hub of the wheel. These might include the high Andes, the Amazon basin, the northern region, the Patagonian grasslands, and the Chilean coastline. Next, make balanced associations between these hub regions and the spoke subjects in order to identify lesson topics on art, music, customs, lifestyles, and languages. Included in the lessons might be map study with depiction of populations, ethnic distribution, and distances between cities and landmarks; study of animals indigenous to the various areas; family life in areas of dense and sparse population; popular music, folk songs, and instruments; illustrations of typical clothing, dwellings, and artifacts; words important in the study of South America; and stories and nonfiction accounts of life in South America.

A review of state and local standards will help identify appropriate reading, writing, and math, as well as social studies and science standards that should be addressed in this study. Once the standards and lesson topics are identified, specific activities and materials

FIGURE 2.1   Interdisciplinary Concept Model

(From *Interdisciplinary Curriculum: Design and Implementation* edited by Heidi Hayes Jacobs. Alexandria, VA: Association for Supervision and Curriculum Development. Copyright © 1989 Thomas Armstrong. Reprinted by permission. All rights reserved.)

can be selected and time segments allocated. Because activities are the crux of all units, the planning process involves questions about activities and materials such as

- What can the children read?
- What can they look at?
- What can they listen to?
- What can they construct?
- What can they write?
- What can they discuss?
- What can they work on individually, and what cooperatively?
- What can they perform, produce, or display?
- What evidence will indicate their degree of learning and enjoyment?

As you can see, a unit is extensive and can be expanded or contracted as needed.

It has long been said that when humans learn they remember approximately

10 percent of what they read
20 percent of what they hear
30 percent of what they see
70 percent of what they say
90 percent of what they do

And yet education still most strongly emphasizes reading and hearing.

Smoothing and Sparkling

Units should be organized to alternate between times of quiet routine work and tasks that have higher excitement and interest value. Carol Mercer, a fourth-grade teacher, refers to such alternations as *smoothers* and *sparklers*. She explains:

> By smoothers I mean the things I do to provide calm, purposeful work, routine but necessary. In my math units for example, for smoothers I
>
> 1. Establish skill groups and assign them names
> 2. Establish routine schedules and procedures
> 3. Use monitors to distribute and collect materials
> 4. Begin all skill lessons in the same way
> 5. Give explicit directions
> 6. Post all assignments on the board
> 7. Allow time for follow-up work
>
> For sparklers in my math units I
>
> 1. Use games, flash cards, fun sheets, and puzzles
> 2. Relate math skills to other areas of the curriculum
> 3. Post a math riddle and special problem each day
> 4. Use department store advertisements for various applications of math skills
> 5. Have students act out math processes
> 6. Let students solve puzzles cooperatively.

A Word about Individual Lessons

Units of instruction are accomplished through the individual lessons that comprise each unit. These individual lessons should be planned carefully so that activities, materials, work, space, procedures, homework, and means of assessment can all be communicated clearly to students.

Suggestions for planning, sequencing, and communicating lessons to all concerned are presented in Chapter 6. However, before considering such detailed aspects of instructional management, we need to explore how, in keeping with the curriculum and calendar, the physical environment of the classroom should be organized and managed. That is the topic of Chapter 3. Before proceeding to Chapter 3, take time to explore these end-of-chapter activities.

Parting Thought

Here is the truth about making a plan: It never works. (Not in the way you plan it, that is.) If, however, you do make a plan, the chances of getting what you want significantly increase.

—John-Roger and Peter McWilliams

SUMMARY SELF-CHECK

Check off the following as you either understand or become able to apply them.

❏ Before planning a year's program of studies, mark important dates on a yearly calendar (vacations, celebrations, special events, school assemblies, conferences, and report card dates) and make note of themes and available blocks of time.

❏ In curriculum management we hope to bring about a purposeful and efficient interaction between students and what they are supposed to learn in school.

❏ Curriculum maps help identify redundancies and gaps in standards, content, and skills.

❏ In the backward design process of planning, teachers identify desired results and determine acceptable evidence before they plan the learning experiences and instruction.

❏ Curriculum standards help define skills, knowledge, and content mastery for students.

❏ A large portion of elementary teaching is done through instructional units, which are related lessons that work together to build larger learnings.

❏ Before planning specific units of instruction, first decide on the daily schedule, then lay out the desired instructional units for the year.

❏ Appropriate national, state, and district standards must be considered when planning instructional units.

❏ Preorganized units are often found in teacher editions of student textbooks, but most teachers plan many units of their own.

❏ Authorities recommend planning units by
  - Identifying standards most appropriate for the unit of study
  - Formulating overall goals or essential or guiding questions
  - Formulating interim objectives
  - Selecting and sequencing activities and materials for the achievement of each interim objective
  - Evaluating student learning in terms of the stated objectives

❏ Many teachers plan their units by
  - Identifying important topics
  - Identifying appropriate state and district standards
  - Thinking of beneficial activities and materials related to the topics
  - Fitting those activities into lessons and time slots
  - Deciding how students are to be evaluated
  - Deciding how students can demonstrate their accomplishments and learning

❏ Thematic units that integrate several subject areas are popular.

❏ Backward design planning can be used for planning the year's curriculum, as well as for unit planning.

❑ Activities are of prime importance in all units; when planning units, teachers should continually think in terms of the following questions:

- What can the children read?
- What can they look at?
- What can they listen to?
- What can they construct?
- What can they write?
- What can they discuss?
- What can they work on individually, and what cooperatively?
- What can they perform, produce, or display?
- What evidence will indicate their degree of learning and enjoyment?

ACTIVITIES FOR REFLECTION AND GROWTH

For Cumulative Skills Development

1. Take a moment to review the statements in the Anticipation–Reaction Guide at the beginning of this chapter. Put a check mark in the Reaction column next to any statement with which you now agree. How have your thoughts changed since reading this chapter?

2. Suppose that January 2 falls on Monday. Lay out the January calendar to determine teaching days and any celebration days that might influence your curriculum.

3. How do lessons, instructional units, and thematic units differ? How are they similar? Why is so much of the elementary curriculum organized into units? Illustrate your conclusions by summarizing what might be done in a short primary-grade unit on dinosaurs, first as a traditional unit and then as a thematic unit.

4. It has been suggested that many teachers do not plan their units as authorities recommend. Describe the purported difference. Based on your experience or supposition, would you say the assertion is correct or incorrect?

5. Suppose you wanted to plan a very short unit (perhaps consisting of only a lesson or two) on the life cycle of the trumpeter swan. Do your planning in two ways:

    First, make a plan beginning with two or three specific objectives, written in terms of what we can later actually see or hear students do as a result of what they have learned (e.g., "Students will demonstrate understanding of the trumpeter swan's habitat by describing the unique environment in which it lives and by indicating its nesting areas on a map of North America."). Your lesson activities should be aimed directly at helping students reach your stated objectives.

    Second, make a plan beginning with two or three experiences you'd like your students to have concerning trumpeter swans. Your lesson activities and materials should be elaborations or manifestations of the experiences you named.

    What do you see as the comparative advantages and disadvantages of these two planning approaches?

6. For a grade level of your choosing, work in teams to outline the major elements of the language arts/literacy curriculum found in an area school (step one of curriculum mapping).

List the standards, processes, skills, essential content and topics, and the products and performances that are expected to demonstrate student learning.

REFERENCES AND RECOMMENDED READINGS

Doll, R. (1992). *Curriculum improvement: Decision making and process* (8th ed.). Boston: Allyn & Bacon.

Eisner, E. (1985). *The educational imagination: On the design and evaluation of school programs* (2nd ed.). New York: Macmillan.

English, F. (1983). Contemporary curriculum circumstances. In F. W. English (Ed.), *Fundamental curriculum decisions.* Alexandria, VA: Association for Supervision and Curriculum Development.

Evertson, C., Emmer, E., Clements, B., Sanford, J., & Worsham, M. (2003). *Classroom management for elementary teachers* (6th ed.). Boston: Allyn & Bacon.

Goodlad, J. (1984). *A place called school: Prospectives for the future.* New York: McGraw-Hill.

Harvey, S., & Goudvis, A. (2000). *Strategies that work: Teaching comprehension to enhance understanding.* New York: Stenhouse Publishers.

Jacobs, H. (1989). *Interdisciplinary curriculum: Design and implementation.* Alexandria, VA: Association for Supervision and Curriculum Development.

Jacobs, H. (1997). *Mapping the big picture: Integrating curriculum & Assessment K–12.* Alexandria, VA: Association for Supervision and Curriculum Development.

Keene, E., & Zimmermann, S. (1997). *Mosaic of thought: Teaching comprehension in a reader's workshop.* Portsmouth, NH: Heinemann.

McWilliams, J., & McWilliams, P. (1995). *The portable life 101.* Los Angeles: Prelude Press.

Newmann, D. (1997). *The compleat teacher's almanack: A daily guide to all 12 months of the year.* New York: Fine Communications.

Rosales-Dordelly, C., & Short, E. (1985). *Curriculum professors' specialized knowledge.* Lanham, MD: University Press of America.

Thousand, J., Villa, R., & Nevin, A. (2002). *Creativity and collaborative learning: The practical guide to empowering students, teachers, and families* (2nd ed.). Baltimore: Paul H. Brookes.

Tomlinson, C. (1999). *The differentiated classroom: Responding to the needs of all learners.* Alexandria, VA: Association for Supervision and Curriculum Development.

Traver, R. (1998). What is a good guiding question? *Educational Leadership, 55*(6), 70–73.

Tyler, R. (1949). *Basic principles of curriculum and instruction.* Chicago: University of Chicago Press.

Wiggins, G., & McTighe, J. (1998). *Understanding by design.* Alexandria, VA: Association for Supervision and Curriculum Development.

CHAPTER

3

Managing the Physical Environment of the Classroom

A bare room is like a boring teacher. Both lack the pizzazz which is the soul of teaching.

—Kathy Paterson

ANTICIPATION–REACTION GUIDE

Before you read the chapter, take a moment to put a check mark in the Anticipation column next to any statement with which you agree.

	Anticipation	Reaction
The main purpose of bulletin boards should be to beautify the room.	❑	❑
Experience has taught that the overall best class environment emphasizes the chalk- or whiteboard and rows of student seats.	❑	❑
Ceiling space is an important but often forgotten facet of the physical environment.	❑	❑
Modular clusters seem to provide the greatest seating advantages, including benefits for students with special needs.	❑	❑
A main disadvantage of modular clusters is that they encourage students to talk and interact with others, even when this is not appropriate.	❑	❑
Ambience is, in reality, a synonym for teacher personality.	❑	❑
Any music can be used effectively in the classroom, as long as the children like it.	❑	❑
The main principle underlying management of physical space is that the physical classroom should enhance the activities included in the curriculum.	❑	❑
An important guideline for managing the physical environment is to keep it clean and in good order.	❑	❑
All students should have responsibilities for helping to maintain the physical environment.	❑	❑

Once the calendar and curriculum have been interwoven and tentatively set, the next step in overall classroom management is to organize the interior of the classroom so it not only reflects but also substantially contributes to the learning and behavior goals of the program. This can be done in elementary school classrooms better than anywhere else (with the possible exception of secondary school laboratories and athletic facilities). Some classrooms are works of art, richly equipped and beautifully laid out, in which you would consider children fortunate to spend their days. Other rooms are austere, dull, and uninspiring; you would pity students trapped in them.

Classrooms often reflect the personality of the teacher. However, beautiful classrooms can be run by teachers who are punitively harsh and cold, and uninspired classrooms can be the domains of warm and nurturing teachers. This fact reminds us that quality of teaching cannot be judged solely on the basis of room appearance. That, however, does not detract from this basic point:

> The physical environment can and should be organized so as to further the
> program of instruction and activity.

This bears repeating, and should be understood before you read on. What you put into your classroom should have instructional purpose. There is little point in loading it with decorations that have no instructional value and do not contribute to the program, except perhaps to charm parents and administrators. But the classroom just as easily can be made attractive—and more usefully so—by setting it up with interesting activities and stimulating materials. Teachers have a free hand in setting up their workplaces—almost anything is permitted, within reason of course, and it begins with their own mental image of a classroom.

The Pictures We Hold in Our Heads

All of us hold some mental picture of what school classrooms should look like. Many of us imagine rows of desks with a chalkboard and teacher in front, one or two doors on the side, perhaps a coatroom in the back, and windows with shelves of dusty reference books. While such classrooms have been used to advantage by thousands of teachers over the decades to teach millions of students, there are better ways of setting up the classroom—ways that affect attitudes, efficiency, and overall learning. Suppose, for example, you plan to have your students do the following:

> Make stick puppets to use in retelling a story.
> Write and share original haiku poems.
> Create a *Who's Who* book of class members.
> Write letters to a class in a foreign country.
> Build a model of a community.
> Make graphs of daily weather phenomena.
> Monitor and record the growth cycles of plants from seeds.
> Learn a folk dance from another country.
> Compare the latitudes of foreign capital cities.
> Make a video of life in the school or classroom.

As you consider these activities, you begin finding hints for organizing the room. The guiding question might be: How can my room best help me do justice to what I want my students to experience and learn?

As the question suggests, the classroom should be made to accommodate and to further a variety of educational activities. Math and language, for example, may require students to quietly work at their seats with furnished materials. Social studies may call for active collaborative work in construction, drawing, or discussion. Science and art often require special workspaces and materials. Dance, music, and drama require open space for movement. Each type of activity calls for its own space, seating, movement, materials, and interactions.

Just how classrooms can be made both rich and flexible will be explained presently, but let us first take a moment to remind ourselves of a seldom-remembered but fundamentally important fact: The room should be set up for the teacher's pleasure, too. Some teachers are more comfortable—and possibly more effective—when working in highly structured programs that hold students under tight supervision and that direct them through assignments. Other teachers are more comfortable—and possibly more effective—when giving students leeway in selecting activities, obtaining and using appropriate materials, and working cooperatively with fellow students. We go too far when we expect all teachers to teach in a single, specified way, especially when that certain way changes from year to year, as is often the case. Teachers are different and have different styles, and most of them would benefit from being allowed to use their talents to their fullest.

Remember, too, that just as teachers show different styles of teaching, so will they set up their classrooms differently. Some prefer their rooms to be richly furnished with materials, charts, pictures, animals, decorations, and slogans, believing that this keeps the classroom fully stimulating. Others prefer their rooms to be clean and efficient, with materials at hand only when relevant to what is being studied at a particular time. Such teachers find heavily decorated classrooms distracting and believe that students find them distracting, too. Effective teaching can occur in both these physical settings, which again suggests the desirability of allowing serious-minded teachers to rely on their own best judgments. Regardless of their differing styles, teachers should consider all areas of the classroom when organizing the physical environment.

Six Facets of the Physical Environment

This analysis breaks the physical classroom into six components: (1) floor space, (2) wall space, (3) countertop space, (4) shelf space, (5) cupboard and closet space, and (6) ambience. Many teachers use a seventh facet as well—the ceiling. The ceiling does offer many possibilities but is not considered here because attaching materials to it may increase fire hazard, and is often a violation of local fire codes. Let's explore some of the possibilities afforded by the other six facets.

Floor Space

One of the first things a teacher has to decide is how to position students for the various activities that involve individual and group work. This not only affects seating arrangements, but also traffic patterns and work/activity areas (including interest centers, teacher's station, and special-effects areas). Because today's classrooms are inclusive and teachers can expect physical and language diversities among their students, it is also important to consider floor space as it relates to any special needs for students, including proximate space for related service providers.

Seating. In the not-so-distant past, student desks were anchored to wooden runners, where they remained unmoved until rusted out or ripped up. You probably won't see that now except in museums. Seating in today's schools is intended to be flexible so various groupings can be made and space opened for multiple purposes, according to the needs of the subjects taught. Teachers arrange seating at their discretion, keeping in mind two cautions: First, students shouldn't be placed so they have to look directly into strong light—the resultant strain causes tension and makes concentration difficult. Investigators, including Hathaway et al. (1992), have documented possible health effects of lighting. Second, when students are asked to rearrange their desks and tables, they show a penchant for shoving, bumping, making noise, and pestering each other. Accept this as a fact of teaching, and when you ask students to rearrange their seating areas, remind them in a positive tone to do so in accordance with class rules.

When students are taught as a total group, they should be seated as near to the teacher as feasible, facing a chalkboard or dry erase board. Primary students may come together on a small carpet area for whole-group instruction. The teacher may sit with them on the carpet or in a chair, often near a small board or an easel. Well-behaved students can be placed close together, but some students may have to be separated a bit. Designating marks or colored squares on the carpet is a common method of arrangement. During guided study, students sometimes will be asked to work alone and sometimes in cooperative groups. Normally the teacher will circulate among students to monitor and help. For ease of movement, aisles and gaps in seating should be maintained, but the distance between the teacher and the farthest student should be as minimal as possible.

When students are taught in small groups, they may be called to special areas where extra chairs are kept or to which they bring their own chairs. Ideally, the floor arrangement will keep the teacher, while interacting with the small group, in fairly close proximity to students working at their desks. The teacher must be able to oversee everyone in the class, and such watchfulness should be evident to students.

Popular seating arrangements include rows, circles, semicircles, and long tables. Jones (2000) advocates creating an interior loop or walkway, with the least distance and the fewest barriers between the teacher and every student in the classroom, so the teacher can easily and efficiently "work the crowd" (see Figure 3.1).

Others find that modular clusters seem to best meet the demands of modern classrooms, where large- and small-group instruction, cooperative group- and teamwork, and individual seatwork are routinely interchanged. Kagan (1994) recommends group arrangements that enable students to engage in classbuilding and teambuilding activities for successful cooperative learning. For example, four students sitting in pairs on opposite sides of a table (or with their desks placed so they face each other) can work as shoulder partners, as face partners, or as teams of four. Kagan further suggests that placing students with comparable language and achievement abilities on the same side of the table so they

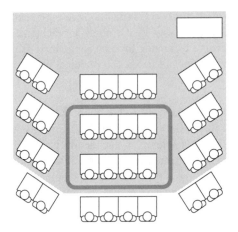

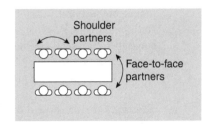

FIGURE 3.2 Kagan encourages group arrangements so students can interact with shoulder partners, face partners, and teams of four.

FIGURE 3.1 Jones's interior loop: Walkways that allow teachers to "work the crowd" with the fewest steps are created by bringing students forward and packing them sideways.

(Fred Jones *Tools for Teaching,* 2000, www.fredjones.com)

can work as shoulder partners ensures the best mix for partnering and processing information and tasks (see Figure 3.2).

Modular clusters of five or six students afford fairly good eye contact among students and between the teacher and individual students, enable easy transition into cooperative work, allow good traffic flow, and provide the flexibility for obtaining extra floor space when needed. Such small group clusters are also most effective in facilitating the inclusion of students with disabilities (Udvari-Solner, 1995). Figure 3.3 shows an example of modular seating for thirty-six students.

Beth Davies, a fifth-grade teacher who prefers modular cluster seating, describes how she uses it:

> Initially I choose the places where the children sit. Once they become acquainted I let them contract to sit by a person of their choice but still within their original cluster. By this time they understand about my right to teach and their right to learn without disruption, and they know I will immediately move any person who abuses their contract. In each cluster of desks I try to balance the lower-achieving students with the higher achieving, in order to mix minds and provide help during group work.

Work and Activity Areas. These areas are affected, in turn, by the room's seating arrangement. Compact seating makes space available to begin with, and rearranging the seats provides still more space. Of course, you don't need extra space for all activities. Reading, math, spelling, handwriting, and guided seatwork are frequently conducted with students in their assigned seats. Activities in social studies, science, art, music, drama, and dance often involve movement and require extra space.

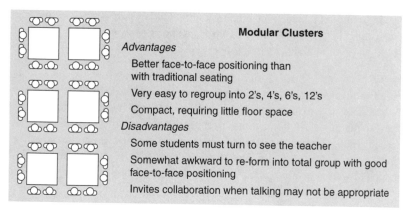

Modular Clusters

Advantages

Better face-to-face positioning than with traditional seating

Very easy to regroup into 2's, 4's, 6's, 12's

Compact, requiring little floor space

Disadvantages

Some students must turn to see the teacher

Somewhat awkward to re-form into total group with good face-to-face positioning

Invites collaboration when talking may not be appropriate

FIGURE 3.3   Modular Cluster Seating

Space is needed for other purposes as well. Most teachers like to include one or more special centers, corners, or interest areas. An art center with easels may be present. Freestanding learning centers may be on the floor, though they are more commonly placed on tables or countertops. Special corners for quiet reading, science projects, map and globe study, or individual investigations are frequently seen. Most classrooms also have at least one computer for students to use in writing, math, and other areas. Because of their operating noise, lighting needs, and potential distractibility, computers require additional considerations. Teacher Jearine Bacon, who makes extensive use of computers in her primary classroom, describes some of the cautions to keep in mind concerning the classroom computer:

Classroom computers are extremely motivating and useful in the classroom, but care should be taken in their use. The computer should be away from liquids, dust, and extreme heat, and some distance from the chalkboard. The screen should be shielded from other students so that it will not be a distraction, and students should be reminded frequently of the rules for use and care of the computer. Computers are expensive to repair and frustrating to use when not working properly.

Some teachers also like to set aside a special space in the classroom as a reward for responsible student behavior or good work. Here, teachers sometimes put cushions, a thick rug, a computer, interesting books and magazines, individual slide viewers, and headsets for listening to music or stories.

The teacher's station—normally a desk—should be placed in a position that oversees the entire class, ideally to the side or the back of the room. It is a good idea to make the teacher's station attractive and special, as it enhances one's position as authority and can help students feel honored when called there. It should begin with a clean desk (a good example for students), an attractive file cabinet, and shelves for a small collection of personal books. Photographs of family, friends, or pets add touches that students like. Artifacts, weavings, and art prints contribute tastefully. One or two articles of high prestige for students can be kept there, such as a puppet, a sports team pennant, or a large toy animal. A special chair for students can provide a pleasant place for individual conferencing.

Traffic Patterns.   Student movement around the room must be given careful attention, because congestion, waiting, and unnecessary contact usually lead to disruptive behavior. For students with disabilities, traffic patterns must be free from barriers and allow easy access to materials. Students routinely enter and exit the room, obtain and return materials, sharpen pencils (some teachers keep a supply sharpened, to exchange when needed), get drinks, go to learning centers, feed the fish, approach the teacher, and so on. Traffic routes for such movements must be kept open, a concern not to be taken lightly when deciding on the layout of the room. Figure 3.4 shows floor space arrangement for a hypothetical elementary school classroom.

Wall Space

Classroom walls are rarely used to full advantage, but they offer excellent instructional possibilities. Chalkboards and whiteboards remain one of the most valuable of all teaching tools. They are routinely used to post daily information, assignments, math problems, and vocabulary words. Most teachers use them for explanations and demonstrations. Often overlooked, however, is the delight many students find in going to the board to work.

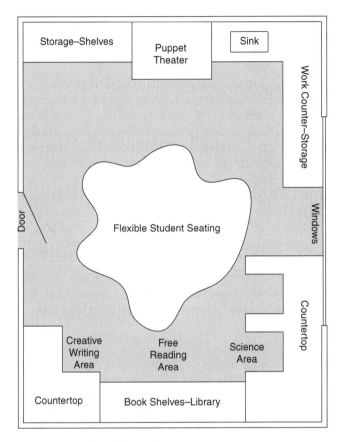

FIGURE 3.4 Floor Space Arrangement

Bulletin boards, though present in practically every classroom, tend to be used mostly for decoration and rarely for instruction. Decorations can make a room pleasant to look at, but with a bit of thought they can also serve the more important purpose of instruction. More valuable than mere decoration are displays such as puzzles that draw students' attention and make them think, clippings from newspapers and magazines that serve as focal points for class discussion, and interactive and creative ideas and problem situations that stimulate writing and debate. Perhaps best of all, bulletin boards are excellent places for displaying student work, art prints, or other visual materials.

Displays of Student Work. It's advisable to give all students the opportunity to display samples of their work in the classroom. Not just any work should be shown, especially when the work is not commensurate with student ability. However, when excellence is obvious or marked improvement is evident, putting that work on display—with the student's permission—is a good way to provide recognition. This recognition gives students a sense of ownership in their classroom, as well as a sense of accomplishment and the understanding that others care about their performance. It also builds self-esteem and is highly motivating.

Art Prints and Other Visual Materials.   Art prints that relate to the curriculum tend to be overlooked by students unless attention is drawn to them in art lessons. The same can be said for most maps, globes, and charts, though students often enjoy simply exploring maps once they learn how to use them.

Wall space should be used for posting graphic models, visual instruction plans, and reminders. Such materials are chronically underutilized given the help they provide students and teachers. These visual materials illustrate and help explain products or procedures such as the parts of a business letter, elements of sentences and paragraphs, steps in long division, proper use of the computer, proper editing notations and publishing procedures, and any number of explanations and reminders that teachers must otherwise repeat, sometimes to the point of exasperation.

You also may consider posting inspirational slogans and class mottoes, class rules, reminders on how to help substitute teachers, and a synopsis of the class goals for the year. Adelheida Montante Castañeda, a sixth-grade teacher, describes four of her favorite visual materials:

Across the room from the entry door is my largest bulletin board, where four posters hang, visible to anyone who comes into the room. I have treasured these posters over the years because they emphasize positive learning, good citizenship, challenge, and determination.

1. My greatest challenge in life is doing what others think I cannot do.

2. Tell me, I forget Show me, I remember Involve me, I understand.

3. My Classroom Rights
  a. I have the right to be happy and to be treated with compassion in this room. This means that no one will laugh at me or hurt my feelings.
  b. I have a right to be safe in this room. This means that no one will kick me, punch me, push me, or hurt me.
  c. I have a right to hear and be heard in this room. This means that no one will yell, scream, shout, or make noises.
  d. I have a right to learn about myself in this room. This means that I will be free to express my feelings and my opinions without being interrupted or punished and as long as the rights of others are not infringed.

4. How to Get Better Grades
  a. Be on time and ready to work.
  b. Follow directions.
  c. Work neatly and accurately.
  d. Ask for help when you need it.
  e. Check your work.
  f. Find a time and place to study.
  g. Take responsibility for yourself.

Countertop Space

A good deal of useful space is available in most classrooms on the countertops that often run beneath windows. Because they are near a good source of natural light, such countertops are well suited to many kinds of science activities, especially those involving living plants. They are also good places for aquariums and terrariums if the outside light is not too strong or hot. Other kinds of science projects find useful placement here as well—experiments, projects in progress, and models of human torsos, sense organs, skeletons, dinosaurs, atoms, molecules, and the like. Globes fit nicely on countertops and can be wonderful instructional devices since they show not only the shape of the earth, but also the relative locations of and distances between landmasses, oceans, countries, and cities. They are important to the study of history, geography, astronomy, and current events. Kits of various kinds that are in most classrooms, often on countertops, typically contain science projects or materials to supplement instruction in reading, spelling, social studies, and mathematics.

Shelf Space

Shelves, if not built into classrooms, can be inexpensively added by stacking pine boards on concrete blocks. Textbooks, reference books, class libraries, and other special materials are typically stored or displayed on shelves.

Textbooks usually accompany the core curricular areas: reading, mathematics, social studies, science, and language. Many teachers keep the textbooks on shelves and distribute them to students when needed.

Reference books are heavily used in the curricula above primary grades. They are normally kept on shelves and typically include dictionaries, encyclopedias, almanacs, atlases, thesauruses, and special reference books such as the *Guinness Book of Records, The Farmer's Almanac,* and the *Golden Library.*

If not kept on a book carousel, a small class library is often found on classroom shelves. A class library usually consists of easy-to-read books of high interest to students, plus magazines such as *National Geographic Kids.* Teachers scour many sources to find such materials at low prices, and students' caregivers often donate such materials. The library may also include student-written materials that are laminated or bound into small books and often contain illustrations by the authors. Rebecca Cummings, a third-grade teacher, describes how her students share their published stories:

> My third-graders write, illustrate, and bind their own stories into books. They read the books aloud to the class, and then take them home to read to their parents. When the books are returned, they are placed on a special shelf in our classroom library. When children finish their work, they may select a classmate's book to read. These books are treated like genuine treasures. At the end of the year, the children take their books home, though I always beg to keep a few to show next year's class.

Special materials to motivate and extend students' experiences are kept on shelves in most classrooms. Examples include video and audio CDs and tapes, games, puzzles, puppets, toys, photo collections, collections of shells and fossils, and the like. Some teachers create a video lending library that includes videotapes of the children as they work on projects and activities during the year. Of course, before children are videotaped, parents or guardians must grant permission, and when taping, equal time must be given for every child. The videotapes are kept on a library shelf and checked out to be viewed at home by parents, grandparents, and others who are not able to be in the classroom during the day.

Cupboard and Closet Space

Classroom cupboards and closets are useful places for keeping student supplies, work sheets, audiovisual equipment, physical education or subject specific equipment, and cleaning materials. They are also good places to store materials used for special occasions such as sports days and certain times of the year such as the winter holidays.

Student supplies include such things as writing paper, construction paper, pencils, scissors, glue, paints, crayons, rulers, and pens. In most schools, smaller quantities of supplies are kept in classroom cupboards while larger quantities are stored in a central teachers' supply room or workroom.

Work sheets are used—overused, many believe—in great quantities in most classrooms. Usually the teacher, aide, or volunteer duplicates them. Work sheets are useful for drilling skills and preparing students for timed tests, but they are of little value when used only to keep children busy.

Audiovisual equipment is usually kept in a central area of the school from where it is checked out. Many classrooms now have their own television and VCR either mounted on a wall or on a moveable cart. Classrooms may also have tape recorders, CD players, overhead projectors, smaller three-dimensional models, and sometimes, slide viewers. Some of these will be kept on tables, and others in cabinets, to be brought out when needed. More expensive items, such as micro-projectors, larger models such as human torsos, large art collections, motion picture projectors (although these have mostly been replaced by VCRs), and so forth, are checked out from a central repository for short-term use.

Physical education equipment or equipment used for specific content areas are often kept in containers and stored in closets. Physical education equipment, usually consisting of little besides balls and jump ropes, with the room number clearly written on each, is kept in closets, frequently in large plastic garbage bins. Manipulatives for math are kept in appropriately sized storage containers. Plastic boxes that are the same size, stackable, and clear for easy viewing of the contents work well for this purpose and can be purchased, on sale, at many stores.

Each room's personal set of cleaning materials is also found in the classroom closet and usually includes a broom, dust cloths, cleanser, paper towels, and rags. A small vacuum cleaner is very useful but will probably not be provided by the school. These materials permit students and teachers to take care of routine spills, dusting, and other necessary cleaning that is beyond what the custodians are available to do. Student monitors can be helpful in this regard.

Finally, collections of special materials for Presidents' Day, Saint Patrick's Day, Valentine's Day, Thanksgiving, winter and spring holidays, and other themes are usually kept in large cardboard file boxes and stored in closets.

Ambience

Ambience refers to the totality of intangible impressions that pervade the physical classroom—an atmosphere that at its best conveys excitement, aesthetics, comfort, security, and pleasure. It is created in large part by the contents of the room, which many teachers further enhance with art and music. Most schools or district media centers make available prints, carvings, weavings, and photographs, which provide focal points for learning about artists and media. Cassette tapes and CDs can provide music that is excellent for relaxation and mood setting, not to mention the opportunity they provide for learning about composers and performers.

Research, including the "Mozart Effect" study (Rauscher, Shaw, Levine, Ky, & Wright, 1993; see also Campbell, 1992, 1997, 2000), is investigating the effectiveness and use of music in the classroom. We now know that music effects changes in the mind and body. With this knowledge, teachers can play the right type of music for the desired objective: thinking, relaxing, learning, destressing, concentration, inspiration, and productivity.

Appropriate music can help reduce stress and can heighten alertness, excitement, relaxation, and emotional well being, as well as creativity. Sometimes we want students to reflect and relax. Music with 50 to 60 beats per minute, as well as environmental music of birds, waterfalls, and the like, works best for this. Sometimes we want students to work independently or quietly, for example during journal or creative writing, or problem solving. For these times we should use music that is 60 to 70 beats per minute. Best for this is baroque-style music and some of the "gentle modern classics" of the nineteenth and twentieth centuries by Beethoven, Chopin, Debussy, and others. Sometimes we want to energize students. We now know that upbeat music with 120 beats per minute, such as many of the songs of the 60s and 70s, works well for managing and energizing transitions.

We know that music contributes to the classroom ambience. As an aside, it is important to be knowledgeable about the ethics and legalities of using music. If you use music only with your students and in your classroom, you do not need a license. If, however, you use music in other venues (workshops or other presentations) a license may be required. When in doubt you should contact the performing rights organization. You can email questions to Broadcast Music, Inc. (BMI) at genlic@bmi.com or call them directly at 877-264-2137.

Many teachers enhance ambience through special themes built around children's literature, professional athletics, popular music, cartoon characters, favorite motion pictures—whatever seems to attract students' interest. Both the room and lessons can reflect elements of the selected theme—characters, emblems, photographs, drawings, colors, sayings, music, and so forth. Students respond well to such themes and like to help in their selection and organization.

Finally, a number of special touches and events add to the room ambience—videos, popcorn parties, classroom pets, favorite plants, class murals or quilts, and time lines that depict the history of the year's dates, events, and accomplishments. Ambience deserves this attention because it helps teachers provide students comfort, enjoyment, stimulation, and satisfaction.

Confusing or Engaging?

Attention to physical environment should not result in a confused mess. It is the teacher's responsibility to ensure that it does not. Each of the six facets that comprise the classroom's physical environment should be carefully considered and used to best advantage. As mentioned, best advantage for some teachers means keeping the environment relatively lean, efficient, and nondistracting, whereas others may see it differently. It depends on teacher and students. In any case, the physical environment should always be kept clean and in good order.

Toward that end and to the extent their maturity allows, students should be given major responsibility in taking care of the classroom and the materials it contains. As they keep things orderly and clean, students have the opportunity to build sound values of aesthetics, ecology, and responsibility.

Teachers who succeed in making their classrooms enjoyable, engaging places in which to work and learn leave impressions such as the one Carlos Bachicha has of Miss Osborne's classroom:

> I don't remember much about my fourth-grade year in school, except that I rode on the same bicycle with my brother and carved a soap elephant that looked much like a pig. My sixth-grade year is even more blank. But my fifth—that's a different story. The teacher was Miss Osborne, and she had red hair and freckles and was forever having us do something interesting in class. We performed plays while wearing paper costumes we cut and stapled together—we thought they looked real enough. We parched corn and smashed it into cornmeal, and a mom baked it and we ate it with butter.
>
> Miss Osborne took us to her house one day to run a spinning wheel, a real one. A bee from her lawn stung me on the toe—I guess she let us go barefoot. That was a long time ago, but I remember her and that year like they were yesterday.

This brings us to the end of our brief exploration of purposes, arrangements, and contents of the physical environment of the classroom. Before proceeding to Chapter 4, which deals with the psychosocial environment of the classroom, take time to explore these end-of-chapter activities.

Parting Thought

Vision is the ability to make a dream a reality.

S U M M A R Y   S E L F - C H E C K

Check off the following as you either understand or become able to apply them.

❑   The physical environment of the classroom should be arranged and managed so as to enhance the activities called for in the curriculum. Keeping in mind preferences of teachers and students, give attention to six facets of the physical environment

■   Floor space: seating, work, and activity areas; teacher's station; special centers and special-effects areas; traffic patterns; students with disabilities and special needs

- Wall space: chalk- and whiteboards; bulletin boards and display areas; prints, maps, and charts
- Countertop space: science projects; globes, kits, and models
- Shelf space: textbooks, reference books, popular library books, special materials
- Cupboard and closet space: student supplies, work sheets, audiovisual equipment, physical education or subject specific equipment, cleaning materials, special decorations or collections
- Ambience: art objects, background music, themes, other special touches

ACTIVITIES FOR REFLECTION AND GROWTH

For Cumulative Skills Development

1. Take a moment to review the statements in the Anticipation–Reaction Guide at the beginning of this chapter. Put a check mark in the Reaction column next to any statement with which you now agree. How have your thoughts changed since reading this chapter?

2. Discuss your feelings concerning the degree to which you'd like your classroom to include various items (materials, photos, models, collections, and so on). Comment on (1) your personal preferences concerning richness/leanness of classrooms you have attended, (2) student interest, involvement, and motivation, and (3) how you would manage the types of items you would use.

3. For which aspects of physical classroom management would you assign student responsibilities, not only to help but also to increase the sense of student ownership of the classroom?

4. In the text the statement was made that "the room should be set up for the teacher's pleasure, too." To what specifically do you think that statement refers? Do you consider it a valid point?

5. Suppose you are teaching a third-grade class. In the afternoons you like to rearrange the seating to provide additional floor space for movement activities. Describe specifically how you would train your students to move furniture so that everything is done quickly, correctly, and with no horseplay.

6. Schools provide custodians whose duties include cleaning the classrooms. To what extent, if any, would you want your class (and yourself) to be responsible for cleaning and tidying the room? Justify your opinion in terms of its value to students and their program.

REFERENCES AND RECOMMENDED READINGS

Campbell, D. G. (1992). *Introduction to the musical brain.* St. Louis: MMB Music.

Campbell, D. G. (1997). *The Mozart Effect: Tapping the power of music to heal the body, strengthen the mind, and unlock the creative spirit.* New York: Avon Books.

Campbell, D. G. (2000). *The Mozart Effect for children: Awakening your child's mind, health, and creativity with music.* New York: William Morrow.

Evertson, C., Emmer, E., & Worsham, M. (2003). *Classroom management for elementary teachers* (6th ed.). Boston: Allyn & Bacon.

Hathaway, W., et al. (1992). *A study into the effects of light on children of elementary school age—a case of light robbery.* Unpublished manuscript, Planning and Information Services, Alberta Department of Education, Edmonton, Alberta, Canada.

Hebert, E. (1998, September). Designing matters: How school environment affects children. *Educational Leadership, 56*(1), 69–70.

Jensen, E. (1998). *Teaching with the brain in mind.* Alexandria, VA: Association for Supervision and Curriculum Development.

Jones, F. (2000). *Tools for teaching: Discipline instruction motivation.* Santa Cruz, CA: Fredric H. Jones and Associates.

Kagan, L. (2003). *The successful dynamic trainer: Engaging all learners course workbook.* San Clemente, CA: Kagan Publishing.

Kagan, S. (1994). *Cooperative learning.* San Clemente, CA: Resources for Teachers.

Rauscher, R., Shaw, G., Levine, L., Ky, K., & Wright, E. (1993). Music and spatial task performance. *Nature, 365,* 611.

Udavari-Solner, A. (1995). A process for adapting curriculum in inclusive classrooms. In R. Villa & J. Thousand (Eds.), *Creating an inclusive school* (pp. 110–124). Alexandria, VA: Association for Supervision and Curriculum Development.

4 Managing the Psychosocial Environment of the Classroom

Don't be out in front of them to rescue or over them to punish, but as they are falling down, stand beside them and guide them. One of the ways we guide them is with the six critical life messages: I believe in you . . . I trust you . . . I know you can handle this . . . you are listened to . . . you are cared for . . . and you are very important to me.

—Barbara Coloroso

ANTICIPATION–REACTION GUIDE

Before you read the chapter, take a moment to put a check mark in the Anticipation column next to any statement with which you agree.

	Anticipation	Reaction
The qualities of good character should be imbedded into the way we teach rather than taught as separate lessons.	❑	❑
Looping is a fairly modern concept in which teachers and students stay together for two or more years.	❑	❑
Students cannot learn in an environment that is harsh, cold, punitive, and rejecting.	❑	❑
In addition to words, teachers communicate with tone of voice and body language.	❑	❑
Giving regular personal attention to students is best done by speaking with them individually every day.	❑	❑
Verbal reinforcement should be directed at students' character traits rather than at their efforts.	❑	❑
Teachers should help students acknowledge that learning is their main responsibility in school.	❑	❑
Modeling refers to teaching through example so students can learn through imitation.	❑	❑
When they team teach, teachers work with students only part of the time.	❑	❑
It is the students' responsibility (with teacher guidance) to maintain a warm, pleasant, and supportive environment.	❑	❑

Psychosocial environment encompasses the overall emotional climate or "feeling tone" that exists in every classroom, a mixture of pleasure, distress, intrigue, boredom, happiness, sadness, excitement, love, fear—all human emotions seem to be included. This environment is intangible, yet all teachers and students are aware of it. Its effects on learning, productivity, and self-concept are even more powerful than those exerted by the classroom's physical environment.

Think about that contention as it applies to you. Like most other people asked to recall their best educational experiences, don't you find yourself remembering teachers or groups of students who enlivened, invigorated, and supported your efforts?

The Positive and Negative Sides of the Psychosocial Environment

The positive side of the psychosocial environment is the warmth, caring, and support that make the classroom a friendly, pleasant, encouraging place. Most students flourish best in such an environment. But the psychosocial environment can have a negative tone as well—cold, uncaring, harsh, punitive, aloof, and sarcastic—further burdening children whose psychological well-being is already threatened by social ills outside the school, and even fear from bullies in school.

Individuals who intentionally instill fear in others are bullies; they intend to hurt, and they enjoy it. Bullies often engage in activities that are verbal or physical, often while bystanders do nothing to stop them or even encourage them. However, not all bullying takes place through obvious activities. Relational bullying undermines the bullied child's sense of self by shunning, isolating, excluding, or ignoring, and is more difficult to recognize.

When the climate feels threatening because of the actions or attitudes of other children or the teacher, students fear making errors, hope they will not fail or be embarrassed, and pray that if they make mistakes the teacher will not take reprisal against them. Few students do well in such environments, though there are exceptions. For most, achievement in such climates is suppressed and pleasure is nonexistent. Most of us during our years as students have experienced or witnessed this extreme as well as the good.

Perhaps you recall from experience that learning can occur rapidly within a climate of fear, provided the fear is not paralyzing. Fear has long been used to motivate learners, but it is doubtful that fear of physical or psychological hurt should ever be used in today's classrooms. At best it has a short-term effect, and it is known to produce detrimental side effects of stress, anger, and resentment, all of which are counterproductive to what we hope to accomplish with young learners.

Toward an Optimal Psychosocial Environment

Research into psychosocial classroom environments tends to focus on five factors: satisfaction, friction, competitiveness, difficulty, and cohesiveness (Fraser & O'Brien, 1985). Such research suggests that teachers may safely proceed on the premise that classrooms function best when they provide a positive and structured climate, one that reflects warmth, support, and pleasant circumstances with very low levels of fear. Fear should be limited to anxiety of not living up to one's own potential, of letting other people down, or of not acting in one's own best interest. It should never be a fear of personal danger.

It is the teacher's responsibility to establish and maintain a positive psychosocial environment, though students can and should help in this effort. Before you conclude that such climates are devoid of structure, expectations, or enforcement, be assured that this is not the case. In fact, it is doubtful that a positive climate can be maintained in the absence of well-enforced regulations governing interpersonal conduct.

Because establishing a positive climate is the teacher's responsibility, and because such a climate is usually best for enhancing learning and building good self-concept, this chapter explores what you can do to ensure that your classroom environment provides the warmth and support prized by students and teachers alike.

Cynthia Scott, a second-grade teacher, describes how she first tries to set the tone in her classroom:

> I begin the year with a discussion about my expectations for the year. I tell the children that I consider them my "school family." I explain that just as in any family we might not always agree on everything, but that I will always care about them. I say that each and every one of them is special and important to me, and that I want them to have the best possible school year. Because they are so important to me, I will not tolerate any cruelty or unkindness to each other. I expect them to be the best-behaved and well-mannered class in the entire school, both in the classroom and on the playground. I tell them that good behavior is really just good manners, because it shows respect for others, whether children or adults.
>
> I also go over the golden rule, and I make a bulletin board on that theme. I refer to the golden rule as our class motto. That is the only rule we have in the class, and I discuss with them how it covers everything. If you don't want to be called names, then don't call other people names. If you want people to listen to you, then be sure to listen to others. And most important, if you want to have friends, then be a friend.
>
> The children seem to understand and accept all of this very well. They see it as a fair and sensible way to do things, and I think it helps them know they have a teacher who cares about them.

Gloria Anderson has taught every elementary grade. However, when she teaches fifth or sixth grade, she explores the psychosocial environment in an unusual way.

> I begin the year with an unusual writing prompt. I show students a *No Hunting* sign, the kind you can buy in a sporting goods store. The students are to write about what they think about the sign and why I have it in the classroom. The next day, after I have read all the quick writes, the students and I discuss what the sign means in their room. This discussion leads to their development of class rules and expectations.

A Quick Look at Looping

Looping, a concept that dates back to the one-room schoolhouse, is reappearing in some areas of the country. In looping, a teacher keeps the same class of students for two or more consecutive years. The first year of looping is very typical—teacher and students get to know one another. The second year, however, has some unique benefits, several of which are related to the psychosocial environment. Among the benefits of looping are familiarity, stability, and strong communication. During the second year they are together, teachers know the strengths, contributions, and abilities of their students, and students know the teacher's expectations and routines. Looping provides stability, particularly for children who might be experiencing difficulties outside school. Teachers, students, and caregivers have more opportunity and a longer time to bond and work together as a team for the child's success.

When Marilyn Cox moved into a new school, she was able to loop with her fourth graders from the year before. She found the experience to be rewarding for everyone.

What a wonderful experience this year has been. I've taught for 30 years, but this is my first fifth-grade class. Being new to fifth grade has been infinitely easier because I brought my students along with me. (Last year I taught fourth grade in another nearby school.) As school started I didn't lose the usual chunk of time from my schedule needed to build the classroom environment. It was established last year. We just caught up on each other's summer experiences and moved right into fifth grade.

This is my first experience with looping. Having the privilege of starting a brand new school at a brand new grade level gave me the opportunity to take a risk on an entirely new concept to me! It has been wonderful to see how great the students have responded to this new environment. Our relationship, established last year, gave us a history to build on. We didn't have to start from dirt and build up from there. Our structure was already in place.

Not only did I know the students and their strengths and weaknesses, I also knew their parents, and I wasn't the least bit hesitant about contacting them. Back to School Night was very well attended. In the past it has been the rule that, by the time students get to fifth grade, parent participation goes down drastically. That hasn't been true with this class. At parent conference time all meetings went smoothly, due in no small part of their having done this with me last year. Parent helpers are coming out in droves to help in the classroom. Forms are returned faster. It seems incredible that we continue to work as such a tight team. Having the same parent group for two years has afforded me a tight relationship with the families. And having the same students again definitely has kept unacceptable behavior in the classroom down to a minimum.

Factors That Contribute to the Psychosocial Environment

Many factors contribute to and significantly influence the psychosocial environment of the classroom. Factors under control of the teacher can be grouped into three categories: human relations skills, teacher and student responsibilities in human relations, and maintenance of the psychosocial environment.

Human Relations Skills

Good human relations enable people to interact pleasantly and productively, both of which are essential to a participative environment that promotes school learning. Four aspects of human relations skills merit attention here: (1) general human relations skills, (2) human relations skills with students, (3) human relations skills with colleagues, and (4) human relations skills with parents and guardians.

General Human Relations Skills.   Certain skills in human relations are pertinent to all people in almost all situations. Those skills involve being friendly, maintaining a positive attitude, demonstrating the ability to listen, and offering genuine compliments.

Friendliness is a trait that is admired everywhere, yet many of us have difficulty being friendly toward others, especially when we find ourselves in threatening situations or with people we dislike. We can, however, learn to be friendly even toward people who do not please us, by smiling, speaking in a considerate way, using their names, asking how they are, and inquiring about family and work. When we do these simple things, we find that others tend to respond to us in the same way.

Maintaining a positive attitude is a skill that should be kept foremost in mind. We show it by generally looking on the bright side of things and by avoiding complaining, backbiting, faultfinding, or hurtful gossiping—behaviors known to undermine positive climates. We maintain a positive attitude by remembering that although all of us have difficulties in our lives, we also have some measure of control over how those difficulties affect us. People with positive attitudes believe that no problem exists that cannot be solved and focus on dealing with problems rather than complaining about them.

Ability to listen is a skill we appreciate in others but that many of us have trouble practicing. Most of us would rather talk than listen, but demonstrating the ability to listen is very helpful in promoting good relationships. It shows genuine interest in the other person, indicates that the other's observations are valued, and enhances the quality of communication by bringing about a genuine exchange of ideas.

Ability to compliment genuinely is not often discussed, but is a skill of considerable power. Both the giving and receiving of compliments make most of us uncomfortable for a time, partly because people sometimes use compliments to manipulate others. Too often, compliments are worded to sound like criticisms rather than acknowledgements or appreciations for what someone does. But it is evident that most people like to receive compliments, even when unable to accept them gracefully, and that they react positively toward individuals who compliment them.

Effective compliments are both genuine and explicit. For example, when complimenting someone on a presentation, we might say, "I found your talk entertaining and helpful, especially your suggestions on conducting evaluation conferences between principals and teachers." Ask yourself how you react to people who give you genuine compliments. In all likelihood, you not only feel good but you also feel more interested in working with and associating with those people.

Human Relations Skills with Students.   General human relations skills can be applied in all situations, but when dealing with students there are additional skills that serve teachers well. Before all else, teachers should (1) infuse qualities of good character into the way they teach. They should also (2) model courtesy and good manners, (3) give regular attention, (4) display genuine caring, (5) show continual willingness to help, and (6) use verbal and behavioral reinforcers.

When teachers infuse qualities of good character into the way they teach, they go beyond lessons that teach about ideals. Lessons are single events. Teachers too often miss opportunities for students to acquire and practice qualities of good character when they simply teach about ideals. For example, when they teach about honesty, they merely provide students a definition that may or may not be learned. On the other hand, when teachers hold honesty as an ideal of good character and provide opportunities for students to practice being honest, honesty is more likely to become a characteristic of each student.

Modeling courtesy and good manners closely complements this way of teaching and is extremely important in establishing a positive classroom climate. Teachers should hold high standards of decency and courtesy and should model these qualities when dealing with students. They should never act cruelly, speak sarcastically, or show favoritism. Nor should they allow students to bully or be cruel or sarcastic. Courtesy and other qualities of good character are held as ideals, imbedded into the way we teach, and practiced at all times. Laughing and joking are not forbidden; they are prized—but never used hurtfully.

Giving regular attention is best done by speaking personally with each student every day, on matters not necessarily related to schoolwork or behavior. In most classrooms, the majority of a teacher's attention goes to two small groups of students—those who do exceptionally well academically and those who chronically misbehave. Now that more classrooms are inclusive, a third group is also requiring extra attention—students with disabilities or special needs. This leaves a large group of students that receives relatively little attention. Because this group causes teachers neither special joy nor special annoyance, it is natural that teachers tend to overlook them. If these students are to do their best, however, they too need attention from the teacher.

"I'LL SAY THIS IS AN OLD MOVIE... THERE'S NO SECURITY GUARDS PATROLLING THE SCHOOL HALLS!"

Some teachers make a point of speaking to students as they enter the room to begin the day. Others speak with students while taking attendance. Still others speak with them individually during small-group instruction. To help them distribute personal attention equitably, some teachers keep class rosters at hand and put tally marks beside names as attention is given. Mary Brewer, an itinerant resource specialist, offers several suggestions for communicating with each individual student.

> One way to keep the lines of communication open between teacher and student is to use a daily journal entry, in which children can express their feelings in a nonthreatening atmosphere via private written conversations.
>
> Another suggestion is to have regular "office hours" scheduled throughout the week. Students who want to discuss something with you can sign up for the time(s) that are best for them.
>
> Students who are otherwise reluctant to express themselves are often eager to draw pictures that illustrate their feelings or to utilize the services of bilingual personnel to draw out hidden concerns.
>
> Students new to the school are often reticent about expressing themselves, often because they feel themselves to be "outsiders," unwelcomed in the "in" group. It is good idea to pair such students with those more at ease. Cooperative learning provides many opportunities for this type of pairing.

Displaying genuine caring should be both verbal and visual. All of us want to believe that we are cared for and that others value what we say and do. Because we also want to feel that we belong and are able to contribute to the group, we look and listen for signs from others that this is so. Teachers should be able to say to students, "I care for you and I want to support you in all that you do here," and then be able to show it. Approximately 20 percent of what a teacher communicates to students is done with words. The other 80 percent is communicated through body language. Teachers need to make sure that what they say and what the body says are really the same.

Continual willingness to help is another trait that is universally admired but seldom seen. We almost confer sainthood upon people such as Albert Schweitzer and Mother Teresa who devote their lives to helping the abject poor. You should not expect your students to look upon you as saintly (though some will) when you show that you will do whatever you can to help them learn. Let it be enough that your students gravitate to you, admire you, and remember you positively in later years. How often we adults are heard to say of our teachers, "That Mrs. Smith was strict, but she always went out of her way to help us."

Verbal and behavioral reinforcers are the teacher's words and actions that show support, encouragement, and approval. Reinforcers increase student attention and work output. Some teachers use tangible reinforcers such as stars, tokens, and even food and candy, but in most classes gestures and verbal reinforcers are sufficient—a wink, nod, smile, thumbs-up, "nice going," "I can see how much work you have put into this," "you must have thought about this a great deal," and "you are improving every day."

Again, reinforcement should be given to all students, not only for achievement but also for effort and improvement. Notice the fine distinction between reinforcing a student's *efforts* and reinforcing *character traits*. Be careful of saying things like "You are very intelligent" or

"You are a good boy" when commenting on work. Praise of this type often brings undesirable side effects of uneasiness, inhibited communication, and an increased need for personal validation. It is preferable to say, "I can see you worked hard. Thank you."

Human Relations Skills with Colleagues.   Every teacher spends a good deal of time working or dealing with colleagues—fellow teachers, administrators, support staff for students with special needs, student teachers, beginning teacher support providers, secretaries, librarians, custodians, nurses, and others. It is very important to be able to interact well with colleagues. In addition to the general skills of friendliness, positive attitude, listening, and complimenting, four additional considerations should be kept in mind: (1) supporting others, (2) sharing the load, (3) compromising, and (4) leading or following as appropriate.

Teachers who work together as partners have an even greater responsibility to practice these skills. Ideally, teams are the result of mutual agreements that form to highlight the strengths of the partners. Teaming allows teachers to arrange students and instruction in a variety of ways to best support both teaching and learning. In addition to the considerations below, team teaching requires excellent communication, cooperation, mutual respect and trust, and careful planning.

Supporting others means standing behind them and what they are trying to accomplish, unless you absolutely cannot do so. This support can be active, as when actual assistance is given, or passive, as when acceptance and encouragement are shown.

This attitude of support is not found in overabundance, and it seems that the larger the school, the shorter the supply. All too often school personnel denigrate the work of colleagues, make snide remarks, and belittle efforts and accomplishments—behind that colleague's back, of course. It has been documented that in faculty lounges, about 90 percent of teachers' comments are negative in nature. Negativism such as this is very detrimental to good working environments.

The paucity of support that teachers show for each other is probably due in part to teacher isolation, frustration, and absence of tangible success. When we don't feel the world is treating us fairly, we tend to lash out at others who have little if anything to do with the real problem.

Another unattractive trait of human nature is that we all want to look good, in our own eyes as well as in the eyes of others, and we seem to believe that we can build ourselves up by tearing others down. As they look worse, we think that we look better in comparison. The result, of course, is never what one had hoped. For example, those who gossip and malign in an attempt to show their

"THEY MEET IN THERE.
SOME KIND OF SUPPORT GROUP."

superiority rarely lack an attentive audience. But does that audience hold the complainer in high regard? Rarely. Complainers and backbiters seldom earn the sincere trust of others. As they tear others down, they taint their own reputations. If you want to build yourself up, the way to do so is by building others up. If you learn only one thing from this book, let it be what you have just read.

Sharing the load is one thing you must do if you hope to earn the respect of your colleagues. In any school, there are many jobs to do and tasks to complete: committee work that no one likes very much; team, Individual Education Plan (IEP), and student concern meetings; open houses and parent–teacher meetings; school musicals and carnivals; safety patrols; curriculum groups; materials evaluations; and in-service education sessions. Typically a few people carry most of the load while the rest do far less than their share. If we are to get along well with colleagues, and it is essential to our professional lives that we do so, we must undertake our part even when it is unpleasant. Sharing the load builds trust; shirking produces resentment.

Compromising is a way of life for those who get along well with others. Compromise doesn't mean giving in to others any more than it means demanding to have your own way all the time. It is a matter of give and take, with resolution coming after everyone has had a say. In any professional group there will be strong differences of opinion regarding purpose, procedure, and workload. You will want to express and stick by what you believe, but also try to understand others' feelings and points of view. If a faculty's work is to go forward in a positive way, an acceptable middle ground must be found.

Leading and following are both important in any endeavor, especially when undertaken democratically. We should assume leadership roles in which we can effectively plan courses of action, obtain resources, guide decisions, and rally support. When others lead, we should do our best to help make decisions and share the load. This does not mean following the leader's dictates uncritically, but it does imply that criticisms and countersuggestions should be expressed in open forums, and support should be given once a group decision has been made.

Teaching in teams requires additional considerations to be most effective and efficient. In addition to giving teachers more time for students, team teaching encourages reflection and evaluation of what the partners themselves are doing. In teams, teachers find someone to provide feedback on their ideas, someone whose strengths they can build on, and someone who will support their successes and challenges. However, for team teaching to work, partners must share a mutual philosophy, trust, and compatibility. Successful teaching teams require a lot of give and take, and the shared mindset that this is *our* classroom, and we work together for the success of our program and our students. First-grade teachers Jamie Rubin and Patti Petersen have twenty-five years of combined teaching experience and have shared a teaching contract for eight years. They say that the past years have been the most rewarding and the best, and they would not teach any other way.

> We have shared a teaching contract for eight years. Being friends for six years prior to this helped in making the situation a strong one. Once, when a child was asked the name of the teacher for whom he was running an errand, he replied without pause, "Mrs. Rubinsen."

> Our teaching styles are very similar and compatible. We both exhibit organiza-
> tion, fairness, structure, and a sense of fun in a fairly strict classroom. We each have
> our own strengths. One of us has a master's degree in reading and is very strong in lan-
> guage arts. The other loves science and music. When parents ask us how their child
> will be able to balance two teachers in a first-grade classroom, our response is, "If the
> child is lucky enough to have a two-parent family, then so it is in this classroom."
>
> What makes our partnership work and thrive? First, our friendship. We respect,
> trust, and love each other. We often try to outdo one another in the kindnesses we per-
> form so that the next day's workload for our partner is lessened. Second is our com-
> munication. We email each other daily with information about the day. Rarely is there
> a time when either of us is left in the dark concerning anything, be it related to parent,
> student, or peer.

In many school districts, teachers now find themselves communicating directly with
district support persons whose attention and efforts help beginning teachers grow in their
professional skills. It's critical that novice teachers are comfortable and able to communicate classroom realities and concerns so support providers can give efficient mentoring and
assistance.

Human Relations Skills with Parents and Guardians.   Teachers have the responsibility to communicate and work with the parents or guardians of the students they teach. Many
teachers accept this responsibility willingly and capitalize on it. Others avoid it as much as
possible, though such avoidance, under most circumstances, is counterproductive. Why?
Alliances with caregivers—teachers working with parents or guardians in a collaborative
effort—further the goal of supporting the student. Teachers who communicate well with
caregivers find that they enjoy increased home support in matters of discipline and curriculum. As an extra bonus, parents and guardians give higher ratings to teachers who take the
trouble to communicate about what caregivers consider the most important element of
schooling—their child.

How teachers reach out to caregivers makes a difference in the response they get from
them. When communicating with parents or guardians (details of which are presented in
Chapter 10), keep in mind the four traits of friendliness, positive attitude, listening, and
complimenting genuinely. Also make sure to (1) communicate regularly and clearly,
(2) describe your program and expectations, (3) emphasize the child's progress while
downplaying his or her shortcomings, (4) mention future plans for the child's instruction,
and (5) arrange for productive parent conferences. Fourth-grade teacher Karen O'Connor
describes how she routinely calls parents and guardians of her students:

> I still remember a reaction the first year I taught from the mother of a student who was
> chronically disruptive in class. The mother said resignedly, "Oh, hello, Mrs. O'Con-
> nor. What has Bobby done wrong today?" When I reassured her that I had called to
> tell her what an interesting oral report Bobby had given in front of the class that day,
> I could hear her relief, even disbelief, as she listened to the details.
>
> I think we need to break the "no news is good news" mind-set by taking time to
> make positive phone calls about our students. That one phone call to Bobby's mother

turned a potentially adversarial relationship into a partnership that helped both of us support Bobby's efforts.

Communicating regularly and clearly establishes a basis of mutual concern about the child. As a general rule, some kind of communication should go to caregivers every week— a note, instructions for homework, a written commentary on a piece of student work, a class newsletter, or a phone call. Parents or guardians of a student with a disability or other special need should be actively involved in their child's educational program. Also, when language diversity is an issue, arrangements should be made to translate communications into the primary language of the caregivers. The importance of frequent regular communication can hardly be overemphasized; a system should be implemented at the beginning of the year and followed thereafter.

This regular communication must be done very clearly, with no possibility of parental misunderstanding. Education is filled with jargon and acronyms, such as *multi-age classrooms, cooperative learning, authentic assessment, portfolios, clinical teaching, inquiry training, grade level expectancies, curriculum standards, inclusion, IEP, GATE, SAT*—you can probably add several others. Don't take it for granted that caregivers understand any of these terms. Avoid such terms if you can, but if you must communicate about them, explain what they mean.

Describe your program and expectations early in your communication, and repeat them occasionally. Caregivers will forget, but many will prove to be so interested in what you have to say that they will actively help their child achieve your stated goals. Inform them of the daily schedule. Tell them something about the activities you will use to reach your goals. Let them know about homework, the grading system, and anything else central to your program. They will appreciate it and will become more predisposed to cooperate. Third-grade teacher Pam Klevesahl goes so far as to communicate with some parents and students prior to the first day of school.

An important part of classroom management is having parents as allies. It is important to develop a strong working relationship from the beginning. Often, when I receive a class list, I find that by the names of certain children there are notes regarding behavioral and/or academic concerns. These are the students who frequently require more teacher time. Addressing these issues prior to the beginning of school pays dividends later.

I try to meet with each of these students and their families in their home. The week before the first day of school I call the family, introduce myself, and explain that I would like to come by the house to meet with them and discuss their child. Often they are surprised and inquire about why I want to come by. I tell them that I try to meet as many students and families as I can before school begins. In this way I put the parents as well as the student at ease, and arrange to stop by their home for approximately twenty minutes.

When I arrive I introduce myself and then ask the child if he or she is looking forward to the start of school. I tell a little about our year and the plans I have for learning units. I then ask the child if he or she has any questions about our year together. Following my discussion with the child, I ask the parents if they have any questions or concerns that I can answer. Frequently parents tell me that their child has difficulty paying attention, working quietly, or the like. When I hear this I turn directly to the child and say, "Oh my gosh! I sure hope that doesn't happen this year." I then explain that they are growing up and will be expected to work independently, and that if they do not, they will have to complete their work during their recess time. In this way I am letting the child and the parents know my expectations as well as the consequences. I then return to the parents and discuss my behavior plan so they will understand what will happen in the event inappropriate behavior occurs. The child, of course, is listening intently and benefits from the discussion as well.

Finally I conclude by saying how much I have enjoyed meeting everyone, and that I look forward to seeing them on the first day of school.

Emphasize progress when communicating about the child. Also identify the child's difficulties, indicate your plans for remedying these shortcomings, and ask for parental help. Caregivers' thoughts about their child are fragile. Parents see their child as an extension of themselves, the child's difficulties as their own, and criticism of the child as leveled at themselves. Dwelling on a child's shortcomings probes at parents' most sensitive feelings.

When discussing the child, consider this sequence: (1) mention something positive about the child personally, (2) show progress the child has made and is making, (3) describe plans for producing still greater achievement in the child, and finally, (4) mention difficulties that are interfering with the child's progress, but assure parents or guardians that you are working to overcome these difficulties, that you have a plan for doing so, that you need the caregivers' support in your efforts, and that you will appreciate any insights or suggestions they might offer. Caregivers usually respond well when treated in this manner. They want their child to learn and behave in school, and when the teacher shows interest, they usually support and help.

Future plans for individuals and for the entire class should be communicated. If a student has unusual difficulty in math, formulate a definite plan you can share with the student and caregivers. If a child excels in science, plan how that child might stretch talents or move into other topics. If the class shows unusual ability in art or music, plan to further those abilities, perhaps through a special performance for caregivers.

Conferencing productively with caregivers, although closely related to the points already made, refers specifically to the parent–teacher conferences scheduled early in the school year in most schools. Have at hand the individual student's folder, which shows progress, strengths, weaknesses, and work samples. Greet the parents or guardians and have them sit at a table beside you, not across from you. Engage them in a few words of small talk and make them feel at ease. Go over the child's good qualities, strengths, progress, difficulties, and your plans for increasing the strengths and countering the difficulties. Request their help in supporting the child and, if necessary, in working with the child at home. In fact, if possible, help the caregivers create a home action plan that parallels and supports your plan. Assure the parents or guardians that you will do your best for the child, and request their cooperation toward that end. Further details of what should be included and said in parent–teacher conferences are presented in Chapter 10.

Responsibilities in the Psychosocial Environment

The psychosocial environment of the classroom keys on warmth, stimulation, and helpfulness. These qualities are unlikely to occur routinely unless planned for, and an important part of that planning lies in recognizing who is responsible for what.

Teacher Responsibilities.   The teacher is responsible for communicating and modeling the sort of psychosocial environment desired, initiating the conditions that lead to it, and maintaining a good environment once it is achieved.

The *desired environment,* as described previously, is one in which students work hard, help each other, and enjoy success, all in a pleasant setting of encouragement and absence of threat. You will want to talk with your students frequently about these desired conditions, in terms suited to their level of understanding. They will want the same conditions you do, and they will, if allowed, make suggestions for achieving them. They will understand and support your reasoning. However, they will not always abide by what is necessary to keep the environment healthy.

Conditions that initiate and sustain the environment must be set forth by the teacher, through explanations, modeling, class-building, and team-building. Students closely watch and often imitate the teacher's attitude and behavior. Teachers must set the tone by using appropriate classbuilding and teambuilding activities throughout the year. During classbuilding activities, students are meeting and interacting with all members of the class. Teambuilding activities give students opportunities to interact and support their teammates in positive ways. Kagan et al. (Kagan, Robertson, & Kagan, 1995; Kagan, Kagan, & Kagan, 1997) describe numerous classbuilding and teambuilding structures (step-by-step sequences of action) that support a positive and safe class environment.

In addition to their own attitudes and behavior, and their classbuilding and teambuilding efforts, teachers must demonstrate the following as they establish and maintain a sound emotional environment in their class.

Enthusiasm.   Enthusiasm is a key element to which students react positively. They find it motivating, energizing, and contagious. Students like seeing teachers who enjoy what they do. Teacher enthusiasm should be shown for the curriculum as well as for working with children, in a stable, ongoing manner throughout the day.

Importance of the Individual.   The importance of every individual in the classroom should be established quickly. Teachers should continually communicate that students are worthy and have a place in school and society, that they have contributions to make, and that the class would be diminished without them. The feeling of importance will grow as students experience success, assume responsibilities in the classroom, and receive deserved acknowledgement from others.

Belonging.   Belonging is a primary goal in life—all of us want to know we are important to family, friends, class, and school. When that goal is not reached, students tend to either withdraw or to misbehave, neither of which is good for teacher, student, or class. Therefore, it behooves the teacher to foster a sense of belonging in every member of the class by stating, and repeating, that every student is important, will be valued, and will be treated fairly. It also helps to follow through with acknowledgment, friendliness, help, support, and assigned responsibility for some aspect of the room or program. Again, classbuilding and teambuilding efforts help affirm belonging and the sense of community.

Important underlying psychosocial values for inclusive classrooms are the ABCs (acceptance, belonging, and community) and the three Rs (reading, writing, and relationships). Inclusive classrooms also focus on how to support the special gifts of every student in the school community and how to meet those students' needs to feel welcomed and secure and to become successful (Pearpoint & Forest, 1992).

Fairness.   Fairness is required if the psychosocial environment is to remain positive. Students don't like the teacher to play favorites or enforce rules unevenly. They expect standards, but don't want them to be impossibly high. They expect rules and enforcement, but don't want them to be harsh. In other words, students will comply with standards and rules if they consider them to be fair.

Responsibility.   Responsibility goes hand in hand with belonging. It is important that all students accept their roles in furthering their own learning, as well as other classroom roles. Classroom monitors can be assigned responsibilities for many of the ongoing requirements of the class. Mirroring some of today's business practices, some teachers use students as "one-minute managers" to help run the class. Group discussions should emphasize that every student has a stake in making things good for all students collectively, and for the teacher as well, and that this responsibility should carry over to friends and family. Such responsibilities do not weigh students down, but instead give them a sense of purpose, with attendant motivation for supporting group endeavors.

Consistency.   Students want to know what to expect from their teachers day to day. They like surprises, but only pleasant ones. When their teacher vacillates between warm and cold or tolerant and harsh, students become uneasy and their behavior becomes unpredictable.

Friendliness.   Friendliness projects the warmth and consideration that contribute to productive work. This is not "best-pal" friendliness, but that which is shown through having a pleasant demeanor, acknowledging individual students, speaking with them regularly and personally, and remembering their birthdays and something about family members or pets. This friendliness dispels threat and helps reduce fearfulness while increasing willingness to attempt difficult tasks. Irresponsible choices and poor behavior will not be tolerated, but standards will be maintained and enforced in an even-handed way. Students are not hurtfully punished; logical consequences give them the opportunity to right their wrongs or to make up for them.

Success.   Success should be established and maintained from the beginning. Success is highly rewarding, motivating, and effective in building positive self-concept. Students should not believe, however, that they will always succeed in what they do, or that success always comes easily. But it is important that every student experience success, especially from diligent effort and improvement.

"YOU ALWAYS GO THAT EXTRA MILE, DON'T YOU MONICA."

Understanding. When students are struggling with personal difficulties, they want to be understood. Understanding includes recognition of illness, discomfort, personal problems, or traumatic occurrences, so that a greater than normal degree of tolerance can justifiably be shown. This is not to be confused, however, with unquestioning acceptance of whatever a student might say or do. We can be understanding of difficulties, excitements, and problems without approving or ignoring a student's disruptive or inappropriate behavior in the classroom.

Help. Help should always be available to students, though in many cases it should not be provided until after they have made a serious effort on their own. Knowing that help is available provides a sense of security and support, and engenders positive attitudes. But there can also be a downside to providing help. A phenomenon known as the "helplessness syndrome" occurs when students will not make or sustain effort without constantly seeking attention from the teacher. Often this occurs simply because students like the teacher's attention, and showing helplessness is a way of getting that attention. In such a case, teachers should give the student attention when help is *not* needed; for example, after the student has made a good effort.

Humor. Finally, humor should be a mainstay of the psychosocial environment. Humor is the trait most often identified by older students when asked what they most like in teachers. (Younger children most often identify niceness.) Students like to laugh, share jokes, and find the humor in situations, and they appreciate teachers who make humor a part of the environment. Unfortunately, students also like to laugh hurtfully at each other, and that is a problem. You never should allow your students to laugh at the expense of others. If everyone is enjoying a laugh, fine. But when it is done in demeaning or cruel ways, it is not to be tolerated. Simply point out that the class will have a good time in their work and there will be plenty of humor and laughter, but there will be no horseplay, no abject silliness, and no laughing at another's expense.

Organizing the Conditions That Build a Good Environment.   Conditions that indicate and sustain a positive psychosocial environment must be brought into play in an organized manner. You must be sure to show every student that he or she is cared for and wanted, will be encouraged but treated fairly, and will enjoy learning in a nonthreatening environment. Every student should have important responsibilities in the class. You should not leave such matters to chance or assume they will occur because of your good intention. Even the smartest teacher cannot keep in mind all of the conditions and responsibilities of a classroom. A checklist, kept in a record book, serves as a useful reminder of the eleven attitudes and conditions just discussed, and ensures that they will be given attention thoroughly and consistently.

Student Responsibilities.   Students have responsibilities to the psychosocial environment just as teachers do, and the act of discharging those responsibilities is very powerful in building the classroom environment. Responsibilities should be clarified in class discussions and reemphasized regularly. Students' main responsibilities include the following:

Learning.   Learning is the main reason students are in school. They are there to acquire the skills, attitudes, values, and understandings that will permit them to function to the fullest while contributing to the societal good. This also includes learning to make responsible choices for themselves. They should be helped to recognize that fact and comply with it as their fundamental responsibility in the classroom.

Contribution.   Contribution to the class is a second major responsibility students have in helping maintain a good psychosocial environment. They are to participate in discussions, help with class duties, assist other students and the teacher, and conduct themselves in accord with class expectations and regulations. Students become more productive and secure and gain more from the educational experience when they participate than they do when they merely serve as passive or reluctant space-fillers.

Making Responsible Choices.   Making responsible choices related to their learning situations as well as their behavior is an important skill for all students. Students benefit from watching teachers model how they make choices to solve situations and problems. We all learn from our mistakes. When students are first guided through the process and then trusted to make choices and decisions, they grow through the results of their decisions.

Being Dependable.   Dependability on the part of all students does wonders for the class environment. When they do what they are supposed to do, well and on time, students help create a climate of enjoyment and productivity. Students can help themselves fulfill this responsibility by using self-reminders concerning tasks and deadlines. Older students can employ checklists of duties; younger students can rely on verbal reminders. All students can be asked periodically to evaluate themselves on dependability.

Being Considerate.   Consideration for others should be shown at all times. Everyone—fellow students, teachers, the principal, custodians, and staff—have difficulties, egos, and sensitive feelings. Students profit from practical discussions of the Golden Rule that help them decide how they can show friendliness and helpfulness toward others throughout the day.

Supporting Others.   Support for others' efforts, shown through acceptance and encouragement, is another important student responsibility. Students must quickly learn that they are not to be passive captives in the classroom but active members who help each other succeed. They should be helped to understand that the best way to be liked and helped is to like and help others.

Relating Positively.   Finally, relating positively means showing good manners, being polite and courteous, and avoiding words and actions that hurt others. Teachers can help students see that everyone profits when they get along with each other and that they should work to maintain that attitude.

Maintaining the Psychosocial Environment

The preceding discussed the many responsibilities of teachers and students in fostering a positive psychosocial environment—a place where students can learn amidst helpfulness, encouragement, and the absence of threat. We return again to responsibilities that fall mainly to the teacher, this time regarding what can be done to sustain a positive psychosocial environment once it is begun. Receiving attention are modeling, verbal reinforcement, class meetings, classbuilding and teambuilding activities, and private discussions.

Modeling.   Modeling refers to teaching through example to help students learn through imitation. The majority of our life learnings occur through this process. We see how others act, dress, and talk, and we imitate them. Modeling is especially powerful in social learning and making responsible choices, which are central to the psychosocial environment. Teachers should consistently model what they hope to see in their students, and provide students with opportunities to practice and model for fellow students as well.

Verbal Reinforcement.   Verbal reinforcement was mentioned earlier as a process in which verbal rewards are given when we see behavior we approve of in others. With words such as "thanks," "good work," "you tried hard on this," "this work shows a lot of thought," "I appreciate how helpful you've been," and "you showed that you cared about John's feelings," teachers encourage, guide, and support behavior that contributes to the good of the total class. Verbal reinforcers should be short and describe the behavior being approved. Teachers should also teach their students how to give reinforcement to others so when classmates behave in pleasing ways, their behavior can be encouraged.

Class Meetings.   Class meetings, a technique for dealing with class problems devised by William Glasser (1969), calls for the identification of concerns, followed by searching for solutions. Teachers and/or students can raise the concerns in the meetings. No fault-finding or blaming is allowed; all focus is on finding positive solutions. Students sit in a tight circle for these discussions so they can see each other face to face. The meetings can deal with social problems in the classroom or school (e.g., noise or playground fighting), academic problems (e.g., lack of class interest, effort, or progress), or problems outside of school (e.g., conditions that interfere with home study). Class meetings also provide an additional setting for discussions and for practicing effective ways to deal with conflicts. Regular class meetings can help students carry out their responsibilities in perpetuating a healthy classroom environment. Nelsen, Lott, and Glenn (2000) clarify this further with eight discrete building-block skill areas to ensure successful and effective class meetings.

Classbuilding and Teambuilding.   Classbuilding and teambuilding, according to Kagan, are essential for creating caring, cooperative classrooms and communities. Classbuilding activities, during which students stand up, move around, and interact with someone new, should be done at least once weekly beginning the first day of school. Random groups can be effective and efficient during the first three weeks as teacher and students get to know each other. Then teambuilding, with fun and easy activities, should occur at least twice weekly. Teambuilding activities are nonacademic and can be very quick. Their purpose is to strengthen team functioning.

Private Discussions.   Private discussions should be held with individual students when necessary to solve problems that are not appropriate for group discussion, such as refusal to work, defiance, theft, vandalism, or personal home or health problems. Individual conferences can focus on conflict resolution or on problem solving when appropriate. Kagan, Kyle, and Scott (2003) share numerous step-by-step suggestions to use with individuals at the moment of disruption, for follow-up, and for long-term solutions.

This concludes our survey of purposes and responsibilities in managing a quality psychosocial environment in the classroom. Now we are ready to move ahead to Chapter 5, in which consideration is given to encouraging students toward greater effort and productivity in the classroom. Before proceeding to the next chapter, take time to explore these end-of-chapter activities.

Parting Thought

Teachers have the right to teach.
Students have the right to learn.
And no one has the right to interfere with either of these events.

—Author Unknown

SUMMARY SELF-CHECK

Check off the following as you understand or become able to apply them.

❑ Teachers strive for an emotional tone in their classrooms that is warm, supportive, and pleasant, as opposed to cold, rejecting, and unpleasant.

❑ Because looping keeps teachers and students together for at least two consecutive years, the climate for the second year is actually created during the first.

❑ Achieving the desired emotional tone calls attention to
- General human relations skills: being friendly, maintaining a positive outlook, demonstrating the ability to listen, offering genuine compliments
- Relations with students: infusing character into the way we teach, setting a good example, giving regular attention, displaying genuine caring, showing helpfulness, providing reinforcement
- Relations with colleagues: being supportive, sharing the load, compromising, leading or following as appropriate, teaching teams, support programs for beginning teachers
- Relations with caregivers: communicating regularly, describing program and expectations, emphasizing the child's progress, giving future plans for the child's instruction, conducting productive parent–teacher conferences
- Teacher responsibilities in the psychosocial environment: communicating the desired environment, classbuilding and teambuilding, setting conditions that initiate and sustain, showing enthusiasm, stressing the importance of each individual, ensuring a sense of belonging, ensuring fairness, stressing responsibility, showing consistency, exhibiting friendliness, ensuring success for all, showing understanding, being helpful, showing a sense of humor, doing all in an organized way
- Student responsibilities in the psychosocial environment: learning, contributing, making responsible choices, being dependable, showing consideration, being supportive, being positive with others
- Maintaining a good psychosocial environment: modeling desired behavior, providing verbal reinforcement, providing opportunities to practice, holding class meetings, using classbuilding and teambuilding activities to build community, holding private discussions as needed.

ACTIVITIES FOR REFLECTION AND GROWTH

For Cumulative Skills Development

1. Take a moment to review the statements in the Anticipation–Reaction Guide at the beginning of this chapter. Put a check mark in the Reaction column next to any statement with which you now agree. How have your thoughts changed since reading this chapter?

2. Suppose that you are meeting your class (select a grade level) for the first time and you want students to understand (a) the psychosocial environment you want for the class and why it is important, (b) the responsibilities you will assume in establishing and maintaining that environment, and (c) the responsibilities that students need to assume in furthering that environment. What will you say to get your ideas across? To what extent will you hope for student response and input?

3. Describe how you would begin the year with a class that had looped with you from the previous year.

4. What will classbuilding and teambuilding look like and sound like in your class? Describe some activities that you might use for each.

5. Suppose you write a class constitution concerning classroom climate. Keeping its length to no more than two pages, what would you include in the document?

6. Class meetings and private discussions were suggested for maintaining a good psychosocial environment. List five topics you would consider appropriate for each. How do you differentiate between topics to be discussed privately and those to be discussed in a group? Are there any topics that you would consider inappropriate for either class meetings or private discussions?

REFERENCES AND RECOMMENDED READINGS

Albert, L. (1996). *Cooperative discipline.* Circle Pines, MN: American Guidance Service.

Charles, C. (2000). *The synergetic classroom: Joyful teaching and gentle discipline.* New York: Addison Wesley Longman.

Coloroso, B. (1994). *Kids are worth it! Giving your child the gift of inner discipline.* New York: Avon Books.

Coloroso, B. (2002). *The bully, the bullied, and the bystander.* Toronto, Ontario, Canada: HarperCollins.

Creating a climate for learning [Special Issue]. (1996, September). *Educational Leadership.* Alexandria, VA: Association for Supervision and Curriculum Development.

Creating caring schools [Special issue]. (2003, March). *Educational Leadership.* Alexandria, VA: Association for Supervision and Curriculum Development.

Fraser, B., & O'Brien, P. (1985). Student and teacher perceptions of the environment of elementary school classrooms. *Elementary School Journal, 85*(5), 567–580.

Freiburg, J. (1996, September). From tourists to citizens in the classroom. *Educational Leadership, 54*(1), 32–36.

Ginott, H. (1972). *Teacher and child.* New York: Macmillan.

Glasser, W. (1969). *Schools without failure.* New York: Harper & Row.

Glasser, W. (1988). On students' needs and team learning: A conversation with William Glasser. *Educational Leadership, 45,* 38–41.

Glasser, W. (1998). *The quality school: Managing students without coercion.* New York: Perennial Press.

Kagan, L., Kagan, M., & Kagan, S. (1997). *Cooperative learning structures for teambuilding.* San Clemente, CA: Kagan Cooperative Learning.

Kagan, M., Robertson, L., & Kagan, S. (1995). *Cooperative learning structures for classbuilding.* San Clemente, CA: Kagan Cooperative Learning.

Kagan, S., Kyle, P., & Scott, S. (2004). *Win-win discipline.* San Clemente, CA: Kagan Cooperative Learning.

Kaufman, J., & Burbach, H. (1997). On creating a climate of classroom civility. *Phi Delta Kappan, 79,* 320–325.

Lewis, C., Schaps, E., & Watson, M. (1996). The caring classroom's academic edge. *Educational Leadership, 54,* 16–21.

Nelsen, J., Lott, L., & Glenn, H. (2000). *Positive discipline in the classroom.* Rocklin, CA: Prima Publishing.

Pearpoint, J., & Forest, M. (1992). Foreword. In S. Stainback & W. Stainback (Eds.), *Curriculum considerations in inclusive classrooms: Facilitating learning for all students* (pp. xv–xviii). Baltimore: Paul H. Brookes.

Schools as safe havens [Special issue]. (1997, October). *Educational Leadership.* Alexandria, VA: Association for Supervision and Curriculum Development.

Sollman, C., Emmons, B., & Paolini, J. (1994). *Through the cracks.* Worcester, MA: Davis Publications.

5 Managing Student Motivation to Learn

Imagination is the true magic carpet.

—Norman Vincent Peale

Mistakes are simply invitations to try again.

—Dian Ritter

ANTICIPATION–REACTION GUIDE

Before you read the chapter, take a moment to put a check mark in the Anticipation column next to any statement with which you agree.

	Anticipation	Reaction
Traditional teaching diminishes children's inborn interest in learning.	❏	❏
Students don't try very hard in school because lessons are not usually very interesting to them.	❏	❏
Unmotivated students rarely misbehave; they just sit and do nothing.	❏	❏
When teachers speak of *motivation* as part of their lessons, they refer to students' innate desire to learn.	❏	❏
Glasser claims that motivation and discipline cease to be problems when schooling is organized to meet students' needs.	❏	❏
Kagan would have teachers use cooperative learning, activities built around multiple intelligences and classbuilding and teambuilding experiences to motivate students.	❏	❏
Students are better able to engage in instruction and demonstrate their learnings when teaching is enriched with multiple intelligence strategies.	❏	❏
Incentives should be given early in the day or week to ensure that students will continue to work hard the rest of the time.	❏	❏
With Preferred Activity Time, (PAT) students are allowed to do anything they want as an incentive for work and good behavior.	❏	❏
Four principles are needed to make cooperative learning more than simply group work.	❏	❏

Ask any group of elementary teachers what brings them the greatest professional pleasure, and they will almost certainly mention working with students who have good intentions and who try hard to learn. Conversely, if you ask those teachers what troubles them most about teaching, they will likely mention disruptive student behavior and an inability to get some of their students interested in learning.

By *learning,* they of course mean school learning, for all students are interested in learning certain things and make intensive efforts to do so. The problem is simply that students' interests in learning often do not correspond with what teachers are required to teach. Most students enter kindergarten eager and open to the entire curriculum, but within a year or two they have clearly distinguished between school activities that intrigue them and those that do not. From that point on, teachers continually search for ways to attract student attention and engage students in learning activities. In other words, they forever look for ways to motivate their students.

What Is Meant by Motivation?

The word *motive* comes from a Latin root meaning "to move" and is defined as an emotion, desire, or physiological need that incites a person to do something. Motive is the "why" of behavior. The associated term *motivation* has two meanings that are used rather differently. One of those meanings refers to a condition within individuals that disposes them toward an activity or goal, such as motivation to learn, motivation to succeed, or motivation to gain acceptance. For example, Mr. Garcia's sixth-graders routinely forgot most of what they read about the Greeks and the Romans until Mr. Garcia arranged a contest on ancient civilization facts against Ms. Espinosa's class. His students suddenly began to remember the material much better. Their internal motivation to learn and to succeed was increased.

Teachers frequently use a second, and different, meaning for the term *motivation.* This meaning refers to a process by which motives are instilled into students—that is, what one (such as a teacher) does to get students interested in lessons and to facilitate willingness to work at them. When teachers speak of motivation as a component of a lesson, they refer to what *they* do to attract students' interest and engage them more or less willingly in the work provided. Thinking in a short-term sense, they might ask themselves, "What can I do for motivation in this lesson?"

Why People Don't Do What We Want Them To

When we ask people to do something, sometimes they will do it, but sometimes they won't. Understanding the reasons why people will or will not do what we ask them is a valuable insight for teachers as they think about how best to motivate students. Fleming and Kilcher (1991) identified the following five reasons why people don't do what we want them to do:

1. They don't know what to do. Students without requisite knowledge or who don't understand the expectations are not likely to do what teachers ask.

2. They don't know how to do it. The same is true regarding students' abilities and skills.
3. They don't know why they should do it. Students want to know the reason for and the importance of their work.
4. They aren't suited or matched to the task. For example, a student who is especially energetic will have a difficult time sitting still for a forty-minute lecture.
5. They don't want to. Sometimes it's simply a lack of will.

Motivation and Lessons

Motivation that resides over time within individuals is *internal or self-motivation,* while motivation that is supplied from outside the individual is *external motivation.* Teachers would love to work with students who are always internally motivated to learn, but they know that most of the time they will have to supply at least some of the motivation for their students.

Teachers know that learning is both exciting and fun when it matches the interests and abilities of their students. They also know that most students enjoy hands-on activities. And they know that when they teach the right way, motivation happens by itself.

Consequently, teachers pay close attention to students' known interests, such as animals, sports, cars, entertainers, music, and cartoons. They look for ways to include those interests in lessons, and are often amazed that young students can quickly learn such vast amounts of information about dinosaurs and sports heroes.

Sometimes something as simple as a coupon booklet works. Students begin the year or semester with coupons from the teacher (see Figure 5.1). For example, booklets may include forgiveness coupons for single specific assignments, an assignment the student chooses (with teacher approval). Clever clip art designs and colored paper make these a fun gift. Students are allowed to redeem their coupons according to simple directions. For example, a general assignment coupon might read, "This coupon is good for one assignment from any subject. Check with your teacher to see if the assignment is a coupon event. Coupons may only be used once."

Teachers also rely heavily on student wants. *Want* is an imprecise, nonscientific term that simply means something students desire, something they wish to have or do. Some wants stem from *needs,* a scientific term referring to what students require in order to live enjoyably in reasonably good health. As Maslow (1943) pointed out, everyone needs food, water, and air, and most of us need acceptance, love, and association with others. To say we need those things is to say that we feel best when we have them—healthy, content, fulfilled.

Most student wants have little to do with psychological needs. For example, students may strongly want to eat ice cream, watch a film, get a new comic book or video game, or play with a particular person—none of which, if denied, interferes with personal well-being. Nevertheless, such wants play important roles in students' lives, and they provide practical insights into how teachers can motivate students.

The major interests and wants of elementary students of different age levels have been well documented and, in general, have remained fairly constant over time. Table 5.1 shows examples of wants and interests that predominate in elementary students.

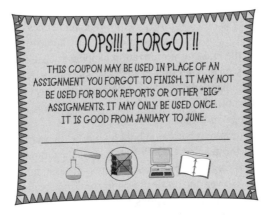

FIGURE 5.1   Sample Pages of a Coupon Booklet

TABLE 5.1 Age, Wants, and Interests

Age	Wants (things students seek and/or respond well to)	Interests (specific activities)
5 to 8 years	assurance, physical activity, direct sensory experience, encouragement, praise, warmth, patience, concrete learning tasks	relating experiences, stories, dramatic play, pictures, songs, poems, rhythms, and animals to organized games, models, dolls, jokes, gangs and clubs, collecting, comics, adventure books, animals, and foreign lands and people
9 to 10 years	praise, physical activity, group membership, being admired	riddles, jokes, puzzles, sharing, competitive games, trips, reading, maps, letters, animals, arts and crafts
preadolescent	affection, warmth, greater independence, peer group acceptance and belonging	riddles, jokes, puzzles, gangs and clubs, sports, competitive and outdoor games, hobbies, construction, pets, movies, TV, comics, reading, drama
adolescent	acceptance by and conformation to peer group; kind, unobtrusive guidance by adults; security with independence	music, dancing, cars, opposite sex, sports, trips, TV, movies, magazines, gossip, intrigue, adult roles

What Does Motivate Students to Learn?

The following is a review of information available to teachers about motivation, accumulated from experience and scholarly research. Also included is an examination of contributions by William Glasser (1998a, 1998b, 1998c, 2000), Howard Gardner (1991, 1993b, 1997), Fred Jones (1987, 2000), and Spencer Kagan and his colleagues (1994, 1995, 1997, 1998).

Motivation for Elementary Classrooms

Brophy (1987, 1998) offers a helpful synthesis of research on classroom motivation. He presents a number of suggestions for teachers, of which the following are most pertinent to elementary-grade teachers:

- Make yourself and your classroom attractive to students.
- Adapt lessons to students' interests.
- Focus attention on individual and collaborative learning goals.
- Teach things that are worth learning, in ways that help students appreciate their value.
- Include novelty and variety.
- Provide for active, hands-on response.
- Include fantasy and simulations.
- Project your enthusiasm.

"FINGER PAINTING IS FUN, BUT WILL WE EVER USE IT IN REAL LIFE?"

Jones (1987, 2000) presents an overview of motivation in the classroom setting that he feels is adequately supported by research. He concludes that students become actively involved in lessons to the extent they expect success, value successful completion of the tasks, and find the climate of interpersonal relationships acceptable. Jones presents conclusions for students at all age levels. For elementary students, academic needs would include

- Being quickly and actively involved in lessons
- Experiencing success
- Seeing learning modeled by adults as exciting and rewarding
- Relating the learning to their own lives
- Having positive contact with peers

Tomlinson (1999, 2002) describes what she calls invitational learning that embraces five student needs: affirmation (acceptance and significance), contribution, purpose, power, and challenge. Children want affirmation, to feel they are significant in the classroom. They want to contribute and make a difference in the community. Students look for purpose when they come to school. They want to know that what they learn is useful and that their choices contribute to their success. Finally, students want to feel challenged and/or stretched. They want to feel that their work contributes to their success and the growth of others. The learning environment contributes to meeting these five needs.

Consolidating the ideas of Brophy, Jones, Tomlinson, and others, the following generalizations are warranted and offer concrete, practical advice concerning student motivation:

Students like to work with others at ideas, activities, and objects that they find novel, intriguing, and related to their perceived life concerns.

Students seek out people and conditions that help meet needs important in their lives.

Students try their best to avoid associating with people and conditions they find unpleasant.

Students engage in tasks that are unpleasant to them in order to please people they see as important, including the teacher.

As a teacher, therefore, you are well advised to capitalize on students' needs, interests, abilities, and curiosity. Use these to full advantage. Students will appreciate the effort you make, and because of their excitement, so will you.

But remember that students detest looking bad in front of their peers; they don't want to appear stupid or to have their failures displayed. Therefore, you should encourage your students and help them feel secure. And as you show your helpfulness and support, students will try to please you with effort, good behavior, responsible choices, and quality work.

These points generally hold true, and teachers who capitalize on them often accomplish much with their students. However, experienced teachers find that these suggestions do not solve all problems of motivation. Thus, they set up systems of reinforcement for good student work and behavior. Many teachers are uncomfortable with such a system, feeling that they might be paying students for doing only what they are supposed to do anyway. They wonder if children will learn to depend on others for approval and recognition and ask questions such as the following: What's in it for me? What's the payoff? Does it count for anything? Do you like it? Did you see me do it? Did I do it right? (Coloroso, 1994). But it is evident that elementary students become excited about receiving smiley faces, stickers, popcorn, extra time at recess or the computer, the honor of helping the teacher, the privilege of feeding the class pet, and many other similar rewards for their good effort. In fact, students will study their spelling and arithmetic in order to get those rewards.

Teachers also have learned, many of them through distressing experiences when they themselves were students, that children can be frightened into working. Many students would rather do their homework than get yelled at, study for their tests than get failing grades, or feign paying attention than receive reprimands. But these days, not all students will comply out of fear. Regardless of the work or behavior it induces, motivation through fear is an area for teachers to avoid. If you genuinely want your students to make an effort to learn and have a reasonably enjoyable time doing so, don't try to motivate through fear or intimidation. Ultimately, the results are not worth the costs. Students won't like you, you won't like them, and worse, you won't feel very good about yourself either.

It is much better to motivate students through what they enjoy and respond to positively, and through things you feel comfortable with as well. Your program doesn't have to be insipidly easy; it can be rigorous and still be enjoyable. First-grade teacher Rose Mary Johnston describes how she uses her own interests to motive her students.

Teachers can be most interesting when they teach about something they love or know well. I love geography and science. Most people believe you can't teach much science and geography in first grade. I teach sophisticated theories and processes, but in ways appropriate for my students.

I teach the steps of the scientific process through very simple experiences (such as things that float or sink). For each step of the process, I use the formal name (observation, experiment, or hypothesis); however, I also have a picture I show the children that goes with the term or means the same thing. After modeling, the children slowly begin using the processes in dealing with simple problems.

The same idea works for geography. My students learn to recognize the shapes and names of the seven continents and some interesting facts about each of them. We incorporate these experiences into the literature and reading program, and we do a number of activities such as making pop-up books of the continents. This enables us to accomplish the goals of writing, reading, and learning sentence structure, but in a way that interests both my students and me.

William Glasser's Contributions

William Glasser is a psychiatrist-psychologist who writes and consults on behalf of school students. His landmark books on education are *Schools without Failure* (1969), *Control Theory in the Classroom* (1998b), *The Quality School* (1998c), *The Quality School Teacher* (1998d), and *Every Student Can Succeed* (2000). For Glasser, motivation is virtually synonymous with needs satisfaction, specifically the needs he emphasizes in his writings. He maintains that when teaching and learning produce needs satisfaction, motivation to work and behave properly follows naturally.

In 1986, Glasser explained that "all of our behavior, everything we do, can be considered our best attempt to control ourselves so as to satisfy our needs" (p. 17). What are these needs we so desperately try to satisfy? According to Glasser they are: (1) to survive and reproduce, (2) to belong, (3) to acquire power, (4) to be free, and (5) to have fun. Glasser contends that these needs are alive and working in every one of us, from the toddler to the elderly, and he says that we can no more deny the urge to fill these needs than we can deny the color of our eyes. He also contends that schools, as traditionally designed, fall quite short of satisfying these needs.

Glasser goes on to say that education—schools, the classroom, and the teaching–learning process—should be reorganized and conducted so that students, while working at lessons, can satisfy their needs. Then students will learn, behave well, and take an interest in education. To this end Glasser would have students work together in small learning teams and have teachers function as "lead-managers" instead of bosses, emphasize quality in all student work, and transform the classroom environment into what he calls a "friendly workplace."

Glasser feels that teams are inherently motivating and give students a sense of belonging. Stronger students find it need-fulfilling to help weaker students, and weaker students find it need-fulfilling to contribute to a team that is getting somewhere. Students with disabilities find themselves able to contribute and participate along with the other team members. Teams provide freedom and fun as they work with less dependence on the teacher and are allowed to assume more authority. Many students working in teams find a good deal of belonging, power, freedom, and fun—the very things Glasser says we all seek in life.

Glasser distinguishes between "boss style" and the "lead-manager" in the Preface to *The Quality School* (1998):

A boss drives. A leader leads.
A boss relies on authority. A leader relies on cooperation.
A boss says "I." A leader says "We."
A boss knows how. A leader shows how.
A boss creates resentment. A leader breeds enthusiasm.
A boss fixes blame. A leader fixes mistakes.
A boss makes work drudgery. A leader makes work interesting.

Glasser has continually refined his thinking, and does so again in *Choice Theory in the Classroom* (1998a) and *Every Student Can Succeed* (2000), his most recent works. Consultants and trainers Kathy Curtiss and Steven English describe practical classroom applications of choice theory. Expanding on Glasser's ideas, they advocate classroom meetings, portfolios and assessment rubrics based on standards, character development as part of the curriculum, and student self-assessment and reflection. They also believe in partnerships between teachers and students and use instructional strategies that support student ownership and responsibility for learning.

Howard Gardner's Contributions

Howard Gardner is a Harvard Professor of Education and the author of several books, including *Frames of Mind* (1983), *The Unschooled Mind: How Children Think and How Schools Should Teach* (1991), and *Multiple Intelligences: The Theory in Practice* (1993). In 1983, Gardner first proposed his theory that human beings possess more than a single, fixed intelligence and learn in a variety of ways. He has identified eight intelligences, and asserts that we all possess all eight intelligences, although each in varying degrees of strength. He also observes that schools tend to develop only two of theses intelligences to any useful extent—verbal/linguistic and logical/mathematical. Overly simplified, the eight intelligences embrace the following understandings:

- Verbal/linguistic—capacity to use words and oral and written language effectively
- Logical/mathematical—capacity to use numbers effectively and to think in logical patterns and relationships
- Visual/spatial—ability to perceive the visual–spatial world accurately, with awareness of color, line, shape, form, space, and the relationships among these elements
- Bodily/kinesthetic—expertise in using one's whole body to express ideas and feelings, with specific physical skills of coordination, balance, dexterity, strength, flexibility, and speed
- Musical—ability to perceive, discriminate, transform, and express musical forms
- Naturalist—ability to perceive and function in nature, with sensitivity to the interdependence of the plant and animal ecologies and to environmental issues

- Interpersonal—ability to perceive and make distinctions in the moods, intentions, motivations, and feelings of other people
- Intrapersonal—self-knowledge and the ability to act adaptively on the basis of that knowledge

Gardner says teachers should not be asking "How smart are my students?" but rather, "In what ways are my students smart?" Many now believe that understanding Gardner's ideas is essential to effective teacher thinking and planning, and key to student motivation.

In the early 1990s, Gardner proposed a radical school restructuring, where students would spend most of their time engaged in project-based learning, both in and out of classroom settings. He believes that life is a series of projects, and that school matters, "but only insofar as it yields something that can be used once students leave school" (Gardner, n.d.). By applying Gardner's ideas of multiple intelligences and project-based learning to motivation, students transform into active participants engaging in meaningful experiences that have real world applications for them. They are motivated.

Fred Jones's Contributions

Fred Jones is a clinical psychologist and consultant who has made extensive field observations of effective teachers, particularly those he describes as "naturals." His observations are translated into ways to improve teacher effectiveness in motivating, managing, and instructing students. Jones gives a prominent place in his program to incentives as a means of motivating students. Jones found that most effective teachers use incentives systematically. Specifically relating to motivation (and behavior management) is his work that focuses on responsibility training through incentive systems.

As do others, Jones says that incentives are something outside of individuals that prompt them to act. Incentives are promised as the consequence for desired behavior, but delayed to occur or be provided later. One way teachers can use incentives as motivators is by applying Grandma's Rule to the classroom—students first do what they are supposed to do, and then, for a while, they can do what they want to do. A sort of bonus portion of the incentive encourages students to save time they would normally waste in order to get it back in the form of preferred activities. It gives students a shared interest in cooperating to save time rather than wasting it in small bits throughout the day.

Jones has found that incentives work best when they are integrated within the context of the instructional program and the classroom structure. He describes this Preferred Activity Time, or PAT, as time allotted for activities such as learning games and enrichment activities. Activities are ones that students enjoy, such as reading a class book for pleasure, using vocabulary words to play hangman, working on an art project, or working with manipulatives. When selecting activities for PAT, teachers must consider three things. First, the activity should be attractive to the students. Second, students should earn time toward PAT through their work effort and responsible behavior. And third, teachers should choose activities that are acceptable to them.

PAT can be earned in several ways. Mrs. Foster gives her fifth graders three minutes to put away their math work and prepare for language arts. Any unused time from the three minutes is added to their PAT. Mr. Bjorka gives the class two extra PAT minutes if everyone is seated and ready when the bell rings. However, the class loses the amount of wasted time if a few students continue to be noisy. PAT can be used the day it is earned, or it may be saved for the end of the week or a future activity such as a field trip.

As incentive motivators, there are several differences between PAT and other rewards. PAT has these important qualities.

- PAT is genuine. In other words, preferred activity time is desired and available to all students, in exchange for making the extra effort to obtain it.
- PAT has educational value because it is found in enrichment activities and team learning games. Saying that students get to do anything they want is misleading. The activities that they want to do are really linked to a full load of academic work.
- PAT motivates all students by encouraging group concern for everyone to complete assigned work and behave well. Only then can students earn the PAT for the entire class.
- PAT can be earned as an individual bonus. Teachers can work individually with students who would lose PAT for the class because of their irresponsible choices. With a contract, the teacher can give consequences to the individual, but can also reward the class when behavior improves or the student makes responsible choices.
- PAT is easy for the teacher to implement.
- PAT is as creative as the teacher and students can imagine. Teachers continually post their PAT ideas to Jones's website, www.fredjones.com.

Spencer Kagan's Contributions

Spencer Kagan is another clinical psychologist and consultant who specializes in teacher effectiveness in classrooms. He, too, has spent hours observing and researching effective teachers and their methods. Kagan sees close connections among curriculum, instruction, and management, with motivation affecting the success of all three. Kagan's work in classroom management gives considerable attention to using cooperative learning, classbuilding and teambuilding, and the multiple intelligences as ways to motivate students.

So, how is cooperative learning a motivator? We realize that most of life and work involves cooperative interaction with others. Success, however, comes in learning how to work cooperatively. The basic principles of cooperative learning rest on critical questions, which Kagan refers to as PIES:

- Positive Interdependence: Is a gain for one a gain for another? Is help necessary?
- Individual Accountability: Is individual public performance required?
- Equal Participation: How equal is the participation?
- Simultaneous Interaction: What percent are overtly active at once?

Cooperative learning groups (like Glasser's learning teams) give students opportunity to learn and apply these skills. Students collaborate with others, with a degree of group autonomy to make decisions about the project, and have fun while they work.

And how are classbuilding and teambuilding motivators? Kagan (Kagan, Robertson, & Kagan, 1995) defined classbuilding as "The process by which a room full of individuals with different backgrounds and experiences become a caring community of active learners" (p. vi). His use of classbuilding as a verb reinforces that it is a process—classbuilding doesn't happen; it is done. Classbuilding activities have students, at least once a week, stand up, move around, and interact about noncontent topics with students they normally don't work with.

According to Kagan, teambuilding sets a climate for learning. Teambuilding has five aims: (1) getting acquainted, (2) team identity, (3) mutual support, (4) valuing differences, and (5) developing synergy. Teambuilding activities are essential when teams first form, but then can be used effectively when energy lulls. Quick teambuilding can take only a minute or two away from instruction time, but reenergizes the learning potential. Occurring at least twice a week, teambuilding activities are fun, nonacademic, and well within the ability of all the children.

And finally, how are the multiple intelligences motivators? Students are smart in different ways—remember Gardner's eight kinds of smart. Kagan has observed that classrooms seem to come alive when teachers (and students) use multiple intelligences strategies to teach and show their learnings. In *Multiple Intelligences: The Complete MI Book* (Kagan & Kagan, 1998), Kagan describes enriched classrooms that have three MI visions: matching, stretching, and celebrating. The goal of matching is to maximize academic success by teaching to the intelligences of the students. The goal of stretching is to maximize the development of all intelligences by making each student more intelligent in all ways. The goal of celebrating is to extol the uniqueness of every student and thereby sharpen students' abilities to understand and work with diversity.

Kagan's work ties to student motivation. In order to best motivate students to make responsible choices regarding their work and behavior, Kagan has written literally hundreds of step-by-step structures for teachers to use. Because the structures are content- and activity-free, they can be used in an infinite range of content areas.

Personality Traits of Good Motivators

Several personality traits are frequently seen in teachers who are especially effective in classroom motivation. As you reflect on these traits, remember that although nobody shows all of them all of the time, everybody shows some of them some of the time. These traits are greatly appreciated by students, and you probably can increase them in your behavior.

Charisma

Charisma is hard to define and harder to acquire, but we have all seen it—that ephemeral quality of personality that attracts and inspires. It is very difficult to say what makes one person more charismatic than another. Reasonably attractive appearance makes one appealing, at first. So does a sparkling personality, though some of the most appreciated teachers could never have been the life of any party. Ability to envision potential helps, as does steadfastness of purpose and faith in students' capabilities. Add to that some wisdom, enlightenment, experience, normal human frailties, a measure of vulnerability, and determination to persist, and you are getting somewhere in the neighborhood of charisma. If you happen to be an individual fortunate enough to possess it, motivation won't be much of a problem for you.

"BECAUSE WHEN YOU'RE DRAFTED BY THE CUBS, YOU'LL HAVE TO BE ABLE TO SIGN YOUR CONTRACT. THAT'S WHY YOU HAVE TO ATTEND FIRST GRADE."

Caring

Practically all teachers would prefer that their students learn and lead happy and productive lives. But caring in teaching implies considerably more than simple concern. It refers to teacher willingness to work on behalf of students, to keep trying when little progress is evident, and to persist even when students show no appreciation for efforts expended on them, as often will be the case. It means showing friendship—not to confuse with being a buddy—to every student, no matter how undeserving the student might seem. Depending on circumstances, it means encouraging, cajoling, supporting, or demanding. It may call for a warm heart or fire in the eye, but it always communicates that you are not willing to let any student drop by the wayside, to let students be less than they should be, or to say, "Oh well, what difference does it make anyway?"

Caring is within the grasp of everyone. It's a matter of effort and persistence. It brings occasional reward and frequent disappointment. How well you care depends on your personality, your level of conviction, and your ability to roll with the punches.

Enthusiasm

Up to a point, teacher enthusiasm motivates students. Enthusiasm is contagious, as is lack of it. But enthusiasm must be genuine. Students quickly spot a fraud. If you truly believe in the value of what you are teaching and in the virtue of those with whom you are working, your students will respond to your efforts, though not always exactly as you would like. But remember, it is difficult to achieve significant results overnight.

Trust

Trust has two sides. Students must trust that their teacher will support and guide them and is someone they can count on. Students also must believe that their teacher believes in them and will let them make choices, decisions, and mistakes, and learn and grow from the results, without harm or reprisal.

Respect

Respect relates closely to trust, and should be mutual. In fact, respect often comes from trust. Students must respect their teacher as a knowledge facilitator and as an adult who models the good character qualities and the Golden Rule. Teachers must respect a student's right to learn, sometimes by making mistakes, and share responsibility for that learning.

Good Motivators—What Do They Do?

Here we move away from the nebulous area of personality traits to the more definitive realm of teaching skills, acknowledging the considerable overlap between the two. With traits of personality set aside, it is obvious that teachers good at motivation also perform certain skill tasks particularly well. These skills can be learned, practiced, and perhaps even perfected. Teachers good at motivation frequently:

1. *Use novelty, mystery, puzzlement, and excitement* to energize their lessons. Mr. Samuel in the reading lesson says, "There may or may not be a double entendre somewhere on this page. If you think you find one and can explain its meaning, raise your thumb so I can see it."
2. *Use color, sound, movement, and student activity* to attract and hold attention. Mrs. Gomez uses songs, rhymes, and skits to help her students practice Spanish vocabulary, pronunciation, and conversation.
3. *Assign individual and group projects* as a means of adding sense of purpose to what is being learned, and encouraging students toward self-control and responsibility. Ms. Eggleston's students keep separate writing and art portfolios of some of their work to show their parents or guardians.
4. *State clear, reasonable expectations and requirements* to avoid confusion and enlist student cooperation. Mr. Timkins uses visual instruction plans (VIPs), writes assignments on charts, explains them to students, checks understanding by having students describe the assignments back to him, and leaves the VIP or chart on display while students complete their work.

In order to manage expectations during instruction, Kim Anderson learned the following strategy from her cooperating teacher, Ginger DeNigro, when she student taught in a multi-age, first- and second-grade class. Kim found it also worked with her fifth-grade students the next semester.

I've picked up several classroom management techniques from my student teaching. One of my favorites came from my master teacher. At the beginning of an important lesson, Ginger would ask her first and second graders what she needed from them before she could begin the lesson. The students would anxiously raise their hands, eager to demonstrate their knowledge. They would list off the five needs, and as they were described, the teacher would draw a simple descriptive icon on the board.

First, she needed the students in *listening position,* and she drew a chair to show that they needed to be sitting up straight. Second, she needed the students to *raise their hands* if they wanted to speak, and she drew a hand below the chair. Third, she needed *mouths closed,* and she drew a set of lips below the hand. Next, she needed *eyes on her,* and she drew an eye. Finally, she needed the students to *listen* to the teacher and to each other. Her last icon was an ear. The icons stayed on the board throughout the entire lesson.

As I began to teach in Ginger's classroom I used the technique. It helped focus the students' attention on the lesson and I was able to point to an individual icon if the students needed to work on one skill.

My second placement was in a fifth-grade class. I didn't use this technique at first, simply because I assumed it was too basic for their level. I was wrong! I finally used it half way through my field experience and was amazed at its effectiveness. All I had to say was "listening position," and the students immediately straightened up, knowing exactly what I expected of them. This is a strategy that can be used in all elementary classrooms.

5. Provide continual support, help, feedback, and encouragement to assist students over rough spots and keep them on track. As often as she can, Miss Moore teaches her lessons in a cycle. She explains one step at a time, models the step, and then promptly involves her students by having them do the step in the process. When possible, students cumulatively practice the steps—they return to the first step and work through the process to finally include the newest step. As the students work, she circulates quietly among them, making helpful suggestions and giving encouraging comments. Jones (2000) calls this Say, See, Do teaching.

6. Listen to student concerns and remain flexible enough to change when it is warranted. Mr. Proybal holds brief class discussions at the end of each day, in which he asks students to comment on the lessons they liked best, those they liked least, and those they found most difficult. He listens to student suggestions and discusses his own ideas for improvement. In addition to asking students to share one idea they learned today, Mrs. Scott asks: "What can you do so you will learn more tomorrow?" and "What do you want me to do to help you?"

7. Provide numerous opportunities for students to display their accomplishments to both the class and to larger audiences. Mrs. Cooper schedules displays of student science and social studies projects, and toward the end of the year invites caregivers to view the displays.

8. Emphasize student accountability concerning behavior, work habits, and production of quality work. Mr. Adams requires his students to keep records of their work and effort and to periodically reflect on their improvement. Similarly, Mr. Wong has students keep private, ongoing charts and rate themselves each day on their behavior and work. He also schedules brief individual conferences with students to discuss the self-ratings. Mrs. Wilder's students are able to describe their own progress and achievement when they participate in student-led parent conferences.

9. Use student-centered classroom assessment. Mrs. Jacobs involves her students in student-centered assessment to better prepare them for writing term papers. By analyzing sample term papers, one outstanding and one very poor, students are able to discern the qualities of the outstanding paper and apply their observations and understanding to their own work.

10. Give students responsibility. Students are allowed to make decisions about their learning and behavior that may be different from others around them. They know

why they make the decisions and are comfortable with the decisions. They are encouraged to be all they can be, and are shown that they have options in what they do. And if they blow it—and sometimes they will—they experience the consequences for blowing it the first time, and are then given a second opportunity to try the responsibility again.

11. Differentiate instruction. Mrs. Hodgers thinks of alternative ways to provide content instruction, vary the process by which students can make sense of the content, or demonstrate the understanding and learning they take away from the content.

12. Work to build *esprit de corps* which, when successfully accomplished, mobilizes the class for better behavior and achievement. Ms. Iwai uses many classbuilding and teambuilding activities. She challenges her students to surpass expectations, to be their best, and to strive to make their lives works of art, and she pitches in, sharing and discussing their efforts as well as her own.

These are some of the things good classroom motivators frequently do. In fact, many of these suggestions bring the students into the process and make them feel as though they have some control. There are, as well, many things that good motivators assiduously try *not* to do.

What Good Classroom Motivators Don't Do

Most teachers are not born with an ability to be good classroom motivators. In fact, observation and experience has probably taught them to not do a number of things. Consider these six things teachers do not do:

1. They don't bore students to death. They plan against boredom, and at its onset they change the topic or activity, take a short brain break, insert a timely energizer, or simply say, "I know this is not very interesting, but it is important, and I need you to hang in with me for five more minutes. Can you do that for me?"

2. They don't confuse their students. At least they try not to, though they recognize that all learners become confused at times. They make their directions short and explicit, they give clear explanations, and when possible they use visual instructional plans to show students the steps. They check for understanding: "Bobby, please help us remember the three things we are supposed to do. Tell us what they are."

3. They don't vacillate. Hour after hour, day after day, they hold to their expectations and to the way they interact with students. They aren't hot today, cold tomorrow; your pal now, your enemy later. They work to get procedures correct and hold them steady. This is not to say they shouldn't be flexible enough to change when change is needed, or that even the best teachers don't have good and bad days. Illnesses and personal problems affect all of us, and in turn affect our work and interactions. But there must be a steadying force in the classroom: the teacher.

4. They don't frustrate their students. Frustrated students sooner or later rebel. Frustration can come from two sources—unreasonable demands or work that is boringly difficult. Mr. Thaddeus is unreasonable when he says, "If the entire class doesn't make

100 on this test, nobody goes to recess for the rest of the day." He is unreasonable when he says, "You are to have all this [exorbitant amount of] homework done by tomorrow or you get an F in the grade book."

Frustration also comes from boringly difficult work, such as an hour of trying to do hard problems in long division with little if any success, or trying to memorize long lists of facts and dates for which there seems to be no earthly purpose.

5. They do not intimidate their students. Most teachers tend to be intimidating at first and others remain so despite efforts to the contrary. But they do not use a stance of autocratic superiority to make students work and behave, nor do they use sour personality, fierce physical stature, hostility, or thinly veiled threats. Rather, good teachers try to downplay intimidation, knowing that for whatever achievement it might inspire, it certainly will produce a counterdesire to resist, vanish, or become transported elsewhere.

6. They do not punish their students for failure or other shortcomings. That is, they don't punish in the sense of inflicting pain, acute embarrassment, or loss of dignity. They do, of course, follow the provisions of the discipline system used in their class, which often invokes unpleasant consequences for irresponsible choices, disruptive behavior, or wanton failure to complete assignments. But that unpleasantness seldom entails more than staying in at recess and, when possible, correcting whatever was done incorrectly. For students, the impact comes from the certainty of receiving a consequence, not the fact that a consequence is a reward or a discipline. Good motivators rarely punish students for doing poor quality work. They know they can get farther through helpful correction than by hurting students' feelings or making them resentfully angry.

What Are Some Cautions in Motivation?

Although most teachers lament the lack of learner motivation, students can, at times, become overmotivated or overstimulated to such a degree that work and behavior suffer. If during a lesson on animals you bring a pet into the classroom, especially one as unusual as a skunk or raccoon, your lesson will probably be lost in the chaos that ensues. If you overemphasize the dire importance of an upcoming achievement test, students may try so hard that they can't relax and think, and do worse than if you hadn't mentioned it at all.

Aside from the deleterious effects of overmotivation, what teachers do to instill motivation often leaves unanswered ethical questions. For example, if novelty, puzzles, intrigue, and excitement are overlaid onto all lessons, do students come to believe that learning is no good unless a wizard performs magic or a toy bounces and sings? If incentives and rewards are used to spur student work, do you perpetuate the belief that work is to be done only for the reward and not for the personal satisfaction of learning or the sense of responsibility to oneself? Most teachers find such questions troublesome but would still rather see students working, even if for reasons not laudable, than find them not working at all. To a considerable degree, taking to heart some of the teachings of Glasser, Gardner, Jones, and Kagan can ease such concerns.

Their suggestions are important to keep in mind as we prepare to move into Chapter 6, the topic of which is managing instruction. Before proceeding to the next chapter, take time to explore these end-of-chapter activities.

Parting Thought

Learning is not attained by chance;
it must be sought for with ardor and
attended to with diligence.

—Abigail Adams

SUMMARY SELF-CHECK

Check off the following as you either understand or become able to apply them.

❑ Teachers are more concerned about student motivation than about anything else in teaching, with the possible exception of discipline.

❑ To most teachers the word *motivation* refers to what teachers do to get students interested in lessons.

❑ People do not do what we want them to for five reasons: they don't know what to do, don't know how to do it, don't know why they should do it, aren't well suited or matched to the task, or don't want to.

❑ To motivate students, experienced teachers capitalize on students' known interests by including those interest topics or themes in their lessons. They also try to encourage students, help them feel secure and supported, and use systems of reinforcement for good work and responsible behavior.

❑ Although many teachers still motivate through fear and intimidation, the overall results are rarely satisfying.

❑ William Glasser has made some very important contributions to education, including the following contentions concerning motivation:
   ■ All behavior is people's best attempts to control themselves so as to satisfy their needs.
   ■ Humans have five predominant needs, four of which are closely related to classroom motivation: to belong, to gain power, to be free, to have fun.
   ■ Education should be organized so learning activities enable students to meet some of those four needs and feel they belong.

- This is accomplished when students work in teams, and teachers function as "lead-managers," stress quality in all student work, and transform the classroom into what students perceive as a "friendly workplace."

☐ Howard Gardner's theory of multiple intelligences identifies eight areas of intelligence: verbal/linguistic, logical/mathematical, visual/spatial, bodily/kinesthetic, musical, inter-personal, intrapersonal, and naturalist.
  - Teachers should ask: "In what ways are my students smart?"

☐ Jones believes incentives work best when they are mixed with the context of the instructional program and the classroom structure.
  - Preferred Activity Time (PAT) is opportunity for activities the teacher would have had students do anyway, if time allowed.
  - PAT is genuine, has educational value, encourages group concern, can work for individuals, and is easy to implement.

☐ Kagan links motivation to cooperative learning, classbuilding, teambuilding, and multiple intelligences.
  - Three visions of MI are matching, stretching, celebrating.

☐ Traits of teachers good at motivation seem to include: charisma, caring, enthusiasm, trust, and respect.
  - Teachers good at motivation use many skills as they plan and instruct.
  - Teachers good at motivation try *not* to bore, confuse, frustrate, intimidate, or punish students for failure or shortcomings.
  - Dangers in motivation include overstimulation of students and questions about the ethics of using rewards as incentives and payoffs.

ACTIVITIES FOR REFLECTION AND GROWTH

For Cumulative Skills Development

1. Take a moment to review the statements in the Anticipation–Reaction Guide at the beginning of this chapter. Put a check mark in the Reaction column next to any statement with which you now agree. How have your thoughts changed since reading this chapter?

2. Describe one of your teachers from the past who seemed especially able to motivate you to work and learn. What can you now identify in that person that contributed to your motivation?

3. The contention was made that good motivators do not intimidate their students. Yet good high school and college football coaches everywhere yell, scream, swear, berate, and sometimes even strike their player-students, despite which the players usually try very hard and show great respect for their coaches. How do you account for that? Could such an approach be equally effective in the elementary classroom?

4. Glasser contends that students will work at any subject if the process of doing so enables them to meet some of their needs. How would you organize the following social studies

lessons to help students meet their needs: (a) a first-grade study of the family, (b) a fourth-grade study of state geography, and (c) a fifth-grade study of U.S. history?

5. Gardner said, "School matters, but only insofar as it yields something that can be used once students leave school." To what extent do you agree or disagree with this statement?

6. Describe how you will use classbuilding, teambuilding, and multiple intelligences strategies in a grade of your choice to motivate your students.

REFERENCES AND RECOMMENDED READINGS

Ames, C. (1992). Achievement goals and the classroom motivational climate. In D. J. Schunk & J. L. Meece (Eds.). *Student perceptions in the classroom.* Hillsdale, NJ: Erlbaum.

Bandura, A. (1977). *Social learning theory.* Englewood Cliffs, NJ: Prentice-Hall.

Brophy, J. (1987). Synthesis on strategies for motivating students to learn. *Educational Leadership, 45,* 40–48.

Brophy, J. (1998). *Motivating students to learn.* Boston: McGraw-Hill.

Coloroso, B. (1994). *Kids are worth it! Giving your child the gift of inner discipline.* New York: Avon Books.

Curtiss, K., & English, S. (2003). *Choice theory certification.* Retrieved August 2003 from www.kathycurtissco.com/what_we_do.htm

Dembo, M. (1994). *Applying educational psychology* (5th ed.). White Plains, NY: Longman.

Fleming, D., & Kilcher, A. (1991, November). Presentation at Organizing and Managing School Change Workshop, NEA National Center for Innovation National Conference, Colorado Springs, CO.

Ford, M. (1992). *Motivating humans.* Newbury Park, CA: Sage.

Gardner, H. (1991). *The unschooled mind: How children think and how schools should teach.* New York: Basic Books.

Gardner, H. (1993a). *Frames of mind* (10th ed.). New York: Basic Books.

Gardner, H. (1993b). *Multiple intelligences: The theory in practice.* New York: Basic Books.

Gardner, H. (1997). Reflections on multiple intelligences: Myths and messages. *Phi Delta Kappan, 77*(3), 200–209.

Gardner, H. (n.d.). *Eye on San Diego* [Interview on television broadcast].

Glasser, W. (1998a). *Choice theory in the classroom* (Rev. ed.). New York: HarperCollins.

Glasser, W. (1998b). *Control theory in the classroom* (Rev. ed.). Harper & Row.

Glasser, W. (1998c). *The quality school* (Rev. ed.). New York: HarperCollins.

Glasser, W. (1998d). *The quality school teacher* (Rev. ed.). New York: HarperCollins.

Glasser, W. (2000). *Every student can succeed.* Chatsworth, CA: Author.

Johnson, D., & Johnson, R. (1998). *Learning together and alone* (5th ed.). Boston: Allyn & Bacon.

Jones, F. (1987). *Positive classroom instruction.* New York: McGraw-Hill.

Jones, F. (2000). *Tools for teaching: Discipline instruction motivation.* Santa Cruz, CA: Fredric H. Jones & Associates.

Kagan, L., Kagan, M., & Kagan, S. (1997). *Cooperative learning structures for teambuilding.* San Clemente, CA: Kagan Cooperative Learning.

Kagan, M., Robertson, L., & Kagan, S. (1995). *Cooperative learning structures for classbuilding.* San Clemente, CA: Kagan Cooperative Learning.

Kagan, S. (1994). *Cooperative learning.* San Clemente, CA: Kagan Cooperative Learning.

Kagan, S., & Kagan, M. (1998). *Multiple intelligences: The complete MI book.* San Clemente, CA: Kagan Cooperative Learning.

Marshall, M. (2002). *Discipline without stress, punishments, or rewards: How teachers and parents promote responsibility and learning.* Los Alamitos, CA: Piper Press.

Maslow, A. (1943). A theory of human motivation. *Psychological Review, 50,* 370–396.

McClelland, D. (1965). Toward a theory of motive acquisition. *American Psychologist, 20,* 321–333.

Pintrich, P., & DeGroot, E. (1990). Motivational and self-regulated learning components of classroom academic performance. *Journal of Educational Psychology, 82,* 33–40.

Skinner, B. (1968). *The technology of teaching.* New York: Appleton-Century-Crofts.

Slavin, R. (Ed.). (1989). *School and classroom organization.* Hillsdale, NJ: Erlbaum.

Tomlinson, C. (1999). *The differentiated classroom: Responding to the needs of all learners.* Alexandria, VA: Association for Supervision and Curriculum Development.

Tomlinson, C. (2002, September). Invitations to learn. *Educational Leadership. 60*(1), 6–10.

Weiner, B. (1990). History of motivational research in education. *Journal of Educational Psychology, 82,* 616–622.

Whalen, S., & Csikszentmihalyi, M. (1991). *Putting flow theory into educational practice: The key school's flow activities room.* Report to the Benton Center for Curriculum and Instruction. Chicago: University of Chicago.

6 Managing Instruction

A teacher must be a prophet who can look into the future, see the world of tomorrow into which the children of today must fit, and then teach and test the necessary skills.

—Anonymous

ANTICIPATION–REACTION GUIDE

Before you read the chapter, take a moment to put a check mark in the Anticipation column next to any statement with which you agree.

	Anticipation	Reaction
According to the text definitions, *instructional strategy* is narrower in scope than *instructional approach*.	❑	❑
In essence, direct teaching puts students in charge of the curriculum while facilitative teaching puts teachers in charge.	❑	❑
Direct teaching typically has students mainly use lower levels of thought.	❑	❑
The strategy of concept attainment works better for older students than for younger students and language learners.	❑	❑
Teachers seem to prefer using cooperative learning over other strategies of instruction.	❑	❑
Generally speaking, students find it motivating to work in cooperative learning groups.	❑	❑
Cooperative learning supports positive interdependence, individual accountability, equal participation, and simultaneous interaction.	❑	❑
Projects are better for primary-grade children than for intermediate-grade children because projects stress concrete rather than abstract thinking.	❑	❑
To differentiate instruction, modifications are made to content, process, or product.	❑	❑
Computerized teaching is an efficient way to instruct all students.	❑	❑

Curriculum and Instruction

Fostering competencies in the basic skills of reading, writing, and arithmetic was established as law by the Massachusetts Bay Colony's Old Deluder Act of 1647 and has been a major ongoing purpose of elementary education in the United States. The law pointed out that Satan intended to lead people away from the paths of righteousness, so it was incumbent upon all citizens to learn to read the Scriptures as a means of thwarting Satan's unholy intentions. Thus the primary schools became an instrument of God in His work against the devil.

For nearly three hundred years thereafter, the content of the elementary curriculum remained much the same, and to a degree still does, though in the 1930s elementary education slowly began to change. Led by Francis Parker and John Dewey, educators suggested that schools be made consistent with students' lives here and now, and attuned to the daily needs, aptitudes, and interests of young students. Furthermore, schools should help prepare the young for constructive participation in a democratic society that requires cooperation, compromise, group decision making, and personal responsibility. The suggestion that the schools should take the lead in preparing such citizens was revolutionary.

This progressive view gained popularity up through the 1950s. However, in 1957 when the Soviet Union launched *Sputnik,* the first orbital satellite, criticisms were aimed at American schools—it was claimed that schools had gone soft, that they were asking students to do nothing but play, and that they had quit training young minds.

Education weathered the fierce criticism. Teachers had known all along to strive for balance between teaching students facts and teaching them to think for themselves. That has not changed. Teachers still strive to help children acquire knowledge, skills, and concepts on the one hand, and cooperation, creativity, and good attitudes on the other, emphasizing all learnings and slighting none.

Can such a balance be accomplished? And if so, how? The answer is deceptively simple. When students are asked to apply what they've learned to real-life situations, they become better at application. When students are asked to analyze problems and come up with solutions, they learn to problem solve. If given activities that require cooperation, they become better at cooperating. In other words, students usually learn to do what we give them practice in doing. To this end, the intended outcome indicates the instructional approach that teachers should use. Remember backward design planning (Chapter 2)? This logic supports the steps of backward design: identify the desired results, determine acceptable evidence, and then plan learning experiences and instruction.

Four Instructional Approaches

The term *instructional approach* is used to mean a broad orientation to instruction, or a general way of teaching that can lead to a variety of outcomes. Four broad instructional approaches—direct teaching, facilitative teaching, technology-assisted teaching, and differentiated instruction—currently are widely used in education. Within these four broad approaches, many different instructional strategies are used. Joyce and Weil (2000) categorize and describe many of the currently popular strategies. Cruickshank, Bainer, and Metcalf (1999) describe twenty-nine instructional alternatives ("any teaching maneuver used to facilitate student learning and satisfaction," p. 163). Here, we will briefly review four major instructional approaches and some of the tactics used in each.

Instructional Approach: Direct Teaching

Direct teaching has historically been at the forefront of teaching practice, and still enjoys great popularity. Several studies in the late 1970s and early 1980s, focusing on basic academic areas of reading, mathematics, and English, found that students instructed with a structured curriculum and direct teacher involvement learned more than students taught with more individualized or discovery methods. Direct teaching continues to be used to advantage when goals are stated very precisely, content coverage is extensive, student performance is monitored closely, and feedback can be given immediately. Direct teaching is excellent for skill development and for delivering large amounts of factual and conceptual information, but it is not good for attitude development or for teaching creativity or problem solving.

Direct teaching gives teachers control of all aspects of instruction at all times. Teachers align the curriculum to the standards, set the objectives, plan the program, organize activities, arrange groups, give explanations, direct and correct student work, keep records, and evaluate results. Teachers may discuss all these matters with students, but they primarily do so to help students understand what they are being asked to do. They normally do not ask for student suggestions.

Instructional Strategy: Direct Instruction.   Direct instruction is referred to by some as the Hunter model or the five- (six-, seven-, or nine-) step lesson plan. Intending to maximize student learning time, direct instruction is a highly structured strategy that normally involves the following (Hunter, 1982):

1. Anticipatory set is used at the beginning of the lesson to orient, focus, or intrigue students, as a means of motivating and guiding their work. As its name suggests, this first step helps students anticipate what is to come. It usually involves a verbal introduction such as

    "Friends, today there is a great surprise in store for us."

    "Class, have you ever wondered what it would be like if you could have your own pet dinosaur?"

    "Boys and girls, today we are going to learn how to write haiku poetry."

2. Teacher input of new information or skills follows the anticipatory set. Input possibilities are limitless. For example, the teacher can present it directly, or it can be contained in written material or visual media the teacher assigns or shows:

    "Boys and girls, watch carefully how I string these beads so you'll know how to string yours." (Teacher explains while demonstrating.)

    "Group six, you are to use the encyclopedia to find out why dinosaurs are believed to have become extinct."

    "Class, watch the steps I follow when multiplying these fractions." (Teacher refers to chart or visual instruction plan with numbered steps while explaining how the fractions are multiplied, then tells students that the chart will remain on display as a reminder.)

3. Guided student practice follows teacher input. Students practice related work at their desks, individually or in groups. The teacher circulates and provides guidance and immediate feedback, stopping class work if necessary to re-explain what students seem to not understand.
4. Closure, following guided practice, further checks student understanding. Students, in their own words, explain concepts, list procedures, suggest how a new skill can be applied, or reconsider the value or purpose of the learning.
5. Independent practice occurs during homework and subsequent lessons when students review learnings and apply them in a variety of ways.

Teacher and Student Roles in Direct Teaching.   The teacher controls and directs instruction by presenting information in sequential steps and providing prompt feedback about students' efforts. Students do as directed and are not expected to give input about content or procedure.

Strengths of Direct Teaching.   This strategy is very effective for teaching information and basic skills to whole classes. It is highly structured and sequential, keeps students closely on task, and gives them immediate feedback. It enables teachers to cover a quantity of information in a relatively short period of time.

Limitations of Direct Teaching.   This strategy tends to emphasize lower levels of thought. Students are not called on to show much initiative, imagination, creativity, or abstract thinking. The strategy's predictability can become boring for teacher and students alike.

Usability of Direct Teaching.   Direct teaching can be used at all grade levels with students of all levels of ability. English language learners and others will appreciate the presentation pattern: smaller information segments followed immediately with practice and feedback. Its appropriateness for a given lesson depends on the curriculum standards, the lesson objectives, and the time available for teaching.

Instructional Strategy: Concept Attainment.   A concept is a general rule or notion we have about a certain thing—for example, about an object, idea, or procedure. We form this general idea by mentally combining that thing's perceived characteristics. Concepts are the essential elements of thought. To say that we think is to say that we review concepts and combine and manipulate them. Thus, concept attainment—that is, the process by which we acquire and refine concepts—is of prime importance in education.

Concepts begin to develop as we encounter elements of life, whether these elements are tangible or intellectual, and whether we encounter them directly or vicariously. Our clear and accurate concept of a dog is the result of numerous experiences with dogs and what they do. Our concept of a tapir may be less clear and accurate because most of us have not had many experiences with that animal. And even less clear and accurate may be our concept of the energy release that occurs in nuclear fusion, though most adults do have some idea about it.

We refine our concepts as we compare and contrast examples. For instance, a child refines the concept of an apple by contrasting apples' characteristics with those of oranges and bananas.

To help students attain concepts in school, we ask them to categorize objects and ideas on the basis of critical attributes. Apples, based on their attributes, go in one fruit box, and oranges, based on their attributes, go in another. Similarly, nouns go in one category of words, and verbs go in another. To help students further refine their concepts, we give them examples, called *exemplars,* that contain essential traits. In map study, for example, we teach students that representations of the earth's surface are called *maps.* We may show them, as one exemplar, a Mercator projection in which the earth's longitude and latitude are represented as straight horizontal and vertical lines. We may show them, as another exemplar, a polar projection in which the pole is in the center and lines of longitude and latitude look something like a circular spider web. From these exemplars and others, students acquire a concept of map that includes both Mercator and polar projections, but their concept of each differs from the other.

In using concept attainment, teachers first give exemplars and then ask students to develop and test hypotheses about them. Teacher and students then analyze the thinking process used.

Teacher and Student Roles in Concept Attainment.   The teacher selects, defines, and analyzes the concept to be developed, creates the lists of exemplars, and directs the activities. The teacher thus controls the lesson but encourages student interaction and discussion.

Strengths of Concept Attainment.   The strategy is valuable when introducing or refining a concept, or checking student understanding of ideas and processes. Students enjoy lessons in concept attainment. It seems like a game to them; it holds their attention and keeps them involved. Further, it causes them to use analytical thinking and inductive reasoning.

Limitations of Concept Attainment.   The strategy is time consuming, and the teacher must prepare well to avoid the danger of students developing incorrect concepts.

Usability of Concept Attainment.   With grade-appropriate concepts, the strategy can be used for all grade levels and most subjects. It can be used to introduce, identify, or refine and strengthen concepts, and to review and check student understanding. Concept attainment will probably not work well with students who do not have the vocabulary or basic knowledge to understand and then translate the concept exemplars and definition.

Instructional Strategy: Say, See, Do Teaching.   Say, See, Do Teaching is an interactive technique developed by Fred Jones (2000). Jones says you have to consider three things—the way we remember, how much we remember, and how long we can remember it. Simply put, the Say, See, Do cycle has three steps: explanation (say), modeling (see), and structured practice (do), with frequent repetitions of steps two and three. For example, Mr. Wallace prepares to teach the steps for long division to his fourth graders. To ensure that they understand it, he uses Jones's Say, See, Do Teaching model, along with a Visual Instructional Plan (VIP) that consists of review, partner teaching, and frequent repetitions of the cumulative steps. As he and the class work through the steps of example problems, Mr. Wallace has the students repeat the full process to the newest step and then teach their partner as they repeat the full process.

A Visual Instructional Plan is a series of picture prompts that represents the process or thinking, and clearly guides students through the process of the task and performance. As Mr. Wallace prepared his VIP with careful consideration of the complete task of long division, he followed three simple guidelines: one step at a time, a picture for every step, and minimal reliance on words. His VIP for long division looked like Figure 6.1.

We can contrast VIPs with summary graphics and simple visual aids. Summary graphics do not include the individual steps of the lesson. For this lesson in long division, a summary graphic would probably look like Figure 6.2.

Simple visual aids are memory aids. Although they can be useful for test review, they omit information and details needed for students to acquire the skill or knowledge. Thus a visual aid for the same long division lesson would look like Figure 6.3.

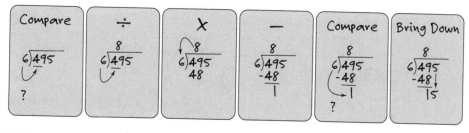

FIGURE 6.1 **A Visual Instruction Plan (VIP) shows each step of the lesson.**

(Fred Jones *Tools for Teaching,* 2000, www.fredjones.com)

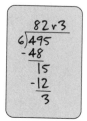

FIGURE 6.2 **A summary graphic hides the individual steps of a lesson.**

(Fred Jones *Tools for Teaching,* 2000, www.fredjones.com)

FIGURE 6.3 **A memory aid is useful for test review, but it omits the information needed for acquisition.**

(Fred Jones *Tools for Teaching,* 2000, www.fredjones.com)

VIPs must answer in a concrete and visual form the question students most ask when they need help: "What do I do next?" Performance illustrations, one type of VIP, are particularly useful for nonreaders because they show the performance steps. The performance illustration in Figure 6.4 shows students the classroom procedure for properly carrying a chair.

Mind maps are another type of VIP. Mind maps are any graphic that shows someone how to organize information or an idea, solve a problem, or perform a series of operations. Thus, mind maps may assume varied forms, such as those shown in Figure 6.5.

Jones has found that VIPs accelerate learning and support independent learning for three reasons. First, VIPs reduce the time needed for teacher prompting because students can be quickly directed to the next step—the explanation is "prepackaged." In other words, teachers can give efficient help, in only a few seconds, by simply saying something like "Look at step five on the board. That's what you do next." Second, VIPs minimize the need for students to remember what is said. Now they can see and refer back to it. And third, because VIPs provide the steps for the entire lesson, students can help themselves rather than ask for help from the teacher.

Teacher and Student Roles in Say, See, Do Teaching.   To reinforce the teaching and learning, the teacher uses the three-step cycle, frequently repeating steps two and three. As students practice and solve the problems, they review each step completely by teaching it to their partner. They are actively engaged in the learning process.

Strengths of Say, See, Do Teaching.   Say, See, Do Teaching reinforces the students' abilities to remember by reducing the amount of new information presented at one time and by quickly involving students. The very nature of the practice allows the teacher to observe students and give prompt feedback as needed.

Limitations of Say, See, Do Teaching.   The teacher must plan instruction in discrete steps. Also, receiving limited pieces of information at a time can be distracting and disruptive for students who need to see the whole picture in order to master the smaller steps.

FIGURE 6.4   For students who cannot read, omit words.

(Fred Jones *Tools for Teaching*, 2000, www.fredjones.com)

Usability of Say, See, Do Teaching. The strategy can be used at all grade levels and in most subjects. Because of the presentation pattern of explanation, modeling, and structured practice, Say, See, Do Teaching can be used to teach new content and skills, as well as review prior learning. English language learners will appreciate its inherent repetition and structured practice.

Instructional Approach: Facilitative Teaching

Direct teaching is rather tightly controlled by the teacher, who aligns the curriculum standards, sets objectives, does the planning, directs the lessons, and evaluates learning. In facilitative teaching, first popularized by Carl Rogers (1969), students play a much more active role in giving input, delving into learning, reflecting on the meaning of what they are learning, and assessing the quality of their efforts. The prime role of the teacher is, as the label implies, to facilitate students' efforts and progress. Notice how these two approaches differ in the following lesson on capitalization.

   1. *Direct Teaching (Direct Instruction Strategy).* The teacher introduces the lesson by stating rules concerning capitalization of first words in sentences, people's names, cities, and states, and has examples of each rule on a chart to which students can refer. Students do two practice sentences together with teacher direction, then complete worksheets while the teacher observes and provides corrective feedback.

   2. *Facilitative Teaching (Inquiry Strategy—described later in this section).* The teacher, presenting a written paragraph containing a number of capitalized words, informs the students that all capitalizations are correct. Students read through the paragraph, circle the capitalized words, and then, working in pairs, attempt to formulate rules that apply to the use of capital letters.

Note that in facilitative teaching the teacher remains in control of the class but does less lecturing and directing and refrains from leading students to conclusions. Instead, students are encouraged to explore problems, come up with their own solutions, and examine the meaning of what they have learned.

Instructional Strategy: Cooperative Learning. Cooperative learning involves two or more students working together to complete specific tasks. This strategy is used in facilitative teaching because it encourages good cooperation, requires positive give and take, shows the value of collective wisdom, and highlights the contributions that every student can make.

   Cooperative learning is a valuable strategy for managing diversity. Students with physical challenges are better able to participate in the learning community because the physical layout of the classroom is planned to best accommodate teams or cooperative groups. English language learners are better able and more likely to communicate with their peers in smaller groupings. As students participate in cooperative activities they gain confidence in their language skills as well as insights into other cultures.

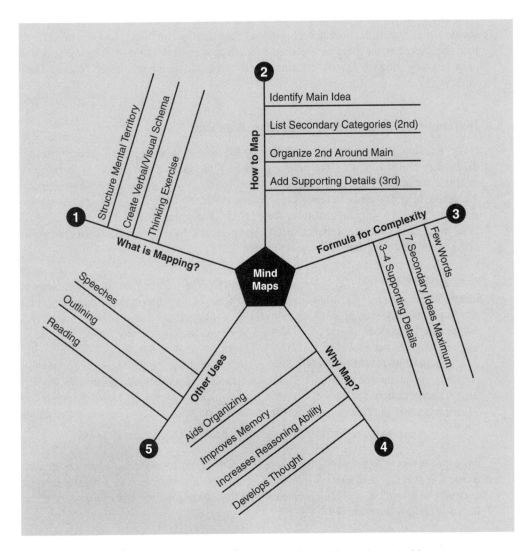

FIGURE 6.5   A mind map shows someone how to organize an idea, solve a problem, or perform a series of operations. In mind mapping, necessity is the mother of invention.

(Fred Jones *Tools for Teaching,* 2000, www.fredjones.com)

Spencer Kagan (1994) asserts that teachers' abilities to successfully implement cooperative learning relates to their competence in six key areas:

- *Teams.* Long-term, teacher-assigned, and small enough for active participation by all members, teams can be heterogeneous (mixed gender, ethnicity, and ability), homogeneous, and random. Four team members can split for even partner work.

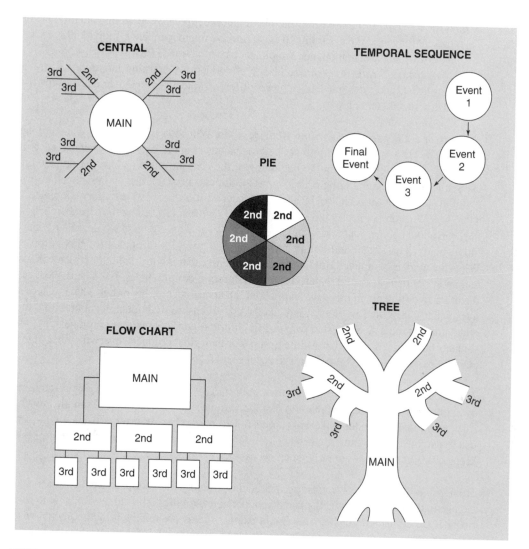

FIGURE 6.5 **Continued**

- *Will.* Students must have the desire, the will to cooperate. Teambuilding and class-building activities enhance the will.
- *Management.* Signals, clear responsibility and role expectations, and other management tools help ensure smooth cooperative learning experiences.
- *Skills.* Social skills help students work together effectively, and teachers can teach these skills in a variety of ways, including role-plays and gambits (specific words to say), modeling and practice, and reflection and planning.

- *Basic Principles.* Four basic principles support cooperative learning, and all must be present for cooperative learning to exist: positive interdependence, individual accountability, equal participation, and simultaneous interaction (PIES).
- *Cooperative Strategies.* An abundance of cooperative learning instructional strategies exist, each designed to achieve different objectives and interactions for the instructional content.

Example of a Cooperative Learning Activity.   Ms. Winston's sixth graders are studying whales. The class is organized into six heterogeneous cooperative learning teams, each of which has five members. From the beginning of the year the students have participated in classbuilding and teambuilding activities. Also, students have learned and practiced a variety of management tools and social skills for successful cooperative learning experiences.

Ms. Winston begins by having students meet as "expert" teams to learn as much as they can about one particular kind of large whale—gray whale, beluga whale, killer whale, blue whale, right whale, and humpback whale. She provides resources for this purpose. When the work is completed, students regroup into five teams with six members each. Each team now contains a student expert on each of the six types of whales. Each expert teaches the other five students in this new team about the appearance of his or her whale, where it lives, what it eats, and whether it is endangered. To ensure individual accountability, the other students are asked to listen for specific information. This process continues until all students have served as teacher for the group. For their final products, every member of the class prepares a booklet that contains drawings and facts about each whale.

Teacher and Student Roles in Cooperative Learning.   Students principally work on their own, in activities that require them to assume various roles in the group. Example student roles might include leader, encourager, questioner, researcher, reporter, artist, summarizer, materials collector, or time manager. The teacher sets up activities, monitors the process, keeps order, and helps—but only when necessary.

Strengths of Cooperative Learning.   Students usually like cooperative activities and engage in them eagerly. In well-planned cooperative activities, all students are able to participate and contribute to their maximum extent. Teams are relatively autonomous, with team members depending on each other. Students learn to think for themselves and show resourcefulness and creativity.

Limitations of Cooperative Learning.   Because students interact in groups, activities can become noisy. Some students wander off task easily, and some rely on others to do the work, which causes irritation. Also, the teacher may have difficulty assessing the quality of an individual student's work.

Usability of Cooperative Learning.   Cooperative learning is appropriate for all age levels and most subjects. However, for successful cooperative learning to occur, teachers must consider the six key areas and the basic principles of PIES. Moreover, cooperative learning is more likely to be successful when activities and projects are designed so every student in the group has a specific role or task to perform. Students must possess adequate skills and self-control for appropriate behavior. With some guidance, language learners can be successful contributors to group activities.

Variations of Cooperative Learning.   Countless books have been written with cooperative learning structures. Among some of the more popular variations are: jigsaw, student teams achievement divisions (STAD), teams-games-tournaments (TGT), think-pair-share, and numbered heads together.

Instructional Strategy: Inquiry.   To inquire is to investigate something in an attempt to understand a situation or resolve a problem. The major purpose of inquiry is to teach students how to learn on their own; thus, the process itself is often considered more important than the ends to which it leads. As renowned psychologist Jerome Bruner (1960) said,

> To instruct someone in [a] discipline is not a matter of getting him to commit results to mind. Rather, it is to teach him to participate in the process that makes possible the establishment of knowledge. We teach a subject not to produce little living libraries on the subject, but rather to get a student to think mathematically for himself, to consider matters as an historian does, to take part in the process of knowledge-getting. Knowledge is a process, not a product. (p. 72)

Examples of Inquiry Topics.   Inquiry can be used to explore topics, find information, and reach conclusions. Consider the following examples of topics that could be profitably explored through inquiry:

Primary Grades
- Find out what your grandparents' lives were like when they were six or seven years old.
- Learn about the life of a favorite author, such as Dr. Seuss, Shel Silverstein, or J. K. Rowling.
- Find out how fast snails can move and what they can crawl over.
- List and categorize things that can be recycled.

Intermediate Grades
- Find out how many television commercials are shown during Saturday morning cartoon programs.
- Find out about games that may have been played by children who traveled west by wagon train.
- Investigate what critics say about popular movies suitable for children, and then see if students in your school agree with the critics.
- Discover as much as possible about how computers work.
- Grow plants in the classroom to discover the colors of light under which they best grow.
- Try to learn how the ages of fossils are determined.

Teacher and Student Roles in Inquiry.   Whether students work individually or in groups, they assume a large responsibility for their learnings during inquiry. Teachers may suggest or present topics, but students decide how they will gather, verify, and interpret information, after which they must demonstrate and explain their conclusions. The teacher may assist in any part of the process.

Strengths of Inquiry. Inquiry teaches students how to learn on their own without the direct control of the teacher. It teaches them to confront a problem, gather information about it, and compose conclusions. The strategy also encourages open-mindedness because students frequently encounter conflicting information and opinions.

Limitations of Inquiry. The process is time consuming and requires access to materials and resources. Many teachers would rather devote time to other matters. Students may get stuck or waste time on inconsequential issues.

Usability of Inquiry. With some modification, inquiry can be used at all grade levels in all subjects, especially science. English language learners and primary children involved in inquiry require tangible topics and much more teacher guidance than do older students.

Instructional Strategy: Projects. Projects are activities carried over longer periods of time that usually result in products such as a models, compositions, drawings, or performances. This instructional strategy is especially useful in social studies, science, art, and language, and it can bring about intense student involvement.

A major advantage of projects is that they help put students in control of their own learning. Though projects are done according to guidelines and suggestions from the teacher, students assume the responsibility of planning, organizing, conducting their work individually or in groups, and finalizing the product. With the teacher's help, students usually have the opportunity to display their products.

Examples of Project Topics. The variety of suitable topics for projects is virtually limitless. The following are illustrative examples:

Primary Grades
- Make a plan for conserving water in your home.
- List your favorite books. Tell what they are about and why you like them. Make and decorate a title page for your list.
- Make a collection of your own drawings, with titles and dates.
- Construct a weather station for your classroom, where temperature, clouds, rain, and snow are recorded and reported daily.
- Plant a class flower garden. See what flowers you can grow indoors during winter.
- Make a guide of your favorite local restaurants and places of recreation, including what you like to eat or do there.

Intermediate Grades
- Grow vegetables without soil.
- Make a video introduction of your class to send to a pen-pal class in another state or country.

- Produce a class newspaper or literary journal.
- Conduct an oral history investigation of a family member or other adult, and learn about an artifact that has particular meaning to that person.
- Maintain cultures of microscopic organisms.
- Plan imaginary trips to selected places in the world, with itineraries, transportation, lodging, meals, places of interest, costs, and so forth.
- Prepare a history of the school, using records, interviews, older photographs, and so forth.
- Make a detailed diary of an imaginary but realistic wagon train trip from St. Louis to San Francisco in 1870.
- Do simulated investments in the stock market. Keep records. Make trades. Follow quotes in the newspaper. See who can make the greatest profit during the year.
- Plan out what you think a good school should be like in twenty years.

Teacher and Student Roles in Projects.   Students do most of the actual work in any project. Though they decide what they want to accomplish, students often require considerable advice from the teacher on how to go about it. The teacher can suggest a number of possible topics, offer suggestions, help students obtain needed materials, set time lines for accomplishment, and arrange for the products to be shown—as advisor, not director. Also, the teacher and students together should create the rubric of expectations for evaluating the project.

Strengths of Projects.   Gardner says, "Life is a series of projects." Projects classrooms are more student- and thinking-centered. They are more likely to inspire motivation, inquiry, collaboration, reflection, personal accountability, and improved self-concept. Projects enable students to plan on a large scale and carry out plans to fruition.

Few in-class activities produce greater student enthusiasm and involvement, in part because they employ a variety of student learning styles and multiple intelligences. Projects that are congruent with curriculum standards and instructional goals and activities, lead to better achievement, behavior, and attitude. Parents and guardians often become involved in their children's projects, too. The resultant products are exciting to students and caregivers alike. Students remember projects as their favorite events in school, and caregivers form high opinions of teachers who use this approach.

Limitations of Projects.   Projects require a great deal of time. Some teachers question the ultimate value of, say, setting up and maintaining a terrarium, when they consider what could be accomplished if that time were devoted to direct instruction. Caregivers can assume too much of the project work.

Usability of Projects.   Projects can be used to good advantage in all content subjects at all grade levels. Of course, primary children require more direct assistance from the teacher than do older students.

Variations of Projects.   Simkins, Cole, Tavalin, and Means (2002) describe multimedia projects as "project-based multimedia learning . . . in which students acquire new knowledge and skills in the course of designing, planning, and producing a *multimedia product*"

(p. 3). In other words, students demonstrate their understandings with technology-based presentations such as computerized slide shows, websites, or video.

Instructional Approach: Technology-Assisted Teaching

The availability of classroom computers and educational software has produced an upsurge in computerized instruction and distance learning (telecommunications). System, program, and equipment costs have dropped, and variety and sophistication of educational software have increased. Using televisions and computers as tools to enhance teacher effectiveness—though not replace it—provides new potential for improving schooling and teaching.

Students learning *from* technology differs from students learning *with* technology. Reeves (1998) explains it this way: Students learning *from* media and technology work with instructional television, computer-based instruction, or integrated learning systems. Fundamentally they use computers as tutors to increase their basic skills and knowledge. Students learning *with* technology use technology as a "resource to help them develop higher order thinking, creativity, research skills, and so forth" (p. 2). Technology in this way is a "tool that can be applied to a variety of goals in the learning process, rather than serving simply as an instructional delivery system" (Ringstaff & Kelley, 2002, p. 2).

In recent years wordprocessors have simplified the processes of writing, editing, and revising. Video has expanded the possibilities for visual presentations. The Internet and hypertext links have increased efficiency for accessing and collecting information. Email now allows students to interact and collaborate quickly with persons who are somewhere else. And other tools, including video cameras, digital editing, presentation software, and web-authoring programs are becoming more commonplace.

Teachers are now able to enrich their overall curricula, as well as differentiate their instruction to respond to special needs with more individualized instruction. Programs that provide at least some tutorial assistance are available for students who need extra help or time. Individual students, able to work at their own pace through a plethora of electronic workbooks and tutorials that provide drill and practice, feel more in control of the kind and quality of their work and progress. They also receive more private and timely feedback and interactions regarding their work, which are likely to be less embarrassing than the more traditional methods. Teachers with easy access to several computers are able to instruct small groups at computers simultaneously. Also, television and cable programming made for classrooms now provide additional curriculum opportunities.

Based on research many believe that technology is most powerful when used as a tool for thinking—problem solving, conceptual development, and critical thinking. This melds with Reeves' thoughts of learning *with* technology, where students work on projects and solve problems by gathering, organizing, and analyzing information.

Learning with technology suggests a shift from student mastery of basic skills to a problem-solving and project-based curriculum. With this goal, teachers and students are in control of the curriculum and instruction, and technology provides assisting tools. "The combination of computation, connectivity, visual and multimedia capacities, miniaturization, and speed has radically changed the potential for technologies in schooling" (Culp, Hawkins, & Honey, 1999, p. 2). Possibilities abound for technology-rich, projects classrooms.

Most students find classroom computers exciting and are intrigued by their color, motion, sound, and interactive capabilities. Jearine Bacon, who teaches upper elementary grades, offers this advice about using computers in the classroom.

> Computers are not just for play. One of their main contributions lies in developing logical thinking. Situations can be created for deductive reasoning with the student guiding the lesson and the teacher serving as facilitator.
>
> Sharing ideas and teamwork on the computer can be used for projects and presentations. Multimedia projects involve the use of many different student talents, so the use of cooperative learning benefits the student while it extends the use of technology. Motivating and empowering students to learn are very positive contributions of the computer.

Using the Internet.   Information accessibility via computer is burgeoning. Today most students rely on this medium to investigate, research, document, and communicate their study and projects. Although millions of such resources are readily available, not all are appropriate. It is important that teachers and students be informed consumers and learn to evaluate the information they access. Here are five tips for assessing the accuracy and value of information obtained on the Internet.

- Try to find out the credentials and affiliation of the author of the information or creator of the website.
- Try to determine the reason the information is posted. Does the author have a personal agenda?
- Find the creation or modification dates. Current information is usually more reliable and useful than older material, unless, of course, the research is historical.
- Try to confirm the information elsewhere. Reporters are taught to confirm their facts with at least two sources.
- Through personal contacts or review guides, try to learn how others feel about the website (Goldsborough, 1997).

Strengths of Technology-Assisted Teaching.   Technology and computer-assisted learning provide several advantages that textbooks cannot. Computers are likely to be more enjoyable because they offer variety, even novelty, to students' studies. They provide easy accessibility to resources and materials (encyclopedias, journals, newspapers, and so on) and tools such as spreadsheets, word processing, text editing, and desktop publishing. Data and information found by computer is likely to be more up-to-date than textbook resources.

Additionally, many programs provide for interaction with students. Some programs challenge students to apply complex databases or solve problems through elaborate simulations. These programs pose a problem, give assistance or instruction when students request it, and then provide immediate feedback and consequences to the students' choices. With links to other technologies such as DVDs, CD-ROMs, and hypermedia, computers can surpass conventional print materials with animation, time-lapsed photography, and other audiovisual techniques for communicating information and demonstrating processes.

When surveyed, teachers in grades 4–12 who had integrated computerized instruction into their teaching believed that computers had substantially changed their classrooms for the better. As their own experience in using computers evolved, the teachers reported a greater use of wordprocessors (students creating compositions) and databases (students doing research), and less use of drill and practice programs. This allowed teachers to expose students to more complex material and provide differentiated and more individualized instruction. This also made classes more student-centered, and allowed teachers to function more as facilitative coaches than dispensers of information (Hadley & Sheingold, 1993).

Limitations of Technology-Assisted Teaching.   Despite its many benefits, technology and computer-assisted teaching suffer limitations as well. Many teachers are hesitant and ill informed about proper use of computers, media, and other technology. In many classrooms there are not enough computers to go around, and student access remains limited. Use of the Internet is risky because students can access many sites that are not suitable for them.

Teachers may need to change their beliefs and understandings about teaching and learning and about learning *with* rather than *from* media and technology. Technology needs to be integrated into the curriculum and instruction. Technology resources may still be inadequate or inaccessible to teachers or students. And, teachers need adequate training and support to use technology.

DAVE CARPENTER...

"I'M LEARNING TO LOBBY."

Instructional Approach: Differentiated Instruction

Students in today's classrooms reflect varying languages, cultures, physical considerations, talents, and experiences. In some schools, students work and study in multi-age classes where they interact with others of very mixed levels of ability. Whether the class is traditional or multi-age, it is the teacher's responsibility to determine, plan, and begin teaching from where the students are, not from the first page of the curriculum guide. These adaptations are called, collectively, *differentiated instruction.* Several principles guide differentiated classrooms.

- The teacher unconditionally accepts all students as they are, attends to their differences, and expects them to become all they can be. The goals for everyone are individual success and maximum growth.
- Assessment is ongoing, responsive to students' needs, and inseparable from instruction. Assessment and instruction are multi-method and multi-source, with student performance determined by individual growth from a starting point.
- The teacher is clear about what is important in subject matter. The teacher then adjusts content, instruction, and products based on student readiness, interest, and learning styles. Activities are used that encourage students to use more than one intelligence, and encourage teachers to use varied instructional approaches, strategies, resources, and materials.
- All students participate in respectful work and help other students as appropriate. Multiple perspectives are sought and valued.
- The teacher and students collaborate to set both whole-class and individual learning goals, and the teacher equalizes group and individual expectations and standards.
- The teacher and students work together flexibly. Time and assessment are also flexible and are often linked to students' needs. The teacher guides students toward self-reliance.

Teachers can differentiate instruction in a variety of ways. In primary grades, for example, learning centers and stations allow teachers to set out varied materials and activities, and thus differentiate instruction. Learning contracts differentiate instruction for older students. So do tiered activities, in which the teacher keeps the same focus for everyone, but provides opportunities of varying degrees of difficulty.

Planning Approaches and Strategies.   Bear in mind that all approaches and all strategies require planning by the teacher. You can't rely on any approach to evolve naturally, but must envision your expectations and foresee what students are likely to do. Successful instruction evolves from this prior attention.

Long-range plans for the year and for longer units of instruction, discussed in Chapter 2, provide teachers with a map of the year's events, content, and activities. The steps in the backward design process—identify desired results, determine acceptable evidence, and plan learning experiences and instruction—help teachers organize their thinking and plan for the year and longer units.

Good daily lesson plans are needed for day-to-day work and, again, backward design can help. First identify the desired results. Then determine how students will demonstrate

"My dog ate my lesson plans for today."

these results. As you plan the learning experiences and instruction, consider skills and knowledge needed prior to the lesson. Then think about the beginning (how you will introduce the lesson), the middle (what you and the students will do), and the end (how you will close the lesson, what students will produce, and how you will evaluate and follow up). Here are considerations for teachers as they make their plans.

Considerations before the Instruction

- *Facts about the learners:* Who they are? How do they learn? Do they have the skills and knowledge to be successful?
- *Content and context:* Why should my students study this lesson or unit? What is the purpose for this learning? What are the grade level and content area? Where does the lesson fit into the unit? What are the state and district curriculum standards? What are the learning goals and/or objectives? How will prior knowledge and skills be assessed before the lesson? What do students need to review?

- *Product and assessments:* How can I tell if students have learned well and enjoyed the work? In what varied authentic ways will students demonstrate accomplishment of the objectives? What criteria will be used to judge students' success?
- *Management and discipline:* What materials and resources are needed? How will technology be used? How will the room be arranged? How much class time is available? How will students be grouped? How will transitions be managed? How will misbehavior be handled?

Considerations in Opening the Lesson
- How will students be motivated and focused?
- What will make students want to learn this material?

Considerations in Proceeding through the Lesson
- *Teacher input:* How much preparation time is available? How will I describe and model skills? What examples and non-examples will I provide? How will I teach to the standards and objectives? How will I actively involve all students? What must I modify to make sure all students learn? What teaching skills and strategies will best help my students accomplish the learning? What materials and resources will I need?
- *Guided practice/monitoring progress:* How will students practice alone, with a partner, or in cooperative groups? How will I check students' understanding?
- *Independent practice/summative assessment:* How will this occur? What will students do to demonstrate their understanding?
- *Closure:* How will I have students summarize and make meaning of their learning?

Considerations in Following through after the Lesson
- *Transfer:* What opportunities will students have to continue practice and transfer learning? What follow-up activities and homework are needed?
- *Reflection:* What went well with the lesson or unit? Was it relevant and worthwhile for the students? What evidence demonstrates this? What teaching skills and strategies worked most effectively? What changes can be made to enhance learning? How will student learning and teacher effectiveness benefit from these changes?

Formalizing the Lesson Plan.   Many experienced teachers plan lessons in their heads and only make notes in their plan book. Most new teachers need to be more deliberate, writing out their plans to ensure coverage and not getting lost in the lesson. Such plans can be written in a variety of ways. Find a way that works well for you. You will probably want to include the following:

- Date
- Standards, objective(s), essential or guided question(s), or intended outcomes
- Teacher input and student output
- List of activities or learning experiences and the time allotted for each
- Modifications for English learners and students with other special needs
- Technology and materials needed for each activity
- Closure and follow-up activities

- Evaluation procedures, scoring guides, and criteria
- Management considerations for room set up; material preparations; student group-ings; content delivery, procedures, and transitions; and student behavior

Before moving from instructional management to Chapter 7, managing students at work, take time to explore these end-of-chapter activities.

Parting Thought

I talk and talk and talk, and I haven't taught people in 50 years what my father taught by example in one week.

—Mario Cuomo

SUMMARY SELF-CHECK

Check off the following as you either understand or become able to apply them.

❑ Four broad instructional approaches are widely used today in teaching—direct teach-ing, facilitative teaching, technology-assisted teaching, and differentiated instruction.

❑ In direct teaching, the teacher plans, directs, monitors, and evaluates all aspects of instruction.

❑ In facilitative teaching, the teacher is in charge but allows much more student input, self-guidance, and responsibility.

❑ In technology-assisted teaching, teacher and students access instruction and resources via computers and the Internet, televisions, and cable.

❑ In differentiated instruction, the teacher modifies content, instruction and process, and product to best meet needs and abilities of students.

❑ Several specific instructional strategies help bring about what is intended in learning:
- Strategies used in direct teaching include direct instruction; concept attainment; and Say, See, Do Teaching.
- Strategies used in facilitative teaching include cooperative learning, inquiry, and projects.
- Strategies used in technology-assisted teaching include tutorials, distance learn-ing, and cyberspace connections.

❑ Teaching approach and instructional strategies become translated into daily lesson plans. Experienced teachers plan most lessons in their heads, with attention to the following:
- What facts are relevant about the learners? (Particularly consider who they are and their prior knowledge and skills.)
- What should students learn, related to the standards and objectives?

- What management considerations, activities, and materials will serve best?
- How much preparation time is available?
- How much class time is available?
- How can students be motivated?
- How should the activities be sequenced?
- How will the lesson be ended?
- What follow-up should there be?
- How will student profitability and enjoyment be assessed?

ACTIVITIES FOR REFLECTION AND GROWTH

For Cumulative Skills Development

1. Take a moment to review the statements in the Anticipation–Reaction Guide at the beginning of this chapter. Put a check mark in the Reaction column next to any statement with which you now agree. How have your thoughts changed since reading this chapter?

2. If you were forced to teach mathematics in either a direct or facilitative approach, which approach would you choose? Explain your reasons, keeping in mind the accuracy, quantity, retention, usefulness, and enjoyment of learning for you and your students.

3. In which subjects typically taught in the elementary curriculum do you think you could best use projects? Bearing in mind that projects are time consuming, how much emphasis would you give to projects during the school year?

4. You have just learned that a new species of animal named zugu has been discovered in the jungle rivers of Zaire. Devise a lesson plan for teaching others verbally (no pictures yet exist) an accurate concept of zugu. Try the plan on fellow students. To check their understanding (and your teaching), have them draw pictures of zugu.

5. Suppose you decided to teach a haiku lesson by using Say, See, Do Teaching. (A haiku is a poem that is usually concerned with nature and has three lines of five, seven, and five syllables. The first line often depicts a scene, the second an action within the scene, and the third the aftermath.) Show how you would break the topic into small sequential steps and monitor each student's progress.

6. Describe how you would use technology-assisted teaching in your third-grade social studies program.

REFERENCES AND RECOMMENDED READINGS

Armstrong, T. (1994). *Multiple intelligences in the classroom*. Alexandria, VA: Association for Supervision and Curriculum Development.

Bruner, J. (1960). *The process of education*. New York: Vintage.

Chamot, A., & O'Malley, J. (1994). *The CALLA handbook: Implementing the Cognitive Academic Language Learning Approach*. New York: Addison-Wesley.

Churma, M. (1999). *A guide to integrating technology standards into the curriculum*. Upper Saddle River, NJ: Merrill.

Cruickshank, D., Bainer, D., & Metcalf, K. (1999). *The act of teaching* (2nd ed.). Boston: McGraw-Hill.

Culp, K., Hawkins, J., & Honey, M. (1999). *Review paper on educational technology research and development.* New York: Education Development Center, Center for Children and Technology.

Gardner, H. (n.d.). *Eye on San Diego* [Interview for television broadcast].

Goldsborough, R. (1997, August/September). Let the reader beware. *Reading Today, 15*(1), 8.

Hadley, M., & Sheingold, K. (1993, May). Commonalities and distinctive patterns in teachers' integration of computers. *American Journal of Education, 101,* 261–315.

Hunter, M. (1982). *Mastery learning.* El Segundo, CA: TIP Publications.

Integrating technology into the curriculum [Special issue]. (1999, February). *Educational Leadership.* Alexandria, VA: Association for Supervision and Curriculum Development.

Jones, F. (2000). *Tools for teaching: Discipline instruction motivation.* Santa Cruz, CA: Fredric H. Jones & Associates.

Joyce, B., & Weil, M. (with Calhoun, E.). (2000). *Models of teaching* (6th ed.). Boston: Allyn & Bacon.

Kagan, S. (1994). *Cooperative learning.* San Clemente, CA: Resources for Teachers.

Orlich, D., Harder, R., Callahan, R., & Gibson, H. (2001). *Teaching strategies: A guide to better instruction* (6th ed.). Boston: Houghton Mifflin.

Personalized learning [Special issue]. (1999, September). *Educational Leadership.* Alexandria, VA: Association for Supervision and Curriculum Development [Interview for television broadcast].

Reeves, T. (1998). *The impact of media and technology in schools: A research report prepared for the Bertelsmann Foundation.* Retrieved August 2003 from www.athensacademy.org/instruct/media_tech/reeves0.html

Ringstaff, C., & Kelley, L. (2002). *The learning return on our educational technology investment.* San Francisco: WestEd RTEC.

Rogers, C. (1969). *Freedom to learn.* Columbus, OH: Merrill.

Simkins, M., Cole, K., Tavalin, F., & Means, B. (2002). *Increasing student learning through multimedia projects.* Alexandria, VA: Association for Supervision and Curriculum Development.

Stull, A. (1998). *Education on the Internet: A student's guide.* Upper Saddle River, NJ: Merrill.

Tomlinson, C. (1999). *The differentiated classroom: Responding to the needs of all learners.* Alexandria, VA: Association for Supervision and Curriculum Development.

CHAPTER

7

Managing Students at Work

A school should not be preparation for life. A school should be life!

—Elbert Hubbard

ANTICIPATION–REACTION GUIDE

Before you read the chapter, take a moment to put a check mark in the Anticipation column next to any statement with which you agree.

	Anticipation	Reaction
The problem with routines is that they inhibit individual thought.	❑	❑
All in all, the best way to begin the day is to allow students to relax and settle in before undertaking the day's arduous work.	❑	❑
Authorities agree that if classroom work is worth doing, it is worth being checked carefully by the teacher.	❑	❑
The use of classroom monitors is valuable in giving everyone some responsibility for what goes on in the classroom.	❑	❑
It is usually possible, during independent work, to give students who are stuck all the help they need to resume work in a few seconds time.	❑	❑
Signaling devices are preferable to raising hands as a way for students to request the teacher's help.	❑	❑
Teachers should not attempt to instruct the class until they have everyone's attention.	❑	❑
Modular cluster seating works well for teachers who wish to use cooperative learning.	❑	❑
Tattling is a normal part of childhood and therefore should not be a matter of concern for the teacher.	❑	❑
Student responsibility is shown adequately when students fulfill duties and obligations promptly, with concern for others.	❑	❑

It might seem that once a teacher has established the physical and psychosocial environments and has taken steps to increase students' desire to learn, students would work diligently with little supervision. Teachers who make that assumption are likely to find that the classroom quickly resembles room 315, described by educational anthropologist Frances Schwartz (1981):

> In room 315 chaos reigns. The room is noisy with the shouting, laughter, and movement of many children. Though most are seated, many are walking or running aimlessly around the classroom. Some stop at others' desks, provoke them briefly, and move on. Several students who are lining up textbooks as "race courses" for toy cars laugh when the teacher demands their attention. As the teacher struggles to ask a question over the noise, few if any students volunteer to answer. When one student does respond correctly, others yell out, "You think you're so smart." (p. 99)

Such classes are familiar to every teacher, and they occur despite good classroom environment and eager students. Missing in room 315 are management procedures that get students to engage in assigned work and stick with it. This chapter addresses management of students at work, giving attention to the following:

1. *Work routines* that involve opening activities, signals for attention, instructions, movement in the room, materials, completed work, student accountability and criterion of mastery, homework, and closing activities.
2. *Providing assistance* through use of student assistants, giving efficient directions and feedback, and directing students in their requests for help.
3. *Incidentals* such as seating, entering and exiting the room, sharpening pencils, using passes outside the room, controlling noise, and dealing with procrastinating, tattling, and bullying.

All of these matters can be handled with routines and procedures that students learn as habits and comply with more or less automatically. Jones (2000) and others agree that students' use of time is a major issue. Routine procedures, far from being restrictive, are very helpful in letting students know what to do, as well as how, when, and where to do it, thus reducing confusion and wasted time.

Work Routines

Opening Activities

Imagine your students arriving like those of Liz Davis, a beginning teacher:

> It is 7:55 in the morning. I have just received and am reading the revised agenda for the school day. There will be a fire drill at 10:15, an assembly for only the best citizens at 10:45, and the nurse will check for lice sometime during the day. In the middle of my desk, amidst the numerous papers, utensils, and miniature toys, an overdue

slip for last week's film glares at me. I look for my attendance sheet. Somewhere a bell sounds and suddenly thirty-one bright and shining faces, complete with loud voices, barge through the door.

"Good morning, teacher!" they cry. "Can I open the windows?" "Guy," one moans, "you always get to do that!" "Teacher! Here is my permission slip for our field trip!"

I stand there in a daze as thirty-one pairs of hands try to bless me with book reports, late homework assignments, and wilted flowers they picked from neighbors' yards on the way to school.

Liz's students were well intentioned; she simply hadn't taught them a better way to begin the school day.

Liz could have eliminated most of the confusion by taking time to teach and practice the classroom structures—all the specific procedures and routines—as lessons (Jones, 2000). Then she would begin the day by having her students immediately get busy on purposeful work when they enter the room. Exactly how this is done depends on the age of the students. In early primary grades, teachers often have the children come in, stop talking, and sit down in their chairs or on the carpet. After this the teacher says good morning and pleasantly interacts with the students individually, calling their names to take attendance before checking the calendar and weather, recognizing birthdays, saluting the flag, and singing a song. This is often followed by a sharing time when selected students are allowed a few minutes to tell of interesting experiences or events in their lives. (A word of caution: Do not allow students to share small toys or new items of clothing. The toys will draw students away from their work. The new clothes may be a source of embarrassment or envy.)

Teachers of older students often have the children come into the room, stop talking, and get to work immediately on a silent activity, such as reading library books, writing in journals, or seeing how many math problems they can do correctly in a given period of time. While students work, the teacher checks attendance, often using a seating chart. Some teachers have group monitors or table captains report who is absent from their group. Some post a daily opinion poll or survey, and have students move their individual photos to indicate how they vote in response to the question for the day. Unmoved photos belong to absent students. Others use a clothespin system in which arriving students clip clothespins with their names to a group chart. Still others use a system in which students take sharpened pencils from loops attached beneath their shadow profiles or photos. The teacher checks attendance by noting which pencils remain.

Choosing is an opening routine once widely popular. Still favored by some primary and intermediate teachers, choosing allows students who are entering the room to move to areas that contain attractive materials and activities. Some students might choose the art center to work with clay, paint, or weaving; others might choose the reading center to read books, magazines, or newspapers; still others might choose the computer center to engage in math or language activities. Once students have chosen their activities, they must be responsible for their conduct, keeping noise down and taking care of the materials with which they are working. This procedure embraces the idea of multiple intelligences (Gardner, 1991, 1993; Kagan & Kagan, 1998) by helping to provide a closer match between student interests, learning styles, and classroom activities, and thereby improve learning and behavior.

Other opening activities popular with teachers are those that go by names similar to *five-a-days*, such as five math problems on the board to try to solve; five vocabulary words to define, learn to spell, and use; or five cities to locate on a map. These are only a few examples of opening activities that students enjoy and that involve them at once. From time to time the opening activities should be changed.

Some teachers open the day with a quick review of the previous day's work and activities. They use the overhead to show key transparencies from the earlier lessons. Others may review the prior day with a mind map of events on transparencies or chart paper, or preview the new day in a similar way.

Signals for Attention

You never should try to instruct the class when you do not have everyone's attention. Normally, all you have to do is say something like "No talking; everyone's eyes on me," or "Listen carefully." But when students are working busily, especially in teams or groups with talking allowed, you can wear yourself out trying to shout over them. Instead, select a signal that tells all students they are to stop what they are doing immediately and give their attention to you. Primary teachers often sound chords on the piano, turn a rain stick, or use a clapping rhythm. Many teachers flick the lights. Some ring a bell, or say "Freeze!" Whatever signal you select, discuss it with your students and practice, practice, practice its use.

Instructions

For assigned work it is very important to inform students precisely what they are to do and when and how they are to do it. Every teacher complains about students' saying, "I don't know what to do," within seconds after receiving directions. Either students don't listen or there's too much to remember, but both can be avoided by stating what is to be done while jotting reminder notes on the board. For example:

> Boys and girls, all eyes on me. Everyone. Thank you. Listen very carefully. At your desks I want you to do problems 2, 4, 6, 8, and 10 on page 32 of your workbooks. [Jot "p. 32" and problem numbers in the corner of the board.] You may work quietly with your partner. [Jot "quiet" and "partner" on the board.] You have 20 minutes to complete your work. [Jot "20 min." on the board.] When you finish, put your papers in the in-basket. [Jot "in-basket."] Then take out your library books and read until time is up. [Jot "library books." Draw a square around what you have listed on the board and point to the notes.] Page 32, problems 2, 4, 6, 8, and 10. Work quietly with partner. Put finished work in in-basket, and then read your library book until I call time. I'll circulate to help you if you need me. All right, let's get to work.

This procedure can apply to most assignments: Get all students' attention, tell them exactly what they are to do, and post reminders on the board or a chart. Jones (2000) advocates the use of VIPs—visual instructional plans (see Chapter 6). You may wish to prepare reminder VIPs and charts beforehand and display them where everyone can see. This may seem unnecessary, but on many occasions it will save your having to repeat yourself several times. Moreover, VIPs will eventually help students learn to be self-directing and take responsibility for their own learning.

Movement in the Room

Movement is necessary before, during, and after many learning activities. Students must move from group to group, obtain and replace materials, turn in completed work, get drinks, go to the restroom, use the wastebasket, come to your desk, perform their monitor duties, and so forth. Older students may be able to sit still for a while, but young students *have* to move; their natural behavior does not allow them to sit still and quietly for more than fifteen or twenty minutes at a time. Teachers should alternate quiet, still activities with those that allow talk and movement, albeit restrained.

Movement management requires close attention because, although movement is necessary, it has high potential for creating discipline problems. Even when no trouble occurs, movement can cause congestion, wasted time, and annoyance. Therefore you must discuss—and practice—movement with your students, and establish appropriate regulations. A basic rule should be that students are to remain seated and working unless otherwise directed. A code system, posted in the front of the room, can remind students of movement expectations for different activities. For example, a red sign tells students they should sit in their seats and talk only when called on. A yellow sign tells students they should remain in their seats, but they may whisper with their neighbors. This is allowed when partners, teams, or small groups collaborate and cooperate on activities. A green sign means that students may do group or individual project work, with quiet talking and movement allowed as necessary for obtaining materials and references.

Materials

Poor materials management can wreck efficiency, especially when it comes to small materials that are used daily—textbooks, workbooks, worksheets, paper, pencils, crayons, scissors, glue, paints, and brushes. The logistics of your materials management must allow materials to be stored out of the way yet remain easily obtained, distributed, and replaced.

Storage and Distribution.   Students with desks can keep many of their small materials there, especially textbooks, workbooks, pencils, crayons, rulers, and paper. Teachers use various techniques to encourage students to keep their desks orderly, ranging from simple inspection to procedures intended to be interesting and motivating. For example, the class may earn time toward a preferred activity when they are able to quickly get out their supplies for math because their desks are tidy and organized. Or, the "desk elf," an imaginary creature, might check all desks at the end of the day. When the elf finds desks that are especially neat, it leaves a surprise such as a sticker.

When students sit at tables instead of desks, as is typically the case in primary grades, or when space limitations make it difficult for students to keep materials in their desks, other arrangements must be made for the storage of small materials. Some teachers provide each student with a container such as a basket, dishpan, or tub, marked with the student's name and kept on a shelf. At appropriate times students go to their baskets and obtain supplies for use at their tables.

In rooms where student desks or tables are arranged in clusters, some teachers prefer to place a large tub in the center of each cluster. The tub contains materials that are arranged in the order they will be used for the day.

Materials are often distributed by the following procedures: (1) Teacher or aide distributes before school, during recess, or lunch, so materials are waiting for students when they arrive. (2) Monitors are trained to distribute materials as needed at recess, lunch, or during class activities. (3) Students get the materials as instructed. Ted Saulino describes how he manages materials in his kindergarten class:

> I place a small, inexpensive, yet durable plastic basket in the middle of each cluster of tables, full of the supplies that students will need on a given day: pencils, scissors, glue, markers, colored pencils, red correction pens, and rulers. The basket sits on top of a folder of good ruled paper and scratch paper.
>
> To avoid arguments and to distribute power at each station, I name rotating team captains. A wall chart, divided into sections representing the workstations, lists the students' names. The name at the top of the list is the first team captain. Next to the captain's name I clip a small star, which I move down to the next name when the week is over. The child whose name is below the captain's acts as the substitute if the captain is absent.
>
> Captains distribute the supplies and distribute and collect all handouts. If someone is absent at a station, captains start an absent folder for the child's return. At the end of each day, captains assess the team's supplies and replenish paper, sharpen pencils, and make sure the team has a clean station.

Use and Care.   Use and care of materials present opportunities for students to practice conservation. Students should be instructed that they are to make good use of paper, crayons, and pencils, and are not to waste any materials. Likewise, books, workbooks, charts, and other materials that can be reused should be kept clean, undamaged, and orderly. The inherent value in taking proper care of materials is important in itself, especially in times of fiscal difficulties. When supply budgets dwindle, it becomes a matter of necessity for teachers and students alike to make better use of materials.

Replacement.   Good management calls not only for efficient distribution and care of materials, but also for attention to how materials are to be replaced after use. Materials are typically replaced in one of four ways: (1) students themselves quietly return the materials; (2) monitors collect and replace the materials; (3) students place materials in folders or containers that are later collected and scored by the teacher; or (4) the teacher or aide collects, organizes, and replaces the materials.

Large Materials.   Larger materials that play key roles in instruction must also be managed and used efficiently. These larger materials include reference books such as dictionaries and encyclopedias, art supplies, globes and maps, models, and other items such as materials for aquariums and terrariums, physical education equipment, and audiovisual equipment. Although monitors can handle most management duties associated with large materials, many teachers prefer to involve all students in procedures and responsibilities.

Maps and projection screens should be mounted on the wall or above the board so they can be pulled down and used as needed. Maps and screens on rollers can be used to cover material, such as test items and directions that have been written on the board, or to hide larger instructional props or resources until needed.

Physical education materials are best kept in a crate or large plastic trash container near or just outside the door until after school, then placed in the corner or a closet in the room.

A wheeled cart makes moving audiovisual materials easy. The top shelf can hold an overhead projector or a television (if one is not mounted on the classroom wall). It also can hold various other projectors—motion picture, filmstrip, or slide. Equipment such as CDs, video and audiotapes, and tape recorders can be kept on the bottom shelf.

Globes and models should be placed where students can easily see and approach them—on countertops or a special table. Reference books should be kept on shelves at the side of the main seating area, also easily accessible to students. Art supplies are best kept near the classroom sink in cupboards with closeable doors, and easels should be folded and stacked nearby. Materials for aquariums and terrariums, such as sand, plants, animal food, rocks, and cleaning equipment, should be kept in cupboards and used only by the teacher and designated monitors.

Completed Work

One of teachers' most time-consuming tasks is dealing with completed work. Teachers commonly take home stacks of daily papers to be checked, graded, recorded, and returned. The following suggestions are intended to help teachers manage this complex and burdensome task.

Should Teachers Check Everything?   It is not necessary that all student work be checked in detail. Much independent work is for practice only, and necessary feedback can be given immediately as the teacher circulates and monitors student efforts.

Further, there is nothing wrong with allowing students to check their own work or exchange papers. As much work as possible should be corrected by students in class, to relieve the teacher as well as to motivate and instruct. Students lose interest when feedback is delayed, and teacher-corrected work, even when returned the next day, has little instructional value. In-class correcting gives quick feedback on performance and errors. Aides or parent volunteers can check routine student work. Of course work that requires judgment or very accurate correction should be carefully checked by teachers. Ginny Lorenz teaches a fourth/fifth multi-age class. She checks her students' work in this way:

> I like to read carefully student work, but I am not willing to bury myself with thirty papers at a time. I have my thirty students divided into eight groups. Every two weeks, Mondays through Thursdays, I am able to collect, read, and give constructive individualized guidance and feedback to everyone's written work by closely looking at about four papers a day, and we all are able to enjoy Fridays and weekends.

Organizing Completed Work.   Some teachers use a folder system to keep track of student work. The folders, kept on students' desks, are compartmentalized with labels such as

Unfinished Work, Ready for Checking, and *Completed and Checked.* At day's end the teacher goes through items in the *Ready for Checking* compartment, and moves them to the *Completed and Checked* compartment.

In classes in which folders are not used, monitors collect completed work, perhaps by tables, teams, or groups, and place it in a receptacle. The teacher or an aide checks the work and returns it the next day.

Acknowledging Good Work.   Student work that has been done well should be acknowledged, usually privately through comments or stickers. Barbara Coloroso (1990) suggests that teachers allow students to decide themselves if their work needs a sticker. Occasionally good work should be posted for all to see. This provides a sense of success and is highly motivating to most students, though not all; ask the student for permission beforehand. Additionally, samples of completed work—both inferior and superior—should be kept privately in student folders to show parents and guardians at conferences or open house. These work samples are intended to present a well-rounded and accurate profile of the habits and accomplishments of the student.

Student Accountability and Criterion of Mastery

Teachers should consider both quality of work and student accountability: How much work is enough? How many math problems should students complete for homework? How many sentences should they diagram? Teachers should answer these questions in terms of the criterion of *mastery.* Some teachers say, "Boys and girls, you are to solve the odd problems on this page. Problems you don't finish before recess will be homework." This statement supports a criterion of *speed.* Students will hurry with their work so they can enjoy recess and have no homework. Nothing the teacher said will encourage students to be accurate or to learn the concept.

In contrast, other teachers say, "Boys and girls, you are to solve the odd problems on this page. You may stop when you correctly answer five problems in a row." Now students have a genuine interest in accuracy and perhaps even mastery. If they answer the first four problems correctly and miss the next problem, they must begin counting from number one again for their five in a row. The teacher has encouraged both mastery and student accountability. With each correct response, students invest in solving the next problem correctly.

Homework

Most teachers above early primary grades assign homework. The value of homework lies not so much in learning new material as in (1) practicing and strengthening skills already learned, (2) developing an interest in more pleasurable learning activities, such as reading, and (3) allowing caregivers to show interest and support for their child's education.

For the most part, homework should focus on activities such as practicing and applying math skills, reading library books or magazines, reading together with a caregiver, writing anecdotes and reports, drawing pictures related to school work, or making up work missed because of absence.

"I COULDN'T DO MY HOMEWORK BECAUSE MY COMPUTER WAS DOWN AND I COULDN'T FIGURE OUT HOW TO PLUG THIS THING IN!"

Such work might encourage, but should not require, caregiver assistance other than that of providing a workplace and insisting that the work be completed. This is particularly true when the caregivers speak a language other than English in the home. When students are weak in a particular skill, such as spelling, the caregiver can be asked to work with the child, perhaps with remedial drill games. Caregivers want to know about homework and how they can help. They should be told that the best things they can do are

Provide a quiet place for the child to work.

See to it (good-naturedly) that the child does homework as scheduled.

Read to or with the child.

Play games with the child that encourage spelling, math, and other types of thinking—Parcheesi, checkers, Yahtzee, dominoes, and Scrabble.

Ask and answer questions about news events and a variety of other topics.

Closing Activities

Teachers who simply wait out the last fifteen minutes of the day miss one of the best opportunities for teaching and reflecting. Here are some ideas for ending the day: Spend five minutes taking care of closing assignments, notices, cleaning, and tidying so the last ten minutes can be used for review and reflection. Have students give their views on what occurred during the day—accomplishments, high points, excitements, disappointments, things that went well, and those that could be done better next time. Review the day's events by creating a mind map with the students on overhead transparencies or chart paper. Give students a preview of what the next day will bring. Promise at least one interesting surprise and live up to it, so they will look forward with anticipation.

Providing Assistance

Student Assistants

Students can assist with many chores in the classroom. Often called *monitors,* these student assistants can take care of tasks such as watering plants, distributing work sheets, and any other routine chores in the room. Some teachers use "one-minute student managers" to handle the variety of jobs that arise from the particular needs for their class. For example, a kindergarten teacher may take advantage of a skilled youngster to serve as "shoe-lace monitor." This student would help classmates tie their shoelaces, and in doing so, save the teacher's time and back. These managerial activities add mutual teaching and learning time to the day and allow students to become real partners in the classroom (Freiberg, 1996).

Monitors can be assigned to most routine duties. For example, Mary Martinez, an experienced fifth-grade teacher, identified sixteen categories of responsibilities, which provide jobs for thirty students:

- Class president—manages class business and classroom meetings as needed.
- Flag monitor—leads the daily flag salute and other lessons and activities that have to do with the flag.
- Lights monitor—sees that the lights are turned on and off.
- Window monitor—sees that windows are opened, closed, and shaded as necessary during the day.
- News, weather, and map monitors (two)—report on two or three news items per day, including weather forecasts for city, state, and nation, and locate on the map where the news and weather events occur.
- Class news reporters (two)—make daily entries into the class log about highlights of the day. Kept as a class record, the log is used as a source for the teacher's monthly newsletter to caregivers. From time to time, the students reread the log to affirm their sense of history, accomplishment, and growth.
- Messenger—delivers messages to the office, library, and other teachers.
- Line monitors (two)—head lines and model good behavior for entering and leaving the room and for movement to other parts of the school.
- Physical education equipment monitors (two)—distribute, collect, store, mark, and take care of equipment used on the playgrounds at recess and lunch.
- Table or group monitors (five to six)—manage tables or identifiable groups of students, with such duties as taking attendance, distributing and collecting materials, seeing that the area is kept clean and orderly, and sometimes, reporting as the group spokesperson.
- Plant and pet monitors (two)—water and care for plants, clean and care for aquarium and feed fish, and feed and care for animals in the terrarium.

- Materials monitors (two)—handle, store, distribute, and collect small materials such as workbooks, work sheets, pencils, paper, glue, and scissors.
- Audiovisual monitors (two)—obtain projectors and VCRs; operate and return equipment; and manage films, tapes, slides, micro-projectors, and models.
- Librarians (two)—manage the class library and the system used for students to check out books and other materials. Library monitors are trained to process checkout cards to keep track of materials.
- Substitute teacher monitors (two)—assist substitute teachers. The teacher keeps these monitors updated on daily routines, the location of lesson plans and materials, standards of behavior, and the discipline system used in the class.
- Visitors monitor—greets classroom visitors and offers them seating.

Assignments to tasks are made in different ways. Some teachers arbitrarily assign the duties. Others allow students to choose, in alphabetical order or on a first-come basis. Still others have students make written requests or complete application forms and interview for the duties they wish to monitor. In such cases, selection can then be made by the teacher or by class vote.

Directions and Feedback

As students work individually at assigned activities such as seatwork, they invariably encounter difficulties that require teacher help. Effective management requires that teachers provide this help quickly and effectively so students can stay on task and complete work on time. Jones says that the teacher's job is to answer the question "What do I do next?" as efficiently as possible. This is best accomplished when the teacher (1) gives clear, understandable directions, (2) posts reminders and visual instructional plans, (3) uses signal systems for requesting assistance, (4) moves easily and quickly to students in need of help, and (5) provides assistance quickly and effectively.

Directions and Reminders. Earlier in this chapter you saw how directions can be given briefly and clearly so students know exactly what they are supposed to do, how much time they have, what to do with completed work, and what to do while waiting for the next activity to begin. In Chapter 6 you saw a VIP for long division. By posting this on a wall, most students can work through the math problem with little additional teacher help. Graphic models are helpful in most content areas. They can depict spelling rules, paragraph construction, math algorithms, and steps in conducting experiments. Teachers should have students review such models before requesting further help. Other reminders, not directly pertinent to a given lesson, may also be posted, such as "i before e except after c," "keep your area clean," and "invert and multiply." These reminders, models, and written directions should answer most of the questions students are likely to ask during independent work.

Teacher Movement. Teacher movement and proximity are key factors in managing assistance. The teacher must be able to reach each student as quickly as possible to minimize wasted time and forestall misbehavior. If the desks are arranged with an interior walking loop or modular clusters or shallow semicircles, the teacher will be fairly close to all students. Some teachers prefer to move in a predetermined pattern among the desks to be near students, comment on their work, and give help in regular rotation. Others prefer to observe from a central location and move quickly toward any student who show signs of difficulty.

Efficient Help. Assistance should be given very quickly—in no more than a few seconds time. Research shows that teachers spend an average of about four minutes per student when giving individual help (Jones, 2000). In a mini-tutorial, teachers question the student and then wait for a reply, which may be erroneous, fumbling, or nonforthcoming. Jones claims that effective help can be given in twenty seconds or less, as follows: (1) At first contact, quickly find anything the student has done correctly and mention it favorably, such as "Good job up to here." (2) Give a straightforward prompt that will get the student working again, such as "Watch the decimal," "Borrow here," "Look at step three on the chart," or "That word means. . . ." (3) Leave immediately, being sure to pay brief attention to the work of nearby students who have not requested help. This third step might appear inconsiderate of the feelings of students needing help, but Jones maintains that it has two positive effects: (1) rapid movement gives attention to a greater number of students during work time, and (2) it begins to break down the dependency syndrome and helpless handraising in which students require the teacher's presence before they begin work. As Jones (2000) says, "Be positive, be brief, and be gone" (p. 54).

Student Requests for Help

Signals. We all remember scenes of students congregating at the teacher's desk or sitting dispiritedly at their desks with arms waving limply, waiting for teacher help. Confusion and arms in the air can be avoided through use of signal systems that advise teachers when students need assistance. Some teachers use folded or colored construction paper that students place on their desk. A variation of this is for students to prioritize and signal their need for assistance by setting a red, yellow, or green cup on their desks. Devora Garrison, a fifth-grade teacher, found this strategy to work with one of her students:

> I have one of those students this year who constantly is standing in front of me with a question. She never raises her hand, but feels the need to be under my feet the moment I give an instruction. I discussed ways she could get answers rather than relying on me to do her thinking for her. Finally, to get her to think, I gave her three sticks each day with "Garrison/Anderson" written on them. When she comes up to Mrs. Anderson, my student teacher, or me, she has to give us a stick. When the sticks are gone, she's out of opportunities for the day. There has been an immediate drop in her leaving her seat.

Partner Helpers. A hallmark in differentiated classrooms is that all students participate in respectful work and when they can, they help each other. In classrooms that utilize cooperative learning teams, the strategy of team questions works well—"Ask three, then me."

" I'M LIVING A SOAP OPERA! — 'THE YOUNG AND THE RESTLESS.' "

Continue Working. While waiting for the teacher to arrive, students needing help should know they are to move ahead to the next problem or exercise. If this is not possible, they should take out a book and read silently until the teacher arrives to help.

Incidentals

Seating

As mentioned in Chapter 3, various seating arrangements have served teachers well—rows, U-shapes, circles, semicircles, and clusters of various kinds. Most teachers today want space flexibility for different kinds of activities. They also use a good deal of cooperative team and group work and want to be able to circulate easily among students. Modular cluster seating, with four to six students per cluster, usually serves these needs well.

It is best to begin the year with the teacher assigning students to seats and making tagboard name tags for each student. Students should not be allowed to select their own seats until the class shows that it is capable of self-control.

Entering and Exiting the Room

For entering and exiting the room, lines are still favored by most teachers. Various procedures are used for forming lines. In the past, the most common procedure was to have boys and girls in separate lines, but now boys and girls line up together in one or two lines. Let your students know how you want them to form lines, and give them ample practice in doing so.

Lines for entering the room are usually formed on a first-come basis. For exiting the room, teachers often excuse students according to (1) where the students sit, (2) alphabetical order by first or last name, (3) arbitrarily by work groups, or (4) as a reward for students or teams who have behaved or worked well. For occasional variety, teachers may have students move according to prompts: "Line up if you are wearing something I can see that is red," "if your birthday is in a month that begins with *J*," and so on.

Pencil Sharpening

Pencil sharpening can be very disruptive to class instruction. Some teachers keep a large metal can of pencils sharpened by a monitor before the day begins. If lead breaks or wears down, the student simply exchanges the pencil. Thus the pencil sharpener is not used during the day, and no time is lost because of noise, wandering, or waiting.

Other teachers feel that this system does not encourage self-responsibility. They allow students to keep two pencils in their desks and be responsible for sharpening them at appropriate times, such as before school. Whatever procedure you prefer, it is important to teach the routine to the students and then adhere to it.

Out-of-Room Passes

Passes are used when students must leave the room to go to the restroom, an outside drinking fountain, the library, or the office. Teachers should not allow students to leave the room without permission—or even with permission—unless clearly necessary, because there are always students who will look for any excuse to leave the room as often as possible.

Some teachers make their own passes from large pieces of wood that students cannot inadvertently misplace. Six passes should be sufficient: one drink pass, one office pass, two library passes, and two for the restroom—one for boys and one for girls. The number of passes should be adjusted according to classroom need, but it is usually not a good idea to allow two or more students to go together to unsupervised areas such as drinking fountains or restrooms. Some schools provide teachers with laminated passes, on which are written the teacher's name and room number. Students in Julia DePew's fourth/fifth multi-age class use laminated passes:

> On the first day of school every student in my class receives a laminated pass with his or her name on it. Students are reminded at that time to use the bathroom before school, at recess, and at lunch. Every morning one student distributes the passes to the others. If students need to leave the room, they return their pass to a small basket near the door. However, if they need to leave more than once, they must sign in for a consequence. Students say, "We like that we can leave once a day if we need to." They also say, "We don't like to sign in, so this lets us be responsible."

This pass allows you to one bathroom and drinking fountain visit. Remember to use the bathroom before school, at recess, and at lunch!

Name:_____

Noise Control

Some teachers tolerate noise well; others don't. Regardless of teacher tolerance, every class occasionally (sometimes daily) gets noisy to a degree that greatly interferes with teaching and learning. If this happens in your room, you will almost certainly hear complaints from neighboring teachers. Kathryn Krainock, a second-grade teacher, explains how she keeps classroom noise from annoying fellow teachers:

> Because I teach in an open classroom where there are no doors between classes, we have developed silent waves, silent claps, and silent cheers so we won't distract others. We give silent waves (index finger gently waving) to a parent or administrator who comes into the classroom. Silent claps (two fingers quietly clapping) and silent cheers (arms quietly moving up and down as though cheering) are for fellow students when they give a speech or do other fantastic feats. I feel these methods would work successfully in any classroom because they take minimal time and don't distract others.

To keep noise within acceptable limits, discuss with your students the negative effects that loud noise has on learning and teaching. Explain that different amounts of noise are allowable for different activities. During silent reading, for example, there should be no talking. During discussions, one person at a time can talk in a normal voice. During cooperative work, quiet talking is allowed as needed. For other activities such as drama and singing, more noise is allowable.

You should also use a clear signal for indicating when the noise level is too high. Consider using a color signal system or sounding a tone bell whenever the noise level goes above acceptable limits. Another alternative is to play background music. When you can no longer hear the music, the noise level is too high.

Procrastination, Tattling, Bullying, and Other Annoyances

Procrastination drives teachers crazy, as do tattling, bullying, messiness, tardiness, and irresponsibility. Teachers should model the appropriate behaviors continually, and signs of these behaviors among the students should be redirected quickly. The following suggestions help bring these problem areas into manageable proportions.

Procrastination.   The exasperating habit of putting things off until the last minute afflicts many students. Everyone has difficulty working at unexciting tasks, and most of us cannot maintain enthusiasm when tasks are overly long or complicated. But when students regularly fail to begin work promptly and fool around instead of working, consider remedies such as the following:

- Keep instructional tasks as interesting and as short as possible while covering what is intended.
- Break long tasks into a series of shorter steps, and place a deadline on the completion of each step. Say, See, Do Teaching, for example, involves students quickly and guides them actively through the learning one step at a time.
- Insert timely brain breaks and energizers into your lesson. For example, have students stand and dance in their teams to music. "The Freeze" is a movement energizer that can be done to music by Greg & Steve on their *We All Live Together* CD (1978), or to some other song the children enjoy.
- Emphasize a time limit and call out the time occasionally, for example, "Ten minutes. You should be about half finished." Or use a Teach Timer, a management tool that displays time (either counting up or down) on the overhead projector. Because students can see this from anywhere in the classroom, they can monitor their progress and the time themselves.
- Use incentives. "As soon as you have finished this work, you may . . . " (some quiet preferred activity, such as free reading).
- If other remedies do not work, take the student aside and say, "You are just not getting your work done. I know you can do it. I wonder what we can work out so you will complete your assignments?"

Tattling.   Tattling can become a virulent disease that affects almost everyone in the group. It is habit forming and causes students to focus on the negative, lose respect for each other, and forever look to an authority to adjudicate minor problems the students should settle or ignore. For teachers, tattling can become a major irritation. Fortunately, tattling can be controlled rather easily. Try the following steps:

- Have class discussions or class meetings regarding the nature of tattling, its negative effects on cooperation and good feelings, and the desirability of solving one's own minor differences. Indicate that it is all right to inform the teacher when another student seriously violates one's rights by stealing, bullying, or inflicting physical harm.

Role-play tattling behaviors and proper alternatives. When tattling occurs anyway, and if the matter is insignificant, as most are, proceed to the following steps.

■ Tell the tattler to write out the complaint, together with a constructive suggestion for resolving the problem.

■ Ask the tattler to wait until lunch or after school to make the complaint, assuring the student that you will carefully consider it at that time.

■ Have the disputants meet together to discuss the matter and come up with an acceptable solution with which they both agree to abide.

Nelsen, Lott, and Glenn (2000) suggest using classroom meetings as opportunities to practice effective problem-solving skills. After discussion and role-play, students are taught to brainstorm ideas for logical consequences and nonpunitive solutions. Then they vote on a suggestion they think will be most helpful.

Barbara Coloroso (2002) stresses the importance of teaching children to think for themselves and to believe that no problem is so great it cannot be solved. To help students develop decision-making skills she continually encourages them by saying "You have a problem; you can solve it. What's your plan?"

To help children discern the difference between tattling and telling, Coloroso (2002) recommends this formula: "If it will only get another child in trouble, don't tell me—that's tattling. If it will get you or another child out of trouble, tell me. If it is both, I need to know" (p. 135).

Bullying. As discussed in Chapter 4, bullying is a regular occurrence at school. Bullies are individuals who instill fear in others, who intend to hurt, and who enjoy it. They may use verbal or physical bullying, or they may ignore or exclude their targets with relational bullying. Bystanders follow or support bullies, or do nothing to stop the action. Teachers can approach bullying by doing the following:

■ Continually model and provide practice for appropriate behavior and acceptance. Infuse expectations for good character into the way you teach.

■ When bullying occurs, gather information directly from students. Do this anonymously, and with sensitivity to the students' safety and needs.

■ Ask the children what they need from adults to feel safe.

■ Establish clear school and classroom rules and consequences for bullying.

■ Provide adequate supervision, particularly in areas such as the playground and lunchroom.

■ Inform parents or guardians and try to involve them in solutions to the problem.

Messiness. A chronic problem for some students, messiness is evidenced in the work students do and the care they give school materials. Messiness annoys teachers and reinforces unattractive habits in students. To deal with messiness, consider the following suggestions:

■ Model neatness. Keep your own work station tidy and in order.

■ Have group discussions about pride in oneself, schoolwork, and the classroom. Talk about how pride is often related to neatness.

■ Let students know you are keeping their neatest papers to show parents and guardians.

- Establish an incentive system in which a series of neat papers earns a reward such as a certificate, sticker, or preferred activity.
- Encourage students to exchange ideas about organizing their desks for maximum neatness and efficiency.

Tardiness.   Although it often occurs for legitimate reasons, when tardiness is habitual, it can be annoying and disconcerting, causing the student to miss out on important instruction and instilling a general lack of responsibility. When left unchecked the habit often becomes worse. Though chronically late students may blame the caregiver or an unending series of catastrophes, they may have fallen into the tardiness habit because it is their nature to procrastinate, they have not yet accepted responsibility for their own educational process, or they are finding something very interesting to do on the way to school.

Although one or two students will arrive late every day, the incidence of tardiness, especially for the chronically late, can be reduced through the following measures:

- Have class discussions or meetings about student responsibilities in supporting and participating in the school program. Make sure students understand the need to arrive a few minutes before school begins.
- Make the opening activities attractive, enjoyable, and important so students will want to participate and will feel left out when they do not. Coloroso (1994) believes in sharing information that is "a little nice to know" first thing in the morning—(for example, tell students to answer only the even problems on today's math quiz).
- Show you mean business by establishing consequences for tardiness and by giving rewards for continued punctuality. Let students help decide the consequences and rewards.
- If other measures do not correct the problem, call the parents or guardians and ask for their input and help.

Irresponsibility.   Irresponsibility refers to student disinclination to work up to capacity; mistreatment of materials, equipment, and facilities; and failure to live up to ordinary obligations. An important goal of education is to build within each student a sense of responsibility for the common good and for one's own acts. Responsibility is shown when obligations are fulfilled promptly and correctly with concern for others. To help instill this sense in students who are not otherwise inclined, consider the following:

- Periodically discuss with students what *responsibility* means and how it contributes to the good of everyone. Also discuss what students should do in the classroom to show they are being responsible.
- Assign specific responsibilities to all class members for helping manage the classroom, as with monitors (described earlier).
- Have students evaluate their own behavior on several points, such as being punctual, completing work, doing their best, taking care of assigned duties, and helping others when necessary. Have them fill out contracts for future improvement, and reward them appropriately when they live up to their promises.

This concludes our consideration of the management of students at work and directs us to an examination of how to manage the special needs of students in today's classrooms. This is the topic of Chapter 8. Before moving ahead, take time to explore these end-of-chapter activities.

Parting Thought

Never, never, never, never give up.

—Winston Churchill

SUMMARY SELF-CHECK

Check off the following as you either understand or become able to apply them.

❑ Good management of students at work contributes greatly to time availability, class control, rapid learning, sense of responsibility, and sense of security.

❑ Routine management calls attention to
- Work routines
- Opening activities: attendance; sharing; silent reading; journal writing; choosing; five-a-days; clear, succinct instructions for doing work; movement in the room (traffic patterns, permission)
- Signals for attention
- Materials: storage and distribution, use and care, replacement, large materials
- Completed work: what to do with students' completed assignments
- Student accountability and criterion of mastery
- Homework: its value and purpose
- End-of-day closing: a wonderful instructional time

❑ Providing assistance
- Monitors: responsibility for everyone
- Helpful directions and feedback: clear directions; visual instructional plans and posted reminders; rapid, effective assistance
- Partner and team help

❑ Incidentals: seating (matched to program); entering and exiting the room; pencil sharpening; out-of-room passes; attention signals; noise control; procrastination, tardiness, tattling, bullying, and other annoyances

ACTIVITIES FOR REFLECTION AND GROWTH

For Cumulative Skills Development

1. Take a moment to review the statements in the Anticipation–Reaction Guide at the beginning of this chapter. Put a check mark in the Reaction column next to any statement with which you now agree. How have your thoughts changed since reading this chapter?

2. Think about the schedule of a normal school day. (Refer back to Chapter 2 if necessary.) Decide on the level of noise that you would consider acceptable for the various activities. What would you discuss with the students about noise? What kinds of signaling devices, if any, would you use as reminders?

3. For a grade level you select, decide what classroom monitor duties you want students to fill. How would you make the assignments? How would you instruct monitors concerning their duties and responsibilities? What would you do if a monitor proved to be irresponsible?

4. Custom design a fifteen-minute closing routine (not clean up) that you consider most beneficial to your students and program. What variations might you make during the week? (Some districts provide one shorter day, or *minimum day,* each week to give teachers planning time without students. How would that routine then vary from the regular days? Between Monday's routine and Friday's?) What variations might you make from month to month?

5. Make a list of the various work products that students regularly complete—tests, practice papers, compositions, artwork, and so on. What would you want your students to do with their completed work? Describe how you would have this process carried out.

6. Describe what you would do to control tattling, procrastination, messiness, irresponsibility, cheating, swearing, bullying, and temper tantrums.

REFERENCES AND RECOMMENDED READINGS

Charles, C. (2005). *Building classroom discipline* (8th ed.). Boston: Allyn & Bacon.

Coloroso, B. (1990). *Winning at teaching . . . without beating your kids* [Videotape from the series *Kids Are Worth It!*]. Littleton, CO: Kids Are Worth It!

Coloroso, B. (1994). *Kids are worth it! Giving your child the gift of inner discipline.* New York: Avon Books.

Coloroso, B. (2002). *The bully, the bullied, and the bystander.* Toronto, Ontario, Canada: HarperCollins.

Freiberg, H. (1996, September). From tourists to citizens in the classroom. *Education Leadership, 54*(1), 32–36.

Gardner, H. (1991). *The unschooled mind: How children think and how schools should teach.* New York: Basic Books.

Gardner, H. (1993a). *Frames of mind* (10th ed.). New York: Basic Books.

Gardner, H. (1993b). *Multiple intelligences: The theory in practice.* New York: Basic Books.

Jones, F. (2000). Tools for teaching: Discipline instruction motivation. Santa Cruz, CA: Fredric H. Jones.

Kagan, S., & Kagan, M. (1998). *Multiple intelligences: The complete MI book.* San Clemente, CA: Kagan Cooperative Learning.

Nelsen, J., Lott, L., & Glenn, H. (2000). *Positive discipline in the classroom.* Rocklin, CA: Prima Publishing.

Olweus, D. (1999). *Core program against bullying and antisocial behavior: A teacher handbook.* Bergen, Norway: Research Center for Health Promotion, University of Bergen.

Schwartz, F. (1981). Supporting or subverting learning: Peer group patterns in four tracked schools. *Anthropology and Education Quarterly, 12*(2), 99–120.

Scelsa, G., & Millang, S. (1978). *We all live together* (vol. 2). [CD] Los Angeles: Little House Music.

Winning the tattle battle. (1998). [Back to school issue]. *The Mailbox Teacher, 27*(1), 52–55.

8 Managing Special Groups

There is only one child in the world and that child's name is ALL children.
—Carl Sandburg

ANTICIPATION–REACTION GUIDE

Before you read the chapter, take a moment to put a check mark in the Anticipation column next to any statement with which you agree.

	Anticipation	Reaction
Inclusive education is a fairly new concept, with little history or legal support.	❑	❑
Exceptionality best describes children who are especially bright, gifted, or talented.	❑	❑
Students with higher-ability are usually self-starters, capable and willing to take responsibility for their own learning goals.	❑	❑
Attention deficit disorder (ADD) and attention deficit hyperactivity disorder (ADHD) are best treated with medication because the child is likely to outgrow the disorder.	❑	❑
Children who are emotionally disturbed can understand the signs and triggers for their outbursts, and can learn to control them.	❑	❑
Language diversity has little to do with ethnicity and race.	❑	❑
Language diversity describes the presence of more than one language in a student's home.	❑	❑
Children of separated or divorced parents are likely to take sides with one parent rather than grieve their loss.	❑	❑
Children without permanent housing are likely to attend school in order to receive the adjunct services such as the free lunch program.	❑	❑
Differentiated instruction contributes little toward managing diversity among students.	❑	❑

The Legislation of Inclusion

Children come to school from diverse cultures and family structures, some speaking languages other than English, some with physical challenges or other special needs, and some with behavior disorders. We have long held that all children have the right to a free public education. However, debate continues as to the best educational approach to meet the diverse needs of all children.

Following the 1954 Supreme Court ruling of *Brown v. Board of Education* and a myriad of related court cases, schools were opened equally to students of all races and ethnic groups. Subsequently, other federal laws were passed regarding the schooling of non-English-speaking children. Included among these are the Supreme Court ruling in *Lau v. Nichols* (1974), Title VI of the Civil Rights Act of 1964, and the Bilingual Education Act of 1974, amended in 1988. As a result, students with varied skin colors, facial features, heritages, values, and ceremonies are now able to come together for their formal education. In 1975, Congress passed the Education of All Handicapped Children Act, PL 94-142. The law provided for inclusion of all students in "the least restrictive environment," "to the maximum extent appropriate," and "with the use of supplementary aids and services." One amendment to the law was the Education of All Handicapped Children Act Amendments of 1986. Known as "The Preschool Law," this amendment expanded the services to infants and young children who have disabilities or who are at risk in their families. The original law and its amendments merged into the Individuals with Disabilities Education Act (IDEA) in 1990 and the Reauthorization of IDEA of 1997. In recent years, children with special needs have been recognized, supported, and included in regular classrooms (to the extent their abilities allow) for a maximum portion of their day. Thus, children with special physical and intellectual needs are able to join a teaching and learning community in which everyone's individual needs are met.

Disabilities that Qualify Children and Youth for Special Education Services

As defined by IDEA, children are considered to have disabilities if they have any of the following thirteen conditions:

1. Autism, affecting verbal and nonverbal communication and social interaction
2. Deafness
3. Deafness-blindness
4. Hearing impairment (DHH)
5. Mental retardation (MR), significantly below-average general intellectual functioning, together with inadequate adaptive behavior
6. Multiple disabilities, simultaneous impairments such as mental retardation and blindness
7. Orthopedic impairment (OI)
8. Other health impairment (OHI), chronic or acute health problems, such as a heart condition, asthma, or diabetes, that limit strength, vitality, or alertness
9. Serious emotional disturbance (SED), including schizophrenia

10. Specific learning disability (SLD), visual and auditory processing difficulties including dyslexia and Central Auditory Processing Disorder (CAPD)
11. Speech or language impairment (SLI)
12. Traumatic brain injury (TBI), caused by external physical force rather than congenital or degenerative injuries
13. Visual impairment (VI), including blindness

The Concept of Inclusion

Inclusion refers to involving all students in the educational setting that best meets their needs, regardless of background, creed, or level of ability. For all practical purposes, this educational setting is considered to be the public school classroom. Inclusion has a broader meaning as well. It refers to a way of life, an attitude, a value, a belief system that holds that all children are entitled to the best education we can provide *and* that an association of diverse students provides benefits for all. Schools and teachers who adopt the attitude of inclusion show it by their decisions and actions. They focus on "how to support special gifts and needs of each and every student in the school community to feel welcomed and secure and to become successful" (Falvey, Givner, & Kimm, 1995, p. 8).

Exceptionality

Among the students who present some of the special challenges for teachers are (1) students whose work is academically below or above grade level, (2) students with physical or emotional challenges, (3) students with limited English proficiency, and (4) students whose family and life experiences lend themselves to potential problems. Some twenty-seven different categories (Ysseldyke & Algozzine, 1995) have been identified relating to exceptional students, those formerly labeled as learning-disabled. In general, six categories, as listed in Figure 8.1, show the range of exceptional students that may be present in a classroom.

FIGURE 8.1   Categories of Exceptionality

- *Intellectual.* Includes both students who have superior intelligence as well as those who are slow to learn.
- *Communicative.* Students with special learning disabilities or speech or language impairments.
- *Sensory.* Students with auditory or visual disabilities.
- *Behavioral.* Students who are emotionally disturbed or socially maladjusted.
- *Physical.* Students with orthopedic or mobility disabilities.
- *Multiple.* Students with a combination of conditions, such as cerebral palsy and dyslexia.

Kirk & Gallagher (1996)

The U.S. Department of Education National Center for Education Statistics (2003) reports a gradual increase, to about 13 percent in 2000–2001, in the number of children being served in programs for the disabled. This increase probably resulted from the Education of All Handicapped Children Act Amendments of 1986 that mandated public school special education services for all handicapped children aged 3–5.

Students of Lower Ability

Some children have achievement rates in certain academic areas that are lower than their general ability levels would indicate. They are apt to be disorganized, forgetful, and frustrated, and they tend toward anger, hopelessness, or low self-concept. To support these students, teachers should

- Follow predictable routines and structure.
- Model acceptable and appropriate actions.
- Signal important information and assistance clues.
- Provide ample practice for smaller portions of information.
- Have students repeat directions aloud.
- Limit confusing trial-and-error activities.
- Emphasize students' achievements rather than their mistakes.
- Have students keep records of their own work and behavior.

Several assistive tools are available for teachers of children with lower abilities. To help students with their reading, teachers may use audiobooks, talking computers, captioned films and videos, and semantic mapping software. To help students with their writing, teachers may have students use word-processing programs with spelling and grammar checks. Manipulatives and calculators can help students with math and problem solving. Personal organizers, electronic calendars, and a variety of organizing software programs are available to help students with their organization. Finally, the Internet and computer-based instructional programs can help students with their studying and learning.

Students of Higher Ability

Students of higher ability, sometimes referred to as gifted and talented (GATE) are those who significantly surpass the norms in achievement. The Gifted and Talented Students Act of 1978 defines gifted and talented students as " . . . possessing demonstrated or potential abilities that give evidence of high performance capability in areas such as intellectual, creative, specific academics, or leadership abilities, or in the performing and visual arts, and who by reason thereof require services or activities not ordinarily provided by the school" (p. 8). The act further distinguishes gifted as referring to above-average intellectual ability, and talented as referring to excellence in drama, art, music, athletics, or leadership, and states that students can have these abilities separately or in combination.

These children require differentiated educational programs and services beyond those normally provided by the regular school. They can be high achievers who are self-starting, persistent, able to work independently, and resourceful. They have direction in their personal learning goals and need minimal guidance to proceed. For these students, management relates to strong articulation of personal goals, of plans to accomplish them, and of tools to assess their progress.

Other students with higher ability, however, may appear more difficult to manage. They are likely to be divergent thinkers who approach situations and problems with perspectives different from those of other students. Teachers often view divergent thinkers either as very creative individuals or as noncompliant students with behavior problems.

Students with higher abilities, both the self-starters and the creative, divergent thinkers, benefit most from open-ended activities. Such assignments allow students to adapt an assignment, a situation, or a problem to match their own uniqueness, ability, and interest. This allowance can be highly motivating for both quality work and behavior. Guided conversations and jointly designed scoring rubrics that clearly set expectations and standards help teachers and students manage this nontraditional approach.

Additional ideas for students who are higher achievers might include bonus activities, questions, and projects that are motivational, challenging, and meaningful. Though these students have the potential to contribute to everyone's learning, they should not be made team teachers for lessons or be kept occupied with busy work. In other words, students who are high achievers should be given *other,* not *more,* and it is especially important that higher-ability students feel valued and appreciated.

Students with Communication Disorders

"A person has a communication problem when that person's speech differs from the speech of others to the extent that it calls attention to itself, interferes with the intended message, or causes the speaker or listener to be distressed" (Van Ripper, 1978). Speech impairment is defined under PL 94-142 as "a communication disorder, such as stuttering, impaired articulation, a language impairment, or a voice impairment, which adversely affects a child's educational performance" (*Federal Register,* 1977, p. 42479). Cartwright, Cartwright, and Ward (1984) distinguish speech (expressive) from language (receptive) disorders: "Speech problems are those associated with the production of the oral symbols of language, whereas language problems are difficulties with the linguistic code or rules and conventions for linking the symbols and symbol sequences" (p. 115).

Many children with speech (expressive) and language (receptive) disorders receive individual help outside the classroom. Sometime during the day, or several times during the week, a resource teacher provides additional assistance to individuals or small groups of students with the same speech or language disorder.

Within the classroom, potential negative consequences of speech and language disorders may affect the child's self-concept and interpersonal relations with peers. To prevent these negative consequences from occurring, teachers should

- Model acceptance for all children.
- Model appropriate language (words, expressions, sounds) at all times.
- Encourage children to talk about activities they participate in outside of school.
- Give children many opportunities to speak without interruption or pressure.

- Ask open-ended questions and wait for responses.
- Listen attentively to what children have to say.
- Plan and deliver instruction so students can easily rejoin the class when they return from their time with the resource teacher.

Assistive technology provides a variety of alternative and augmentative communication (AAC) devices for students with communication disorders. AAC devices can be made for individual students; can be electronic or nonelectronic, simple or complex; and are intended to supplement oral or written language production. Communication boards are fairly low tech. High-tech equipment such as speech synthesizers and speech talkers allow individuals with communication disorders to "talk." Machines that create speech and language use icon systems that are accessed by touch or switches. With technological advances, AAC devices are now smaller (some can be worn on the wrist), more capable, and more affordable.

Students with Hearing Impairments

Hearing impairments fall into two categories—being deaf and having partial hearing (or being hard of hearing). It is possible that mild hearing loss may go unnoticed. Children with hearing impairments usually function well in the classroom, provided certain accommodations are made. For example, some may require a paraprofessional to assist them through the day. Arrangements must be made to accommodate the paraprofessional. Others may use a hearing ear dog as helper. It is crucial that the other children understand the dog is there to work, not to play. It may help to have the dog's owner introduce the dog to the class and share about how they work together. To best help students with hearing impairment, the teacher should

- Ask the student what can be done to help him or her. Teachers should not assume that their ideas of help are what the student needs.
- Use adaptive devices such as microphones and receivers, as available.
- Seat the student near the front and center of the room and close to the primary instructional area.
- Always face the student when speaking, particularly when giving important information or instruction, so the student can see your face and read your lips.
- Learn and use basic sign language during instruction.
- Use the overhead projector rather than the board so you face forward as you talk, and provide the student with a copy of the transparency text.
- Consider the lighting in the room and the location of windows and doorways in relation to you as you talk.
- Repeat and rephrase instructions, information, questions, and discussion comments made by other students.
- To the extent possible, minimize noise—particularly auditory and visual distracters—both in and outside the classroom.
- Encourage all students to ask questions.
- Partner the student with someone who will take good, legible notes to share.

- Partner the student with someone who will provide cues about instruction and when to watch the teacher, and who will help in emergency situations.

Assistive technologies for students who are deaf or hard of hearing allow them to experience instruction with amplification or through their other senses. Assistive learning devices (ALDs) include hearing aids and a variety of FM (frequency-modulated) transmission devices. With FM technology, the speaker uses a microphone that transmits directly to the student's receiver. This helps overcome the distance and noise problems of classrooms, including background noise that can interfere with appropriate hearing and the hearing of subtle language sounds. Captioning on broadcast and media presentations is another tool that is readily available.

Students with Visual Impairments

Students with visual impairment usually function quite well with the use of supplementary aids and services. For example, they may use a cane or a guide dog, use a braille machine, or have a paraprofessional who works with them throughout the day. As with the hearing ear dog, the other children must understand that the dog is there to work, not play. Arrangements will need to be made in the classroom so a braille machine, if used, can be placed where it is accessible to the child and not distracting to classmates. Again, the other children must understand the purpose of the machine. Likewise, arrangements must be made to accommodate the paraprofessional who accompanies the child to class. To best help students with visual impairment, the teacher should

- Ask the student what can be done to help him or her. Teachers should not assume that their ideas are what the student needs.
- Seat the student as close to the main instructional areas as possible.
- Provide the student with clear oral instructions and perhaps even provide the paraprofessional with written instructions for his or her reference.
- Modify lessons to include numerous auditory and tactile experiences.
- Partner the student with others who are able to verbalize expectations and procedures, and who will help in emergency situations.
- Use vigilance in watching and listening to children for signs of behavior, appearance, and complaints that might signal possible visual impairment.

Assistive technologies for students who are blind or visually impaired also allow them to experience instruction by means of enlarged print or through other senses. Closed-circuit television (CCTV) displays enlarged print on a television monitor. The Magni-Cam also enlarges print. This is a camera embedded in a mouselike tool that can be rolled over printed pages. When it is connected to a computer, the computer screen displays the magnified image. Word-processing features allow changes to print style and fonts, and copy machines allow for page size adjustments. Some braille machines are more compact, portable, and convenient than before. In fact, the Kurzweil 1000 is a personal computer and desktop reading system that turns print into speech or braille. Audiobooks may be available on request. Finally, bar magnifiers and writing guide sets are relatively inexpensive visual aid tools.

Students with Behavior Disorders

Behavior disorders is a general category in special education for students who exhibit serious and persistent inappropriate behaviors that result in social conflict and personal unhappiness that affect school performance (Dembo, 1994). Behavior sometimes is characterized in terms of *excesses* and *deficits* (Whelan & Gallagher, 1972). Excesses are the more blatant behaviors, such as tantrums and frequent fighting. These obvious behaviors have teachers' attention. However, students with deficit behaviors (shy or withdrawn students who have few friends or who seldom participate in class) also need attention.

Student Who Have Attention Deficit Disorder and Hyperactivity Disorder.   Volumes are written about attention deficit disorder and attention deficit hyperactivity disorder (ADD and ADHD), what they are, how to recognize the conditions, and how to treat the problems. However, it almost seems that the more we learn about the disorders, the more remains to be learned. Caregivers and teachers say they readily spot the symptoms. In primary grades, children with ADD have short attention spans or are easily distracted. In the intermediate grades, the children daydream or have difficulty staying focused on work.

Students with attention deficit hyperactivity disorder generally have difficulties with attention, hyperactivity, impulse control, emotional stability, or some combination of these. Children who are hyperactive show excessive, almost constant movement. They jiggle and wiggle and squirm and fuss, blurt out comments and answers, and generally bother the teacher and other students with their noises and movements. "Some say that up to 35 million children, mostly boys under 18 (about 4 percent) display symptoms" of ADHD (Cruickshank, Bainer, & Metcalf, 1999, p. 43).

Although attentional distractibility and behavioral hyperactivity often go together, their exact relationship fluctuates. During the 1970s, evidence emerged to suggest that distractibility was the key to the hyperactivity syndrome. However, more recent research suggests that this view overemphasizes the role of attention deficits in leading to hyperactivity problems, and that hyperactivity is linked more closely to oppositional and aggressive conduct disorders (Good & Brophy, 2002). Here are two important things to remember: (1) ADD can be diagnosed without hyperactivity but one does not have hyperactivity without ADD, and (2) for the most part these behaviors are not deliberate, and it takes a long time for these children to learn ways to compensate for or control them. Figure 8.2 lists thirteen statements that seem to characterize an ADHD child.

The following are some things you can do to help children who have ADD or ADHD, or who show some of the symptoms:

- Be sure you have everyone's attention when giving oral instructions. Make instructions brief and clear and, when possible, teach them one step at a time.
- When preparing for a transition, use clear directions and cues (such as a five-minute warning before a transition).
- Have students repeat instructions back to make sure they were understood.
- Use visuals in conjunction with oral instructions.
- Carefully monitor work, especially as students begin a new activity or step.

FIGURE 8.2   Does a child you know possibly have attention deficit hyperactivity disorder?

If eight or more of the following statements seem to characterize a child you know, he or she has traits common to ADHD. A medical diagnosis may be helpful.

1. Often fidgets or squirms when sitting
2. Has difficulty remaining seated
3. Is easily distracted
4. Has difficulty awaiting turns
5. Often blurts things out
6. Has difficulty following directions
7. Has difficulty paying attention
8. Often shifts from one incomplete activity to another
9. Has difficulty playing quietly
10. Often interrupts or intrudes
11. Often doesn't seem to listen
12. Talks excessively
13. Often engages in dangerous play without considering consequences

Source: Adapted from Wallis, C. (1994, July 18), Life in overdrive. *Time, 144* (3), 50. In Donald R. Cruickshank, Deborah L. Bainer, & Kim K. Metcalf (Eds.), *The act of teaching* (2nd ed.) © 1999, McGraw-Hill. Reprinted by permission of The McGraw-Hill Companies.

- Adjust work time so it matches attention spans, and provide breaks.
- Insert timely energizers and brain breaks into longer lessons and activities.
- Establish and use a secret signal to remind the student when he or she is off task.
- Remind students that accuracy, not speed, is important by encouraging a criterion of mastery.
- When students work with printed material, let them use cards with a cut out area to frame their attention and cover irrelevant information.
- Allow students to use their fingers as pointers to avoid skipping words or lines.
- Plan for students to move around every few minutes.
- Have a study carrel or a place in the room that is free from distractions, and give them the option to go there when they need to.
- Teach relaxation techniques for longer work periods or tests. These might include deep breathing and muscle stretches while sitting.
- If medication is prescribed, monitor and cue their trips to the nurse as needed.

Students Who Are Emotionally Disturbed

Generally speaking, children who are emotionally disturbed differ from others in the degree of emotionality they exhibit. You should read their school histories, if available, and consult with the school psychologist, administrators, and other teachers who are involved with the student, taking note of any recommendations. Children who are emotionally disturbed are easily frustrated and are prone to outbursts of temper. They need your patience and help learning to manage their self-control. Here are some suggestions:

- Learn to recognize clues in behavior that may signal outbursts in order to anticipate their loss of control.
- Overlook minor inappropriate behavior, reinforce acceptable behavior, and reduce stressors. (This even means temporarily adjusting expectations if the student is having a bad day.)
- Provide a supportive, predictable, and safe environment.
- Give the student structured choices whenever it is possible to do so. ("Are you able to concentrate on this work at your desk right now, or would you rather move to the study carrel?")
- Provide a safe and supervised area for the student to cool down.
- Develop a plan of action with the principal, counselor, and others for when the student has a tantrum or outburst.
- Avoid dwelling on past outbursts and incidents, because often the student does not understand an outburst and will not be able to have meaningful conversations about it. Rather, try to help the student learn from the current incident to prevent future outbursts.

Computers have been found to be especially helpful assistive tools for children with emotional or behavioral disorders. Computers are emotionally neutral systems with which to interact, have fun, achieve success, and engage actively in learning (Lucent Technologies, 1999). Computers provide safe environments in which children are not judged or criticized. Answers in computer-assisted instruction are simply right or wrong.

Students with Physical and Health Impairments

Orthopedic impairments are skeletal and muscle problems that adversely affect a child's educational performance. These impairments might be congenital (such as a clubfoot or absence of a limb); caused by disease (such as tuberculosis); or be the result of physical trauma such as cerebral palsy, amputations, fractures, or burns (*Federal Register,* 1977).

Health impairments involve limited strength, vitality, or alertness, due to chronic or acute health problems (such as a cerebral palsy, diabetes, epilepsy, heart condition, leukemia, tuberculosis, and others) that adversely affect a child's educational performance (*Federal Register,* 1977).

Many students with physical or health disorders remain in regular classrooms. Because some of these students may need medication, or they may miss school for long periods of time, teachers must carefully consider both the academic as well as the social experience of the child. Supportive actions include

- Consulting with the school nurse, previous teachers, or other resources to understand the condition.
- Asking the student what can be done to help him or her. Teachers should not assume that their ideas of help are what the student needs.
- Spending time helping the class understand the condition and develop realistic attitudes and ways of interacting with the child.
- Adjusting assignments and time considerations to allow students to participate and complete work.

- To the extent possible, continuing to support the child who is hospitalized during the school year.
- When welcoming a child back to school from an illness, allowing sufficient time for catching up and making up work.

Students from Diverse Language Groups

Language diversity obviously includes the presence of a language other than English. In addition, however, it includes issues of slang, pronunciation, and usage within a single language, such as with African American or Hispanic American English. The National Clearinghouse for English Language Acquisition reported in 2002 that about 4.4 million students have limited English proficiency. According to the U.S. Census Bureau, in 2000, one in five U.S. residents aged five and older spoke a language other than English at home, an increase of approximately 15 million people since 1990. The report *Language Use and English-Speaking Ability: 2000* found that in addition to English and Spanish, other languages spoken in the home included Chinese, French, German, Italian, Russian, and other Asian and Pacific Island languages. The report also said, "55 percent of the people who spoke a language other than English at home also reported they spoke English 'very well' " (U.S. Census Bureau Public Information Office, 2003, p. 1). However, for teachers these numbers have great implication, for they will have English learners in their classes. To be more specific, 7.9 percent of their students will receive ELL services (National Center for Education Statistics, 2002).

Cary (1997) points out that in past years language learners were given a variety of negative-sounding labels such as limited-English speaking/non-English speaking (LES/NES) or limited-English proficient/non-English proficient (LEP/NEP). His preference is to emphasize the student's growing resource advantage—having two languages instead of one—by simply referring to them as English learners.

A variety of philosophies and programs have been put forth for instructing English language learners. Examples include:

- Separate ESL curriculum—grammar, heavy skill and drill, and worksheets (1970s).
- Natural approach—developmental and low stress, with practice of real language meaning and communication (Krashen & Terrell, 1996).
- Submersion—"sink or swim" for language learners who are placed in all-English classrooms with instruction designed for native English-speaking students.
- Dual immersion—a 50/50 split of instruction in English and the other language.
- Sheltered instruction—another meaning- and communication-based approach, with language made understandable through context (also called bridging) (Schifini, 1988). Also referred to as Specially Designed Academic Instruction in English (SDAIE), this approach helps language learners learn core curriculum and expand English skills (Krashen, 1985).

Most common and successful today are second language programs that utilize English Language Development (ELD), Specially Designed Academic Instruction in English (SDAIE), and long-term primary language support and development (Cary, 1997).

"MY FRIEND EDWARD IS BILINGUAL.
HE CAN TALK TO BOYS AND GIRLS."

Teachers who follow today's research of language acquisition understand language development differently than their predecessors. They understand that second language learners need many opportunities to practice both their basic interpersonal communication skills (BICS) and cognitive academic language proficiency (CALP), and the practice must be meaningful and with low stress. Teachers also believe that listening, speaking, reading, and writing skills should be linked and developed at the same time. Thus their instructional strategies and classroom environment include the following:

- A concrete, context-rich environment that builds connections of context to objects, manipulatives, models, and multimedia
- Showing rather than telling directions and instructions
- Repeating, summarizing, and paraphrasing
- Preview–review format
- Frequent and varied understanding checks, such as thumbs up, partner sharing, and journal writing
- Opportunities for partner and group work
- Nontraditional assessment options, such as role play, media, and art
- Speech modification so it is slower, with fewer complex sentences, free of idioms and fused words ("okayeveryonedoyahaveanyquestions?"), and using specific naming words

- More wait time and think time
- Integrating students' interests, backgrounds, and personal experiences from their home country
- High but reasonable expectations, in keeping with the language level of each student

Rebecca Cummins teaches third grade. Here is how she works with students with language difficulties in English.

> For my students who cannot speak English, I provide notebooks in which I encourage them to draw a picture or write in their native language during writing time. The story can be told or read to a buddy who speaks the same language, then told aloud to the teacher in English by the buddy. If no one speaks the children's native language, show them that you want a picture. When they finish, admire the picture and point out two or three main parts. Say the names of those parts and label them on the picture. As the children begin learning English, I have them label parts of their drawings and write summary sentences in English.

Students from Unstable Family Structures

The areas of diversity that we have just described are well recognized. However, another area of diversity is on the rise, and its very nature also affects the classroom and instruction. Under a broad category of family and life come hard realities of family structure, involving separation, divorce, blended families, latchkey children, and children who are homeless. Students who come from these situations sometimes (but not always) bring with them yet another set of challenges.

Children of Separated or Divorced Parents, and Blended Families.   "Half of all children will witness the breakup of a parent's marriage. Of these, close to half will also see the breakup of a parent's second marriage" (*Divorce Rates*). Between 1970 and 1996, the proportion of children under eighteen years of age living with one parent grew from 12 percent to 28 percent (U.S. Census Bureau, 1998, p. 3). For some children this means they spend time with each parent, sometimes split by school year and vacation and summer, but other times split during the school year itself. When a parent remarries, children may find themselves members of blended families, possibly with new brothers and sisters in addition to a new parent.

Wallerstein and Kelly (1980) identified some common responses to divorce related to the development level of the child. Primary-aged children (between five and eight years old) frequently cried and fretted about rejection. Boys in particular missed their fathers and were angry with their mothers for making them leave. Often, their school performance declined.

Children between nine and twelve were apt to be particularly angry with the parent they believed caused the divorce. They were inclined to side with one parent, often with the mother against the father. They grieved for their loss and were anxious and lonely. Some children also had academic problems.

Teachers with children of separated or divorced parents should be prepared for the probability of adjustment and custody concerns. Both can affect a child's behavior and academic achievement. As a constant adult for the child, teachers should

- Recognize and accept emotions.
- Listen and talk to the child, encouraging healthy expressions of these emotions.
- In activities and class discussions, be sensitive to a variety of personal and family situations.
- Make information about divorce available to children and their parents or guardians.
- To the extent possible, maintain communication with both parents.
- When possible, consider mentors (such as male teachers who can support children without fathers).

Latchkey Children. For a multitude of reasons, large numbers of children spend time without adult supervision. A report in 1992 published that about 64 percent of children did not have a parent at home full time (Center for the Study of Social Policy). This meant that an estimated range of 2 million to 6 million children was unsupervised before or after school. Current reports by the U.S. Census Bureau indicate that approximately one of every ten elementary school children spends four and one-half hours a week unsupervised by

"BILLY GOT HIS IQ FROM A DAD FROM A PREVIOUS MARRIAGE."

adults (although younger children may be supervised by an older sibling). The Bureau also found that 6.9 million school children between the ages of five and fourteen regularly care for themselves without adult supervision. These children are referred to as *latchkey* because they are responsible for letting themselves in and out of the residence. Research reports that latchkey children, compared to children who are supervised, are more likely to experience stress, are more afraid to be alone, are angrier, have more academic and social problems, skip school more frequently, and are more likely to commit antisocial acts founded in peer pressure (Long & Long, 1989; Dwyer et al., 1990).

Teachers, as well as some communities and business organizations, are working with caregivers and children to reduce unsupervised time for children. Structured before- and after-school activities, Boys and Girls Clubs, homework clubs, and mentors are in place for this purpose.

Children Who Are Homeless.   The *National Coalition for the Homeless Fact Sheet #7* (2001) provides statistics regarding a fast-growing segment of the homeless population. According to the document, a 2000 survey by the Conference of Mayors of twenty-five cities in the United States found that families with children accounted for 36 percent of the homeless population, and that homelessness among families is increasing. In 2002 almost 20 percent of children living in the United States lived in families that fell below the poverty line (Annie E. Casey Foundation, 2002). This is almost twice as high as the poverty rate for any other age group. Approximately 25 percent lived with parents who did not have full-time, year-round employment (Annie E. Casey Foundation, 2002). Further, some two to three million people, about 1 percent of the population in the United States, experience homelessness. Approximately 60 percent of homeless women and 41 percent of homeless men had minor children (U.S. Department of Health and Human Services, 2002). The increasing poverty and subsequent homelessness among families has resulted from several causes: changes in welfare programs, unstable employment, low wages, loss of benefits, diminishing supply of affordable housing, and a rise in domestic violence.

Children without permanent housing may suffer physically, emotionally, and educationally (Children's Defense Fund, 1994). Children who live in cars, shelters, and other such places are more likely than other children who are poor to miss school because of higher mortality rates, more severe health problems, and fewer immunization opportunities.

Some communities have come together to support homeless students. For example, a magnet school and adult volunteers and mentors in Phoenix provide stability, support, and opportunity for students who are homeless throughout the Phoenix area. The Steward B. McKinney Homeless Assistance Act (1987, amended 1990 and 1994) attempts to protect the educational needs of homeless children. In addition to tracking attendance and addresses of students who are homeless, The Home, Education, Readiness, and Opportunity (HERO) program, developed in 1993 in Nashville, provides parent training, after-school tutoring in shelters, school supplies and clothing, and community locations where children can play with friends. The After-School Corporation (TASC), established in 1998, grants money raised from contributions and foundations to community-based organizations to run after-school programs in schools. Federal and local programs such as these are working to curtail this cycle, but homelessness is a reality, nonetheless, and teachers are faced with the challenges of students who appear at school one day and then miss the next because they do not have a permanent residence.

Teachers can be powerful forces in the lives of children who are homeless, helping them both emotionally and academically. On an emotional level, teachers can

- Recognize and accept emotions.
- Listen and talk to the child, encouraging healthy expressions of these emotions.
- Be sensitive to a variety of family situations in activities and discussions.
- To the extent possible, maintain communication with caregivers and provide information regarding appropriate and available support services.

On an academic level, teachers can

- Partner students with classmates who can help show them the ropes around the school and in the classroom.
- Find volunteers or mentors who can tutor and support the child at the shelter.
- Improvise a portable desk (such as a clipboard or notebook) so the student can do homework at the shelter.
- Offer nontraditional options for students to display their understandings and for teachers to assess (such as role-play, media, and art).
- Find appropriate services and donations of clothing and school supplies from local civic organizations.
- Be informed of appropriate services from the school, such as the free lunch program.
- Meet with parents at the shelter rather than at school.
- Minimize enrollment delays.
- Provide shelter staff with copies of homework assignments, newsletters, and calendars.

This has been a discussion of but a few of the special challenges teachers face every day with their students. The list of potential special needs is far from exhausted. The important thing for teachers to remember is that all children are entitled to life, liberty, and the pursuit of happiness. Our job as teachers is to support these rights. We can begin by making all children feel welcome, wanted, secure, and successful.

Instructional Strategies for Individual Differences

We now consider some of the broader approaches to managing today's diversity. However, remember this: Before you do anything with your students, you must get to know them. It is essential that you observe and evaluate your students so you know what their special gifts and needs are. Then remember to frequently reevaluate the effort and progress of each of your students.

Assistive Technology

Assistive technology gives students with special needs access to instruction. With this assistance, regular education teachers are better able to include all students in the instruction and learning.

Differentiated Instruction

When teachers differentiate instruction, they use alternative ways to deliver content instruction. They also vary the process by which students can make sense of the content or they provide various ways for students to demonstrate the understanding and learning they take away from the content.

Multi-Age Classes

When students of varying ages and abilities come together as a community, they are able to contribute to the learning environment. Successful multi-age classes practice differentiated instruction.

Looped Classes

Keeping teachers and students together for two or more years results in increased familiarity and understanding for the teacher, the students, and the caregivers. It increases the teacher's understanding of the students' needs and provides a better-matched academic program for them. It also increases student and caregiver confidence in the teacher.

Team Teaching

Teachers at the same grade level can agree to team teach. They share students, but because they teach specific subjects or ability levels, they may see different students at different times. Team teaching maximizes the teachers' instructional time and energies, but requires cooperation, planning, coordination, and flexibility.

Student Study Teams (SSTs)

The regular education teacher generally initiates these teams of interested adults. In addition to the teacher and the parents or guardians, the team may include former teachers, an administrator, and a counselor or other service provider. The primary goal of the participants is to review the student's apparent needs and develop a plan of action to further investigate and then best meet the needs.

Individualized Education Programs (IEPs)

PL 94-142 describes the conditions of IEPs. Regular and special education teachers, parents or guardians, and other involved parties together develop educational plans for individual students. IEPs must be referenced to the core curriculum. Also, they must include statements of the student's current performance, long- and short-range goals for the student, details of the nature and duration of instructional services for meeting the goals, as well as an overview of the intended evaluation methods.

Supplementary Pullout Instruction

Sometimes students are best taught when they leave a classroom for special instruction. Although this sounds out of line with the essence of inclusion, it is not. For some students, pullout instruction is used to reinforce skills being taught in the classroom. For students with higher abilities, pullout instruction is another way to enrich their educational program.

Probably the biggest challenge related to pullout programs is organizing the schedule. Schedules must be planned carefully so students do not miss or interrupt important instruction. This means coordinating times with other teachers, service providers, and resource specialists, and staying on schedule in your own classroom.

Transitions require finessing, as well, so they are not disruptive. Teachers must think about students both as they leave and return to the class. Because students need to be brought into the current instruction or activity quickly, teachers should

- Establish and practice routines for transitions: leaving and entering the classroom, locating appropriate materials, and the like.
- Establish and practice clear behavior expectations.
- Post organizers and visual instructional plans for activities and assignments for students to refer to as they begin to work.
- Arrange for partners or buddies to help students settle into the activity or assignment.
- Have shorter activities available for the rest of the class to work on while the teacher helps the returning or new students.

Contracts

Contracts provide individualized agreements for student's work, effort, and behavior. They include the specific goals or objectives, relevant materials, assessment expectations, and incentives. Further, contracts are agreed to by the teacher and the student. Because contracts are individualized, they give the teacher and student the opportunity to modify the activity or assignment in ways that are best for the student. Contracts may also extend to involve parents or guardians and align with home behavior and work expectations.

Learning Groups and Partner Learning

Partners or groups of up to six students often provide learning benefits. Spencer Kagan (1994) describes four principles that are essential for cooperative groups: positive interdependence, individual accountability, equal participation, and simultaneous interaction (PIES). Additionally, teachers should remember two other facts about groups: (1) Group structure must be taught and rehearsed; groups don't simply happen. To be successful, students must learn and practice the skills of cooperation such as listening, sharing, and being responsible; (2) Groups seem to work best when every student in the group has a specific job with specific responsibility to contribute to the group effort, and is accountable for that responsibility. For example, literacy circles in groups of five might have a discussion director, a character captain, a summarizer, an illustrator, and a materials manager. (You may wish to revisit Chapter 6 about cooperative learning.)

Peer and Cross-Age Tutors, and Cross-Grade Partnerships

Most of us learn better when we have to teach someone else. Cross-age tutors and cross-grade partners provide another opportunity for individualized assistance and attention. For the older students, the experience provides the opportunity to be a mentor and a role model to someone younger. The younger children enjoy individual attention from someone who is closer to their age and experience.

Special Programs

Special programs involving community, businesses, and foundation partnerships exist around the country. Several of these were mentioned in the chapter. These programs support academic achievement and social growth and offer enrichment activities for all children.

This brings to an end our consideration of the management of special groups of students. In our next chapter we look deeper into how to manage overall student behavior. Before moving ahead, please take time to explore these end-of-chapter activities.

Parting Thought

Knowledge is of two kinds:
We know a subject ourselves or
We know where we can find information upon it.

—Samuel Johnson

SUMMARY SELF-CHECK

Check off the following as you either understand or become able to apply them.

❑ Inclusive schools are a way of life, an attitude that values all children.

❑ Exceptionality includes a wide range of students, including
  - Students with lower abilities
  - Students with higher abilities
  - Students with communicative disorders

❑
- Students with sensory challenges such as hearing or visual impairment
- Students with behavioral concerns
- Students with physical and health disorders

❑ Students with attention deficit disorder and attention deficit hyperactive disorder have difficulties with attention, hyperactivity, impulse control, emotional stability, or some combination of these.

❑ Language diversity is independent of ethnicity and race.
- *English learner* is a more positive label that celebrates the student's growing resource advantage of having two languages instead of one.
- English learners need many opportunities to practice basic interpersonal communication skills (BICS), cognitive academic language proficiency (CALP), and listening, speaking, reading, and writing.

❑ Family diversity is a broad category of family and life situations that includes challenges related to separation, divorce, and blended families; latchkey children; and homelessness.

❑ Strategies for managing individual differences include differentiated instruction, multi-age classes, looped classes, team teaching, Student Study Teams (SST), Individualized Education Programs (IEP), supplementary pullout programs, contracts, learning groups, peer and cross-age tutors, and cross-grade partnerships.

ACTIVITIES FOR REFLECTION AND GROWTH

For Cumulative Skills Development

1. Take a moment to review the statements in the Anticipation–Reaction Guide at the beginning of this chapter. Put a check mark in the Reaction column next to any statement with which you now agree. How have your thoughts changed since reading this chapter?

2. In your opinion, which of the diversity issues discussed in the chapter pose the greatest challenge to the teacher? To the students who are in that group? To other students in the class? Describe how you will include these students (and their caregivers) into your class community.

3. Anticipate that you have a new fifth grader who is an English learner. How will you instruct that student in language arts and reading? Math? Social studies or science? How will your instruction be different if the student is a primary (K–2) student rather than an intermediate (3–6) student?

4. How will you adapt your classroom, instruction, and activities to include a student who is in a wheelchair?

5. Describe how you will use peer and cross-age tutors and a buddy class for your first graders. What kinds of activities might you have the two classes work on together?

6. Write a sample contract to use with a student with higher ability who is interested in studying about immigration during the fifth grade unit on the topic. Write a sample contract to use with a student with lower ability for the same unit.

REFERENCES AND RECOMMENDED READINGS

Annie E. Casey Foundation. (2002). *Kids count data book, 2002*. Baltimore: Author.

Cartwright, G., Cartwright, C., & Ward, M. (1984). *Educating special learners* (2nd ed.). Belmont, CA: Wadsworth.

Cary, S. (1997). *Second language learners*. Los Angeles: Galef Institute.

Center for the Study of Social Policy. (1992). *What the 1990 census tells us about children*. Washington, DC: Author.

The changing lives of children [Special issue]. (1997, April). *Educational Leadership*. Alexandria, VA: Association for Supervision and Curriculum Development.

Children's Defense Fund. (1994). *Child poverty data from the 1990 census*. Washington, DC: Author.

Cole, R. (Ed.). (1995). *Educating everybody's children: Diverse teaching strategies for diverse learners*. Alexandria, VA: Association for Supervision and Curriculum Development.

Cruickshank, D., Bainer, D., & Metcalf, K. (1999). *The act of teaching* (2nd ed.). Boston: McGraw-Hill.

Da Costa Nunez, R., & Collignon, K. (1997, October). Creating a community of learning for homeless children. *Educational Leadership, 55*(2), 56–60.

Dembo, M. (1994). *Applying educational psychology* (5th ed.). White Plains, NY: Longman.

Divorce Rates in Families with Children. (n.d.). Retrieved December 18, 2003, from www.divorce reform.org/chilrate.html

Dwyer, K., Richardson, J., Danley, K., Hansen, W., Sussman, S., Brannon, B., et al. (1990, September). Characteristics of eighth grade students who initiate self-care in elementary and junior high school. *Pediatrics, 86*(3), 448–454.

Falvey, M., Givner, C., & Kimm, C. (1995). What is an inclusive school? In R. Villa & J. Thousand (Eds.), *Creating an inclusive school*. (1995). Alexandria, VA: Association for Supervision and Curriculum Development.

Federal Register. (1977, August 23). Washington, DC: U.S. Government Printing Office.

Gifted and Talented Students Act of 1978, PL 95-561. (1978).

Glick, P., & Lin, S. (1986). Recent changes in divorce and remarriage. *Journal of Marriage and the Family, 48*, 737–741.

Good, T., & Brophy, J. (2002). *Looking into classrooms* (8th ed.). New York: Longman.

Individual with Disabilities Act (IDEA) of 1990, PL 101-476. (1990).

Kagan, S. (1994). *Cooperative learning*. San Clemente, CA: Resources for Teachers.

Kirk, S., & Gallagher, J. (1996). *Educating exceptional children* (8th ed.). Boston: Houghton Mifflin.

Krashen, S. (1985). *Inquiries and insights*. Hayward, CA: Alemany Press.

Krashen, S., & Terrell, T. (1996). *The natural approach: Language acquisition in the classroom*. Oxford: Pergamon.

Long, L., & Long, T. (1989). Latchkey adolescents: How administrators can respond to their needs. *NASSP Bulletin, 73*, 102–108.

Lucent Technologies. (1999). *Reinventing today's classrooms with wireless technology*. www.wavelan.com/educational

National Center for Education Statistics. (2003). *Digest of Education Statistics, 2002* (NCES 2003-060). Washington, DC.

National Center for Education Statistics. (2003). *Overview of Public Elementary and Secondary Schools and Districts School Year 2001–02*. Retrieved December 18, 2003, from http://nces.ed.gov/pubs2003/overview03/table_10.asp

National Clearinghouse for English Language Acquisition. (2002). *Survey of the states' limited English proficient students and available educational programs and services*. Washington, DC: George Washington University, National Clearinghouse for English Language Acquisition.

National Coalition for the Homeless (2001, June). *Homeless families with children* (NCH Fact Sheet #7). Retrieved December 15, 2003, from www.nationalhomeless.org

Orlich, D., Harder, R., Callahan, R., & Gibson, H. (2001). *Teaching strategies: A guide to better instruction* (6th ed.). Boston: Houghton Mifflin.

Pearpoint, J., & Forest, M. (1992). Foreword. In S. Stainback & W. Stainback (Eds.), *Curriculum considerations in inclusive classrooms: Facilitating learning for all students.* Baltimore: Paul H. Brookes.

Poplin, M. (1992). Educating in diversity. *Executive Educator, 14*(3), A18–A24.

Race, class, and culture [Special issue]. (1999, April). *Educational Leadership.* Alexandria, VA: Association for Supervision and Curriculum Development.

Reauthorization of IDEA of 1997. (1997).

Rief, S., & Heimburge, J. (1996). *How to reach and teach all students in the inclusive classroom.* West Nyack, NY: Center for Applied Research in Education.

Ryan, K., & Cooper, J. (2000). *Those who can, teach* (9th ed.). Boston: Houghton Mifflin.

Schifini, A. (1988). *Sheltered English: Content area instruction for limited English proficient students.* Downey, CA: Los Angeles County Office of Education.

Schools as safe havens [Special issue]. (1997, October). *Educational Leadership.* Alexandria, VA: Association for Supervision and Curriculum Development.

Smith, D. (2004). *Introduction to special education: Teaching in an age of opportunity* (5th ed.). Boston: Pearson/Allyn & Bacon.

U.S. Census Bureau (2003). *Language use and English-speaking ability: 2000.* Retrieved December 18, 2003, from www.census.gov/prod/2003pubs/c2kbr-29.pdf

U.S. Census Bureau Public Information Office. (2003, October 8). News release. Retrieved December 18, 2003, from www.census.gov/Press-Release/www/releases/archives/census_2000/001406.html

U.S. Conference of Mayors. (1994). *Status report on hunger and homelessness in America's cities.* Washington, DC: Author.

U.S. Conference of Mayors. (2000). *Status report on hunger and homelessness in America's cities.* Washington, DC: Author.

U.S. Department of Health and Human Services. (2002). *HHS programs and initiatives to combat homelessness.* Retrieved December 18, 2003, from www.hhs.gov/news/press/2002pres/homeless.html

Van Ripper, C. (1978). *Speech correction: Principles and methods* (6th ed.). Englewood Cliffs, NJ: Prentice-Hall.

Villa, R., & Thousand, J. (Eds.). (1995). *Creating an inclusive school.* Alexandria, VA: Association for Supervision and Curriculum Development.

Wallerstein, J., & Kelly, J. (1980). *Surviving the breakup.* New York: Basic Books.

Wallis, C. (1994, July 18), Life in overdrive. *Time, 144*(3), 50.

Whelan, R., & Gallagher, P. (1972). Effective teaching of children with behavior disorders. In N. G. Haring & A. H. Hayden (Eds.), *The improvement of instruction.* Seattle: Special Child Publications.

Woods, C. (1996, November). Hope for homeless students. *Educational Leadership, 54*(3), 58–60.

Ysseldyke, J., & Algozzine, B. (1995). *Special education: A practical approach for teachers* (3rd ed.). Boston: Houghton Mifflin.

9 Managing Student Behavior

Everyone stood in awe of the lion tamer in the cage, with half a dozen lions all under the control of his "consequences." Everyone, that is, except the teacher . . .

—June Dostal

ANTICIPATION–REACTION GUIDE

Before you read the chapter, take a moment to put a check mark in the Anticipation column next to any statement with which you agree.

	Anticipation	Reaction
Discipline usually heads the list of teacher concerns about education.	❏	❏
Kounin says successful behavior management relates to *withitness* and lesson management.	❏	❏
Dreikurs and Albert believe that behavior comes from a need to belong, and individuals may choose mistaken goals in order to satisfy this need.	❏	❏
The Canters insisted that nothing should be allowed to interfere with students' right to learn and teachers' right to teach.	❏	❏
After studying teachers who seemed naturally adept at discipline, Jones made his greatest contribution by identifying and focusing on several clusters of teacher skills.	❏	❏
Glasser contends that cooperative group work helps meet students' need for belonging.	❏	❏
Kagan, Kyle, and Scott define student positions as where the student is coming from.	❏	❏
Coloroso, in responding to student mistakes, mischief, and mayhem, applies the three Rs (restitution, resolution, and reconciliation) to all situations.	❏	❏
Looking at situations in light of a hierarchy of social behavior removes the action from the person.	❏	❏
A good discipline plan meets students' needs; teacher needs are basically irrelevant to its success.	❏	❏

How Serious Is Disruptive Behavior?

Disruptive behavior in the classroom is any behavior that interferes with productive teaching and learning. Charles (2005) pinpoints it as any behavior that, through intent or thoughtlessness, (1) interferes with teaching or learning, (2) threatens or intimidates others, or (3) oversteps society's standards of moral, ethical, or legal behavior. Fred Jones (2000) noted that teachers in a typical classroom lose about one half of their teaching time because of students' disruptive behavior. Such behavior is not always bad behavior. It is usually nothing more than talking, goofing off, or moving about the room without permission. Disruptions, even those considered benign, lower achievement and often damage class morale. Consider the following:

- Regarding students' right to learn: Students who make irresponsible choices disrupt learning for themselves and others, which in turn leads to lowered academic achievement.
- Regarding teachers' right to teach: Disruptive behavior interferes with the teacher's basic right to teach, which also affects student learning and produces much teacher frustration.
- Regarding wasted time: Teachers dealing with classroom disruptions lose enormous amounts of time that would and should be devoted to instruction—the 50 percent that Jones observed.
- Regarding stress, motivation, and energy: Disruptive behavior increases stress and weakens motivation and energy by wearing on teachers and students and perpetuating a poor attitude toward learning.
- Regarding classroom climate: Disruptive behavior can at times produce a climate of fearfulness and stress for students and teachers alike.
- Regarding teacher–student relationships: Disruptive behavior dissolves trust so cooperative relationships never adequately develop.

Many beginning teachers have naive expectations of students. They believe that if the teacher is caring, students will make responsible choices and will behave appropriately—they will be orderly, courteous, respectful, honest, considerate of property and others, willing to work, and relatively quiet. But what those teachers often encounter are minor but ongoing misbehaviors and even unruliness that in some cases escalate to open hostility, defiance, and physical aggression. Although 95 percent of disruptive behavior involves little more than talking, moving about the room without permission, and simply wasting time, almost all teachers report that disruptive behavior interferes with their teaching, sometimes greatly (Jones, 2000).

The disquieting fact is that student behavior, reflective of society in general, continues to worsen. In fact, Curwin and Mendler (1997) have observed these trends:

- More students now are disruptive than in the past, and the rate is increasing.
- Children are becoming more disruptive at younger ages.
- Children are more violent.
- Many children lack any feeling of caring or remorse.
- Teachers describe students as more aggressive and hostile.

It is no wonder that for more than three decades, both the public and teachers have repeatedly ranked discipline (meaning misbehavior in the classroom) at or very near the top of their concerns about teaching. (See the Gallup polls concerning attitude toward education, published annually since 1969 in *Phi Delta Kappan.*)

Is the Discipline Situation Hopeless?

The answer to that question is clearly no. The best elementary teachers have long practiced the time-honored Golden Rule to reach their students. They treat children as they want to be treated themselves. They are humane. They care and try. They love their students, or try to, and want to be respected in return. When that didn't work in the past, teachers could demand, scold, speak sternly, threaten, and keep students in after school—all to force students to conduct themselves appropriately. Teachers also had the backing of administrators, caregivers, and the community.

But that condition has changed. Students have lost their respect for teachers and principals. They can—and do—swear at and argue with the teacher with impunity. Caregivers are likely to side with their child in disputes with the teacher. Principals fear, with good reason, that a disgruntled parent will protest before the school board or even file a lawsuit against the teacher, the principal, or the school. The old coercive tactics for enforcing behavior are no longer viable, and teachers who still rely on them, for the most part, are doomed to ineffectiveness and depression.

The Movement toward New Discipline

Thousand, Villa, and Nevin (2002) depict effective discipline as a pyramid (see Figure 9.1). Prevention is the base and strength of the pyramid. Prevention is accomplished by establishing a classroom of caring and interdependence, with effective routines and procedures. The next level in the pyramid consists of quick, nonintrusive responses to stop distractions and disruptions. When a disruption cannot be resolved in the classroom, children go somewhere else. In a place away from others, students can calm down, think, and problem solve under adult guidance in order to return to the classroom quickly. The apex of the pyramid consists of caring individuals who collaborate to establish plans to bring about long-term change in student behavior.

What Major Authorities Say about Discipline

A number of authorities, past and present, have made suggestions and devised techniques that greatly help teachers minimize disruptive behavior in the classroom. Here we will briefly review selected contributions.

Jacob Kounin. Jacob Kounin (1970) explored differences between teachers good at classroom control and those poor at it and found that good managers (1) project an image of being in charge in the classroom and (2) efficiently manage lessons and transitions between lessons.

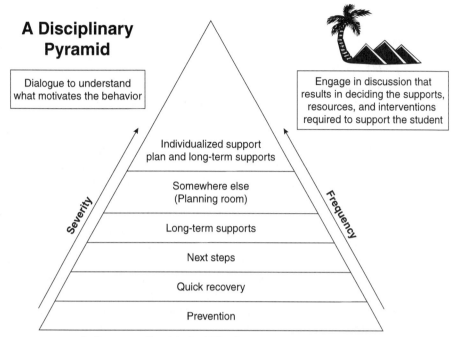

FIGURE 9.1   A Conceptualization for Effective Disciplinary Systems

(From Villa, R. A., Udis, J., & Thousand, J. S. (2002). Supporting students with troubling behavior. In J. S. Thousand, R. A. Villa, & A. I. Nevin (Eds.), *Creativity and collaborative learning: The practical guide to empowering students, teachers, and families* (p. 143). Baltimore: Paul H. Brookes Publishing Co.; reprinted by permission.)

With regard to being in charge, Kounin isolated two significant skills, which he called *withitness* and *overlapping*. Withitness is knowing what is going on in every part of the classroom at every moment, in a way that is evident to students. Overlapping refers to the ability to deal with at least two issues simultaneously. For example, if the teacher is working with a small group and disruptive behavior occurs elsewhere in the room, the teacher overlaps by correcting the disruptive behavior without leaving the small group or interrupting its activity.

With regard to lesson management, Kounin identified several important skills, among them focus, attention, accountability, pacing, momentum, and efficient transitions between activities. Each of these skills, if not accomplished well, allows for inattentive dead time that encourages disruptive behavior. *Focus* is obtained by making sure students know what they are supposed to do and why. *Attention* is obtained through motivation and specific directions. *Accountability* (student responsibility) is obtained by calling on students to respond, interpret, comment, discuss, and demonstrate. *Pacing* depends on timing that ensures efficient coverage of activities, ending at the appropriate time. *Momentum* is evident in steady progression through the lesson, without slowdown or frantic rush. *Transitions* from one activity to another depend on established routines that ensure rapid changeover.

Kounin's work focused on the role good lesson management plays in discipline. Because he did not study techniques used by good disciplinarians to correct disruptive behavior, his work was never considered a well-rounded approach to discipline. However, his suggestions on lesson management are incorporated into most of the discipline systems used today.

Rudolf Dreikurs and Linda Albert.   Psychiatrist Rudolf Dreikurs (Dreikurs & Cassel, 1972; Dreikurs, Grunwald, & Pepper, 1982) considered discipline to be an ongoing process in which students learn to impose limits on themselves. His procedure made no use of punishment because he considered it counterproductive in teaching students to control themselves. Dreikurs suggested that teachers and students should collaborate on procedures that offer order, limits, firmness, kindness, freedom to explore, teacher leadership, and frequent opportunities for students to choose their own acceptable behavior.

Dreikurs maintained that all students are motivated by a predominant goal: to feel that they belong—to the group, to the classroom, to the school. They behave acceptably if they attain that goal of belonging. Otherwise, they turn progressively to mistaken goals—attention getting, power, revenge, and withdrawal. The essence of classroom discipline for Dreikurs involves teachers helping students to gain a sense of belonging and to choose acceptable behavior. Dreikurs made four suggestions for dealing with student misbehavior.

He suggested that teachers first establish democratic classrooms that allow students to gain their primary goal of belonging. This will cause most, though not all, discipline problems to disappear. Second, when disruptive behavior does occur, teachers should identify the student's mistaken goal and confront the student with it: "You would like me to pay attention to you, wouldn't you?" or "Could it be that you want to show that I can't make you do this work?" Third, teachers must make sure that disruptive behavior is always followed by reasonable consequences. Consequences, never hurtful acts, are activities students dislike, such as staying after school or completing an assignment at home that should have been done in class. Fourth, teachers must always remain helpful and encourage students to improve.

Dreikurs's work has been widely acknowledged as beneficial in developing student self-control and responsible behavior. Linda Albert (2003) has built on Dreikurs's work by providing a process that teachers, students, administrators, and caregivers can easily implement. Her approach, called *cooperative discipline,* holds that behavior is based on choice, and the choices students make are based on the basic need to belong. To this end, students must feel capable, connected, and able to contribute to the group. Students unable to feel belonging misbehave in ways that correspond to the mistaken goals Dreikurs had described. Albert's program of helping strategies for students also includes a classroom code of conduct, cooperative conflict resolution, school and home action plans, and student and caregiver involvement as partners in the discipline process. Fifth-grade teacher Devora Garrison tells a story about the school code of conduct she uses in her class.

> For behavior I use the school code of conduct, which we call "Life Skills" in class. If students break a school rule (such as no homework, which falls under "responsibility"), they sign in the binder under that section and then take a reflection sheet. The sheet has spaces for the student's name; the life skill that needs work; what the student specifically did; why it's important not to break that life skill; and parent, teacher, and student signatures. I don't accept "so I don't get in trouble" as a reason.

Imagine the shock of one of my students when we went into parent–teacher–student conferences and I reminded him that reflection slips would be discussed—he effectively had been forging his dad's signature. One chastised boy and two embarrassed parents showed up to discuss the slips!

The Canters.   Lee Canter and Marlene Canter (Canter & Canter, 1992, 1993, 2001) are authors of *Assertive Discipline,* a widely used system of classroom discipline today. Their approach, originally published in 1976, was an instant success. The Canters insisted on students' rights to learn and teachers' rights to teach, and said that nothing, especially student misbehavior, should be allowed to interfere with either.

The Canters went on to say that teachers have the right to a calm, quiet classroom if that's what they need in order to teach well. Teachers have the right to expect students to behave in ways that do not defeat their best interests. They have the right to expect backing from their administrators and support from parents or guardians. And they have the right to a classroom in which quality teaching and learning can occur. Teachers appreciated this approach because no one ever so strongly championed their cause before.

According to the Canters, the logic of assertive discipline holds that

- Teachers have the right to teach in a professional manner, without disruption.
- Students have the right to learn in a safe, calm environment, with full support of professional educators and others.
- These rights are best met by in-charge teachers who do not violate students' best interests.
- Trust, respect, and perseverance enable teachers to earn student cooperation.

The Canters maintain that these goals can be met by

- Maintaining a calm, productive classroom environment
- Meeting students' needs for learning and ensuring that their rights are attended to
- Helping the teacher remain calmly and nonstressfully in charge of the classroom

Overall, assertive discipline is an approach that allows teachers to apply positive support and corrective actions calmly and fairly. It provides techniques for teaching students how to behave properly, for gaining student trust and cooperation, and for dealing with students whose behavior is difficult to manage.

Fred Jones.   Fred Jones (1987, 2000), formerly a clinical psychologist, developed and now directs popular training programs in procedures for managing classrooms and discipline. Unlike Kounin and Dreikurs, whose suggestions were valuable but not capable of achieving quick results, Jones intended his program to be effective, easy to implement, and able to quickly produce results.

Jones's research found that although most teachers fear crisis events such as fighting and blatant defiance to authority, these rarely occur, even in hard-to-manage classes. The reality is that about 80 percent of all disruptive behavior is little more than talking without

Dave Carpenter...

" I LEARNED THAT FIFTEEN MINUTES OF FAME ON
THE PLAYGROUND EQUALS ONE HOUR OF DETENTION.

permission, and another 15 percent is almost entirely students moving about the room when they should be in their seats, or generally goofing off by daydreaming, making inappropriate noises, and the like.

Jones also found that most teachers can recoup teaching time that otherwise is lost. They begin by arranging the room to allow for them to work the crowd as they move among students during seatwork and by setting limits through effective body language. Then they use several clusters of skills—Say, See, Do Teaching; providing incentive systems; and giving efficient help.

Efficient classroom arrangement improves the likelihood of successful teaching, learning, and behavior. Limit setting involves clarifying the boundaries of acceptable behavior, then formulating rules accordingly. Jones's rules describe procedures: how students are to do their work, what they should do if materials are needed, what to do when unable to proceed on their own, and what to do when finished with an assignment.

Because body language, according to Jones, is the teacher's most effective tool in enforcing boundaries on acceptable behavior, it receives considerable emphasis in this system. Effective body language projects the message that the teacher means business. Jones claims that teachers can prevent 90 percent of normal discipline problems with calm breathing, physical proximity to students, body position, facial expression, tone of voice, and eye contact. Here are two examples:

An Li stops following the math lesson and is thinking about the new puppies at home. She hears Ms. Eckert pause. She looks at Ms. Eckert and finds her looking at her (eye contact). An Li straightens herself and waits attentively.

Shawn stops working and talks to Jerry. Suddenly he sees Ms. Eckert's shadow (physical proximity). Immediately he gets back to work, without anything said.

Say, See, Do Teaching keeps students actively involved during instruction by asking them to respond frequently to teacher input. Incentive systems are like carrots before the horse's nose. Jones suggests using preferred activity time (PAT) because it offers something students want, and students know they will get it only if they work and behave as they should. Ms. Eckert tells her class that all who completely finish their homework assignments every day for a week can participate in a game of Jeopardy at the end of the day on Friday. Questions for the game will reinforce what the students study during the week.

Providing efficient help is one of Jones's most useful suggestions. Suppose that Ms. Eckert demonstrated a long-division algorithm and students practiced under her guidance before she assigned them problems to complete at their seats. Soon eight students raise their hands. Describing situations such as this one, Jones asked teachers how much time they thought they spent helping individual students during seatwork. Teachers thought one or two minutes, but Jones observed that the actual average was four minutes per student. This is a long time for other students to sit doing nothing—until they misbehave.

To keep students working instead of misbehaving, Jones offers two suggestions. First, teachers should use visual instructional plans and graphic reminders to which students can refer instead of calling for the teacher. Second, teachers should give students enough help *in twenty seconds or less* to get them back on track. Teachers give this help in three steps: (1) comment on what the student has done correctly (an optional step after the first interaction), (2) give a direct suggestion or clue to get the student back on track, such as "The next thing to do is . . . " and (3) leave immediately. This rapid procedure enables teachers to provide help to all who need it while deterring helpless handraising and the dependency syndrome in which students rely on the teacher's presence before doing their work.

William Glasser.   William Glasser has developed, refined, and popularized an approach to teaching that provides motivation and helps students make good behavioral choices while taking responsibility for their actions. He calls his approach *choice theory,* which Glasser says helps everyone become more realistic about human behavior (see Glasser, 1998). He describes how choice theory can be used to establish learning environments that lead to success and quality. The following are some of the main tenets of choice theory:

- We can control no one's behavior except our own.
- We cannot successfully make a person do anything. All we can do is open possibilities and provide information.

- All behavior is best understood as *total behavior,* composed of four components: act-ing, thinking, feeling, and physiology (how we function).
- All total behavior is chosen, but we only have direct control over the acting and think-ing components. In other words, we can choose how to act and how to think. Feeling and physiology are controlled indirectly through how we choose to act and think.
- What we do is not automatically determined by external causes. It is primarily deter-mined by what goes on inside us.
- One way to improve behavior is through clarifying what a quality existence would be like, and planning the choices that would help achieve that existence. In the class-room, this process occurs best when teachers establish warm, trusting relationships with students.

Applications of choice theory to the classroom are seen in the work of consultants and trainers Kathy Curtiss and Steven English (2003), who have been providing services to schools across the country for many years. Curtiss and English advocate using classroom meetings, integrating character development into curriculum content, and developing instructional strategies that lead to student ownership of learning. They also work on strengthening student reflection and self-evaluation, with the aim of increasing students' responsibility for making the most of their educational opportunity. They recommend the use of portfolios and assessment rubrics (procedures) based on standards, as well as devel-oping stronger partnerships between teachers and students. They point out that these provi-sions accomplish little unless the classroom is imbued with trust and respect and students learn to resolve their problems without hurting each other. Instructional strategies that make this possible include cooperative learning, conflict resolution, classroom meetings, and character education.

Spencer Kagan, Patricia Kyle, and Sally Scott.   Spencer Kagan and Patricia Kyle have independently researched and written about classroom discipline for nearly twenty years. Together with Sally Scott, they have collaborated to describe an approach they call *win-win discipline* (2004). Kagan, Kyle, and Scott say that the ultimate goal of discipline is for stu-dents to be able to manage themselves autonomously and meet their needs through respon-sible choices. They believe that responsible behavior links closely to curriculum, instruction, and management, and that discipline is something acquired by students, not something done to students. Any behavior that interrupts the learning process reflects a lack of acquired dis-cipline and is a good opportunity for students to learn skills of self-discipline.

Accordingly, win-win discipline emphasizes a "we" approach to working with stu-dents to produce long-term learned responsibility. This approach involves three fundamen-tal principles that Kagan, Kyle, and Scott call "the three pillars":

- Same Side: teacher understands where the student is coming from and teams up with the student to find discipline solutions
- Collaborative Solutions: teacher and student share responsibility for co-creating dis-cipline solutions
- Learned Responsibility: student acquires long-term responsible behavior that is nondisruptive

Kagan, Kyle, and Scott show teachers how to identify the type of misbehavior as well as the condition that is prompting students to misbehave at any given time. The four main types of disruptive behavior are aggression, breaking rules, confrontation, and disengagement (ABCD disruptive behaviors). They tell teachers *what* students do. Kagan, Kyle, and Scott refer to the conditions as *positions*. Positions tell teachers *why* students do what they do. The positions are

- Attention-seeking—seeking to be recognized; to receive caring, concern, love
- Avoiding failure—seeking to avoid looking foolish or unsuccessful in front of others
- Angry—seeking to express one's anger
- Control-seeking—seeking to establish the sense of being in charge and able to make one's own choices
- Bored—seeking stimulation
- Energetic—seeking to release energy
- Uninformed—not knowing which behavior is appropriate for the situation

These positions are part of the human condition. We all find ourselves in these positions regularly. What one does is seek responsible, nondisruptive ways of behaving when in these positions. Identifying and understanding a student's position does not mean that the teacher allows or affirms the disruption. Nor does it mean that the teacher tries to change the position. The teacher deals with the disruption by validating the position, maintaining the student's dignity, and helping the student toward responsible behavior.

Kagan, Kyle, and Scott give teachers a myriad of concrete structures—step-by-step sequences of interactions—to use for the moment of disruption, follow up, and long-term solutions. They place heavy emphasis on preventative strategies aligned with each of the positions, as well as the importance of integrating life skill instruction as part of the discipline program. They also advocate that teachers and students create jointly written class agreements, and that teachers develop parent and community alliances to make win-win solutions work for everyone. Ginny Lorenz shares something one of her fourth graders wrote about class rules:

> Perhaps the best statement for allowing students a hand in the writing of classroom rules came from one of my students. At the end of the year I ask students to write a letter to the incoming fourth graders. Alex wrote, "I will always remember fourth grade because I finally felt good about me. When I came to fourth grade everybody didn't like me because I always got in trouble. Nobody would let me play at their house because they had heard about me at school. This year we talked about rules and picked the ones we wanted. I found out I could be good. I found out I could even be a good student." Alex was correct; he found out that when he controlled his own behavior he could be a good student. I did not control Alex's behavior. He and the other students took care of their own behavior because they felt that they had a say in what was important and they felt that they truly belonged.

Barbara Coloroso. Barbara Coloroso, who writes and consults widely on discipline, believes that all students are worth the effort teachers can expend on them—not just when they are bright, good looking, or well behaved, but always. She asserts that in order for teachers to have good discipline, they must do three things. Teachers must treat students with respect and dignity. They must give students a sense of positive power over their own lives. Finally, teachers must give students opportunities to make decisions, take responsibility for their actions, and learn from their successes and mistakes.

Proper discipline, according to Coloroso, does four things punishment cannot do. First, it shows students what they have done wrong, in contrast with punishment that merely tells. Second, it gives students ownership of the problems. An important goal is for children to develop an inner discipline by learning how to think, not just what to think. To this end, teachers must give students responsibility and ownership by allowing them to make mistakes, and by guiding them to accept the natural or reasonable consequences of their actions. For students the certainty, not the severity of consequences will have effect. Third, proper discipline provides students with ways to solve subsequent problems they may encounter. And fourth, proper discipline leaves students' dignity intact.

Coloroso explains her ideas in her books *Kids Are Worth It! Giving Your Child the Gift of Inner Discipline* (1994), *Parenting with Wit and Wisdom in Times of Chaos and Loss* (1999), and *The Bully, the Bullied, and the Bystander* (2002). She describes three categories of misbehavior, with indications of what teachers can do to help students. The categories are called mistakes, mischief, and mayhem.

Mistakes are simple errors that provide opportunity for learning better choices. When an excited Brent accidentally scribbles on the table rather than his paper, he can help scrub the table clean, and the teacher can cover the table with paper to avoid future mishaps.

Mischief, while not necessarily serious, is intentional misbehavior. It provides opportunity to help students find ways to fix what was done wrong and to avoid doing it again, while retaining their dignity. If Beth tears apart a book because she likes the pictures and wants to keep them in her desk, she should work out a payment plan with the teacher and her parents to replace the damaged book.

Mayhem is willfully serious misbehavior. It calls for application of the three Rs (restitution, resolution, and reconciliation) for guidance in helping students take responsibility and accept consequences. *Restitution* has the student repair or compensate for the damage. *Resolution* allows the student to identify and correct whatever caused the misbehavior so it won't happen again. *Reconciliation* helps students complete the process of healing the relationships with people who were hurt by the misbehavior. Consider fifth grader Marcy. When she was not selected for the soccer team, Marcy broke the team captain's arm by willfully pushing her against the wall. With the help of an insightful and supportive coach, Marcy offered to take notes for Amy, the captain, so Amy could keep up in class. In addition to apologizing to Amy and her parents, the coach, and the other team members, Marcy participated in an anger management program sponsored by the neighborhood youth club. There she was able to clarify what she did, why she did it, and what she learned from the experience. She was also able to develop alternative anger management strategies so she could make better choices in the future.

In her newest book, Coloroso examines the bully, the bullied, and the bystander, all participants in the cycle of violence, a reality in today's schools. Bullies instill fear in others; they intend to hurt, and they enjoy it. Bystanders follow or support bullies, or do nothing to stop the action. Teachers must be willing to confront the problem and work with students for awareness, a safe environment, and solutions.

Marvin Marshall.   Marvin Marshall has been a teacher, counselor, and administrator at all levels of public education. He presents a system for managing student behavior based on raising students' levels of responsibility. He explains the approach in his book *Discipline without Stress, Punishments, or Rewards: How Teachers and Parents Promote Responsibility and Learning* (2002), and in his monthly newsletter entitled *Raising Responsibility.*

Marshall's plan is to raise individual responsibility so students choose to do what is right and proper. He believes that almost all students are inclined to behave responsibly. Because students may need help in doing so, Marshall believes in teaching them about the four levels of social development. With this understanding, students can reflect on their personal behavior, and with encouragement and guidance from their teachers, find ways to avoid outside destructive influences and make responsible decisions.

Marshall depicts social behavior as a hierarchy of four levels. Level A *Anarchy* and Level B *Bothering/Bossing/Bullying* are unacceptable levels of behavior. Level C *Cooperating/Conforming* is acceptable in the classroom, although students are generally relying on external motivation such as peer pressure, to guide their actions and behavior. Level D *Democracy* is the most desirable level. Through the activities Marshall suggests, students learn to make decisions based on internal motivation and take the initiative to do what is right and proper. Level D leads to self-discipline.

" YOU CAN'T REALLY WIN WITH TEACHERS. ALL YOU CAN DO IS
SEE HOW MUCH YOU CAN GET AWAY WITH. "

Marshall insists students cannot be forced to learn or behave responsibly, but they can be influenced to do so through a noncoercive approach. For example, if the student misbehaves, the teacher asks, "At what level is that behavior?" The student replies with the appropriate level (usually A or B), and the teacher asks, "What would a responsible person do?" By focusing on the hierarchy, rather than naming the misbehavior, the teacher separates the action from the student's character. This helps students understand choices and consequences, while directing students toward better self-control and self-management.

Building a System of Participative Discipline

You have seen ideas from a number of different approaches to discipline. You can use those ideas to build a system that works for you and your students. In most cases, a participative approach will serve you best. *Participative discipline* is a system in which teachers and students cooperate in making decisions about expectations, behavior, and consequences for violations of class rules or agreements. To develop a participative discipline plan, you should compile discipline techniques, sketch out the plan using those techniques, and then fine-tune the plan with your students.

Compiling Techniques

Compile a list of discipline ideas and techniques that suit the needs of your students and that match your philosophy of working with students. For example, you might (or might not) include such ideas as basic rights to teach and learn, rules, withitness, student positions, good lesson management and transitions, efficient help, incentive systems, focus on belonging, use of body language, levels of social behavior, focus on student needs, shared responsibility, and joint teacher–student ownership of the discipline plan.

Sketching Out a Plan

Outline a basic plan. At the outset, think of your discipline system as requiring the following:

1. Understanding between you and students
2. Balance between your needs and theirs
3. Formal agreements between you and them
4. Practicality of implementation
5. Vitality in ongoing use
6. Gentility in application
7. Flexibility and renewability

Summarize your ideas clearly, but wait until your discussion with your students to finalize them. Together, agree to a plan of action.

Launching Your Plan

Implement the class discipline plan by discussing your ideas with students and asking them for their reactions and suggestions. Following are some of the things to consider in each of the seven points listed above. The first three provide a sample dialogue to have with students as you launch your plan with your class. The other four are general considerations before you finalize the plan.

Understanding

1. This is our class, and if we all work together, we will create a place in which each of us feels comfortable and in which we can all enjoy the process of teaching and learning. I have a responsibility to create an environment in which this can happen, but I need your help to really make it work. Each of you must know that you are an important member of this class with important responsibilities, and you can help make it a pleasant place to be. One of your important responsibilities is to help us create a positive learning atmosphere, one where everybody's needs are met. To accomplish this, we all must work together. I suggest we begin by creating a class agreement.
2. We all have very important jobs in this class. Your job is to learn as much as you can. That means you must try your hardest, do your best work, and help everyone in the class do better. My job is to teach you as best I can, to help you, and to make learning as much fun as possible.
3. We all have very important rights in this class, and we must not let anyone interfere with them. You have a right to learn without anyone bothering you. I have a right to teach without anyone bothering me. We must not allow any kind of irresponsible behavior to take away your right to learn or my right to teach.
4. Throughout the year, we must try to do the best we can do—the best teaching from me, the best learning from you, and the best work from all of us, so we can be proud and your caregivers can be proud of you. We can have a good time doing this, working together and getting along and doing excellent work. That is how we make the best of ourselves.

Balance

1. There are many things you need to have in this room in order to do your best—you need good teaching from me, good things to learn, and pleasure in what we do together.
2. There are many things I need as well, in order to teach you best—a calm, quiet atmosphere, good manners from you, and cooperation and helpfulness toward each other.
3. What I need must be balanced with what you need. We can't have a good class if we do everything only to suit me or only to suit you. We have to balance things so that all of us can have what we need to make this class exceptionally good, and that means that all of us must be kind, considerate, and helpful to each other.

Formal Agreement

1. Suppose you were trying your best to learn something in this room. How would you want the other students to act while you were trying to learn? Let's name some

behaviors we could choose that would make us happy to be in this class and able to get our work done. (Record student responses, guiding the process so the behaviors are stated positively and apply to everyone.) What are some examples of what these behaviors look like and sound like?

2. Do you think we need rules to help us remember how we should behave when I am trying to teach and you are trying to learn? (discussion) Let's see if we can think of a rule about how each of us will try to do our work, and a rule about how each of us will behave toward others. (discussion) These are fine rules. I'll write them here on the board.

3. Let's think about what they mean, about what they tell us to do and not do. How do you feel about this list? (discussion) You seem to like these rules, and I do, too. I believe they will help us. Are you willing to adopt them as our class agreement?

4. Now suppose that most of us follow these rules, but one or two students don't. Suppose they talk loudly or run around the room. What should we do if that happens? (discussion) I think your suggestions will be good for our class.

5. You and I need to be on the same side and work together to create a classroom in which we all want to be and all can learn. You will help make decisions about the class. You will be able to have your say. We will learn and practice skills that are important for being citizens in a democratic society. Choosing responsible behavior will be one of the most important things we will learn. Tomorrow I'll have the class agreement, with the rules as well as what happens if they are broken, written on a sheet of paper. We will write our names on that paper to show that we agree with the rules and agree to follow them. Then I will make copies for you to take home for your caregivers to see.

Practicality.   Before finalizing the rules and consequences and considering the remainder of your discipline plan, keep this point foremost in mind: You have to live with the plan. It is supposed to serve your class; your class is not supposed to serve it. It must not be so complicated, difficult, or time-consuming that you are enslaved by it. Make sure the plan is easy to implement, serves its purpose, requires little extra time from you, and produces a minimum of irritation, resentment, and lost time.

Vitality.   Ideally, your discipline plan is not something apart from instruction but rather something incorporated into instruction, as essential as directions and feedback. Assuming that students see your plan as fair (and that's why you spend so much time discussing it and making sure students buy into it), it will serve wonderfully as you inject interest, novelty, fun, and importance into learning activities. It will earn continued support if, when you invoke consequences, you can stop disruptive behavior at once, then follow through calmly and helpfully, showing the personal support students prize. Also, for students, it should not be the severity but the certainty of receiving the consequence that has impact. Further, caregivers and administrators will back the plan if it is humane, obviously serves students, and is communicated well.

Gentility.   Despite the workload, frustration, and stress with which you always must contend, remember that it is your responsibility to ensure that the classroom remain a place of gentility, where students speak and act courteously, where no one's character is attacked, and where you, especially, serve as the finest model. If you and your students are to prosper, you must keep the classroom a good place in which to live and work. This requires ongoing modeling of the qualities of good character and behavior, and opportunities for students to practice them.

Flexibility and Renewability. You should begin with what you believe to be best for your students and yourself, then stick by your resolve so long as there is reason to do so. But you must remain, at the same time, eminently flexible. If something is not working, then try to change it so that it will. Discuss the problem with the students and together come up with an alternative that promises better results. It is good to routinely discuss discipline in classroom meetings, which should be held regularly. Some teachers take time at the end of every day for a short discussion of what went well and what did not, and when problems surface they arrange times for longer discussions. They want to know students' views of how things are going and what needs to be done differently. They willingly make new beginnings when warranted, knowing that sometimes a simple change for change's sake is valuable.

This concludes our consideration of discipline—of how to manage student behavior so good teaching and learning can occur within an atmosphere of gentility and helpfulness. Before we turn to the topic of how to manage the assessment of student progress, along with record keeping and reporting to caregivers and administrators, take time to explore these end-of-chapter activities.

Parting Thought

Simplicity is an acquired taste. Mankind, left free, instinctively complicates life.
—Katharine Fullerton Gerould

SUMMARY SELF-CHECK

Check off the following as you either understand or become able to apply them.

❑ Disruptive behavior causes more wasted time, more teacher stress, and more teacher burnout than all other factors combined.

❑ Student behavior is growing worse, evident in apathy, failure to work, disrespect, and open aggression.

❑ The old disciplinary technique of authoritative teacher demands no longer works.

❑ Many valuable new ideas in discipline have appeared in the past four decades:
  ▪ Jacob Kounin: withitness, effective lesson management
  ▪ Rudolf Dreikurs and Linda Albert: genuine goal of belonging; mistaken goals of attention, power, revenge, and withdrawal; choice
  ▪ Lee Canter: teacher and student rights, clear limit setting and consequences, assertive discipline
  ▪ Fred Jones: setting limits and body language; Say, See, Do Teaching; incentive systems; efficient help
  ▪ William Glasser: student choice as fundamental in teaching, discipline, and quality
  ▪ Spencer Kagan, Patricia Kyle, and Sally Scott: Same Side, Collaborative Solutions, Learned Responsibility, ABCD disruptive behaviors, student positions
  ▪ Barbara Coloroso: dealing with three categories of misbehavior (mistake, mischief, mayhem); three Rs of guidance (restitution, resolution, reconciliation); the bully, the bullied, the bystander
  ▪ Marvin Marshall: external and internal motivation; levels of social behavior (Level A Anarchy, Level B Bothering/Bossing/Bullying, Level C Cooperating/Conforming, and Level D Democracy); helping students behave more responsibly

❑ Teachers typically construct their own systems of discipline, consistent with their personality, their philosophy, and the traits of the students they teach.

❑ Steps in formulating a good personal system of discipline:
  ▪ Compile preferred techniques.
  ▪ Outline a plan that includes understanding, balance, formal agreement, practicality, vitality, gentility, flexibility and renewability.
  ▪ Fine-tune the plan after discussions with students.

ACTIVITIES FOR REFLECTION AND GROWTH

For Cumulative Skills Development

1. Take a moment to review the statements in the Anticipation–Reaction Guide at the beginning of this chapter. Put a check mark in the Reaction column next to any statement with which you now agree. How have your thoughts changed since reading this chapter?

2. Virtually all elementary students will agree that they would like to learn. Why then do they so often misbehave and make no effort to do what teachers provide for them?

3. Compile a list of specific discipline techniques that you feel best match your personality, philosophy, and needs.

4. When you were a third-grade student, under which of the various systems of discipline described in this chapter would you have preferred working? Explain.

5. Review the seven student positions that Kagan, Kyle, and Scott identify. Create kinesthetic signs (and add sounds) to convey their meanings.

6. For a grade of your choosing, describe an example of Coloroso's degrees of disruptive behavior. For the most serious misbehavior, also describe how the student might display the three Rs of restitution, resolution, and reconciliation.

REFERENCES AND RECOMMENDED READINGS

Albert, L. (2003). *Cooperative discipline.* Circle Pines, MN: American Guidance Service.

Canter, L., & Canter, M. (1992). *Assertive discipline: Positive behavior management for today's classroom.* Santa Monica, CA: Canter & Associates.

Canter, L., & Canter, M. (1993). *Lee Canter's succeeding with difficult students: New strategies for reaching your most challlenging students.* Santa Monica, CA: Canter & Associates.

Canter, L., & Canter, M. (2001). *Assertive discipline: Positive behavior management for today's classroom* (3rd ed.). Los Angeles: Canter & Associates.

Charles, C. (2000). *The synergetic classroom: Joyful teaching and gentle discipline.* New York: Addison Wesley Longman.

Charles, C. (2005). *Building classroom discipline* (8th ed.). Boston: Allyn & Bacon.

Coloroso, B. (2002). *The bully, the bullied, and the bystander.* Toronto, Ontario, Canada: HarperCollins.

Coloroso, B. (1994). *Kids are worth it! Giving your child the gift of inner discipline.* New York: Avon Books.

Coloroso, B. (1999). *Parenting with wit and wisdom in times of chaos and loss.* Canada: Viking.

Curtiss, K., & English, S. (2003). *Choice theory certification.* Retrieved August 2003 from www.kathy curtissco.com/what_we_do.htm

Curwin, R., & Mendler, A. (1997). *As tough as necessary: Countering violence, aggression, and hostility in our schools.* Alexandria, VA: Association for Supervision and Curriculum Development.

Dreikurs, R., & Cassel, P. (1972). *Discipline without tears.* New York: Hawthorn.

Dreikurs, R., Grunwald, B., & Pepper, F. (1982). *Maintaining sanity in the classroom.* New York: Harper & Row.

Elam, S., Rose, L., & Gallup, A. (2000). Thirty-fifth annual Phi Delta Kappan/Gallup poll. *Phi Delta Kappan, 85*(1), 41–66.

Glasser, W. (1969). *Schools without failure.* New York: Harper & Row.

Glasser, W. (1998a). *Choice theory in the classroom* (Rev. ed.). New York: HarperCollins.

Glasser, W. (1998b). *The quality school teacher.* New York: Perennial Press.

Jones, F. (1987). *Positive classroom instruction.* New York: McGraw-Hill.

Jones, F. (1992). *Positive classroom discipline.* New York: McGraw-Hill.

Jones, F. (2000). *Tools for teaching Discipline instruction motivation.* Santa Cruz, CA: Fredric H. Jones and Associates.

Kagan, S., Kyle, P., & Scott, S. (2004). *Win-win discipline.* San Clemente, CA: Kagan Cooperative Learning.

Kounin, J. (1970). *Discipline and group management in classrooms.* New York: Holt, Rinehart & Winston.

Marshall, M. (2002). *Discipline without stress, punishments, or rewards: How teachers and parents promote responsibility and learning.* Los Alamitos, CA: Piper Press.

Nelsen, J., Lott, L., & Glenn, H. (2000). *Positive discipline in the classroom.* Rocklin, CA: Prima Publishing.

Olweus, D. (1999). *Core program against bullying and antisocial behavior: A teacher handbook.* Norway: Research Center for Health Promotion, University of Bergen.

Thousand, J., Villa, R., & Nevin, A. (2002). *Creativity and collaborative learning: The practical guide to empowering students, teachers, and families.* Baltimore: Paul H. Brookes.

10 Managing Assessment, Record Keeping, and Reporting

What we want to see is the child in pursuit of knowledge, not knowledge in pursuit of the child.

—George Bernard Shaw

ANTICIPATION-REACTION GUIDE

Before you read the chapter, take a moment to put a check mark in the Anticipation column next to any statement with which you agree.

	Anticipation	Reaction
Authentic assessment places less reliance on testing than traditionally has been the case.	❏	❏
Portfolio is a term synonymous with *student work folder.*	❏	❏
Assessment should be part of the instruction process and should help students learn.	❏	❏
Among assessments that guide improvements in student learning are those that teachers administer regularly in their classrooms.	❏	❏
Overall, test scores are the most useful records for teachers to keep, since those are what most parents and guardians understand.	❏	❏
Corrective instruction is the same as remedial work.	❏	❏
Lists of standards and objectives, as well as continuums, can be found in newer curriculum guides and teachers' editions of textbooks.	❏	❏
Teachers should display comparison records of students as a means of motivating all toward higher achievement.	❏	❏
Parents and guardians resent being asked to help with their child's schoolwork at home.	❏	❏
Performance should be observed during class time, but records entries should be made in the privacy of the teacher's home.	❏	❏

Assessment, record keeping, and reporting are necessary requirements of teaching, but few teachers enjoy dealing with them. Traditionally, these tasks have been seen as unpleasant burdens to be endured while experiencing the pleasures of teaching children. But in recent years, new practices in both teaching and assessment have made these tasks more enjoyable and beneficial to everyone concerned.

This chapter explores assessment methods that are under teacher control, then discusses effective means of keeping records and reporting to parents and guardians. The following overview summarizes details relevant to the processes of assessment, recording, and reporting.

The Push for Better Assessment and Reporting

A nationwide movement is now underway to ensure positive learning outcomes for our nation's students. The Goals 2000: Educate America Act (1994) and the No Child Left Behind Act (2001), have set the tone for curriculum standards and provided impetus to their development. This national attention has led to the creation or revision of state learning goals along with standards for each grade level. These standards relate to the broad areas of content, performance, and opportunities-to-learn. *Content standards* focus on what should be learned in various subject areas, as well as critical thinking and problem-solving skills. *Performance standards* attempt to answer the question "How good is good enough?" They specify the level of satisfactory performance when students apply and demonstrate what they know, often in authentic or real-life situations. *Opportunity-to-learn standards,* controversial because of the potential for more federal involvement, have to do with the condition and resources necessary to give students an equal chance to meet the performance standards (Morrison, 2002).

The Nature of Assessment

Assessment is the preferred term for what educators formerly called *measurement.* In education, assessment refers to the process of finding out, as objectively as possible, how well students are progressing. Because it should be ongoing, assessment can drive instruction as teachers use this information to plan their next steps in instruction. Full assessment involves multi-trait, multi-method, and multi-source estimations of student status or progress. Measurement, by contrast, tends to be one-dimensional, often reduced to scores made on short-answer tests.

Some assessments, as part of the instruction process, are fundamental for helping students learn. These are the quizzes and tests, writing assignments, and other in-class work that teachers administer regularly. These assessments relate directly to instructional goals and should align to state and district standards. They provide immediate results about both student and instruction success, because teachers are testing what they teach.

Other assessments probe learning—the intended outcomes of instruction. They ask students to produce products and demonstrate skills and understandings in realistic situations.

This is typically done through discussion and role-playing or through conducting investigations, completing projects, producing tangible products, and analyzing ideas and procedures.

In the past, test scores were entered and averaged in the teacher's grade book as evidence to support final grades. But in the movement toward more satisfactory means of assessment, evidence has been expanded to include the quality of student productivity, often in class or cooperative team assignments. Attempts are made to help students demonstrate nuances of understanding over time, indicate how they think and process information, and show their ability to apply learned skills realistically. This type of assessment is generally considered to be more genuine, less contrived, and less test-like, than former attempts at measurement.

At this time, there is considerable controversy concerning the use of standardized testing. Such norm-based measurement (showing how students compare to each other) is emphasized in the movement to establish national standards of performance. Tests such as the SAT 9 are intended to measure student achievement of grade-level standards. Many educators dislike standardized tests because too often they measure only knowledge and provide sparse insight into learning outcomes such as critical thinking and creativity. Furthermore, they are usually inadequately aligned with district and state curricula. It is believed that, as states develop their own assessment tests, reliance on national standardized tests may decrease (Ryan & Cooper, 2000).

"ANOTHER DAY, ANOTHER STATE-MANDATED TEST..."

Authentic Assessment

Authentic assessment has been gaining favor rapidly among educators. It is explained as that which "involves students in challenges that approximate or at least better represent the 'tests' likely to face them as professionals, citizens, or consumers" (Wiggins, 1994). With feedback from their teachers and others, students analyze, refine, and improve their work over time. In this approach, a student essay might be written and rewritten until polished to high quality (see Glasser, 1998). You can see the contrast between this approach and what used to occur—the student wrote an essay, turned it in, received it back with red marks and a grade on it, and threw it away. Authentic assessment encourages students to investigate possibilities, make judgments, rethink efforts, and even redo work until the student considers it a quality product. It is the student, not the teacher, who decides when the work is good enough. The resultant *improvement* can be as objective an indicator of quality as grades on tests.

Unlike testing, authentic assessment is at the center of the teaching–learning process. Students are judged by what they do and produce during and after instruction. They do not have to try to translate what they learn into test responses. That fact makes authentic assessment appealing to teachers and students. Taking improvement into account makes the process even more appealing.

As teaching and assessment practices change, a rethinking of grading is also occurring across the country. Marzano (1998) believes the primary purpose of grading is to provide feedback that is as accurate and precise as possible so students can improve their work; letter grades usually fall short of that goal. Letter grades are symbols, but they are generally not aligned to any common standard and they are essentially arbitrary in levels (A versus B versus C and so on). Further, letter grades do not carry much information about students' strengths and areas for growth, or give any insight into how to help students improve. Consequently, what they represent is often unclear.

In some areas teachers are being asked to maintain records in Internet portals so parents and guardians can use their home computers to check on their child's homework, attendance, and scores. To accomplish this, some publishers are providing districts and teachers with the needed software with adoption of their materials. Caregivers can track their child's progress daily. This program is intended to strengthen alliance between teacher and caregivers. In some schools, paper report cards will continue in addition to this program (Alphonso, 2003).

Educators are seeking better ways to report student accomplishments and areas of growth. Some current recommendations even go so far as to advocate the elimination of letter grades, particularly during the primary years. Teachers are now encouraged to monitor student growth in terms of performance, work samples, and long-term projects that show students' capabilities in light of predetermined standards and intended learning goals. They can then report this with holistic narratives or continuum checklists of competencies. Vermont was the first state to use portfolios in a statewide assessment program when in 1991 it required all students in fourth and eighth grade to keep portfolios for writing and mathematics. Fourth and eighth graders took a *uniform test* (timed writing samples and a series of mathematics problems) and presented their portfolios to demonstrate their progress and understandings over time. Well-crafted standards have been developed for judging the portfolios.

Student Portfolios in Authentic Assessment

Students use portfolios to show their work, efforts, and talents, just as models, artists, architects, and others use portfolios to showcase their work. Portfolios play a central role in authentic assessment. They can contain work samples from most areas of the curriculum, as well as written tests. And though the name can suggest a large and unwieldy container, a portfolio may simply be a file folder or a three-ring binder. The important thing is not how they look, but how they are created and used.

Paulson, Paulson, and Meyer (1991) explain that the portfolio concept requires collection, selection, and reflection. From a collection of all their work products, students select for inclusion in their portfolios pieces of work—not necessarily their A work—that they consider particularly noteworthy. Then they reflect and articulate orally or in writing why they selected each sample—why it is special and what they learned by completing it.

This process has significant benefits for students and teachers. Portfolios make students active participants in the assessment process. They show individual students' ranges of interests, abilities, and achievements over time. This provides teachers, students, and caregivers much to discuss about student learning at school. The process of selection, articulation, and improvement over time provides a broad window into students' experiences and learning and can provide tangible profiles of growth over time.

Portfolios in Different Subject Areas.   Student portfolios are suitable for use in all subject areas. Examples for the traditional areas of reading, writing, and arithmetic at the sixth-grade level might include

For Reading
- Written responses to reading, such as character or problem analysis
- Book reports
- Literature-based projects, or photographs with supporting details of projects
- Audio- or videotapes of dramatic readings

For Writing
- Examples of free or creative writing
- Writing targeted for different audiences
- Writing for different purposes, such as persuasion, information, or entertainment
- Work in a variety of forms, such as poetry, journals, letters, and scripts

For Mathematics
- Math journals
- Projects and investigations
- Diagrams, graphs, charts

Grading of Portfolios.   Portfolios are whole efforts, not collections of individual items. The following general criteria are used for grading portfolios (based on Paulson et al., 1991, p. 60):

Depth: Evidence of personal growth through reflection, critical thinking, and insights.

Breadth: Evidence of personal growth through multiple and varied experiences.

Emphasis: All entries and reflections contribute to the theme of personal growth.

Unity: Clear evidence of the process of collection, selection, and reflection.

Mechanics: Correct sentencing, spelling, capitalization, and punctuation.

From the basis of these expectations the teacher is able to make evaluations that ultimately may be converted to grades for records and report cards, described in the broadest of terms as follows:

Exceptional achievement, earned by a portfolio that is particularly well presented, well organized, insightful, and technically correct.

Commendable achievement, earned by an impressive and interesting portfolio that is more loosely organized, less insightful, and not as informative as the exceptional portfolio.

Adequate achievement, earned by a portfolio that, although acceptable, does not show good organization or display much critical thinking, insight, involvement, or growth.

Minimal evidence of achievement, earned by a portfolio that lacks depth and is weak in content, thought, and presentation.

No evidence of achievement, earned by a portfolio that is completely off track, reveals no insights or other redeeming qualities, or is not the original work of the student.

It is important to remember that portfolios are viewed as whole products. Although they are made up of individual samples of student work already reviewed and graded by the teacher, it is for the student to determine the items that are noteworthy and that provide evidence of progress and achievement.

Nancy Rutherford, who teaches first grade, explains how she uses portfolios with her students.

When I first heard about portfolios, I thought they were too advanced a concept to be used in first grade. I was put off by the logistics of storing the many oversized projects that were part of my curriculum. I also envisioned the portfolio as purely an assessment tool, so all in all the use of portfolios didn't appeal to me.

I have since changed my mind 180 degrees. I have found portfolios to be a great asset in monitoring work in progress. Students realize that writing is not a one-time try. They learn to look at their work reflectively in terms of predetermined criteria, to assess strengths and weaknesses, and to rewrite accordingly. My favorite use of portfolios is to show individual progress. Students review their own work over time and are generally astonished at the differences they find. Even those who had top papers see how much they have improved.

Portfolios also provide concrete examples for parent conferencing. The teacher can say, "Here's what we'd like to accomplish. Here's where your child is. Here are some examples."

Rubrics and Their Use

A *rubric* is a scoring guide or assessment scale that is devised to match the standards, objectives, and learning goals of a specific assignment. Because rubrics reflect both broad evaluation standards and specific evaluation criteria, they provide clear descriptions of what students are expected to achieve.

Rubrics require teachers to think more clearly about intended goals and quality work. They can be written for any subject and adapted to any grade level. Well-written rubrics help teachers to score students' work more accurately and fairly because they match student work to predetermined scoring standards rather than to other students' work, as do standardized tests. Teachers should share rubrics with students. Students profit from clear knowledge of expectations, and that knowledge then guides their work. It can be very beneficial for teacher and students to discuss learning goals, and from those discussions develop the rubrics together.

There are, however, things teachers don't like about rubrics. For one, they don't match other systems, such as letter grades. For another, it takes time to develop successful rubrics, especially those that describe multiple aspects of performance, each with its own criteria and attainment levels. In addition, rubrics can be difficult to explain to caregivers.

When developing rubrics, the right language is critical because rubrics must clearly articulate the qualities of student performance that distinguish the levels of work and effort. Over a period of time, teachers may write and refine a project rubric several times in order to make it closely resemble what they actually expect to see in the student work. To ensure the quality of rubric criteria, Wiggins (1994) states this guiding thought: "If a student can achieve a high score on all the criteria and still not perform well at the task, you have the wrong criteria." Depending on grade level, a variety of descriptors can be used:

- Exemplary, proficient, progressing, or not meeting the standard
- Level four, level three, level two, or level one
- Exemplary achievement, commendable achievement, adequate achievement, limited or minimal achievement, or no response
- Star, smiley face, or straight face

Records and Record Keeping

With ongoing assessment, good records of student progress must be kept to promote effective teaching, good learning, and efficient reporting to caregivers and administrators. Other reasons for keeping accurate records are to furnish data to other schools; to keep attendance, on which financial aid is based; to show student achievement; and to evaluate and modify the school curriculum periodically. Additionally, the No Child Left Behind Act now requires that records be used in evaluating school districts.

What Teachers Want Records to Show

From the teacher's perspective, good records can quickly indicate, at any time during the year, where individual students stand academically and socially. Teachers need this information for teaching, evaluating students, planning for the future, and conferring with and reporting to caregivers. Records should show the following for individual students:

- Instructional level
- Progress
- Unreached standards, goals, and objectives
- Strengths and weaknesses
- Social adjustment

Instructional Level.   A student's instructional level in any part of the curriculum is the level at which new learning is challenging yet possible. These levels are especially important in classrooms in which differentiated instruction occurs. Instructional level is determined through observation, ongoing monitoring of student performance, and occasionally, formal testing. The scores, work samples, and anecdotal comments that serve as indicators are recorded in formats that will be illustrated later.

Progress.   Teachers, students, and caregivers appreciate evidence that the student is making genuine progress. But lack of progress must be noted as well, for this is where replanning, corrective instruction, and second chances begin. Second chances help determine whether the corrective instruction was effective, and they give students another opportunity to be successful in their learning. Progress can be shown in several ways. One of the most common is to compare pre- and post-test scores, useful in spelling and math. Another is to compare samples of work, as in writing and art, done a few weeks apart. Yet another is to show increased performance through standards and objectives that have been reached, and through books that have been read.

Students enjoy seeing graphic depictions of their improvements. They like making the graphs themselves to show increases in scores, quickness, accuracy, and quantity. Because graphs seem to motivate students toward higher performance and are appealing to parents and guardians as well, they are valuable inclusions in individual records folders. To avoid showing a student in a bad light when compared to others, these graphs should be individual and private.

Unreached Standards, Goals, and Objectives.   Parents and guardians are interested not only in their child's progress, but also in what remains to be accomplished. Well-managed records provide this information, either in a list of standards or objectives that can be checked off when attained, or in notations of material to be covered in textbooks.

Strengths and Weaknesses.   Student strengths and weaknesses become apparent by examining test scores, other records, and the contents of portfolios or work folders. Teachers will note error patterns as they analyze student work, develop ideas for appropriate corrective instruction, and provide opportunities for students to have a second chance to be successful in their learning. Occasionally, specialists may be asked to administer diagnostic tests to individual students. Such tests reveal specific weaknesses and error patterns as well as general overall scores.

Social Adjustment.   Among the most important outcomes of schooling are the abilities to relate acceptably and work cooperatively and productively with others. Evidence of

"PUT IT UNDER SOMETHING."

social adjustment is obtained on an informal basis by the teacher, who notes how a student gets along with classmates, shows manners and courtesy, cooperates, takes turns, accepts responsibility, and abides by class rules. Teachers compile this evidence by entering brief comments on progress forms for each student. This information is of special interest to caregivers, most of whom want their child to behave, cooperate, and learn as much as possible.

As older students work in cooperative learning groups and teams, they should be taught to judge the quality of their own work and the efforts of their group. The teacher can help by providing a review sheet such as that shown in Figure 10.1. Note that the contributions of every group member are recorded as positive comments. If a member makes no contribution, the space is left blank.

Future Instructional Plans. In every parent–teacher conference, attention should be given to future instructional plans for the student. For the most part these plans will be carried out at school, but they sometimes require assistance at home from the parents or guardians. Student records substantiate the need for assistance, indicate the areas in which it should be provided, and demonstrate how caregivers can help provide assistance.

FIGURE 10.1 Contributions Review

Project Activity ———————————— Date ————————————

Leader ———————— Contributions ————————————

Recorder ———————— Contributions ————————————

Member ———————— Contributions ————————————

Member ———————— Contributions ————————————

Member ———————— Contributions ————————————

Member ———————— Contributions ————————————

Problems: Describe any problems the group had and tell what you did to help correct the
problem. ————————————————————————————————

Forms and Formats for Good Record Keeping

Forms and formats for keeping records include (1) master continuums of standards, objectives, or learning goals; (2) individual student folders; (3) progress forms; (4) graphs; and (5) work samples. It is crucial for teachers to know the state standards, the district expectations and benchmarks, and what is expected on the district report cards.

Standards and Continuums.   Standards or benchmarks may be written statements or checklists. They are listed in newer curriculum guides and teachers' editions of school textbooks. Objectives are written statements that precisely describe the intended outcomes of instruction—what students will know or be able to do because of the instruction. When organized into a particular order or sequence, standards or objectives form what is called a *continuum*. Continuums are helpful to teachers in keeping track of student progress. Normally, they are simply checked off when attained. Marilyn Kimbell, a kindergarten teacher, uses a skills continuum as follows:

> When I begin a school year, I prepare a continuum of skills, which I list across the top of a grid. Down the side I list the names of my students. Examples of skills are writing name; writing numerals; writing letters; circling objects that are above, below, larger, smaller, and so forth. Children are assessed on these skills by me, my aide, and trained parent volunteers. My aide records the results and I study them. If there seems to be a need for further assessment, I do it myself. The results usually merely document what I have already discovered in working with the children. We have tried to correlate our skills continuums with the school report cards. I make copies for myself, the parents, and the office.

An excerpt from Marilyn's math skills continuum is shown in Figure 10.2. Codes are frequently used for marking the continuum form. One of the simplest is to enter a slash (/) to indicate that the concept or skill has been introduced. When the student masters the concept or skill, the slash is crossed to make an X. Other systems indicate the date on which the standard or objective was reached, the number of attempts before mastery, and the degree to which the standard or objective was attained—for example, mastery (M), satisfactory (S), and improvement needed (I).

Individual Records Folders.   A personal records folder should be made for each student, but kept separate from portfolios that include work samples chosen by students. Records folders contain all essential information about students and are indispensable for conferencing with caregivers and administrators, as well as students themselves. The following suggestions help make folders attractive and useful:

- Folders. Use legal-size manila folders. The extra length accommodates oversized materials.
- Front cover. Teacher affixes student name, room number, teacher's name, and grade level. Students decorate the front cover with their own design or artwork. (Have them practice first.)
- Inside front. Teacher attaches progress form sheet, such as Figure 10.3.
- Inside back. Teacher affixes graph forms (such as Figure 10.4) to indicate individual progress in math, spelling, and other areas.

FIGURE 10.2   A Portion of a Kindergarten Math Skills Continuum

Student Names	identify & complete pattern	match set members	identify set with most	match set of 6 to numeral	identify set 1 less than 5	identify set 1 more than 2	identify greatest numeral	identify least numeral	identify counting order (1–4)	identify counting order (11–13)

FIGURE 10.3   Student Progress Sheet

Name _____

	Pretest	*Midtest*	*Posttest*

Reading
   San Diego Quick—level
   Oral Reading Test—level
   Silent Reading Test—level
   Word attack needs _____

Mathematics
   Math grade-level test—
   Basic facts (see graphs)
   Word problem application _____

Language
   Spelling placement
   Word lists and scores (see graphs and samples)
   Capitalization, punctuation, grammar _____
_____

Composition and Penmanship (see samples) _____
_____

Social Studies _____
_____

Science & Health _____
_____

Art (see samples) _____
_____

Music _____
_____

Physical Education (see graphs) _____
_____

Other _____

Social Behavior _____
_____
_____

FIGURE 10.4   Sample Graph Forms

No.	Week 1	2	3	4	5	6	7	8	9	10	11	12

Math: Additional facts, number correct out of 50 in five minutes' time.

```
45–
40–
35–
30–
25–
20–
15–
10–
```

Spelling: Scores on midweek tests, number correct out of 20.

```
20–
19–
18–
17–
16–
15–
14–
```

- Loose inside. This area holds samples of student work in penmanship, composition, and art. Special vocabulary and spelling lists plus individual reading lists can also be included. Before and after samples can be stapled together. Samples should be updated periodically.
- Student responsibility. From third grade upward, consider giving students responsibility for recording, graphing, and updating their folders.
- Location. Keep folders in a secure location where they will remain neat and clean and out of the way when not in use.

Records for Various Curriculum Areas

Assessment scores can indicate instructional level, progress made, and particular areas of strength and weakness. Because different areas of the curriculum involve different content standards and goals, they call for different types of records. Those differences are discussed in this section and desirable types of records are indicated.

Mathematics.   The most useful records for mathematics include standards or objectives continuums, work samples, and progress graphs. The standards or objectives continuum, where student skills and progress are checked off, provides an overall view of the mathematics program, together with indications of student progress. Student competencies and errors can be tracked on a record sheet of the different types of math problems. Graphs such as Figure 10.4 should be kept for certain parts of the math curriculum where they can show dramatic progress in increments. Graphs are best for recording timed exercises in addition, subtraction, multiplication, and division, as well as word problems.

Reading. The most valuable records in reading show assessment scores including comprehension and fluency levels, standards or objectives continuums, and lists of books and other materials read by the student. A progress form such as that shown in Figure 10.3 shows areas in which measures are often sought. A reading standards or objectives continuum, illustrated in Figure 10.5, can be used to document specific standards or objectives reached and not reached by the student. For books read, many students find it motivating to add segments to a bookworm instead of simply listing titles and dates. Others like to add ornaments to a picture of a tree, where each ornament shows the title of a book read.

Teachers can keep running records of students' reading to assess their reading fluency. The teacher or trained volunteer records individual students reading aloud. Then the teacher calculates the percentage of words the student read correctly to determine how well the text matches the student's level at this time. The teacher also analyzes miscues or errors

FIGURE 10.5   Portion of a Reading Objectives Continnuum

Student Names	consonant sounds	short vowel sounds	blends/digraphs	long vowels, final	long vowels, double	vowels modified by letters "r" & "l"	variant & irreg. vowels	affixes	main idea	facts	cause–effect	sequence	prediction	inference & conclusion	bases, prefixes, suffixes	antonyms, synonyms	contractions	compound words
	Word attack								**Comprehension**							**Vocabulary**		

for possible patterns in order to plan mini lessons, tutorials, and other word study activities. Running records, such as Figure 10.6, are made easier when the teacher makes notations directly on a duplicate copy of the text the student reads.

Spelling.   Spelling can be treated almost like math facts insofar as records are concerned, as was shown in Figure 10.4. For each student, records should include the scores on weekly spelling tests, showing continuity of achievement and effort. Student work on special word lists or bonus words should be indicated. Teachers also need to assess spelling in written work—are words mastered on the spelling test carrying over to a student's written work?

FIGURE 10.6   Running Record Form

Student ————————————   Grade ————————   Teacher/Rm ————————

Date ——————   Recorder ————————————   Comments ————————

Competencies: (circle predominant behaviors)
1-to-1 matching   Directionality   Fluent Reading

At an unknown word:			
Makes no attempt	Seeks help	Reruns	Reads on
Attempt using . . .	Visual	Meaning	Structure

Calculations

Error Rate $\dfrac{RW}{E} = 1$

Accuracy % 91%

S/C Rate $\dfrac{E + SC}{SC} = 1$

Level: Easy   Instr   Hard

After an error:			
Ignores	Seeks help	Reruns	Attempts S/C
Self-corrects using . . .	Visual	Meaning	Structure

Level: 4   RW: 53   **Totals:**

Page	Title: Where Is My Hat?	Words:	E	SC	Cues Used E	SC
2	"Where is my hat?" said Ben.					
3	Ben looked under his bed. "It is not here," he said.					
4	Mom looked in the closet. "It is not here," she said.					
5	Ben looked in his toybox. "It is not here," he said.					
	He looked and looked.					
6	Mom looked behind the chair.					
7	"Here it is!" she said.					

Grammar and Vocabulary.   For this part of the language curriculum, records management moves from recording scores to entering notational appraisals and comments. *Grammar* refers to general language usage, both oral and written, including sentence structure, subject–verb agreement, correct verb tenses, and so forth. The teacher notes errors that seem to recur and makes comments, if needed, on the student's progress sheet (Figure 10.3). The same procedure is followed for vocabulary unless the teacher includes a vocabulary development segment in the language program. In that case, students can keep a list of words whose meanings they have mastered, as they do for special spelling words. In some cases, the lists of special spelling words and the new vocabulary are the same.

Writing.   Comments about penmanship and composition are entered here. Composition is further divided into expository and creative writing. Expository writing emphasizes the clear and sequential expression of ideas, and involves skills in organization, paragraph construction, the use of topic and subordinate sentences, and so forth. Creative writing stresses the artistic side of writing—expression, novelty of presentation, and varied forms of prose and verse. In both cases, the records folder should contain samples of the student's efforts, including penmanship. Before and after samples show student progress, though it should be recognized that the contrast (or lack thereof) may be influenced by variations in penmanship that occur normally from day to day.

Social Studies.   The social studies program follows various paths according to grade level. Numerous topics are covered in a given year, usually including current events plus the history, geography, economics, customs, and so forth of particular communities, states, nations, and continents. Skills with maps, globes, charts, and graphs, plus innumerable construction activities are usually involved in the program. With emphasis on multicultural and global education, various styles of art, music, clothing, and other cultural items of particular places and times are also highlighted.

Samples of project work done in social studies often reflect team or group efforts and are too cumbersome to be kept as records unless they are photographed or videotaped. Team or group murals or construction projects can be displayed in the classroom for viewing by others, at which time individual students' contributions can be pointed out. A composite video of all the students as they work on various projects throughout the year makes a nice feature at the spring open house.

Science and Health.   Class work in science and health is similar to that in social studies. Large units of study characterize the curriculum, and group projects are often undertaken. Some teachers like to have students complete one or more individual science projects, which are displayed for others to see. Notational appraisals entered on forms (Figure 10.3), indicate the type of work done, the student's level of involvement, quality of participation, and any extra efforts that might have been undertaken. Science projects can also be included in a composite video.

Art.   The art program usually consists of two aspects, appreciation and production. Art appreciation is difficult to measure, and records are difficult to keep except for notation of experiences in which the student participated (Figure 10.3). Productive art, on the other hand, provides excellent samples, at least two of which should be included in the folder. Legitimate before and after samples show artistic growth, and attention can be drawn to the inclusion of various elements such as line, form, texture, composition, balance, and other specific art techniques.

Music.   Meaningful records are difficult to keep in the area of music. Neither music appreciation nor music production yields scores or products that show relative standing, growth, or attainment of objectives. Notational appraisals can be entered on the progress form (Figure 10.3) to indicate experiences in which the student participated, special talents, and contributions.

Physical Education.   In elementary schools, physical education is rarely presented through formal instruction. Students are taught to play various games and more or less fend for themselves while the teacher supervises their play. Some teachers and schools offer programs in running, cardiovascular fitness, and individual sports that promote coordination and muscle tone. For these programs, times, distances, numbers of repetitions, and so forth can be recorded and graphed.

Work Samples.   As noted, work samples are very useful in judging and documenting student performance. Some subject areas do not yield useful work samples. Always try, however, to include something in math, language, social studies, and art, as appropriate for the grade level. At fourth grade, for example, the following should be included:

1. A math work sheet that reflects different skills emphasized at that grade level, such as regrouping, subtracting, adding, and maintaining correct alignment; that reveals certain types of errors that may occur; and that requires knowledge of basic number combinations.
2. A composition that includes many recently taught spelling words and that reveals organization, sentence structure, spelling, and penmanship. Before and after samples show writing development.
3. Artwork, such as a drawing, that incorporates techniques of line, form, color, contrast, and overall composition—elements that can be analyzed both in isolation and as a total composition.
4. Personal reading lists.

Simplifying Records Management

Good, complete records can be kept rather easily. Record keeping need not be a distasteful and overwhelming burden. Consider the following suggestions:

1. Relate all records directly to the standards and objectives used in the district, curriculum guides, and/or teachers' editions of textbooks.
2. Use record-keeping forms that require a minimum of marking. Combine and summarize so one form contains the records for many activities. (Many districts now allow the teachers to create and revise forms to better match their needs.)

3. Supplement the forms with samples of student work that show progress toward standards and objectives.
4. Do most of the record keeping during school time, not at home in the evening. Have aides or volunteers help, and to the extent possible, involve students, as such participation motivates, shares responsibility, and conveys ownership to students of their own education. It also makes for more timely feedback. Remember, however, that because records are legal documents, you are legally responsible for their management, recording, and accuracy.
5. Make the individual records folders and portfolios sources of pride for students. They show student accomplishments, capabilities, and progress. Help students see them as extensions of themselves.
6. Save time and work by using computers and software to record and access records. They can help organize and manage grades, log standards and objectives that are attained, and print record forms and progress notes for parents and guardians.

Jearine Bacon teaches upper elementary grades. She comments on how she uses a computer to manage many aspects of her program:

> For the teacher, the computer can offer organization and efficiency, and can be used to extend and reinforce the lessons. Forms and templates can be created for use in all aspects of the teaching day. The computer can provide statistics in seconds and display student data in multiple formats. Parent communications can be made to look professional and documented in minutes. Substitute teacher plans can be updated and printed at a moment's notice. Learning to make use of the enormous capabilities of the computer can be an exciting adventure for teacher and students alike. Attitude is the key.

Records Needed for Conferencing

Most teachers personally conference with parents or guardians at least once a year. Some conference more often, and there are times as well when student study teams and conferences about particular students must be held with administrators and specialists. The quality of input that regular education teachers bring to these conferences is sharply increased by good records. Suggestions for the conferences themselves are presented in Chapter 11. The following materials will help you feel well prepared for any conference.

The Individual Student Folder.   The individual student work folder provides your most useful set of materials for conferencing with or about a student. As suggested earlier, the progress form inside the front cover describes the curriculum in a nutshell, with scores and comments about how the student is doing in each area. Inside the back cover are the graphs that show evidence of progress. Work samples and lists that provide concrete evidence of student effort, accomplishments, and progress are loose inside.

Notes about Future Plans.   Student strengths and weaknesses, revealed in the records folder, may suggest future instructional plans for the student. Take a moment before the conference to make notes concerning such plans, to discuss with the caregiver or administrator.

Notes about Suggestions for Help at Home.   Parents or guardians should be informed if necessary about how they can help at home with future plans. Their assistance might consist of setting definite uninterrupted study times, working for short periods of time with drill or spelling, listening to their child read aloud, or discussing with the child the plot of a story or book that is being read. Remind caregivers that their involvement normally serves to increase their child's achievement. This information should be made available to parents and guardians in their primary language.

Student-Involved Conferencing.   Some teachers have found student-involved conferences to be very valuable and powerful. These may be goal-setting conferences in the early fall, or progress and sharing conferences later in the year. Both teacher and student participate in sharing information with the caregivers, although the teacher's role and degree of participation vary with the purpose of the conference.

For fall goal-setting conferences, students begin a fifteen-minute conference time by sharing their personal goals, describing their learnings, and presenting some of their work. Student, teacher, and caregivers recognize strengths demonstrated by the student's work, and then each identifies an area or two that the student needs to work on. The student states one or two goals for future work, and teacher and caregivers promise specific help toward meeting the goals. The teacher then answers questions, summarizes, and concludes the conference.

Conferences that occur later in the school year usually serve a much different purpose. Students use their own portfolio with preselected work samples and artifacts to share progress at this time. In preparing for this type of conference, students who self-assess are able to provide remarkable insights into the quality of their work and what they need to do to improve it.

Teachers must prepare students carefully before they schedule student-led conferences. These conferences are most successful when students have rehearsal opportunities. For older students, peers, parent volunteers, and the teacher can listen to the rehearsal. Cross-age tutors and cross-grade partners can be taught to provide helpful feedback to younger students.

It is essential that students and caregivers understand both the learning goals and their roles for either type of conference. Further, they all must be willing to give thought to the student's strengths and areas for growth, and how each can participate toward improvement. In any event, student-led conferences bring the focus back on the children.

Ancillary Materials.   The records folder and notes are usually sufficient. During the conference, however, you should have standards and objectives continuums, a curriculum guide, textbooks, workbooks, and sample work sheets. These materials should not be referred to unless there are questions about standards and objectives, materials, or activities.

This concludes the review of assessment considerations that fall to the teacher's control—authentic assessment, management of high-quality records, and preparation for reporting to parents and guardians. Before moving ahead to Chapter 11, which deals with managing communication with students, caregivers, and others, take time to review these end-of-chapter activities.

Parting Thought

I have learned that success is to be measured not so much by the position that one has reached in life as by the obstacles he has overcome while trying to succeed.

—Booker T. Washington

SUMMARY SELF-CHECK

Check off the following as you either understand or become able to apply them.

☐ Assessment, record keeping, and reporting are requirements of teaching that few teachers have enjoyed, although with new authentic assessments, the tasks are becoming less burdensome, and for some teachers even enjoyable.

☐ Assessments that relate directly to what teachers cover in class help teachers more accurately test what they teach.

☐ Corrective instruction is part of the instructional process and helps students learn.

☐ Standardized tests are an effort to respond to public concern regarding accountability, but may alter curriculum by making teachers teach to the test.

☐ Authentic assessment minimizes the use of tests while emphasizing products that result from student work. Those products provide greater insight into student abilities and accomplishments than do tests, and they can be judged with equal objectivity with the use of carefully designed rubrics.

☐ Records of student performance should reveal the following for any student at any time: academic instructional levels, specific strengths and weaknesses, progress that has occurred, social behavior, future instructional plans.

☐ Formats for keeping good records: Standards and objectives continuums (simply checked off), progress forms, graphs showing progress, work samples (few in number and specially selected), individual student forms, incentive records.

☐ Record management simplified: Relate records to specific standards and objectives in the curriculum guide and textbooks; use record forms that require a minimum of marking; make most entries during school time; make the individual records folder a source of pride for students.

☐ Records are legal documents, and you are legally responsible for their management, recording, and accuracy.

❏ Records during conferencing: Use individual student folder to describe strengths, needs, and progress; make a note about future plans for the student; make a note about how caregivers can help at home; student-led conferences reveal much about student progress and learning.

ACTIVITIES FOR REFLECTION AND GROWTH

For Cumulative Skills Development

1. Take a moment to review the statements in the Anticipation–Reaction Guide at the beginning of this chapter. Put a check mark in the Reaction column next to any statement with which you now agree. How have your thoughts changed since reading this chapter?

2. Describe how you will balance standardized testing and authentic assessment alternatives in a grade of your choice.

3. Organize a record-keeping system for a grade of your choice. Try to set it up so almost all of the required work can be done at school.

4. Explain how you would use a student records folder to describe to a parent in ten minutes or less a child's achievement and needs in your class.

5. You are to conference with parents who have a history of criticizing and berating teachers for unfairly assigning grades to their child. What have you included in the child's folder to counter or forestall the expected criticisms? Explain.

6. Briefly describe a social studies project for a grade of your choice. Create a rubric to objectively score the project.

REFERENCES AND RECOMMENDED READINGS

Alphonso, C. (2003, August 8). A poor student's worst nightmare. *The Globe and Mail.* Retrieved August 2003 from www.globetechnology.com/servlet/ArticleNews/TPStory/LAC/20030808/USTUDNO

Brimijoin, K., Marquissee, E., & Tomlinson, C. (2003, February). Using data to differentiate instruction. *Educational Leadership, 60,* 70–73.

Carr, J., & Harris, D. (2001). *Succeeding with standards: Linking curriculum, assessment, and action planning.* Alexandria, VA: Association for Supervision and Curriculum Development.

Gardner, H. (n.d.). *Eye on San Diego* [Interview on television broadcast].

Glasser, W. (1998). *The quality school teacher.* New York: HarperCollins.

Gusky, T. (2003, February). How classroom assessments improve learning. *Educational Leadership, 60,* 6–11.

Marzano, R. (1998, December). Advances in grading. *Education Update, 40*(8), 4.

Marzano, R. (2000). *Transforming classroom grading.* Alexandria, VA: Association for Supervision and Curriculum Development.

McTighe, J., & Thomas, R. (2003, February). Toward better report cards. *Educational Leadership, 60,* 52–55.

Morrison, G. (2002). *Teaching in America* (3rd ed.). Boston: Allyn & Bacon.

Paulson, F., Paulson, P., & Meyer, C. (1991). What makes a portfolio a portfolio? *Educational Leadership, 48*(5), 60–63.

Perrone, V. (Ed.). (1991). *Expanding student assessment.* Alexandria, VA: Association for Supervision and Curriculum Development.

Picciotto, L. (1999, August). Let your students take the lead. *Scholastic Instructor, 109*(1), 33–35.

Ryan, K., & Cooper, J. (2000). *Those who can, teach* (9th ed.). Boston: Houghton Mifflin.

Using standards and assessment [Special issue]. (1999, March). *Educational Leadership.* Alexandria, VA: Association for Supervision and Curriculum Development.

What do we mean by results? [Special issue]. (2000, February). *Educational Leadership* Alexandria, VA: Association for Supervision and Curriculum Development.

Wiggins, G. (1994, November). Toward better report cards. *Educational Leadership, 52,* 28–37.

Yancy, K. (Ed.). (1992). *Portfolios in the writing classroom.* Urbana, IL: National Council of Teachers of English.

11 Managing Communication with Students, Caregivers, and Others

The most important thing in communication is to hear what isn't being said.
—Peter F. Drucker

ANTICIPATION–REACTION GUIDE

Before you read the chapter, take a moment to put a check mark in the Anticipation column next to any statement with which you agree.

	Anticipation	Reaction
It is the student's responsibility to communicate with the teacher when concerned about something in the classroom.	❏	❏
The main purpose of the four-way test is to ensure that what you are saying is factual.	❏	❏
Parallel communication in elementary classrooms means that both teacher and student use the "adult" style, as described by Berne.	❏	❏
The main purposes for communicating with caregivers are to inform and to obtain support.	❏	❏
Teachers tend to give less attention to students who behave properly and do their work consistently.	❏	❏
The main purposes of parent–teacher conferences are to become acquainted and to give parents or guardians the opportunity to talk.	❏	❏
The purpose of no-lose conflict resolution is to find a good solution without either disputant feeling put down.	❏	❏
Glasser and Nelsen suggest that a class meeting be scheduled whenever the teacher senses a problem that involves the class.	❏	❏
Good communication is capable of preventing many kinds of disruptive behavior.	❏	❏
When telephoning caregivers, teachers should try to draw out their feelings, even though the process might take a good deal of time.	❏	❏

What are your memories when you think back to your best school experiences, to those classes or rooms where you learned most and found yourself most engaged in education? Chances are you recall teachers and others who were present with you, more than what you actually were taught. That's because so much of school learning occurs from exchanges with others. This phenomenon, also present in work and leisure, helps us understand that interaction with others is what makes life most rewarding and memorable.

The Value of Communication

When it comes to teaching, communication—the interchange of thoughts, feelings, and information—is the vehicle that moves education forward. It is the means by which teachers motivate, inform, guide, encourage, build relationships, meet needs, and otherwise stir the educational pot. Although we think of communication as verbal, much of it is nonverbal, conveying powerful messages through proximity and facial and body cues (Jones, 2000).

Teachers must routinely communicate with students, caregivers, colleagues, support providers, and administrators. Those who do it well earn cooperation, respect, and even esteem. It is not far-fetched to say that communication contributes more to the quality of teaching than does any other skill. It is no accident that teachers who enjoy the greatest success in teaching also happen to be good managers of communication.

Despite its obvious importance, communication is rarely emphasized in teacher education. Most teachers have to learn how to manage it while on the job. This chapter is intended to help by offering an overview of communication requirements and suggestions for their successful accomplishment.

Uses of Communication

Throughout the school day, good communication is repeatedly necessary. Consider the following:

- Giving directions—making them brief and clear
- Conducting instruction—teaching gently, clearly, and patiently
- Holding class discussions and meetings—being receptive, nonthreatening, positive, and helpful
- Holding individual conferences with students—applying the Golden Rule here as elsewhere
- Meeting with student support providers—being open and collaborative
- Meeting with staff, administrators, beginning teacher support providers, and other teachers—shedding all defensiveness and applying the four-way test, which follows
- Meeting individually with administrators and colleagues—being pleasant, helpful, and supportive
- Conferencing with parents and guardians—treating them as equals who prize their child above all else

The Four-Way Test

Keep the four-way test in mind as you speak with students, parents, and others:

1. Is what I am saying true?
2. Is it helpful?
3. Would my silence hurt?
4. Will my saying this build good relationships?

These matters will receive attention in some detail later in the chapter. First, for a better view of what, how, and to whom school communication applies, review the grid shown in Figure 11.1. Notice the groups of persons—students, caregivers, colleagues, and administrators—with whom teachers regularly communicate, and the five primary purposes served by communication—to inform, instruct, build relationships, maintain class control, and build esprit de corps. These points will be explained in sections that follow.

Although communication is a dynamic two-way engagement, understand that teachers must guide the process. The remainder of this chapter is divided into three parts representing the three groups to whom teacher communication is aimed: (1) students, (2) caregivers, and (3) colleagues and administrators.

Communicating with Students

Please make sure you communicate with students and caregivers in a parallel manner. Parallel communication, a concept introduced by Eric Berne in 1964, is communication between two persons when they talk as equals. Berne identified three states individuals exhibit when talking with others. The child state is shown when we talk with someone to

FIGURE 11.1   A Classroom Communication Grid

Purposes	Persons			
	Students	**Caregivers**	**Colleagues**	**Administrators**
1. Inform	x	x	x	x
2. Instruct	x			
3. Relate	x	x	x	x
4. Control	x			
5. Spirit	x	x		

whom we feel inferior. We defer to authority and perhaps behave emotionally. The parent state is exhibited when we talk with someone to whom we feel superior. We tend to act as our parents probably did to us—we correct, admonish, and moralize. In the adult state, used when talking with others on a basis of equality, we express our thoughts logically and firmly, without hostility.

We should always try to use the adult state when we communicate with anyone. The examples of exchanges between teacher and students presented in this chapter reflect adult–adult parallel communication.

Informing Students and Conducting Instruction

Informing.   Informing students is mentioned here because teachers do this regularly. All it means is giving routine information orally, then checking that students understand.

Conducting Instruction.   In conducting instruction, teachers use communication to gain student attention, provide motivation, give directions, explain concepts and procedures, pose questions, provide feedback, reteach by providing corrective instruction and second chances, and redirect inappropriate behavior.

Gaining Attention.   Frequently attention is gained by making statements such as

- "All eyes on me."
- "Everyone, fold your hands and look at me."
- "Freeze!" (to gain attention of a boisterous class)

Often nonverbal signals are used, such as

- Bell tone, rain stick, or chord on piano
- Flick of lights
- Rhythmic hand clap

Students should be taught to respond immediately to these words or signals. No new task or lesson should be started without the attention of every student.

Providing Motivation.   Under ideal circumstances, motivation is inherent in most well-structured lessons. Teachers provide motivation with statements such as

- "Boys and girls, have you ever imagined what it would be like to . . . ?"
- "This is a contest lesson to see if you can set a new record for yourself or for the class."
- "Friends, there is a surprise hidden somewhere in this lesson. Watch for it."

Giving Directions.   Good directions prevent a multitude of problems. Therefore

- Make directions very clear.
- Keep them short.

- Model what you mean and, if appropriate and available, show examples.
- Check to make sure students understand.
- If more than two steps are involved, consider writing reminders on the board, using visual instructional plans, or using Say, See, Do Teaching as described in Chapter 6.

Examples of directions:

- "When I say 'begin,' open your workbooks to page 23 [write page number on the board]. On scratch paper do problems 2, 4, and 6 [write problem numbers on board]. This is for practice only. I'll come around to see how you are doing. All right, let's get to work."
- "Study your map with your team. You may discuss, but use soft voices only [write "soft voice" or place marker on the soft voice icon]. Using the map, find the answers to the five questions I have given you. When you finish, you may read your library book."

Explaining Concepts and Procedures.   Like giving directions, explaining ensures student understanding; therefore, clarity is essential. For concrete concepts and procedures, common in elementary education, it is best to explain orally as you demonstrate the procedure. For example:

- "We will cut out our rabbits by starting here at the tail and cutting up and around [demonstrate]. Cut along the line, like this. Jorge, please show us where to begin cutting. Amelia, where do we try to cut? Now let's all do that."
- "When we multiply two negative numbers, the product is a positive number. Watch what I do [demonstrate on board or overhead $-2 \times -2 = +4$]. Minus times minus equals plus. Kwan, try this one: minus 4 times minus 2. What did you get? Why? Remember class, minus times minus equals plus."

Posing Questions.   Questions keep students focused and active. A question such as the following might be asked to encourage student participation: "Who can tell me what *e pluribus unum* means? Thumbs up if you know." (Wait and look around before calling on anyone.)

Questions also force students to use various levels of thought. Benjamin Bloom (1956) listed six levels in a hierarchy of thinking: memory, comprehension, application, analysis, synthesis, and evaluation. Following the hierarchy, you can pose questions such as the following:

- For recall of information: "In what year did the Spaniards finally drive the Moors from Spain? What else of importance to us happened that year?"
- To show comprehension: "Suppose you have the colors red, yellow, and blue, but you need some green. How could you make it from the colors you have?"
- To show ability to apply learnings: "Let's say you have just written a story. How could you make certain you have spelled all your words correctly?"
- To show ability to analyze learnings: "What do you think the colonists were trying to accomplish by dumping tea into the harbor?"

- To show ability to synthesize from learnings: "How would you go about constructing a map of an imaginary island so we could locate it and identify its various features?"
- To show ability to evaluate: "Do you think Peter Rabbit was doing a good thing when he got into Mr. McGregor's cabbage patch? Why did he do that?"

Providing Supportive and Corrective Feedback.   Making helpful comments, sometimes publicly and sometimes privately, while directing a lesson or circulating during student work can provide both supportive and corrective feedback. Comments may focus on errors and corrections, observations, or encouragement. In general, comments should be private if they single out a student, and public if they give reminders of procedure or are appropriate to the entire class. For example:

Private (Individual Focus)

- "This is some of the best work I've seen you do."
- "You've made a mistake here. How can you correct it?"
- "No, look here: A plus times a minus gives a minus."
- "I don't feel as though you are trying today. I think something else must be on your mind. How can I help?"

Public (Group Focus)

- "This is some of the best work we've done."
- "It seems that many of you are making the same mistake. Look up here. Let me go through this again before we continue."
- "The secret to doing this correctly lies in looking at the time that the driver uses. Think of the problem from that angle."
- "I see improvement today. I see good improvement. We are getting there."

Remember that with very few exceptions feedback should be positive and helpful rather than faultfinding. When you must reteach, also remember that corrective instruction and second chances support students' success in their learning.

Redirecting Inappropriate Behavior.   When students become inattentive, noisy, disgruntled, or reluctant, or when they dawdle, daydream, and play with objects instead of working, they need only gentle reminders. Negative consequences need not be invoked unless the behavior becomes flagrant or is continually repeated. Students can normally be put back on course through redirection such as the following:

- "Justin." (Just say the student's name quietly.)
- "You need to be finished in five minutes."
- "I know you're tired, but let's see if we can finish this. I'll help you."
- "Please remember our rule about working."

Building Positive Relationships

Another important role of communication is that of building positive relationships. Previous chapters, especially Chapter 4, have explained that students have a primary need to belong. They should be reassured that they have place, purpose, and acceptance in the class. Students also have a need to be noticed and acknowledged. The quality of their behavior and work merits comment, always with courtesy and consideration.

Emphasizing Belonging and Importance.   What most of us want, really, is to feel appreciated. As a practicing rule, you should make comments that show you value the presence of every student. (Even if you don't, be a convincing actor for the student's sake and yours.) You may even find that such expressions help troublesome students become less troublesome. Be very free with comments such as

- "We are very glad you are in this class, Michael."
- "I like your drawing, Trish. May I put it on the display board?"
- "Class, I just want to tell you how pleased I am with our agreement to make everyone feel comfortable and important in this room."
- "We can't do our best work in these groups unless everyone contributes. We need that from everybody."

Speaking Personally with Each Student.   Teachers good in communication try to speak personally to each student at least once a day. You might feel that this personal contact will occur naturally, without conscious effort on your part, but in practice teachers tend to give most of their attention to the few brightest students in their class and to those who disrupt or fail to work. In doing so they overlook other students—usually the majority—who follow directions, complete their work, behave themselves, and show no particular flashes of brilliance.

What do teachers say in these personal communications? They ask questions and make observations, as appropriate:

- "I heard you have new puppies at your home, Teisha. What kind are they?"
- "Today is a hot day, isn't it, Manny? Were you too hot on the playground?"
- "Class, Jimmy has a new baby brother. What's his name, Jimmy? What's it like to be a big brother?"
- "I really appreciate how nicely you worked today, Caitlin. Thank you."

These personal touches need not take long, really only a few seconds, and they can be accomplished without using instructional time.

Karen O'Conner, a fourth-grade teacher, tells how she introduces herself and makes each student feel welcome:

> As a fourth-grade teacher and mother of three, I am sensitive to the anxiety that children experience at the start of the new school year. Common worries include: Will my teacher be nice? Will I know anyone in my class? Is fourth grade going to be really hard? Although I can't alleviate all of their concerns, I have been able to relax them considerably on the eve of the new school year by calling every student and personally welcoming them to fourth grade and to my class. Each call takes about four minutes. I tell them how much I'm looking forward to meeting them, and I highlight a few of our major activities and areas of study. I conclude the phone call by allowing them

to ask questions and by suggesting that they have a good night's sleep so that they can be ready for a terrific year.

Although phone calls to 30 or more students takes the better part of the evening, the rewards are great. I have had parents thank me throughout the year for that call and tell me how excited their child was to receive a phone call from the new teacher. On the first day of class the children are less anxious because they have already "met" me. It's a great way to set the tone for the year.

Commenting on Quality of Behavior and Work.   Almost all students like to receive positive comments about their good behavior and work. Younger students like those comments made publicly; older students may prefer that they be made privately so others won't tease them about being teacher's pet or worse. Conversely, no student likes to receive negative comments, especially in front of the class.

It is important that students know when their efforts are appreciated, as well as when they are not. Except for routine comments such as "good," "fine," "thank you," "right," "you're on target," and so on, personal appraisals should be kept between teacher, individual student, and the student's parents or guardians. If a student does well, find a quiet moment and say

- "You really helped our class today with your comments, Pedro. Thank you for that."
- "Sarah, your paragraph showed that you have learned a great deal in the past week. Keep up the good work."

Or write a private note mentioning the same thing for the student to take home and share. If the student does poorly, feedback should be honest, even if sugarcoated:

- "I don't think you did your best today, Anna. Is there a problem I can help you with?"
- "Kevin, you missed eleven spelling words. I'd like to ask your mother to help you at home. I've written a note for her that lists these words and asks if she will work with you tonight."
- "I was really bothered by your behavior in class today, Cassie. I wasn't able to teach well because of it. I think we should come up with a plan so we won't have that problem again."

Stressing Courtesy and Consideration.   Classes tend to reflect the personality of their teacher. Good character among students is more likely when it is infused in the way teachers teach. Classes behave much more humanely when courtesy and dignity are emphasized as prime goals, incorporated into class rules, and intentionally taught and modeled.

Younger students readily accept instruction in good manners, meeting people, speaking courteously, saying please and thank you, and offering help. Older students may snicker and groan, but they privately like learning and practicing these things, too.

- "Don, would you please help Mary? Thank you."
- "Boys and girls, I'd like to introduce Mrs. Sands, Claire's mother. Welcome to our room, Mrs. Sands."

- (After instruction on how to introduce people) "Craig, please introduce our guest."
- "Class, what should we say when someone helps us or does something nice for us? That's right, thank you. Today I will listen hard to hear if any of you say thank you to another student. You listen, too. At the end of the day, we'll discuss what we heard."
- "Room 12, I believe we have been acting very discourteously during our kickball games. I think this goes for winners and losers alike. No one likes to lose, but usually somebody does. How should we act at such times? How should winners act? Let's practice your suggestions before we go outside to play today."

Maintaining a Sense of Community

Sense of community is emphasized as a means of encouraging students to take initiative, show responsibility, and provide support for each other and the teacher. The following help provide a sense of community in the class.

Class Meetings.   William Glasser (1969) feels that most major problems teachers and students face in the classroom can be resolved in what he calls class meetings. Many other authorities in classroom management now place heavy emphasis on classroom meetings. These whole-class meetings are conducted with students seated in a tight circle so they can see and talk easily with each other. The teacher sits as part of the circle and participates with students but does not criticize or try to direct.

The purpose of class meetings is to find constructive solutions to problems identified by students—too much noise during work time, assignments too difficult or no fun, students picking on each other, not enough time to complete work, or too much homework.

Three rules are required for meetings to function as intended. First, only positive and constructive solutions can be considered—no complaining, faultfinding, or backbiting is allowed. (This is the only place where the teacher steps in strongly.) Second, every person has the right to express an opinion without being slighted or put down by others. Third, the teacher plays a subdued role, participating to clarify and encourage but not to dominate, lead, or criticize.

Jane Nelsen, Lynn Lott, and H. Stephen Glenn (2000) describe eight building blocks that lead to effective class meetings: forming a circle, practicing compliments and appreciations, creating an agenda, developing communication skills, learning about separate realities, solving problems through role playing and brainstorming, recognizing the four reasons people do what they do, and applying logical consequences and other nonpunitive solutions.

Win-Win Conflict Resolution.   Even in the best-managed classes conflict occurs between students and between the teacher and students. In the normal resolution of those conflicts, one person usually emerges as winner with an urge to gloat, and the other as loser with a penchant to pout and hold hard feelings. To improve that situation, Spencer Kagan, Patricia Kyle, and Sally Scott (2004) have developed a win-win approach, where all involved get at least part of what they want. For win-win resolutions to occur, teacher and student need to be on the same side, working together toward the same end, and sharing responsibility in the learning process.

Communicating with Caregivers

Caregivers are parents, guardians, or any others who are in charge of children at home. Elementary teachers who are most successful—and who enjoy the highest reputations within the community—are those who communicate best with caregivers. For most caregivers, though nowadays appearances sometimes seem to contradict this point, their child is their most precious possession, their best reflection of themselves, and their best extension into the future. They expect teachers to hold little Johnny or Jennifer central in their thoughts; never mind that there may be nineteen to thirty-five other children in the class whose caregivers expect the same. The wise teacher keeps this reality in mind.

What Caregivers Expect from Teachers

Caregivers don't expect you to turn their child into an Albert Einstein, a Langston Hughes, or an Amy Tan. But they rightfully expect you to

1. *Care* about their child and give attention to him or her as a person, which you show through acknowledgment of the child's interests, joys, fears, capabilities, and special needs.
2. *Excite* their child about learning.
3. *Teach* their child the basics—literacy and life skills; something of the human condition; correct ways of behaving; and the good, right, and beautiful.
4. *Encourage and support* their child's efforts by nurturing, prodding, and encouraging.
5. *Control* their child to prevent self-defeating behavior, and especially to prevent mistreatment by others.
6. *Inform* them about their child's educational program and progress.
7. *Be dedicated* to doing the best you can for their child.

What Caregivers Need to Know, Will Ask, and Will Say

Caregivers need to know a number of things about their child in school but often never ask about what they really need to know. They tend to shy away from school after their child completes kindergarten and first grade. Many feel they shouldn't meddle. Many feel insecure about approaching the teacher. They don't want to feel embarrassed, or their culture doesn't support such an action. Many would like to help but don't know how. Some, because English is not their first language, do not feel able to help. If you take time to inform them about what they need to know, you will earn their esteem and support.

Anticipate the questions caregivers are likely to ask, and be prepared to answer them as though their particular child were always in the center of your thoughts.

- "What is a typical day like?"
- "How's my child doing in school?"
- "Is my child progressing as well as expected?"
- "Does my child seem happy?"
- "How does my child get along with others?"

- "How does my child react to trying new things? To making mistakes?"
- "What is my child best at? What is my child weakest in?"
- "Does my child cause problems?"
- "What after-school opportunities are there for my child?"
- "Is there anything I can do to help?"

As parents or guardians listen to your answers, they are likely to reply with comments such as

- "He was never that way before." (Even though he was, your reply should be, "I hope I can count on your help, because I know you don't want him behaving this way.")
- "She was well liked in her other school." (This may or may not be true, but your reply should be, "She will be well liked here, too, if together we encourage her to be more friendly to others. I'm sure with your help we can.")
- "He is just like his father, who has never learned to pick up after himself." (Your reply should be, "Let's see if we can work on this. How can you help?")
- "Her mother is the same way, just loves to talk." (Your reply should be, "I really like her. It's just that her talking sometimes disturbs the class and keeps her from getting her work done. I'm sure you want her to learn, just as I do.")

"NO SMOKING ON SCHOOL PROPERTY, MS. HANES."

A Note on Communicating with Caregivers.   Caregivers see teachers as professional, knowledgeable, and communicative. They don't want to think of teachers as wishy-washy, silly, or disorganized, nor do they want to see them behave as long-lost best pals. Of course, they don't want teachers to be gruff and intimidating either.

Focus on how you communicate with caregivers. You want to be approachable and nice, but brief, plain, and businesslike. Be considerate, remain approachable, and show caregivers that you value their collaboration. This is no time to show off your impressive vocabulary or your command of complex sentence structure. Neither is it a time to impress caregivers with the number of acronyms you know (GATE, ELP, IEP, SDAIE, ADHD, and so on ad infinitum). Don't be wordy. Use short, direct sentences with words everyone understands.

Means and Opportunities for Communicating with Caregivers

You never know when a parent may appear at your classroom door and want to talk. When that happens, be sure the unexpected visit does not interrupt your instruction time, then mostly listen. But for occasions you set and for which you have time to prepare, consider the following opportunities for communicating well with parents and guardians.

Open House.   As described in Chapter 2, early in the year your school will host an open house. You will be expected to talk about the following:

1. The educational program provided in your class—a summary of your curriculum, the subject area standards, and special activities. (This doesn't have to be communicated all at once. You can spread it out through the year.)
2. The expectations you hold for their child, including class work, behavior, homework, attendance and tardiness, makeup work, and so forth.
3. How you intend to enforce your expectations—your discipline system.
4. How their child is doing in school, both generally (does good work; is a good citizen) and specifically (has improved from 75 percent to 85 percent correct in math). They also need to know about any specific problems their child is having.
5. What caregivers can do to help further the progress of the child.
6. Information about special activities and events.

After your presentation, parents or guardians may wish to ask questions and speak with you individually about their child (refer back to questions caregivers ask). It's good practice to schedule this meeting at another mutually convenient time.

Questionnaire.   Some teachers send a questionnaire (written in English and translated into the primary languages used in the homes of their students) in order to receive specific information from caregivers regarding their child and family. Questions might include: Does your child use the same last name as you? To best work with your family, what do I need to know? (Are parents separated or divorced? Are there stepparents? Is this a blended family? Are separated parents able to meet together, or is it best to have individual communications?) What special needs does your child have (health, allergies, medications)? How will you be able to participate in the classroom (time, sharing a special interest, helping with field trips or special activities, donating wish list items)? Asking caregivers to describe their child to you can be particularly insightful.

Videotapes.   Some teachers find opportunities to videotape students as they work on projects and activities in class. The tapes are then available in the class library for children to check out and share at home. The tapes provide a nice alternative option to communicating with caregivers.

Kindergarten teacher Linda Monedero describes how she uses videotapes to communicate with parents and guardians.

> Videotapes are valuable tools in communicating with home, for they give to parents and grandparents a gift of time. Many caring adults work outside the home and can no longer volunteer in classrooms during the day. However, they still have the desire to know what their child is doing in school. Videotaped lessons and programs share this with them.
>
> To prepare parents for this communication, I first send a letter home to each family listing the purposes of the videotape program and encouraging their participation (which is not mandatory). They are told that the completed videotapes are usually less than fifteen minutes long; this allows families to view tapes when they come home in spite of busy schedules. Each family is encouraged to keep videos for one or two evenings and return them to school as soon as possible so that other families can view them. The rotation for each video varies because children put their names on slips of paper and the helper of the day draws the name of the video student. Video checkout cards or lists are kept in a special location as a record of who has which videotape.
>
> Three basic rules are necessary for making this video program successful. First, the person filming the video is reminded that the tape will go home with each child; therefore, each child should be taped about the same amount of time. Second, children are told that only acceptable student behavior will be taped. This fosters positive behaviors without having to emphasize the negative, which leads to better overall behavior. Third, a short list of desired activities to be recorded is given to filming volunteers so that the tapes always show children actively involved in learning.

Newsletters.   Many teachers send home newsletters every month—or more frequently if possible. Older students can assist with the production of the newsletter within the language arts and computer programs. Results come in the form of parent interest, involvement, and support—well worth the effort.

It is better if newsletters are short and to the point, and caregivers can anticipate them on the same day or week of the month. They should include items such as calendar dates of field trips and other special activities, and class accomplishments. Newsletters also may include a question, learning activity, or website of the week. They should never disintegrate into breezy notes that single out a few students.

Notes.   Personal notes are helpful for sending brief messages to parents and guardians, reminders about snacks and money, and for calling attention to responsible student behavior and accomplishments. Students should be allowed to read these notes, or you should read the notes to them; otherwise if students are uneasy about them, the notes may never reach home. Of course, if appropriate, these notes should be translated into the primary language of the caregivers.

Websites and Home Pages.   More and more teachers, taking advantage of computer technology, create web pages for their class, and are thereby able to stay in contact with caregivers who have computer access. Teachers post announcements, homework assignments, and other news and information that may be of interest.

Setting up a web page is not as difficult as it sounds. First you need someone to host the page. Free space is available on the Internet if the school district doesn't have its own server and site dedicated for this purpose. Geocities is an example of a free host. Many service providers now include a free website in their service package. You should find several from which to choose by searching for keyword *free space* or *free web hosting.*

Although the size of the site may be limited, there is generally plenty of room to have several pages of your own. You will also need a way to edit your page. Where your site is housed will determine this; free sites often include the necessary software and instructions online, or you can use a website-editing package such as Microsoft FrontPage. To include student work and photos you will need access to a scanner or digital camera.

Lynne Harvey, a third grade teacher who uses web pages, shares her discoveries:

> My web page is an effective way to establish and maintain ongoing, interactive communication between school and home. I found that it does not have to be fancy or elaborate, but there are several helpful items to include for parents. The number one requested item by parents is a homework page—this simple posting can be done daily or at the beginning of each week, with updates and changes as needed. A monthly newsletter is an added bonus. Both the homework posting and the newsletter help keep parents informed, and provide an opportunity for them to support student efforts. Including a section dedicated to showcasing student work, photos from class, and field trip photos gives parents a taste of what goes on from day to day, and allows them the opportunity to participate in special events without actually being there.
>
> Here's one final tip. You will want to make sure you have a signed permission form from parents *before* including their child's picture and/or name on a website. Most districts will have a form for this, but if they don't you can make your own. My suggestion would be to get several separate permissions giving parents and students options:
>
> To include work with first name identification only
> To include photo with no name identification
> To include photo and name identification

In Lynne's experience, there is usually no objection to the first two options.

Telephone Calls.   Caregivers rarely receive phone calls from the teacher except when their child is in trouble. It is good to surprise them occasionally with brief, friendly messages such as

> "Mrs. Appleton, this is Miss Cabrera, Leo's teacher. I just wanted you to know that Leo did excellent work in math this week. We can all be very proud of him. Tell him I said so. Thank you for your support, and I'll call you again before long."

With that you say good-bye and hang up, thereby avoiding a lengthy chat from what certainly will be an appreciative Mrs. Appleton. Messages about concerns should be delivered in a way that requests help:

> "Mrs. Engles, this is Mr. James, Rob's teacher. I am calling to let you know there's a problem at school that I need your help with. Rob has received four playground citations in the past two weeks, and I am concerned about him. I know you don't want him misbehaving on the playground and endangering himself and others. I have begun talking with him about following school rules and I'd like to ask you to do the same at home. We don't want to punish Rob. All we want is for him to follow the rules, for his benefit as well as that of others. May I count on your support in helping Rob?"

Performances and Displays.   Like many teachers, you may wish to put on student performances and displays of student work to be attended by caregivers, relatives, and friends. Such events include musical productions, plays, choral verse readings, readers' theatre, science fairs, art exhibitions, and athletic events. Caregivers usually turn out in numbers for these occasions. Teachers can show off what they and the students have done, but also further explain the special activities that contribute to the children's well-rounded education. These events also contribute strongly to teacher's good reputations.

Newer schools may have the technology capability to broadcast events over the Internet with video streaming. Video streaming via the Internet requires a media program such as RealPlayer, a free downloadable program, that has a video streaming tool included. Family and friends anywhere are able to view the production online through the school website.

Parent–Teacher Conferences.   As described earlier, most schools regularly schedule conferences that bring the teacher and caregivers together to confer about each child's progress. In Chapter 10 we looked at two types of student-involved conferences. Conferences, both teacher- and student-led, can be very productive if properly organized. In traditional parent–teacher conferences, that duty falls to the teacher, who must set caregivers at ease, communicate without causing affront, draw out the caregivers' ideas, and when necessary, suggest a plan for improving the progress of the child. The following suggestions help make conferences agreeable and useful.

Before the Conference
1. Prepare a folder for each child, with the child's name attractively written on it.
2. In the folder include a summary of work covered to date; a profile of the child's performance in that work; samples, good and bad, of the child's work; and tests and other products that back up your evaluations.
3. Make notes to yourself about anecdotes that provide insight into the child's behavior and progress.

When Caregivers Arrive
1. Greet them in a friendly, relaxed manner.
2. Sit side by side with the caregivers at a table rather than behind a desk. This conveys a message of cooperation.
3. Begin by chatting about the child as a worthwhile person. Mention good traits. This reassures the caregivers.
4. Guide them through the student's folder, commenting on work samples it contains.
5. Encourage them to talk. Listen carefully. Be accepting. Do not argue or criticize. Caregivers cannot be objective about their own child, and you do not want to cause resentment.
6. Keep in mind that caregivers can be your strongest allies. Let them know you believe this. Show that you, like the caregivers, want the best possible for the child.
7. If appropriate, work with them to create a home action plan for them and their child.
8. End the conference by describing your plans for the student's future progress. Earnestly request their help in supporting your efforts. Thank them for talking with you about the child.

Forming Home Alliances and Home Action Plans

Teachers may find it helpful to involve the parents or guardians as partners to work with the student's progress and behavior. Certainly caregivers can reinforce what teachers do in the classroom. In fact, many of the current discipline practitioners and theorists stress the importance of home alliances and partnerships, and build home communication and cooperation into their plans for managing student behavior. To win parental cooperation, it's important to talk about behavior in clear, objective, nonjudgmental terms; to ask for what is possible to do; and to anticipate success.

Keeping Track of Communication with Caregivers

On index cards or individual sheets of paper, maintain a chart, such as the one in Figure 11.2, for keeping track of contacts with caregivers and to serve as a reminder for contacting them.

A very simple variation of the communication log would be to use a telephone message book such as those found in office supply stores. Every entry is automatically duplicated on carbonless paper. The duplicate record remains in the book as a running chronology of contacts; the original copy is placed in individual student files.

FIGURE 11.2 **Date and Type of Communication**

Surname	Date	Ns	T	Nt	C	U	UC
_____	____	___	___	___	___	___	___
_____	____	___	___	___	___	___	___
_____	____	___	___	___	___	___	___

Ns = newsletter; T = telephone; Nt = note; C = conference; U = unscheduled talk;
UCA = unsuccessful contact attempt

Communicating with Colleagues and Administrators

In Chapter 4 much was said about how you ought to speak with and conduct yourself around colleagues and administrators so as to ensure support and good working relationships. If you remain concerned about this topic, you might wish to refer back to that chapter. Otherwise, we will bring this chapter to a close with the following brief reminder.

Administrators should be kept informed about programs and problems in your classroom. You may communicate this information orally unless otherwise directed. They may or may not be able to offer help, but in any case, administrators like to know what's going on in the school, and they detest being caught off guard by calls from upset parents or guardians and not knowing what the caregiver is talking about.

Administrators want to know about your discipline plan, and you should furnish a written copy. Occasionally administrators will rule against your discipline system or an event you want to organize. By tactfully asking them to suggest alternatives that would accomplish the purpose you had in mind, administrators will feel obliged to help you. Administrators also want to know in advance about class parties, programs, and field trips, and may want to see copies of your newsletter before it is sent home to caregivers.

Colleagues such as fellow teachers, paraprofessionals (such as service providers for students with special needs), beginning teacher support providers, student teachers, clerical staff, librarians, nurses, psychologists, custodians, lunchroom and playground staff and others should also be informed of any activities or needs that might impose on them. They do not appreciate your taking their professional duties for granted, especially when they must change plans for your benefit. On the other hand, when you take pains to communicate such matters fully and they are able to help you, most will do so willingly, and your efforts in communicating will have paid off in friendliness, helpfulness, and mutual respect.

Ginny Lorenz, member of a fourth-grade team of teachers, discusses decision making within her team:

> As the year began at my new school, a meeting with the fourth-grade team members was set up to discuss grade-level expectations, grading system, school and classroom rules, and other such matters. Our discussion was going well until we began to identify our classroom behavior system and classroom rules. I feel strongly that students need to be involved in making the class rules if they are to "buy in." One of my colleagues felt just as strongly that the teacher must be the rule maker. I was afraid we had come to an impasse, but I managed to convince one of my colleagues to try my way of writing rules and consequences; the other person insisted she had to write the rules, but she would agree to identical consequences. Not a perfect solution, but at least there was some consistency. . . .
>
> The end of my first year with my new colleagues has now come. The compromise worked quite well. Substitutes told us that it was very easy to substitute in any of our classes because of the grade-level behavior system. Both students and parents seemed to feel that there was a genuine concern for the needs of all students. And we teachers felt far less frustrated about the need to constantly correct negative behaviors.

This ends our consideration of the effective management of communication. Before moving ahead to Chapter 12, which deals with how to manage the work of other adults—paraprofessionals, substitute teachers, and student teachers—take a moment to explore these end-of-chapter activities.

Parting Thought

What most of us want, really, is simply to feel appreciated.

SUMMARY SELF-CHECK

Check off the following as you either understand or become able to apply them:

❑ Good communication is what makes good education possible.

❑ Good communication is especially needed in giving directions, conducting instruction, holding class discussions, holding individual conferences with students, having staff meetings and individual conferences with administrators and colleagues, and conferencing with parents and guardians.

❑ When communicating, remember the four-way test:
- Is this true?
- Is this helpful?
- Will my silence hurt?
- Will this build good relationships?

❑ Always use parallel (adult–adult) communication with students and everyone else.

❑ Communication considerations when conducting instruction: gaining attention, providing motivation, giving directions, explaining concepts and procedures, posing questions, providing supportive and corrective feedback, reteaching using corrective instruction and offering second chances, redirecting inappropriate behavior.

❑ Communication for building positive relationships: emphasize belonging and importance, speak personally with each student, focus on quality of work and behavior, stress courtesy and consideration.

❑ Communication for maintaining good behavior: no-lose conflict resolution, the win-win approach, class meetings.

❑ Communicating with caregivers:
- What caregivers need to know from teachers: the educational program, student expectations, means of enforcing rules, how their child is doing, how they can help, routine information
- Style of communication with caregivers: friendly but businesslike, clear with no jargon
- Opportunities for communicating with caregivers: open house (the educational program, student expectations, means of enforcing rules, how they can help),

newsletters, notes, websites and home pages, telephone calls, performances and displays, parent–teacher conferences

■ Communicating with administrators and colleagues: keep everyone informed, never take other's services for granted, beginning teacher support providers

ACTIVITIES FOR REFLECTION AND GROWTH

For Cumulative Skills Development

1. Take a moment to review the statements in the Anticipation–Reaction Guide at the beginning of this chapter. Put a check mark in the Reaction column next to any statement with which you now agree. How have your thoughts changed since reading this chapter?

2. What advantages do you see in applying the four-way test to what you say? What dangers do you see? Illustrate with scenarios that involve talking with caregivers, students, and administrators.

3. For a grade of your choice, identify typical contents of a class newsletter you would want to produce. Sketch out the format. How would you mention student work? How would you mention as many student names as possible?

4. Write out the telephone messages you might want to deliver to caregivers concerning (a) Maria, whose work quality has been declining; (b) Linda, who has frequent squabbles with other girls in the class; (c) Marta, who always behaves well and offers to help; and (d) Carla, who seems to try hard but continues to do poorly in spelling.

5. You are due to have a routine evaluation conference with your principal. The principal has only observed you three times, and on two occasions your students were abnormally unruly. You expect to be criticized for poor class control. (a) How will you intend to conduct yourself in the conference? (b) If criticized for class control, what will you say in response? (c) What, if anything, will you say concerning your feeling that you've not been sufficiently observed? (d) What would you intend to say at the conclusion of the conference?

6. Assuming you are able to create one, describe what you would like to include on a web page. What special considerations and permissions will you obtain in order to proceed with this tool?

REFERENCES AND RECOMMENDED READINGS

Albert, L. (1996). *Cooperative discipline.* Circle Pines, MN: American Guidance Service, Inc.

Berne, E. (1964). *Games people play.* New York: Grove Press.

Bloom, B. S. (Ed.). (1956). Taxonomy of educational objectives: The classification of educational goals: Handbook I, cognitive domain. New York: Longmans, Green.

Christopher, C. (1996). *Building parent–teacher communication: An educator's guide.* Lancaster, PA: Technomic Publishing.

Coloroso, B. (1990). *Winning at teaching . . . without beating your kids.* [Videotape from the series *Kids are worth it!*] Littleton, CO: Kids Are Worth It!

Coloroso, B. (1999). *Parenting with wit and wisdom in times of chaos and loss.* Toronto, Ontario, Canada: Viking.

Dembo, M. (1994). *Applying educational psychology* (5th ed.). White Plains, NY: Longman.

Glasser, W. (1969). *Schools without failure.* New York: Harper & Row.

Glasser, W. (1998a). *Control theory in the classroom* (Rev. ed.). New York: HarperCollins.

Glasser, W. (1998b). *The quality school: Managing students without coercion* (Rev. ed.). New York: Harper-Collins.

Glasser, W. (1998c). *The quality school teacher* (Rev. ed.). New York: HarperCollins.

Gordon, T. (1970). *Parent effectiveness training: A tested new way to raise responsible children.* New York: New American Library.

Gordon, T. (1974). *T.E.T.: Teacher effectiveness training.* New York: David McKay.

Gordon, T. (1976). *P.E.T. in action.* New York: Bantam Books.

Gordon, T. (1989). *Discipline that works: Promoting self-discipline in children.* New York: Random House.

Jones, F. (2000). *Tools for teaching: Discipline instruction motivation.* Santa Cruz, CA: Fredric H. Jones & Associates.

Kagan, S., Kyle, P., & Scott, S. (2004). *Win-win discipline.* San Clemente, CA: Kagan Cooperative Learning.

Nelsen, J., Lott, L., & Glenn, H. (2000). *Positive discipline in the classroom* (3rd ed.). Rocklin, CA: Prima Publishing.

Quiroz,, B., Greenfield, P., & Altchech, M. (1999, April). Bridging cultures with a parent–teacher conference. *Educational Leadership, 56*(7), 68–70.

Ribas, W. (1998). Tips for reaching parents. *Educational Leadership, 56*(1), 83–85.

12 Managing the Work of Paraprofessionals, Substitute Teachers, and Student Teachers

It's easy to get good players. Getting 'em to play together, that's the hard part.

—Casey Stengel

ANTICIPATION–REACTION GUIDE

Before you read the chapter, take a moment to put a check mark in the Anticipation column next to any statement with which you agree.

	Anticipation	*Reaction*
A classroom paraprofessional is someone who takes the place of the teacher.	❏	❏
Substitute teaching is considered one of the most difficult teaching jobs.	❏	❏
Teachers are expected to provide detailed lesson plans for their substitute teachers.	❏	❏
Legally, paraprofessionals may administer, correct, and record student tests and scores.	❏	❏
Substitute teachers should not score or grade papers; that is the responsibility and prerogative of the regular teacher.	❏	❏
Substitute teachers should be encouraged to teach some of their own lessons that they particularly like.	❏	❏
Student teachers are technically paraprofessionals.	❏	❏
Paraprofessionals, substitutes, and student teachers, like contracted teachers, can be dismissed from their jobs for reasons of incompetence.	❏	❏
The same standards of professionalism are expected equally of paraprofessionals, substitutes, student teachers, and regular classroom teachers.	❏	❏
Paraprofessionals and substitutes are advised to discipline students in the way they deem best, so long as they do not infringe on students' rights.	❏	❏

Enterprising teachers have always looked for help in operating their classrooms. In the old one-room schools, more advanced students helped the less advanced. In today's class-rooms, students help each other in cooperative learning teams, differentiated and multi-age classes, cross-grade partnerships, and cross-age tutoring. Increasingly, other adults have begun helping teachers in running the class program. It is now rare to find an elementary teacher who does not at least occasionally count on the assistance of another adult in the room, ranging from mothers helping with a class party to the daily services of full-time employed aides. On occasion when the regular teacher must be away, substitute teachers are present to teach the class and make the day productive for the students. Student teachers may also work in a classroom as teachers-in-training.

Adult helpers who undertake regular, assigned duties are commonly referred to as *paraprofessionals. Para* means alongside of; *professional* refers to the teacher. Teachers have come to rely on paraprofessionals, not only to do clerical work, but also to tutor stu-dents; monitor the work of small groups; and supervise in the library, on the playground, and elsewhere in the school. At times, paraprofessionals also deliver basic instruction under the teacher's supervision. Paraprofessionals mostly fall into the following groups: (1) paid instructional aides, (2) paid support providers for students with special needs, (3) caregiver volunteers, and (4) community resource volunteers (often senior citizens). As we will presently see, student teachers also provide help in many classrooms, but are not referred to as paraprofessionals. The same is true for substitute teachers, cross-grade partners, cross-age tutors, district curriculum and instruction mentors, and adults brought in for special purposes, such as to read to children or supervise them on outings. However, all these helpers work under the direction of, or in conjunction with, the teacher. The teacher there-fore must manage the schedules, duties, and activities of those helpers.

Instructional Aides and Support Providers

Instructional aides and support providers have regular work schedules, are salaried, and are expected to meet the same standards of reliability and professional demeanor as teachers. They are recruited, selected, paid, and sometimes trained by the school district before assigned to or selected by individual teachers. The supply of paid volunteers waxes and wanes in accord with economic conditions and special programs and grants. When schools have money, they hire more aides. Mandated programs such as special and bilingual educa-tion usually provide money to hire skilled support providers. Because of the individual attention young students require, paid aides are more common at the primary level than at the intermediate. Mary Brewer, a teacher who works with students who are hearing impaired, describes being a special needs support provider:

> One paraprofessional with whom you may interact is the interpreting aide for chil-dren who are deaf or hearing-impaired. The interpreting aide's role in the classroom is not to teach, but to act as the voice for the deaf student and to provide ongoing sign interpretation of all voiced communication to that student. Classroom teachers must therefore learn how to use the interpreter's services effectively. Toward that end, it is

important that teacher and aide clearly understand their respective roles in working in the classroom.

Family Caregiver Volunteers

The prime source of volunteer help is from caregivers and other relatives of students in the class. Grandparents are especially excellent, because they have more available time and usually relate well with the young. This has been the case for the Senior Motivators in Learning and Educational Services (SMILES) program in the Salt Lake City School District. However, relatives tend to be reticent about volunteering their services, so some gentle recruitment may be needed. This can be accomplished informally through hints and expressions of need, and with formal notes sent home with children, asking for specific kinds of volunteer help. These gentle requests should specify days and times help is needed and should include a response form.

Family caregiver volunteers are an extremely valuable, though sometimes a frustrating, source of classroom help. These volunteers may be highly educated and skilled, or barely literate. They may be conscientious or negligent, reliable or undependable. They may genuinely want to help, or they may have little else to do with their time. They may be good models of language, self-respect, good character, and attitude toward others, or they may fall short in these regards. Not all turn out to be what you might hope, but when you get a good volunteer, it's like finding buried treasure. Teacher Eileen Andreoli comments on parent volunteers:

> I find parent volunteers invaluable in my classroom. At the beginning of the year I make it clear during back-to-school night that I greatly appreciate parents' help and welcome them to share any gifts or talents they have.
>
> When parents come into my class to help, I like to make them feel welcome. On a volunteer table I have work that needs to be done, accompanied by a clear description of what I need, and files for regular volunteers with notes about things they can do. I make sure there is a basket on the table filled with everything the volunteers may need in their work, such as tape, stapler, scissors, glue, paste, and paper clips. This avoids my being interrupted while I work with the class, or having parents search through my desk.
>
> Finally, and most important, I leave letters of thanks and appreciations regularly. A little bit of acknowledgement goes a long way.

Community Resource Volunteers

Community resource volunteers can make marvelous contributions to your program, but rarely can you consistently count on their help. They may be representatives from businesses or agencies. They may be volunteers with a local program, such as the Rolling Readers literacy program. Frequently they are retired persons who held occupations that are receiving attention in the class. Sometimes they are musicians or artists who like to help with the music and arts programs. These individuals tend to be interesting and good communicators, but because they lead busy lives, you cannot regularly count on them.

What Is Expected of Paraprofessionals

A common view persists that paraprofessionals mostly do clerical work and help children with their shoelaces and coats, but the actual range of their contributions is almost as broad as that of the teachers. True, they spend substantial time copying materials, checking papers, and keeping records, but most are also given quasi-instructional duties such as directing instructional games and activity centers, monitoring and assisting individual students during seat work, and working with small groups to provide additional practice in basic skills. They may help teachers prepare instructional materials such as flash cards, art materials, visual aides, and work sheets. They may also organize bulletin boards, administer tests, and be another caring adult with whom students can relate.

Although intended to provide services that supplement and assist the teacher's efforts by handling many of the miscellaneous time-consuming tasks, skilled paraprofessionals clearly supervise most—and in some cases all—of the instruction in art, music, and physical education. It is common to see paraprofessionals who, at least in particular segments of the curriculum, are as skilled in instruction as the elementary teacher.

It is true that paraprofessionals add to the complexity of teachers' lives, which prompts questions about whether they are worth the extra time they require. Most teachers say they are definitely worth having because paraprofessionals help make their programs fuller, richer, and more student oriented. Teachers are quick to point out, however, that good planning is necessary if the paraprofessional is to be used to best advantage.

In elementary classrooms, paraprofessionals may do such things as

- Duplicate materials
- Prepare games and other instructional materials
- Tutor individual students
- Monitor and assist students during centers (such as reading, math, and art) and seat work
- Distribute and collect materials
- Prepare displays
- Assist students on projects
- Supervise playground activities
- Read stories
- Help with media equipment
- Perform innumerable other duties assigned by the teacher

How Paraprofessionals Are Obtained

Some teachers are known for their ability to attract and maintain an unending supply of qualified paraprofessionals and volunteers eager to work in their rooms. How do they do this?

Word of Mouth

Word gets around about teachers who like to work with volunteers and are skilled at doing so. Parents and guardians talk among themselves about teachers and programs. A number of these caregivers, and others to whom they talk, like to work in elementary classrooms. They hear about and gravitate to teachers who treat people kindly and in whose rooms children seem to have fun while learning.

Not all teachers enjoy using paraprofessionals and volunteers. It is perfectly acceptable if you prefer to rely on your own abilities to provide a sound educational program. There is no reason to use an aide unless your program is thereby improved. Paraprofessionals and volunteers can sometimes get in the way of instruction, and many teachers do not like dealing with their assorted trials and troubles.

On the other hand, if you enjoy working with other adults, and particularly if you like to provide activities such as plays, field trips, exhibits, and so forth—activities for which aides are especially useful—let your interests be known. Good aides are available. It is simply a matter of making contact with them.

As mentioned, aides and support providers for students with special needs are the only regular paraprofessionals to receive pay, and they are recruited, selected, and given orientation training by the personnel department of school districts. Other aides—parents and guardians, community resource persons, and student tutors—volunteer their services and receive only the pleasures from their work and contribution. Other arrangements are made for substitutes and student teachers.

Universities and High Schools

Area universities and high schools have many students willing and eager to help in elementary classrooms. Often these students have decided on teaching as a career. For admission to teacher credential programs, university students may be required to provide documentation of experience in elementary classrooms. High school students may be in future teachers' clubs that maintain connections with elementary schools. Volunteers obtained through these sources tend to be highly motivated to do well and to learn as much as possible about teaching.

PTA Bureaus

Schools with active Parent–Teacher Associations (PTAs) may have bureaus run by parents that furnish qualified parent volunteers to aid in classrooms. Teachers usually provide some basic training for these parent volunteers.

Community Agencies

Especially in larger cities, community agencies may provide from among their employed personnel, liaison persons who make school and classroom presentations upon request. Zoos, museums, newspapers, hospitals, and fire and police departments often have educational departments that provide this service.

Other Helpers in the Room

As we noted, many other people not considered to be paraprofessionals also provide important help to the teacher. They include cross-age partners, cross-age tutors, and student teachers.

Cross-Grade Partners and Cross-Age Tutors

Older students in school can offer valuable assistance to teachers of earlier grades. A hallmark of differentiated and multi-age classrooms is the belief that students help students. As with using cross-grade partnerships, teachers can differentiate instruction in such a way that classmates help one another.

Research shows that the use of cross-grade partners and cross-age tutors results in increased achievement and positive attitudes in both the children who are helping and the children being helped. It is very motivating to younger children to have older students sit beside them, read to them, play with them, and help them with their work. Many teachers say, too, that cross-grade partners and cross-age tutors are among their most reliable, conscientious, patient, and valued helpers.

Some schools have formally established cross-age tutor programs. Where that is not the case, primary teachers desiring tutors should check first with the principal, then approach teachers of older grades for suggestions. In this way, students best suited for tutoring can be obtained.

Cross-grade partners are students from higher grades who befriend and provide encouragement to students in lower grades. In many schools, intermediate and primary teachers organize liaisons between older and younger students. This is not primarily done for instructional help, but for moral support, assistance, and helping young students feel there are older students in the school who will help them.

Cross-age tutors provide younger students help in learning. By fifth or sixth grade, some students think they might want to become teachers. They enjoy younger children, and the young enjoy them in return. Primary teachers prize such students, who are selected because of their skill, personality, and reliability. However, some teachers are reluctant to make frequent use of these students for fear of causing them to miss out on important parts of the educational program offered by their own teachers. To this end some primary and upper grade teachers form cross-grade partnerships and make this a regular part of their programs. They have both classes come together from time to time to work on projects and share reading and stories.

Substitute Teachers

Substitute teachers fill in for regular classroom teachers when the latter are ill or are excused for other duties. In many districts, qualified substitute teachers must successfully interview in order for their names to appear on a master list. Substitutes may also be required to participate in an orientation or training before they can work in some districts.

"THE FIFTH GRADE SUBSTITUTE WON'T
BE HERE. SHE CALLED IN CHICKEN."

Teachers can request a substitute any time of the day or night. Substitutes may be called directly by a clerk in the district office. Other districts use a twenty-four-hour telephone hotline system. Potential substitutes have the opportunity to check the hotline throughout the day, and accept positions at any time. Substitutes may still receive a morning call from this electronic "subfinder" for last-minute requests.

Substitute teachers have two main obligations—to keep order in the classroom and to further the class's instructional program. The second obligation, which most people consider the more important, cannot occur without the first. Substitutes fulfill these two primary obligations by being prepared, arriving early and obtaining information at the principal's office, and generally making the day productive for the students. Substitutes make the day productive when they take charge in the classroom, clarify expectations about how students are to behave, and emphasize to the students the importance of learning.

Teachers hope that when they must be absent their substitute will control the class and make a normal day's progress in the curriculum. Substitutes hope that they will find a substitute folder with good lesson plans and discipline standards. They also hope they will have the opportunity to use their own special skills, and even teach a favorite lesson or two not in the teacher's plans. An ideal relationship between teacher and substitute incorporates their mutual hopes. The teacher's responsibilities, then, are to

- Plan well.
- Leave an up-to-date substitute folder with lesson plans and a copy of the discipline plan, current seating chart, and class roster with notations of relevant student information (behavior, students with special needs and support providers, medication, special schedules and routines, and so on), class schedule and duty schedule, classroom monitor and volunteer lists, and school map.
- Teach students how to treat and work with substitutes, and hold students accountable for their behavior.

The substitute teacher's responsibilities are to

- Follow the teacher's plans carefully unless otherwise allowed.
- Follow the teacher's system for discipline, or if a plan is not available, quickly establish one before doing further work.
- Have special lessons ready at all times.
- Creatively use good time-filler and transition activities.

Second-grade teacher Candace Young shares her hope when she needs a substitute.

While I usually want a substitute teacher to follow my schedule as much as possible, I always make it clear that variations are not only acceptable but often, desirable. Substitute teachers often bring delightful learning activities with them. Some play the guitar and teach new songs; some bring favorite stories; some speak of faraway places; and some teach wonderful games, which the children then teach me when I return. Far more than covering material from point A to point B, I would expect a substitute teacher in my class to keep students engaged, successful, safe, and I would hope, happy.

Janet Beyea shares some of her experiences as a substitute in primary grades.

One teacher I worked for includes in her sub folder a sheet of coupons to give students who behave well. These coupons are good for a trip to the restroom, a drink of water, a free pencil, or a free eraser.

A substitute teacher always anticipates walking into a classroom and finding no lesson plans. I once showed up to teach music and ended up teaching a sixth-grade class for a week with no lesson plans, no roll book, and no set routines. The class had had four teachers in the first six weeks of school, so even the students didn't know what they were studying in class. Because the unexpected is the norm in substituting, flexibility and creativity are required.

When I find no lesson plans, I turn to resources I have brought with me. In my briefcase I have a book of games and art projects for all grades and some easy-to-use lessons. I look around the classroom and often find posted the classroom schedule, the discipline rules, and a job chart. I try to find the teacher's edition of the textbooks;

they're filled with suggestions. I use the students and other teachers for guidance. Finally, I remember that I am not expected to be a miracle worker. If at the end of the day the room is tidy, I have had no major discipline problems, and the students have had some fun, I consider my day successful.

Student Teachers

Student teachers work with tenured master or cooperating teachers. For most certification programs, student teachers are required to successfully complete field experiences in both primary (K–2) and intermediate (3–6) classroom settings. Because they are training to be teachers, they are present every day and responsible for portions of the educational program as guided by the cooperating classroom teacher and a university supervisor.

Arrangements for student teachers are usually made by the credentialing university or by the district. Occasionally student teachers may request their field placements, although when doing so they must be certain that the experience will fulfill all the state and university requirements for the student teacher to receive a teaching license.

The duties of student teachers are usually quite clear-cut. They often carry out some of the same duties as paraprofessionals, but there are two main differences: (1) Student teachers are training to be teachers, not teacher helpers, and (2) student teachers, as they progress through their field experiences, are assigned fewer clerical and supervisory tasks and ever-increasing amounts of the instructional program. As teacher trainees, they will eventually assume all classroom responsibilities from curriculum planning and instruction to management.

Therefore, under the guidance of the classroom teacher and university supervisor, student teachers typically do the following:

- Plan lessons and units
- Teach lessons
- Take responsibility for managing student behavior
- Communicate with parents and guardians
- Confer with teachers and university supervisors for suggestions, guidance, and detailed analyses of their efforts and progress
- Perform on a reduced scale most of the professional activities performed by teachers
- Observe and participate for the same hours (contracted hours) as the teachers

It is important to understand the role the master teacher plays in partnership with student teachers. Teachers who are perceived to be highly skilled in instruction and management may at times be asked to have student teachers in their classroom. In this capacity they may be called master, cooperating, or lead teacher, and as such they are mentors, coaches, and counselors for individuals enrolled in a teacher credential program. The cooperating teacher is perhaps the most important resource for the student teacher during the field experience. The cooperating teacher works closely with the student teacher and university supervisor to provide the best guidance and field learning experience possible. Effective cooperating teachers are expected to do many things. They help student teachers understand the role the classroom plays in their development as professionals, and help ease them into the school setting. They help students and caregivers understand the valuable role the student teacher plays in the classroom. Cooperating teachers also help with the following:

- Orientation—helping the student teacher locate key persons; resources; materials; equipment; and district curriculum standards, guidelines, and programs
- Induction—helping the student teacher understand the full-time teaching realities and responsibilities, how children learn, district expectations, and available supports
- Guidance—helping the student teacher with planning, evaluation, lesson delivery, and management; providing demonstration teaching
- Cooperation—through sharing ideas, conferencing and coaching, accepting and respecting the student teacher both as a learner and a coworker
- Reflection—sharing critical assessments of the student teacher's experience and progress, and encouraging the student teacher to use self-reflection productively.

Ginny Lorenz, who has been a master teacher many times, shares her thoughts:

I've been teaching nearly twenty years and I have watched the education pendulum swing from one side to another and back again. During those pedagogical swings one

"THAT WAS A PRETTY TOUGH STUDENT TEACHER. SHE DIDN'T WAVE THE WHITE FLAG 'TIL ALMOST NOON."

thing has remained constant—the need for a master teacher with whom a student teacher can train, and from whom a student teacher can learn.

The master teacher must be willing to mentor a student teacher through all aspects of the educational system, and this mentoring process takes a great deal of time and effort. Is it worth all the time and effort? Each time I have been asked to mentor a student teacher I struggle with a variety of questions and emotions. Questions such as: Do I have enough time to work with a student teacher? Will we (student teacher and I) get along? Will the student teacher have potential? Emotions such as: Do I really want to share my students, my class, my time? If the student teacher is not doing well, do I have expertise to help him or her succeed? Ultimately I always agree to the mentoring process because I feel that if we truly believe in the educational system, we owe it to the new generation of teachers to provide them with a safe place to hone their skills. We, the veterans, the master teachers, need to share our love of teaching. We need to share our enthusiasm for teaching and for learning!

It is through teaching that we learn. And it is though learning that we continue to grow. Mentoring a student teacher allows us to do both.

Requirements for Paraprofessionals and Volunteers

The requirements for paraprofessionals and volunteers are not stringent, but all persons under consideration should understand two things from the beginning. First, their services are needed to support the educational program. Their presence at school is not for socializing, drinking coffee in the lounge, or laughing about inappropriate things children sometimes do. This point is tactfully made to prospective helpers, of course. Second, once they are given responsibilities, professional standards apply to them just as to other school personnel. This point is also tactfully made so that no offense is given. (Professionalism is discussed later in this chapter.) With these two understandings in place, teachers look for three additional traits in paraprofessionals and volunteers: (1) a sincere desire to work with students and to help provide a quality educational experience, (2) a personality suited to working with children and other adults in the school, and (3) an assurance of reliability—that the person can and will appear regularly as scheduled.

Optimum Number of Paraprofessionals and Volunteers

One paraprofessional or volunteer per classroom is desirable; two per room, if they are good, may be better. With more than two, the situation is likely to be counterproductive, cumbersome, and confused. With the exception of support providers for children with special needs, ideally a class profits substantially from the presence of a teacher, one paid paraprofessional present every day, and one caregiver or university student volunteer scheduled as needed. Cross-grade partners and cross-age tutors may be used as needed to work directly with students who require extra help. This amount of assistance permits good instruction and monitoring, individual attention to children, and adequate help so the teacher isn't run ragged.

Ground Rules for Paraprofessionals and Volunteers

There are many expectations of paraprofessionals and volunteers with regards to behavior, authority, and dealing with children. They do not automatically know what is expected of them, especially in professional appearance and demeanor. They will almost certainly know little about legal requirements and danger points. You should be prepared to inform and instruct paraprofessionals and volunteers under your direction, so they are able to function well.

Expectations of paraprofessionals are often stated in handbooks prepared by school districts, and if these are available where you teach, you should see that your adult paraprofessionals receive copies. You should ask that they read the guidelines and discuss the contents with you afterward. If you use parent volunteers, cross-grade partners, or cross-age tutors, take time to carefully explain what you expect. Make sure you discuss with all paraprofessionals and volunteers your expectations concerning authority, reliability, instruction, discipline, communication, professionalism, and legal requirements.

Authority

Adult paraprofessionals and volunteers should be made aware of the lines of authority within the school, which normally flow in the order depicted in Figure 12.1. As illustrated, the principal is in charge of everyone at the school. Below the principal and on an equal level are teachers, librarians, clerical staff, custodians, and district resource personnel such as specialists and psychologists. Classroom paraprofessionals and volunteers are under the authority of the principal and classroom teacher but are directly responsible to the teacher in whose room they work.

FIGURE 12.1   Lines of Authority within the School

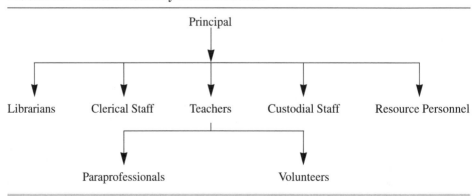

The paraprofessional has authority over students only in areas delegated by the teacher. That authority is usually limited to the classroom and the playground. It should be clearly understood that although the adult may be given considerable latitude, the teacher has final say in all matters related to the class duties of the paraprofessional or volunteer, including instruction, clerical work, the learning environment, and dealings with children and their parents or guardians.

Reliability

Reliability is essential in paraprofessionals and volunteers. Those who are not reliable in attendance or performance of duties are of no value. They need to understand that they must be prepared, that they must function consistently, and that they must let nothing except emergency situations interfere with the performance of their obligations.

Naturally, people become ill and cannot or should not report for work in the classroom, and unexpected emergencies happen to everyone. When these situations occur, paraprofessionals are obliged to inform the teacher as early as possible so the teacher can make other arrangements.

Teachers should not spring surprise duties on paraprofessionals or volunteers that cannot be handled well or gracefully. And they should always anticipate the possibility that the aide may be absent. With a backup plan always in mind, such as change of activity or use of a volunteer, cross-grade partner, or cross-age tutor, the teacher need not panic when an aide will not be present.

Instruction

The instructional program is to be planned and delivered under the direction of the classroom teacher. Many paraprofessionals and volunteers are very good at teaching and do so regularly, but always with the presumption that the teacher has provided suitable guidance. The classroom teacher is not to turn over complete responsibility for significant portions of the instructional program to any paraprofessional or volunteer. The teacher is legally and professionally expected to remain in charge of instruction and is responsible for instructional outcome.

Discipline

Technically, paraprofessionals and volunteers are not to discipline students. Discipline is the province of the teacher, principal, and other credentialed persons. In practice, however, you could not expect a paraprofessional or volunteer to work with students but do nothing to manage or help students manage their own behavior. When it is necessary to correct disruptive behavior, the paraprofessional or volunteer should always do so within the parameters of the discipline system in effect in the classroom, and with the teacher's permission. By no means should paraprofessionals or volunteers punish students physically, berate them, detain them after school, or force them to do unpleasant tasks as punishment for disruptive behavior. Consequences for disruptive or inappropriate behavior are always for the teacher to provide.

Teachers know that students often consider substitutes fair game. Therefore, they should talk seriously with students about class behavior during the teacher's absence. It should be made clear that the substitute will report on the behavior of the class and individual students. Students should be informed that the substitute may use the teacher's discipline plan or an altogether different one, but that, in either case, students are to behave and be as helpful as possible to the substitute.

Linda Monedero uses a video activity to prepare her young students and the substitute for a successful day.

> Videotapes can be helpful communication tools within the classroom. A taped daily schedule and the class rules can be part of the materials left for the substitute when the teacher is absent. The substitute and class view this five-minute tape together at the beginning of the school day. Students are accountable because they were involved in making the tape, and then they hear and see it with the substitute.
>
> To make the short videotape, students are formed into cooperative groups. Each group draws and labels a sign for one subject area (such as "Reading 9:00–10:30"), and another sign for a class rule. The videotape then shows each cooperative group reading its two signs. The signs for subject areas are presented in time line order.

For student teachers, the field experience is a time to find out what works and doesn't work, with a safety net of sorts provided by the cooperating teacher and university supervisor. Consequently, student teachers might hope to develop and present their own discipline system. This would be done only with the guidance and support of the cooperating teacher.

Communication

Paraprofessionals and volunteers should be taught how to communicate with your students—to speak in a calm, reassuring tone of voice, using words that students understand, and to serve as models of correct grammar and polite language. If your paraprofessional, volunteer, or tutor has a problem in this regard, very tactfully explain that you have a certain way of speaking with children that you would like help with; then demonstrate what you say and how you speak. When you notice improvement, acknowledge the effort with thanks.

Communication between teacher and paraprofessional, volunteer, substitute, or student teacher must be open. Provided neither person is put on the defensive, such openness permits an easier resolution of problems than when secrecy or hurt is involved. Teachers must take the lead in communicating openly and tactfully, taking as much care as when communicating with students to never disparage or speak brusquely to a paraprofessional, volunteer, or student teacher.

Professionalism

Paraprofessionals and volunteers, certainly those paid for their services, should be taught how to behave in a professional manner—that is, with a positive and sincere attitude toward one's status, work, and the children in the class. Professionalism includes dependability and the acceptance of responsibility. In addition, it reflects the styles of dress, speech, and demeanor considered proper for school personnel.

Be sure that you take a moment to discuss with paraprofessionals and volunteers the dangers inherent in gossip. Reportedly over 90 percent of the informal talk that occurs in teachers' lounges is negative in nature. Negative talk that criticizes programs, students, administrators, caregivers, and colleagues may be entertaining, but invariably is counter-productive. It encourages further negativism, diverts energy from productive work, and can lead to personal conflicts. Paraprofessionals and volunteers should be helped to understand clearly that they should either keep quiet or speak positively about children and programs to prevent irreparable damage.

Occasionally, frank talk is called for between teacher and paraprofessional, volunteer, or student teacher. Sometimes shortcomings must be discussed, but even then, the teacher must try to point to positive solutions, to better ways of doing things without denigrating the character of others. If you hear paraprofessionals or volunteers at your school speaking derogatorily of school, program, students, or personnel, take immediate steps to correct the problem. Handle the problem yourself if your own paraprofessional or volunteer is guilty, and consider including the university supervisor if your student teacher is guilty. If others are involved, take up the matter with the principal *as a school problem.* Don't point blame at fellow teachers.

Professionalism is also shown in the way one dresses. Adult paraprofessionals and volunteers, and occasionally student teachers, need to be encouraged to dress neatly, more or less in keeping with how teachers in the school and grade level dress. Like everyone else, they want respect, but they should understand that respect is influenced by appearance. For cross-grade partners and cross-age tutors, of course, this caution does not apply.

Responsibility and dependability have already been mentioned as aspects of pro-fessionalism. Responsibility is shown in the assumption of duties and their follow-through without having to be asked. It is also shown through use of common sense, such as paying attention to children when on playground duty. Dependability refers to living up to expectations—doing what one is supposed to do when one is supposed to do it. Of course, it is the teacher's responsibility to clearly inform paraprofessionals, volunteers, and student teachers of expectations, routines, and duties.

Legal Requirements

Paraprofessionals, like teachers, will not be allowed to keep their jobs if they are shown to be incompetent or insubordinate, or to have engaged in criminal or certain immoral activities.

Incompetence refers to an inability or failure to perform satisfactorily those duties normally expected. To be substantiated, this failure must occur repeatedly over a period of time and be documented by the teacher. *Insubordination* means refusal to follow direct, reasonable orders given by a person in authority, or the breaking of a valid school rule in a willful and defiant manner. Generally, *criminal acts* are those activities categorized as felonies under the law—for example, robbery and sale of illegal drugs, but not jaywalking or speeding. *Immoral or otherwise unacceptable acts* come into play only when they directly impact one's job performance or reputation, such as intoxication or drinking while on the job, obscene language at school, and inappropriate sexual activity around the school premises.

Paraprofessionals, like teachers, need to be careful about what they say. The Supreme Court in 1969 guaranteed teachers and students freedom of expression in the schools. Yet that guarantee does not apply as fully for school personnel as for ordinary citizens. For example, teachers are allowed to speak out on controversial matters, including conditions and policies of the schools. They may not, however, make false or reckless accusations that disrupt the educational process, or make abusive and scornful attacks on school officials. Nor are they allowed to use profanity or tell off-color stories within students' range of hearing. Using the classroom as a forum for expressing personal conviction in sensitive matters such as religion, politics, abortion, or sex education is also forbidden.

Liability for student injury or loss is another legal matter of which paraprofessionals and volunteers should be aware. School personnel have a legal responsibility to protect students from harm and injury. If a student is hurt on the playground, for example, and suit is brought to show that the injury occurred at least partly because of negligence, the court will try to determine three things: (1) who was supervising the student at the time of the injury, (2) whether the supervisor exercised reasonable foresight in anticipating danger to the student, and (3) whether the supervisor acted in a reasonable and prudent manner. Teachers, paraprofessionals, and volunteers will not be found negligent unless it can be shown that they violated the requirements of reasonable foresight (e.g., not allowing students to play where there is broken glass or an excavation) and prudent manner (e.g., keeping watch over the students instead of slipping into the lounge for a cup of coffee).

Paraprofessionals and volunteers working in supervisory capacities therefore must be clearly informed that they must be present and attentive, that they must not allow students out of their line of sight while supervising, and that they must make sure students do not play in unsafe areas or use equipment that is obviously unsafe. Paraprofessionals and volunteers should always be apprised of legal danger areas and given suitable instruction on conduct.

When Paraprofessionals Must Be Absent

Most student teachers genuinely want successful field experiences and see them as rich and practical learning opportunities. Many paraprofessionals and volunteers are completely dependable and miss work only out of dire necessity. Others take all the paid absences available, plus a few extras. Volunteers tend to be even less reliable. Thus there will be days when your paraprofessional or volunteer fails to come to work. Absences appear to occur at times when the aide seems indispensable, leaving the teacher out of sorts while scrambling for alternative plans.

This need not be the case, however. Since you know that your paraprofessionals, volunteers, or student teacher may, at any time, be unavailable, you need only to arrange for substitute aides or extra cross-grade or cross-age tutors. And when that is not possible, you can have backup instructional plans ready.

Training Paraprofessionals and Volunteers

As mentioned earlier, some school districts provide training for the paid paraprofessionals they employ. Such training typically deals with the foregoing matters. However, most paraprofessionals, and almost all volunteers, cross-grade partners, and cross-age tutors, are trained on the job, in the classroom by the teacher. As teachers-in-training, student teachers also receive on-the-job training as the cooperating teacher models, mentors, and coaches the routines, management, and instruction of the classroom.

On-the-job training is acceptable—even preferable in most cases—because duties of paraprofessionals and volunteers vary from classroom to classroom. Training done by teachers usually includes an orientation to the classroom; instruction in specific duties; details of where the volunteer is to be stationed, work, or circulate; and demonstration of how duties are to be performed. Legal, ethical, and professional regulations are spelled out clearly. As the paraprofessional or volunteer works in the manner indicated, the teacher provides necessary feedback, both corrections and appreciations.

Paraprofessionals and aides quickly learn procedures and become able to discharge their duties without direct supervision. Still, it is the teacher's responsibility to plan all work included in the instructional program and to supervise these adults at work. Student teachers also learn procedures and become able to perform with less direct supervision, although it is the responsibility of the cooperating teacher and university supervisor to guide and oversee their progress.

Assigning Space and Work Duties

All regular paraprofessionals, student teachers, and aides, whether paid, volunteer, cross-grade, or cross-age, should have a place in the classroom designated as their own, preferably a desk or table if available, where the teacher provides their notes, materials, or other items. Adults should not be asked to sit in small chairs at low tables used by young children.

Work times are scheduled according to teacher need. Paid paraprofessionals are assigned to the classroom for a specified number of hours. Volunteers are scheduled by agreement with the teacher, typically for certain days and times. Volunteers should not be left to simply hang around and observe, not knowing what to do with themselves. If a parent offers unexpected help on a particular morning, the teacher should accept the offer if it is convenient, but only when there is something productive for the parent to do, such as organizing materials, helping individual children, or sorting and filing papers. Otherwise, the teacher should thank the parent, explain that no help is needed at the moment, and ask for permission to call for help in the future.

Many teachers write specific work assignments on cards for their paraprofessionals and volunteers. These notations need not be made in detail but should indicate duties,

FIGURE 12.2   Assignment Card for Paraprofessional

Name: ——————————————————— Date ——————————————

Reading: Take Tom to center and have him read the story aloud to you; keep a record of the errors he makes.

Math: Duplicate tomorrow's paper's. Collect today's paper's and score them. Enter scores in record book.

Spelling: Give today's practice test to the class. Collect and mark the papers.

Language: Help me monitor students as they write their stories. Help with spelling or other questions they have.

sequence, materials, and time allocations. An assignment card might look something like the one in Figure 12.2.

Figure 12.2 is written out as it would appear when beginning to work with your paraprofessional. Later, when duties are understood, brief notes suffice, such as

Reading: Tom to center, read story to you; record errors.
Math: Photocopy tomorrow's papers; score today's and enter.
Spelling: Give practice test.
Language: Help monitor.

When the duties of the paraprofessional or volunteer are mostly supervisory or clerical, oral instructions are usually sufficient, though misunderstandings can be avoided by jotting notes on an assignment card. When the duties involve record keeping, remember this earlier caution: Records are legal documents and you, as the contracted teacher, are legally responsible for their management, recording, and accuracy.

Maintaining Paraprofessionals' Morale

Good morale, easily overlooked, is as necessary to paraprofessionals, volunteers, and student teachers as it is to teachers. It affects the quality of their work and the amount of satisfaction derived from it. To keep the morale level high for paraprofessionals and volunteers, give attention to the following:

1. Acceptance—a sense of belonging to the class and educational program, which grows out of appreciative attention and communication from the teacher, and is furthered by assigning specific tasks and work space
2. Meaningful work and clear directions—the paraprofessional or volunteer should not always do something menial or tedious; give sufficient guidance that the work can be done properly

3. Sense of accomplishment—helps paraprofessionals and volunteers see that their work has been done well and progress made
4. Evidence of appreciation—for contributions made to the instructional program; need only be a sincere thank-you, but an occasional card or small gift is always welcomed

Remember that student teachers are learners, and need morale boosts, too. It is as important for them to hear about what they are doing well, as it is to know what they need to change, correct, or improve. Specific positive feedback can be given during planning or conferences, in an interactive journal, or on short notes to the student teacher.

This concludes our consideration of managing the work of paraprofessionals, volunteers, substitutes, student teachers, and other helpers in the classroom. Before moving ahead to Chapter 13, which deals with how to manage two kinds of stress—the stressful emotions of unexpected events and trauma, and job-related stress that so badly afflicts teachers—take time to explore these end-of-chapter activities.

Parting Thought

Determine that the thing can and shall be done, and then . . . find the way.

—Abraham Lincoln

SUMMARY SELF-CHECK

Check off the following as you either understand or become able to apply them.

☐ Paraprofessionals and volunteers are people who work in the classroom with the teacher to help provide the educational program. They usually fall into the categories of paid paraprofessional, caregiver or university student volunteer, cross-grade partner or cross-age tutor, or community resource person. Substitute teachers and student teachers are other adults who might work in your classroom.

- What paraprofessionals can do: tutor, test, supervise, correct papers, duplicate, record, file, prepare instructional materials, assist as directed by the teacher.
- How paraprofessionals are obtained: recruited by schools or by teachers from parents and guardians of students, friends, and relatives; from high schools and universities; from older elementary and secondary students; from parent–teacher associations; from senior citizens' groups; and from community agencies and companies.
- Other helpers: cross-grade partners, cross-age tutors, substitute teachers, and student teachers.
- Substitute teachers are hired to teach when contracted teachers must be away from the classroom.

- Teachers leave an updated substitute folder that contains lesson plans and a copy of the discipline plan, current seating chart and class roster with notations of relevant student information, class schedule and duty schedule, classroom monitor and volunteer lists, and school map.
- The teacher's obligations: inform students about teacher absences, substitute teachers, how to work helpfully with substitutes, duties of substitute teacher monitors.
- The substitute teacher's obligations: further the program and make the day productive for the students, maintain discipline.
- Mutuality: the ideal relationship between teacher and substitute.

❑ Student teachers, who are not properly called paraprofessionals, are also often seen working in classrooms. Student teachers are different.
- What student teachers can do: plan and teach lessons; take responsibility for discipline; communicate with parents and guardians; confer with teachers and university supervisors; observe, participate, and perform most of the teacher's activities.

❑ Ground rules for paraprofessionals
- Authority belongs to the teacher but can be delegated to the paraprofessional.
- Reliability is an essential trait.
- Instruction can be provided by paraprofessionals under teacher's supervision.
- Discipline is the province of the teacher.
- Communication is needed for good relationships.
- Professionalism standards are explained and exemplified by the teacher.
- Legal requirements require that attention be given to incompetence, insubordination, criminality, immorality; liability for student injury or loss; freedom of expression and restrictions thereof.
- When paraprofessionals must be absent: utilize substitute, cross-grade partner or cross-age helper, backup plan.
- Training paraprofessionals: by schools for paid aides; by teachers, on-the-job training
- Work space and assignments: designated personal area; work assignments clearly set forth; record-keeping duties closely checked and verified.
- Morale of paraprofessionals and student teachers maintained through acceptance, meaningful work and clear directions, sense of accomplishment, evidence of appreciation.

ACTIVITIES FOR REFLECTION AND GROWTH

For Cumulative Skills Development

1. Take a moment to review the statements in the Anticipation–Reaction Guide at the beginning of this chapter. Put a check mark in the Reaction column next to any statement with which you now agree. How have your thoughts changed since reading this chapter?

2. You are told you can choose a paid paraprofessional (or substitute or student teacher) from among three candidates available. List in order the criteria you would use in making your selection. How would you determine the extent to which each candidate met your criteria?

3. You are provided a paid paraprofessional for two hours per day. Put in order of importance what you would have your aide do during that limited amount of time. Give your reasons.

4. You are ready to instruct your paraprofessional on the ground rules of discipline and professionalism. What would you say and what training would you give, if any?

5. Compile what you will provide in a substitute folder to ensure the teacher and students have a productive day.

6. Suppose you teach second grade. Two talented but somewhat troubled sixth-grade boys (they talk back to their teacher and sometimes fight with other boys on the playground) think it would be "cool" to work in your room as cross-grade tutors. Their teacher thinks the experience would be good for them. You hesitantly agree to give them the opportunity. What ground rules would you establish for them? If they proved to be good and worthwhile for your program, how would you let them know that you appreciate their work?

REFERENCES AND RECOMMENDED READINGS

Allard, H. (1977). *Miss Nelson is missing!* Boston: Houghton Mifflin.

Duebber, D. (2000, May). Substitute teaching: Sink or swim. *Educational Leadership, 57*(8), 73–74.

Engaging parents and the community in schools [Special issue]. (1998, May). *Educational Leadership.* Alexandria, VA: Association for Supervision and Curriculum Development.

Foster, E. (1992). *Tutoring: Learning by helping: A student handbook for training peer and cross-age tutors* (Rev. ed.). Minneapolis, MN: Educational Media Corporation.

Kagan, L., Kagan, M., & Kagan, S. (1997). *Cooperative learning structures for teambuilding.* San Clemente, CA: Kagan Cooperative Learning.

Kagan, M., Robertson, L., & Kagan, S. (1995). *Cooperative learning structures for classbuilding.* San Clemente, CA: Kagan Cooperative Learning.

Kagan, S. (2000). *Silly sports and goofy games.* San Clemente, CA: Kagan Publishing.

National Council of Teachers of English. (1989). *Substitute teachers' lesson plans: Classroom-tested activities from the National Council of Teachers of English.* Urbana, IL: Author.

Power, B. (1999, October). Strengthen your parent connection. *Instructor, 109*(3), 30–31.

Salt Lake City School District. (1992). *SMILES (Senior motivators in learning and educational services)* [Senior volunteer program]. Salt Lake City, UT: Author.

Stanley, S. (1991). Substitute teachers can manage their classrooms effectively. *NASSP Bulletin, 75*(532), 84–88.

Supporting new teachers [Special issue]. (1999, May). *Educational Leadership.* Alexandria, VA: Association for Supervision and Curriculum Development.

Tannenbaum, M. (2000, May). No substitute for quality. *Educational Leadership, 57*(8), 70–72.

Thaler, M. (1989). *The teacher from the Black Lagoon.* New York: Scholastic.

There's no substitute for a great sub! A collection of creative tips and lifesavers from substitute teachers. (1998). [Back to school issue]. *The Mailbox Teacher, 27*(1) 32–35.

Youngerman, S. The power of cross-level partnerships. *Educational Leadership, 56*(1), 58–61.

13 Managing Emotional Trauma and Job-Related Stress Productively

There have been no dragons in my life, only small spiders and stepping in gum. I could have coped with dragons!

—Author unknown

ANTICIPATION–REACTION GUIDE

Before you read the chapter, take a moment to put a check mark in the Anticipation column next to any statement with which you agree.

	Anticipation	Reaction
Current brain research suggests that all three parts of the brain work equally in times of stress.	❏	❏
The main purpose for crisis intervention and Critical Incident Stress Management is to handle situations beyond the resources of the individual or site.	❏	❏
Distress is bad for you; however, eustress is good for you.	❏	❏
Teaching is considered to be high on the list of stressful occupations.	❏	❏
Discipline problems and lack of time are two of teachers' worst stressors.	❏	❏
When prioritizing, it is advisable to get the easy tasks out of the way first so you can concentrate on the more difficult.	❏	❏
Selective avoidance is one way to reduce the stress of teaching.	❏	❏
Good cooperation and quality achievement almost certainly render a high level of class synergy.	❏	❏
A good place to cut back if your workload is too heavy is on communication with parents and guardians, provided there are no serious problems with students.	❏	❏
If the work you assign students is important enough for them to do, then it is equally important that you correct it carefully.	❏	❏

In this chapter we explore two aspects of stress. We begin with a topic that relates ever more strongly to our lives today—the effects of emotional stress that result from unexpected events such as tragedy and trauma, with attention to managing that stress. Later, we will explore suggestions concerning management of stress that normally accompanies teaching.

Managing Emotions of Unexpected Events and Trauma

"The best laid plans of mice and men . . . " How many times have we planned and prepared and showed up ready to teach, only to find that something or someone has put an enormous obstacle in our path. It may be something as simple as having to change the schedule for the day, despite its effects on your program. Certainly the move of a child's best friend or the death of a pet can affect a child's attention and interrupt the flow of your plans. But increasingly it seems that these obstacles are taking on a more serious nature: an accident involving a school bus and its passengers, the sudden death of a beloved teacher, the kidnapping and death of a local child, the shooting at a local high school, terrorist attacks on New York, and the other disasters that overflow the newspapers. All such events produce strong emotional reactions in us and our students. We can't change the events, but we can manage the associated emotions in a way that allows us and our students to cope with them more easily.

Important Definitions

In order to understand the nature and results of events that require special care or intervention, we should be familiar with the following terms.

Stress.   *Stress* is anything that causes continuing physical, mental, or emotional strain or tension (California Department of Education, 1997). Later in the chapter we will explore how stress can be positive (eustress) or negative (distress). Here we will talk about distress.

Trauma.   *Trauma* is a physical or emotional injury or shock from experiencing a disastrous event outside the range of usual experience. Here we will focus on emotional trauma. Anyone can experience high emotions when traumatic events occur. A primary question for teachers is how can we manage these emotions, especially in our children? And how do we take care of ourselves as well?

Critical Incident and Crisis Intervention.   Childs (2002) defines a *critical incident* as "any emotionally significant event that overwhelms the coping abilities of exposed individuals or groups" (p. 3). *Crisis intervention* is the assistance rendered after a critical incident. . . ." (p. 3). Crisis intervention is a short-term response to a critical incident. It is intended to decrease or relieve adverse reactions of individuals or groups affected by trauma. Crisis intervention has several goals:

- Interventions attempt to decrease or relieve adverse reactions of individuals or groups affected by trauma.
- Interventions are intended to impact or address the individual or group's ability to cope, and assist in identifying and assessing available support structures.
- They normalize reactions to the event or crisis.
- They assess the individual or group's capabilities and need for further support or referral.

Crisis intervention is not therapy for the individual or group. Teachers do not have the training for that task. Rather, it is to assess and then assist with the immediacy of an event in order to return the individual or group to a normal level of functioning.

Critical Incident Stress Management.   *(CISM) Critical Incident Stress Management* is a systematic crisis intervention model that has become a standard of care for traumatized persons. The model and its structure were conceived by Dr. Jeffrey Mitchell, a military doctor who studied emotional trauma of individuals involved in a crisis. State laws give districts the legal responsibilities for emergency preparedness, school safety, and risk management. To this end, districts have plans in place for such major events. Generally, public school employees are sanctioned as disaster service workers, and as such, teachers are responsible for giving care and support to students in a crisis. Further, the Field Act of 1933 requires that schools are to be available as postdisaster shelters.

Stress and the Triune Brain

Human brain physiology helps us understand how to provide crisis intervention. In the 1980s, Paul MacLean, the former director of the Laboratory of the Brain and Behavior at the United States National Institute of Mental Health, developed the triune brain theory. Maclean describes the human brain as being three brains in one, having evolved in that manner in response to various needs. Although each of the three brains, or layers, specializes in a separate function, all three layers interact.

The three areas of the brain work in this way. The primary function of the brain stem and cerebellum, also called the reptilian complex, controls physical survival and body maintenance (digestion, reproduction, circulation, breathing, and movement). The middle brain controls emotion and survival acts, such as eating, drinking, and sleeping. The outer brain (neocortex) is responsible for language, higher-order thinking, and ability to see ahead and plan for the future. The neocortex seeks a balance of emotions (meaning none becomes extremely high), and until this balance exists, the cortex has a reduced capacity to process information and use logical reasoning.

Here is how all this relates to stress. In times of undue stress or threat, the brain tends to bypass reason. Instead of allowing us to assess situations and plan ahead, it hammers us first with a fight or flight response—we either fight back or we try to escape from the situation. In other words, we react first, after which logic, reasoning, and decision making seem to follow. This also explains why we may behave the way we do during a critical incident—why we may forget the name of our best friend or feel driven to clean the house and polish the silver.

Signs and Symptoms of Emotional Stress

Fear and anxiety are debilitating emotions for everyone. Human reactions to disaster differ from person to person. Adults, when reacting to disastrous events, often engage in a natural grieving process that begins with denial, then anger, and finally a degree of resignation. If their distress is great, they may demonstrate symptoms of post-traumatic stress disorder (PTSD), in which they reexperience the event, either in dreams or in a related context; avoid talking about it; numb their emotions; or assume a high-alert state of being.

Also, children's reactions to trauma may be varied. For example, they may detach from the pain of the moment in emotional shock, and be seen as having an apparent lack of feelings. They may regress to immature behaviors, needing to be held, rocked, or remain close and clinging to a caregiver or someone important to them. They may act out behaviorally, venting feelings of anger, terror, frustration, or helplessness. They may require a lot of extra reassurances or repeatedly ask questions.

The Nature of Crisis Intervention

Critical incidents generally involve traumatic loss (death, serious injury, hostage situations) social unrest or racial conflicts, and man-made or natural disasters. Critical incidents are judged by reaction to the incident, not by the magnitude of the event.

Today, many districts and schools have teams of district and community members trained to assist in the aftermath of a critical incident. A Crisis Response Team (CRT) is called when the event overwhelms the school's ability to handle a situation and operates with consent and concurrence of the site administrator. The CRT command leader meets with administration and keeps them informed as it carries out the approved plan. Typically the team provides direct crisis intervention services to students in the classrooms, in whole or small group settings, and to individual students, as needed. The team is also prepared to assist teachers in handling student reactions and provide personal support to staff. Additionally, the CRT can provide consultation services to administration, and give information and community resources to parents and guardians.

The CRT responds to what individuals need right in the moment. Their interventions deal with the here and now, are designed to prevent further emotional and behavioral disturbances, and are short term. Team members are facilitators who use active and direct strategies and responses. CRT members are not counselors, bound to invest in long-term care and treatment. As needed they will make referrals to counselors and other community resources so individuals receive the best long-term support.

When Crisis Teams Are Not Available

Crisis Response Teams are not always available when needed. In those cases, it is up to the teachers and school personnel to help others cope. Most school districts provide some advice concerning how personnel are to function at those times, recognizing they do not have adequate training or understanding. The following are some things schools do. When applying any of these tactics, one must keep in mind students' emotional maturity and needs.

Sherry Coburn, a sixth-grade teacher, is also the team coordinator who prepares the yearly telephone tree that is used to contact all staff when a serious event warrants their knowledge. She describes crisis response at her school.

> Gilmore's Crisis Response Team was originally designed to aid students in crisis—suffering from such losses as a sibling, parent, or relative. As time has gone on, its purpose has increased. We have been called on to service children who had been friends with someone shot and killed by gang involvement and gang retaliation. We once had to deal with many students when a popular student was hit by a train and killed. We also had an incident when a teacher was killed due to domestic violence.
>
> Our crisis team has had to branch out within the past few years to anticipate problems and work out solutions prior to their happening in order to make our school a safe place for both students and staff. We devised and held the first intrusion drill in our state, and continue to hold them on a monthly basis. We believe that this drill must be second nature to our students, just as a fire drill is.
>
> Last year when a large hall fight broke out we devised a plan to deal with this new type of incident. We called it a "Code Hall Sweep." When teachers hear this over the PA system, they close their classroom doors and do not allow anyone in. Administrators and hall assistants then can handle the situation by rounding up anyone involved.

Through a question and response guide, Berman, Diener, Dieringer, and Lantieri (2003) coach teachers and caregivers about ways to discuss exceptional events with children. These discussions are varied in accordance with age and maturity of the children, as well as their personal connection to the event. Most children appreciate talking with adults they trust and see as supportive, caring, and sensitive. Among the guidelines for discussions are the following:

- Ask the children what they already know, what they think they know but are not sure about, and what questions they have. Ask open questions: "What do you know about . . . ?" "What is upsetting you the most?" "Are you saying that . . . ?"
- Listen and respond to their questions and comments with facts said in simple language and without extraneous details for which the children may not be ready. Simply and factually correct misinformation. Allow children to respond to each of your comments.
- As you listen to and observe the children, respond to what you hear and see in a supportive and sensitive way. Children are reassured when they know you are listening and you care about them and others.
- Avoid talking to children about adult concerns that would likely raise new questions and fears, limit their own expressions, or simply be over their heads.
- Use active listening to clarify without judgment, help you understand the children, and help the children sort out their ideas. Because children may be unable to say what they feel or what they say may mean something different to you than they intended, paraphrase what you hear and invite them to elaborate or clarify: "Can you tell me more about that?" or "What do you mean by that?"

- In addition to talk, provide children with opportunities to explore and express themselves through writing, play, drawings, and props such as clay.
- Look and listen for nonverbal messages such as facial expressions, gestures, posture, and fidgeting; also notice voice rate and tone and watch for significant increases in anxiety, distractibility, despair, or fear.
- Help children explore their feelings. Listen closely for underlying concerns such as personal and family safety.
- Validate that their feelings are OK: "You seem sad when we talk about this. I feel sad too."
- When closure to discussions of feelings is difficult, simply thank the children for sharing and affirm that you care.
- Identify and monitor children with personal connections to the event, and inform the counselor.
- Finally, look for and accept support from other adults who can help you (a caregiver, mentor, etc.).

Of the numerous strategies that have been proven effective, several are fairly easy to remember and implement by teachers, including the SEA-3 Method and the SAFER Method, described in the following paragraphs. As you read these strategies, keep in mind that they can be applied to anyone in need, adults as well as children. Also remember that as the classroom teacher, you know your students. Because you are familiar with your students' behavior and maturity prior to situations of stress or trauma, you will be able to gauge any of the changes listed in the paragraphs below.

SEA-3 Method

This is a five-step method to assess the functioning of individuals—children or adults—in situations of stress or trauma. SEA-3 stands for speech, emotion, appearance alertness, and activity.

1. *Speech:*   Listen to the child's speech. To what degree is it slurred or rapid?

2. *Emotion:*   Evaluate the child's emotion, considering both mood and affect. For example, to what degree is the child depressed or euphoric? Is the child's display of emotions flat or inappropriate? What emotions, if any, are being expressed? Does the child laugh or make jokes about a sad situation? Does the child show overwhelming emotion, such as excessive crying or hysteria?

3. *Appearance:*   Consider the child's appearance—neat, disheveled?

4. *Alertness:*   Pay attention to the child's alertness. Do the child's thoughts seem normal? What is the child's level of abstraction—concrete or conceptual? Is the child hallucinating? How accurate is the child's orientation to time, place, and others? What is the child's judgment and capacity for insight? The teacher can assess the child's alertness and judgment by using nondirective responses to what the child says.

5. *Activity:*   What is the child's activity—lethargic, hyperactive?

SAFER Method

This is a very useful method of crisis intervention, which teachers often use without knowing they do. The SAFER method is designed to stabilize the situation by (1) removing the person in crisis from the source of stress, (2) reinforcing cognitive processing and what is natural in time and place, (3) reinforcing the individual's own coping skills, and (4) referring the person for additional care, if necessary. This process may take only a minute or less to perform. In more easily understood terms, here is what you do:

1. *Stabilize the situation.* Reduce the situational stressors by removing the child from the situation. Turn the child away from the scene or take him or her into another room.

2. *Acknowledge the crisis.* Ask the child to describe what happened and describe personal reactions. The teacher's role is to assist the child in talking about what happened and putting words to the reactions and emotions. Using active listening, the teacher would ask the child to describe what happened, and then retell what he or she heard the child say. ("I heard you say . . .")

3. *Facilitate understanding.* Using language appropriate to developmental and emotional maturity, explain what is going on. This helps the child understand the situation. Validate the child's reactions as being natural. For example, you might say something like: "That was probably really scary for you to hear the sirens when they came into the parking lot."

4. *Encourage adaptive coping.* While continually assessing the child's ability to function, teach the child reasonable and appropriate basic stress and crisis management strategies. Identify appropriate coping skills ("What do you do when you are scared?"); consider personal, school, family, and community resources ("Is there someone at home now who could come here for you?"); and develop a reasonable action plan ("Would you like to put some water on your face or lie down in the nurse's office for a few minutes before you go back to class?" "I know Sarah is your friend. I just talked to Sarah's mother, and after school you can go to their house until your parents come home.").

5. *Restore or refer.* Your goal is to help the child return to normal functioning. If you feel your efforts are not producing that result, you should consider referring the child for additional care.

Attention-Refocusing Strategies

Attention-refocusing strategies also assist teachers as they work with children in stressful situations. This can be done by asking questions that require the use of the five senses or that draw attention to the outdoor natural environment. The teacher may begin this strategy by telling the distressed person, "I'm going to ask some silly questions to help you become less upset." Before returning the child to the class or situation, it's important for the teacher to ask, "Do you feel you are ready to go back to class?"

Up Shifting

Up shifting strategies are intended to shift the child from an emotional focus to a cognitive focus. These strategies involve quick actions and sounds, such as having students echo rhythmic clapping led by the teacher, or blend counting with a word: Example—when counting in sequence, replace every multiple of five with the word *buzz*.

Other Subtle Techniques

Several other subtle techniques can be used to advantage. Examples include:

- Physical contact by gently touching the child's hands or shoulders.
- Physically turning the individual away from the event or distraction.
- Speaking in a calm, quiet, unemotional voice.
- Prompting deep rhythmic breathing.
- Relating only relevant facts, not details.
- Paraphrasing the child's last sentences and using nondirective responses.
- Asking specific questions to check what the child understands and how the child is doing.
- Asking the child what has helped in past upsetting situations.
- Asking the child what he or she needs to help settle down now.
- Reiterating the paradigm: Who was involved? What happened? What comes next?

Throughout the entire contact, the teacher behaves naturally and authentically.

Taking Care of Self

Through all these efforts, it is crucial that teachers and helpers take care of themselves and each other, whether they are individual teachers working with their students or members of a Crisis Response Team. This is necessary because helpers and team members are susceptible to direct or vicarious traumatization when responding to a crisis event and when providing support services for victims.

Self Care.   Make sure that all adult helpers utilize tools to help them more effectively manage their own stress. These tools include proper diet, exercise, and rest; journaling and/or counseling for themselves; reduction of other distractions; and moderation of alcohol and medication.

Debriefing.   Debriefing is a structured process in which adults involved in crisis intervention are helped to process their experience in such a way as to avoid symptoms of PTSD or vicarious traumatization. Debriefings, conducted by trained personnel, are essential for everyone's well-being and should occur regularly.

Managing Job-Related Stress

We now turn attention to stress normally associated with teaching. Teaching can be a good and rewarding job, contributing to individual and collective good and bringing one into contact with many fine people. But it is no secret that teachers' lives are filled with stress.

FACULTY MEETING

"I HAVE SOME GOOD NEWS AND SOME BAD NEWS, THE PROBLEM IS
I DON'T KNOW WHICH IS WHICH."

Teaching makes one nervous and tired, and if students do not behave well, teachers are certain to experience headaches, anxiety, apathy, and an occasional desire to escape from it all.

Teaching used to be easier than it is now. As recently as the 1950s, practically all teachers taught to age sixty-five. Many retired at that time, but others continued on to age seventy and beyond. Teachers can't do that anymore. You rarely see a teacher remain in service until sixty-five; most now retire much earlier, accepting reduced pensions just to escape the pressure. Teachers say the job wears them out, especially now that they no longer can count on the success, respect, and dignity that once came with teaching.

What has caused this unfortunate change? Most teachers say students have become more recalcitrant and increasingly difficult to motivate and manage. They are influenced by a myriad of interests outside of school, often lack a cohesive family structure, are less responsive to adult authority, and are more willing to test limits, which they do with regularity. Increasingly, parents and guardians either seem to do little to support the school program and their child, or they are overbearing and demanding in their expectations.

But not only unruly students or difficult caregivers wear teachers down. Pullis (1992) reported a survey of 244 teachers who considered the school setting and workload pressures more stressful than direct contact with students. Teachers everywhere complain of too much to do and too little time to do it. They see the curriculum change yearly, for reasons sometimes academic, sometimes political. They are constantly required to retool so as to teach in accord with programs, standards, and tests that come into vogue, and they are responsible for fulfilling nonteaching duties that were unheard of three decades ago. Add to that shrinking funds for supplies; the inclusion into regular classes of students with special needs, including children with physical and emotional challenges, English language learners, and exceptionally difficult-to-handle students; the endless in-service workshops; and the increased criticism they endure because of lackluster student achievement, and you can see why teachers feel they are expected to do more and more with less and less, and yet, get less respect for it. Such perceptions, correct or not, bring with them heavy loads of stress.

Stress and Its Effects

We have noted that stress is a state of bodily and mental tension. At times the pressures associated with stress become intense. That is not to say that stress is always bad. Life without any stress at all would be incredibly dull. Stress prepares us for action. As discussed earlier, under situations of threat or excitement, our bodies undergo chemical changes that are manifested in rapid pulse, increased blood pressure, muscle tension, and perspiration. In modest amounts, these changes give us vim and vigor. It only becomes harmful when it reaches such proportions that it produces deleterious effects. Sandy Schuster (1992) describes stress's good side and bad side in her book on teaching stress management. Stress is seen as consisting of two parts—distress and eustress. Distress is negative and occurs when one feels unable to cope. It produces a number of undesirable side effects. Eustress, on the other hand, is positive. It occurs in the presence of interesting, challenging, yet resolvable problems. Eustress energizes, enlivens, and excites. Thus, it would be incorrect to put forth the impression that teachers need *no* stress in their lives. What they need is eustress. Unfortunately, too much of what they get is distress.

What Bothers Teachers Most

Two decades ago, Donald Cruickshank and his associate (Cruickshank & Callahan, 1983) conducted studies to determine what teachers see as their main professional problems. They reported that teachers everywhere share five goals: (1) affiliation, the need to establish and maintain positive relationships with students and colleagues; (2) control, the need to have students behave properly—that is, to be relatively quiet, orderly, and courteous; (3) parent relationships, the desire for mutually supportive relationships with students' parents and guardians; (4) student success; and (5) time to accomplish necessary personal and professional tasks. If any of these goals is not being reached, teachers sense a growing amount of pressure or unease. Similar studies, including the yearly Gallup polls, identify time pressures and management of disruptive children as prime sources of teacher stress. It should be noted that the concerns identified in research produce only modest stress, though the level increases as the problems remain unresolved.

But far worse stress occurs when teachers receive poor teaching evaluations, experience verbal or physical attacks from students or caregivers, endure job transfers, and contend with lawsuits. While most teachers never experience most of these events, they say they frequently feel the threat of them.

What Energizes Teachers?

You might think that teachers would be energized by conditions opposite to those that bring stress—that is, they would be very happy if given adequate time, well-behaved students, high student achievement, close affiliation with colleagues, and cooperation from satisfied caregivers. It has been found, however, that while removal of major stressors results in job

Artwork reprinted courtesy of Jody Bergsma Galleries: www.bergsma.com.

satisfaction, it does not in itself motivate teachers to invest greater amounts of effort into their work.

Few schools make significant efforts to provide positive motivation for teachers. Teachers rarely have the opportunity to do work in areas of special personal interest. They have almost no opportunity to advance unless they move out of teaching into administration or counseling. Given those facts, teachers must find job rewards within teaching itself. Teachers sometimes have classes, and frequently several students, who are fun to work with. Occasionally caregivers express gratitude, sometimes students thank their teachers and show appreciation, and once in a while administrators or fellow teachers make favorable comments. Some teachers are recognized as master teachers and asked to work with and mentor student and beginning teachers. But self-satisfaction, in these hectic days of teaching, is too weak to motivate a continual push for excellence in most people. Slowly most teachers begin to question the value of their efforts, especially as frustration builds.

Carolyn Monnell, a third-grade teacher, comments on playground supervision:

> Yard duty can sometimes be a rewarding experience, but more often it makes you think of hell. Rules are broken, fights break out over disputed game rules, and children ignore all the safety rules. You are asked to listen to one sad story after another as to who took cuts, who hit whom, and now a kid is crying because a disparaging remark was made about his mother. Balls land on rooftops or roll into the street, and children fall and scrape knees. A written note is required or else the damaged child will not get any first aid. If it's a windy day you get lots of nosebleeds, more notes to write, and ubiquitous uneasiness. Those are the rewarding experiences. Now let me tell you about . . .
>
> No, really, yard duty seems like you against 400 kids. How I pray for the wisdom, which so often eludes me, to know not to blame the wrong child for the deviant act of another, to be wise enough to single out the initiator and not the innocent bystander. When there is a confrontation, the kids themselves frequently don't know who started it. I usually ask them to shake hands. Kindergartners love to do that and they go away hand in hand. First and second graders comply, but fourth graders and older kids don't go for it. I also try to make them smile. The power of suggestion helps. I bet them they can't smile by the time I count to three. That rarely fails. If it does, I am alerted to a problem that may have deep roots, one that has little to do with the situation at hand.
>
> Meanwhile, I continue praying that there will be no serious accident on the playground, for which some parent would no doubt sue me for negligence.

Stress Management for Teachers

Much can be done to make teachers' professional lives better, despite the increasing number of stressors with which teachers must contend. There remains hope that someday school districts may decide that education occurs better when teachers are contented and hard working than when they are stressed out and clinging by their fingernails. To accomplish a transformation in teachers' lives, schools need only free up time for teachers; require less busy work; trust teachers' judgment concerning how to teach and manage student behavior; support home and community alliances that lighten teachers' burdens; and energize teachers through recognition of effort and success.

But let's be practical. If teachers want to improve their existence, they must take charge of the matter themselves. Among steps they can take to relieve much of their stress are prioritizing, accepting a new perspective regarding perfection, selective avoidance, time management, discipline, communication with parents and guardians, and maintenance of physical well being. Discipline and communication, though discussed previously, are mentioned here once more.

Prioritizing. To prioritize is simply to put things in order of importance and then to focus on items that require immediate attention, while leaving those of less importance until later. It means considering the best use of time at this moment. Most people operate the other way around—they attend to inconsequential matters first, thinking that when they get them out of the way they can concentrate better on more important matters. Unfortunately, with time restrictions as they are, the important matters never receive the attention they should. Pressure comes from not getting to the matters that really need attention, or that others expect one to do expeditiously. It doesn't come from skipping the junk mail.

Accepting Less Than Perfection.   Many teachers want perfection. They want students to be perfect and they want themselves to be perfect. They set high goals and push everyone to reach them. Certainly nothing is wrong with holding high expectations. The stress arises when individuals fall short, and they will, for a variety of reasons. It is therefore best that we acknowledge that perfection simply isn't possible. Vince Lombardi summed it up: "Practice doesn't make perfect. Only perfect practice makes perfect."

Using Selective Avoidance.   At a conference that dealt with the major problems that teachers have to face, one speaker suggested several ways teachers could deal with stress, the best of which is simply to avoid it. The audience laughed, but the speaker was serious. He went on to explain that teachers can learn to say no as a way to prevent overburdening themselves with an insupportable load of tasks. They can avoid associating with chronic complainers who find fault with everyone and everything and thus adversely affect the attitudes of those around them. They can set aside the trivial matters that consume so much time. They can learn not to take work home with them every night so that once in a while they can enjoy the luxury of thinking and talking about nonschool topics. Finally, they can give students greater responsibility in helping manage the classroom and the instructional program. Here are some suggestions:

Say No.   Most teachers, particularly new teachers, are unwilling to say no to their principal, and most are reluctant to say no to colleagues and caregivers. They want to impress others with their willingness to shoulder the load; they want the principal, caregivers, and colleagues to think and speak highly of them. And they are often afraid that a displeased administrator will give them a bad evaluation or assign them to unsavory duties. That eventuality is unlikely if the teacher says, "I'd like to help, but my schedule is packed. I'll do it if you can help me get a little more time." (Administrators can often reduce one's duties to make the time available.) Similarly, teachers are often afraid that caregivers and colleagues will dislike them if they decline personal requests. Again, say, "I'd like to be able to help you, but I'm so pressed for time. Do you have any suggestions?" Sometimes caregivers and colleagues will surprise you with their willingness to relieve you of certain tasks in order to obtain your assistance with their problems.

It should not be forgotten that teachers, by nature, want to be helpful. They have, after all, chosen a profession based on helping others. But sometimes one has to say no to balance rewards against ravages of overload. It's important to remember, too, that there are many tasks that teachers simply must assume. You can't say no to meetings, keeping good records, filing required reports, planning lessons, obtaining necessary materials for teaching, and so forth. But if you list the incredible number of tasks that teachers routinely contend with, you would find that many of them could be left aside without any negative consequences.

Seek Occasional Solitude.   Teachers can probably accomplish far more if they find a space that is quiet and away from the activity of others. The space should be furnished adequately with the materials and supplies they need for the task at hand.

Avoid Time Robbers and Use Time Savers.   Too much to do and not enough time to do it—that is the teacher's chronic complaint. But let us now bring up a matter that teachers tend to overlook: Most of them could save large amounts of time simply by not wasting time they have available to them.

Time robbers eat up a large portion of teachers' time and give little in return. One such robber is teachers' tendency to deal with matters that could just as well be delegated or even left aside indefinitely. Consider Mr. Monroe:

> Mr. Monroe, a sixth-grade teacher, works in his room for two hours each day after school. Two hours of concentrated work should be more than enough time to take care of all the matters that significantly impact his program. But Mr. Monroe spends the time reading memos, emails, notices, advertisements, and other pieces of mail received at school. He goes to the faculty lounge for coffee and on the way stops to talk with the custodian about a ball game. In the lounge he finds the principal and they chat, tell jokes, and talk about politics. Then he returns to his room; waters the plants; feeds the rat, hamsters, and rabbits; and cleans their enclosures. He dislikes messiness, so he picks up scraps, arranges books, cleans the sink, and tidies his desk. While looking for reference materials for the next day's lesson on ancient Greece, he comes across interesting material on money, coins, mints, and various monetary systems, which he reads though they have nothing to do with Greece. Before he knows it, it is five o'clock and only a few of his necessary tasks have been done. He still has papers to grade, so he takes them home.

Mr. Monroe no doubt needs quiet relaxation time to socialize with colleagues. But the reason he has to work at night, when he would do better to keep his mind free and be with family and friends, is that he falls prey to three of teachers' greatest time robbers—dealing with the trivial, talking instead of working, and working in a disorganized way. By becoming more organized, he could check all his student papers in an hour and then be able to do other things.

In contrast to time robbers, time savers are steps and shortcuts that enable teachers to get necessary work done, while leaving some time for personal needs. The most valuable time savers are working efficiently, delegating work, reducing paper checking, and controlling the number and length of faculty meetings.

Efficiency begins with prioritizing tasks as described earlier, giving attention only to tasks that are absolutely necessary—such as planning, scoring selected papers, preparing instructional materials and activities, keeping adequate records, and preparing for conferences with students and caregivers. Difficult tasks should be completed first and the fun work left for later.

Once you establish priorities, work hard during the time you have set aside. Avoid temptation to chat, gossip, daydream, or gaze out the window. Though these activities are quite restful and valuable, they should come after the work is finished. Score papers and make records quickly and efficiently, then plan for the next day. Normally you can do all this in an hour of concentrated work.

Assign routine tasks such as watering plants, cleaning the room, feeding animals, dusting, straightening, and so forth to students. It's good for them. If students are too young, have aides or volunteers help.

Be Realistic about Paper Checking.   Checking work students have turned in consumes monumental amounts of time for most teachers. This task can be greatly reduced with no detriment to students. Most teachers believe that if they assign written work they are honor bound to mark every single paper carefully. But there are strong counterarguments to this view. First, many written tasks are given to students for practice only. By circulating, you can observe students at work and know how they are doing, identify problems they are encountering, and provide the help they need. Two side-benefits accrue from circulating around the room. You are close to students, and proximity helps maintain discipline. Also, by working the crowd you can provide efficient help (as Fred Jones suggests, in twenty seconds or less). When students have completed their work and you have made notations as necessary on your clipboard, collect the papers and discard them later.

Students profit little, if any, from the marks you make so conscientiously and meticulously. Even by the next day, students will have lost the context of what they were doing and your marks will mean little to them. Their errors should be corrected as they are being made. Moreover, students do not like to receive marked-up papers. Their first and often final inclination is to crumple it and throw it away, unless of course it has a star or happy face on it. If you insist on going to such lengths in scoring student papers, you need to go back over the papers with students, in detail, when you return them. Students don't like this, but that's the only way you can make them learn much from all your hard work.

This is not to say that you should never carefully correct student papers. Toward the end of units, when students are asked to show how much they have learned, you can expect them to do their very best work, which you should then check carefully. Ginny Lorenz describes a procedure she now uses:

> This year I teach a 4/5 multi-age class of thirty-two students. Formerly, I read student papers four nights a week. This year I'm doing something new. I have added a Writer's Workshop where parents and guardians help with the editing of student work. When students have a piece in final draft form, they put a check next to their name on the board. Once I have eight or ten names with check marks, I take that group home and read for grades. This is working well so far.

A note of caution, however: If you are going to send corrected papers home with your students, make sure you mark them accurately! Caregivers invariably find the mistakes you make.

Streamline Record Keeping.   As discussed in Chapter 10, record keeping is another task that can consume great amounts of time. You can reduce the workload by doing four things:

"GOOD. THEN THERE'S NO REASON TO
GRADE ALL THOSE PAPERS TONIGHT."

(1) keep only those records that truly are necessary; (2) train students to assist in keeping their own records; (3) have an aide or volunteer help with recording and filing, and (4) use available computer technology for records management. Remember these two cautions, however—students have the right to privacy regarding their work and progress, and you are legally responsible for the accuracy of these records,

Take a Proactive Role in Faculty Meetings.   If the faculty meetings at your school tend to be too long and tedious, you can take steps to shorten them. You can expect agendas for the meetings, and when discussions stray from the agenda, you can suggest that, in the interest of time, the agenda be followed. Any segment of the faculty can ask to be excused from the meetings when the topics do not apply to them—for example, there is no need for primary teachers to attend meetings that deal with sixth-grade outdoor camp. Also, teachers can agree as a staff to limit the length of discussions.

Remove the Stress from Teaching.   As explained in Chapter 9, disruptive student behavior not only severely cuts into teachers' time but also is a major source of frustration and stress. You can use a number of different tactics (many described in Chapter 9) to dramatically reduce the stress usually associated with discipline. You and your students will very much appreciate the results.

Streamline Communication with Parents and Others.   In Chapter 11 you were urged to communicate well with caregivers as a means of securing family support for your efforts. But when stress and overload make you look for ways to free up some time, you may decide you don't have time for much parent communication, which can be time intensive. However, please remember that communication with parents and guardians is always worth the effort involved and should be given high priority. You can streamline the communication process by using a class website that describes expectations you hold, your discipline system, class activities, and how parents can help. Add e-mail capability so parents can initiate communication with you, to which you can respond briefly. If you need to call a parent on the phone, say, with utmost courtesy and respect, something like, "Hello Mrs. Nichols. This is _____, Betsy's teacher. How are you this evening? I'd like to talk with you for a moment about Betsy. I only have five minutes right now. Is this a convenient time for you?" Prior to calling, rehearse what you want to say and anticipate questions and comments from the listener.

Keep Yourself Physically Fit.   Make sure you have adequate rest, good nutrition, some recreation, and some physical exercise, all of which help in combating stress. Your brain needs food (glucose) and oxygen. When possible, work in natural light; fluorescent lights may cause eyestrain and anxiety. Drink plenty of water to keep your brain hydrated. Get enough sleep. Sleep is critical in order for the brain to process, think, and remember. Also, do some isometric exercises and stretches throughout the day. Involve students. It will help them, too.

Take Occasional Brain Breaks.   Throughout your daily class routines, take time to nourish your brain (and your students' brains, as well). The human brain is not designed to hold constant focus on something for a lengthy period of time. Brain breaks can involve short periods of rest, listening to calming music, thinking about something entirely different, telling a joke or story, and standing and stretching.

Activities That Produce Positive Stress

The first part of this chapter has dealt with the damaging effects of stress, and you have seen a number of suggestions for removing unwanted stress in your work. We now turn attention to what you can do to increase positive, useful stress, known as *eustress*.

Moderate amounts of stress energize us, give us a sense of direction, make us pleased with our jobs and ourselves, provide a sense of accomplishment and importance, and in so doing positively affect our morale. The following paragraphs review sources of eustress that teachers find most readily available in teaching—group efforts, student achievement, newsletters and literary journals, public performances and exhibits, shared responsibility, and class synergy.

Group Efforts

Many teachers enjoy working with other teachers. However, unless they belong to a collaborative grade-level team, they seldom have incentive to do so. When they decide to collaborate on a task or activity such as a field day, art exhibit, or simulated archaeological dig, they find excitement and joy, not only for themselves but for students as well. The eustress they experience is inherent in the activity itself, but another good payoff is student involvement and parental appreciation. Remember, teachers can be resources to one another; they simply need to learn to ask and learn to share.

Student Achievement

Achievement is mainly what schooling is all about. Teachers of high achievers usually feel successful, while those of lower achievers feel somewhat defeated. It is important to realize that student achievement can actually be increased through the way attention is given. For example, when outstanding student work products such as art, compositions, and scale models are put on public display, students become motivated to accomplish work of still higher quality. When students keep personal charts that graphically depict how much they have read or how skilled they have become in math, they strive to reach even greater heights, especially when the results are communicated to caregivers.

To emphasize student achievement, you need to discuss with students what achievement means, show them what makes it possible, illustrate how progress is documented, and explain how results are shown to caregivers and others. Then as students strive to achieve, and later to surpass previous levels of achievement, you will find that everyone's motivation to excel increases.

Newsletters and Literary Journals

Described in Chapter 11 as a vehicle for communicating with parents and guardians, teacher- and student-produced newsletters and web pages provide marvelous opportunities for enlivening teaching and learning. The same is the case for class literary journals. Intermediate-grade students can contribute to the writing and production of newsletters and journals, as writers, designers, and artists, with their names listed somewhere in the work. Teachers can assist in primary grades, but from third grade onward students can do most of the work in print, and they are highly motivated to do their best writing, spelling, grammar, and artwork. Parents and guardians eagerly read such materials, taking pride in their child's work and crediting the teacher for the documented accomplishments.

Kay Ballentine, a kindergarten teacher, tells about her weekly class newsletter:

> Our newsletter, titled *Kindergarten Korner,* is very short. It tells about activities during the week and upcoming events I want parents to be aware of. I try to mention as many children by name as possible each week, and I make sure every child is mentioned frequently. Parents read the newsletter avidly and go out of their way to write or tell me about it. They seem to think it proves I care about their child, which of course I do.

Ronda Royal, a third-grade teacher, adds:

> Although I often like to send home snippets of children's work to show parents what the children are creating in my room, the weekly newsletter is solely my production.

It is always written in complete sentences and full paragraphs. Many parents say they appreciate this type of complete communication because it shows that I am putting effort into informing them of events of our room, of ways to assist their child, and of upcoming guests and activities. I always give a copy of my newsletter to the principal and to any volunteers who do not have children in my room. I use these newsletters to keep everyone informed.

Public Performances and Exhibits

Most schools encourage teachers and their classes to present performances such as plays, readers' theatre, holiday skits, and musicals, as well as exhibitions of art, science projects, and social studies projects. These events produce high levels of excitement and motivation, and students willingly work hard to prepare for them.

Performances and exhibits are most often seen in conjunction with back-to-school nights. But displays of student work for students, teachers, and visitors to see can be posted at any time in various locales in the school. Some events may even be broadcast through a local cable station or via the Internet. Most people may think of performances and exhibits as frills outside the core program, but once you see the level of motivation and pride they engender, you will want to make them prime components of your class's educational program.

Sharing Responsibility with Students

From the beginning of the school year, you should impress on your students the roles and responsibilities they are to assume in regard to their own education. They can be shown how to take an active stance in learning to be participants rather than recipients. As they move into this shared responsibility, a spirit of self-direction and self-responsibility develops that teachers find very satisfying.

Achieving Class Synergy

When you are able to bring about an attitude of shared responsibility and then add to it the desire for significant accomplishment and evidence thereof, there may occur that elusive condition C. M. Charles (2000) refers to as *class synergy,* in which members of the class energize each other through cooperative group efforts. This effect binds students together, spurs them on, and makes school a time of pleasure and fulfillment. Synergy, or esprit de corps, is one of the best things that can happen in a classroom. The class work becomes joyful instead of onerous, and students involve themselves actively rather than comply lethargically. Classbuilding and teambuilding activities do much to foster synergy. They help school days end with a satisfied glow instead of wretched fatigue. As students experience synergy, they provide much positive energy to teachers. As a bonus, word quickly gets to caretakers, who react positively to their child's educational program, becoming in the process more supportive of the teacher.

Before moving ahead to Chapter 14, take time to explore these end-of-chapter activities.

Parting Thoughts

Yes do I hold that mortal foolish who strives against the stress of necessity.

—Euripedes

Rule #1: Don't sweat the small stuff. Rule #2: It's all small stuff.

—Dr. Michael Mantell

SUMMARY SELF-CHECK

Check off the following as you either understand or become able to apply them.

❑ Stress and trauma affect teachers and students.

❑ Critical incident—any emotionally significant event that overwhelms coping abilities

❑ Crisis intervention—short-term response to a critical incident with the goal of helping

❑ Critical Incident Stress Management (CISM)—a systematic crisis intervention model

❑ The three areas of the triune brain work somewhat simultaneously as we react to a critical incident.

❑ Signs and symptoms of emotional stress—children may shut down their feelings, regress to immature behaviors, act out behaviorally, ask questions, require lots of extra reassurance.

❑ Crisis intervention is not therapy.

❑ What teachers and schools can do:
  - SEA-3 Method: speech, emotion, appearance, alertness, activity
  - SAFER Method: stabilize the situation, acknowledge crisis, facilitate understanding, encourage adaptive coping, restore or refer.
  - Attention-refocusing strategies
  - Up shifting
  - Subtle techniques
  - Take care of yourself.
  - Debrief

❑ Stress—some is needed, but too much is harmful.
  - Eustress—a challenge; interesting, helpful
  - Distress—inability to cope; overwhelming, hurtful

❑ What stresses teachers most: disruptive student behavior, lack of time, too much to do, lack of student success, poor relationships with parents and guardians.

❏ What energizes teachers most: student achievement, recognition, interesting work, possibilities for growth and advancement.

❏ Stress management for teachers: prioritize (take care of important matters first), accept that perfect isn't possible, avoid selectively (learn to say no; learn to hide) manage time efficiently (avoid time robbers), develop a nonconfrontive discipline system, communicate well with caregivers, give close attention to your physical well being.

❏ Positive directions—building meaning and spirit: engage in group efforts; work toward student achievement; produce newsletters, web pages, and journals; have your class put on public performances; work for shared responsibility with students; seek the class synergy.

ACTIVITIES FOR REFLECTION AND GROWTH

For Cumulative Skills Development

1. Take a moment to review the statements in the Anticipation–Reaction Guide at the beginning of this chapter. Put a check mark in the Reaction column next to any statement with which you now agree. How have your thoughts changed since reading this chapter?

2. Investigate the crisis response plan at a local school and share your findings with your class.

3. List six important tasks that call for your attention today. Prioritize those tasks by their importance. List nonessential tasks that try to draw you away from your important tasks. How will you deal with them?

4. Do you know a teacher who appears to have reached burnout? Assess that person as to how he or she looks, talks, relates to students, prepares for teaching, maintains discipline, and participates in school activities.

5. The text suggested that your teaching life would be more enjoyable if you had your class produce newsletters, a web page, and journals, and put on public performances and displays. Evaluate that contention objectively: To what extent would those suggestions simply *add* stress rather than reduce it? List and discuss your pros and cons.

6. Suppose you are put in charge of teacher morale and appreciation in your school. Within reason, what would you do and emphasize in order to make teachers' professional lives more joyful and rewarding? Explain your program to the class.

REFERENCES AND RECOMMENDED READINGS

Berman, S., Diener, S., Dieringer, L., & Lantieri, L. (2003, March). *Talking with children about war and violence in the world.* Cambridge, MA: Educators for Social Responsibility. Retrieved August 2003 from www.esrnational.org

California Department of Education. (1997). *Reducing exceptional stress and trauma: Facilitator's guide.* Sacramento, CA: Author.

Charles, C. (2000). *The synergetic classroom: Joyful teaching and gentle discipline.* Boston: Addison Wesley Longman.

Children's reaction to trauma: Suggestions for parents (n.d). National Mental Health and Education Center. www.naspcenter.org/safe_school/trauma.html

Childs, G. (2002). *Workshop and crisis response team guidebook: Critical Incident Stress Management Program.* Poway, CA: Poway Unified School District.

Cruickshank, D., & Callahan, R. (1983). The other side of the desk: Stages and problems of teacher development. *Elementary School Journal, 83,* 251–258.

Department of Defense. (n.d.). *Crisis management toolkit.* Retrieved August 2003 from www.odedodea.edu/instruction/crisis

Fuery, C. (1996). *Winning year one: A survival guide for first year teachers.* Captiva, FL: Sanibel Sanddollar Publications.

Jensen, R. (1998). *Teaching with the brain in mind.* Alexandria, VA: Association for Supervision and Curriculum Development.

Johnson, S., & Johnson, C. (1986). *The one minute teacher: How to teach others to teach themselves.* New York: William Morrow.

Jones, F. (n.d.). *A weekly planner with Fredisms.* Santa Cruz, CA: Fredric H. Jones.

Kabat-Zinn, J. (1990). *Full catastrophe living: Using the wisdom of your body and mind to face stress, pain, and illness.* New York: Bantam Doubleday Dell.

Kagan, S., & Minor, J. (2002). *Boost achievement through brain-based instruction: Course workbook.* San Clemente, CA: Kagan Publishing.

Levin, D. (2003, April). When the world is a dangerous place. *Educational Leadership, 60,* 72–75.

Pullis, M. (1992). An analysis of the occupational stress of teachers of the behaviorally disordered: Sources, effects, and strategies for coping. *Behavioral Disorders, 17*(3), 191–201.

Putnam, J. (1993). Make every minute count. *Instructor, 103*(1), 38–40.

Schuster, S. (1992). *Classroom connections: A sourcebook for teaching stress management and fostering self-esteem.* Spring Valley, CA: Innerchoice.

Sesame Workshop Education and Research Division. (2001). *Tragic times, healing words: Helping children cope.* Retrieved December 2003 from www.sesameworkshop.org/parents/advice/article.php?content ID=49560

Sprenger, M. (1999). *Learning & memory: The brain in action.* Alexandria, VA: Association for Supervision and Curriculum Development.

Talking with kids about war and violence: Learn how to answer children's questions by seeing the world through their eyes. (n.d.). PBS Parents. Retrieved December 2003 from www.pbs.org/parents/issuesadvice/talkingwithkids/war

Waddell, D., & Thomas, A. (1998). *Disaster: Helping children cope: A handout for parents.* National Mental Health and Education Center. Retrieved December 2003 from www.naspcenter.org/safe_schools/coping.html

Wolfe, P. (2001). *Brain matters: Translating research into classroom practice.* Alexandria, VA: Association for Supervision and Curriculum Development.

Woolfolk, A. (2004). *Educational Psychology* (9th ed.). Boston: Allyn & Bacon.

Zabel, R., & Zabel, M. (1996). *Classroom management in context: Orchestrating positive learning environments.* Boston: Houghton Mifflin.

CHAPTER

14 It's Your Turn

The present is the only thing that has no end.

—Erwin Schrodinger

PULLING EVERYTHING TOGETHER

Now it's your turn to pull together everything you have read, observed, discussed, and analyzed. In the preceding chapters you investigated good management skills. It is hoped that the additional information and resources presented in the appendixes that follow will help you to step confidently into your first classroom. The cumulative skills development activities below are extensions to the appendixes.

This short chapter ends with a Capstone Activity in which you can reflect on the nature and operations of your own classroom.

ACTIVITIES FOR REFLECTION AND GROWTH

For Cumulative Skills Development

1. Obtain five or six good resource books for teachers. Review and compare contents. Present the reviews for class information and discussion.

2. Visit five or six websites. Review and compare contents. Present the reviews for class information and discussion.

3. Obtain copies of five or six widely read journals and teacher magazines in education. Review and compare the contents. Present the reviews for class information and discussion.

4. Contact various professional organizations and inquire about their mission, cost of membership, and benefits. (This can usually be done at the local level by contacting organization representatives or members for information.)

5. Obtain a source that provides information on overseas employment. (Your college or university placement office can usually furnish this information.) Share the information with the class. If possible, speak with a teacher or professor who has taught abroad and obtain his or her impressions of the advantages and disadvantages.

6. Obtain a reference that outlines teacher certification requirements in various states. Compare four or five states' requirements and present them in class.

CAPSTONE ACTIVITY

As a group or individual activity, outline in three to four pages the components of classroom management you would intend to employ in your overall operation of the classroom. Explain briefly how your selections reflect your personality and beliefs about teaching and learning.

Parting Thought

The journey of a thousand miles begins with one step.

—Chinese Proverb

Resources for Expanding Horizons and Opportunities

Live a balanced life—learn some and think some and draw and paint and sing and dance and play and work some every day.

—Robert Fulghum

ANTICIPATION–REACTION GUIDE

Before you investigate the appendixes that follow, take a moment to put a check mark in the Anticipation column next to any statement with which you agree.

	Anticipation	*Reaction*
Education differs from other professions in that it uses jargon that is easily understood outside the profession.	❑	❑
In reality, educators would do better to use plain English that every one understands and to avoid jargon.	❑	❑
Quality teacher resource books of ideas and activities can be found in abundant supply.	❑	❑
Resource books are intended to help supplement existing curriculum, not provide a curriculum of their own.	❑	❑
Among the professional journals available, more elementary teachers would be interested in *Instructor* and *The Mailbox Teacher* than *Gifted Child Quarterly*.	❑	❑
One of the most widely read journals of general interest to educators is the *Phi Delta Kappan*.	❑	❑
Each state has one head education official whose office is normally located in the state capital.	❑	❑
Department of Defense teaching opportunities exist worldwide.	❑	❑
Teaching positions overseas, in which instruction is given in English, are rarely available to American teachers.	❑	❑
Teacher certification requirements are essentially the same in every state.	❑	❑

In 1988 Robert Fulghum's delightful best seller *All I Really Needed to Know I Learned in Kindergarten: Uncommon Thoughts on Common Things* seemed to capture many of life's truths, as exemplified in the epigraph presented above. Fulghum reminds us that by the end of kindergarten he and the rest of us had learned such things as: Play fair, Don't hit people, Put things back where you find them, Clean up your own mess, Don't take things that aren't yours, and Say you're sorry when you hurt somebody. Fulghum's book is wonderful and reassuring for teachers to read, as are many of the other resources presented in the following appendixes but it doesn't include all that teachers need to know about teaching. It does not help novices understand the special language that teachers sometimes speak. It does not identify helpful resources and tools. Nor does it help recently licensed teachers take the next step in their career.

In the appendixes that follow we move beyond the ordinary parameters of classroom management to information that is of particular value to teachers new to the profession. This section includes

- Appendix A: brief explanations of frequently heard educational terms
- Appendix B: contact information for professional organizations
- Appendix C: some of the professional journals that teachers have found useful
- Appendix D: selected websites, music, and teacher resource books that contain especially interesting curriculum ideas, activities, and reproducible pages
- Appendix E: contact information for head education offices of each state
- Appendix F: a brief list of contacts for overseas teaching opportunities
- Appendix G: the comprehensive list of references and recommended readings

APPENDIX A

Education Talk

I was still learning when I taught my last class.

—Claude M. Fuess,
Phillips Academy educator

If you are around schools as a teacher, student, paraprofessional, or volunteer, you hear a number of terms and expressions that may not be understood by anyone outside of education. It almost appears that teachers have a language of their own. These special words and labels aren't purposefully used to confuse others, but are conveniently used to refer to all manner of special programs, materials, and procedures that would wear educators to exhaustion if they had to say all the names in full.

All professions use unique jargon, with words, letters, and language patterns understood for the most part only by persons in that profession. For those new to teaching, a brief list of special terms is offered here to ease the rites of passage. This list presents a beginning; it is far from exhaustive. As you hear people use other words and expressions you don't recognize, swallow your pride and ask what they mean.

Term	*Meaning*
Average daily attendance (ADA)	a record kept for administrative and budgeting purposes
Attention deficit disorder (ADD)	a learning disability; characterized by difficulty in concentrating or paying attention for long periods of time, that affects ability to concentrate on learning
Attention deficit hyperactivity disorder (ADHD)	a learning disability; characterized by hyperactivity, impulsivity, and/or distractibility, that affects ability to concentrate on learning
Assistive technology	devices and tools to assist individuals with disabilities
Authentic assessment	assessing students' learning, problem-solving, and ability to analyze, apply, synthesize, and evaluate by having them work on tasks they might experience outside the classroom

Back-to-school night	a scheduled event, usually early in the school year, when parents and guardians visit schools to meet the teachers, see the classrooms, discuss programs, and ask questions
Backward Design	teachers identify desired results and acceptable evidence before planning learning experiences and instruction
Beginning Teacher Support Program (BTSA)	usually a district-sponsored program that matches beginning teachers with veteran teachers for support and guidance
Bilingual education	varied approaches to educate students who speak a primary language other than English
Certified personnel	teachers, administrators, and sometimes librarians and media specialists whose positions require a credential or license earned through programs of higher education and issued by the state in which they are employed
Charter schools	self-governing public schools that operate outside the boundaries of existing district and union structures according to a special contract or charter that is often made by educators in the local community
Classified personnel	nonteachers who make up the support staff, including secretaries, custodians, attendance clerks, aides, and other school employees
Combination class	a class of two grade levels in which a teacher instructs independent grade-level programs; homogenous, usually fewer discipline problems, and less instruction time because of the dual curricula
Convergent thinking	a type of thinking that focuses on finding a single correct response, answer, or solution (the opposite of divergent thinking)
Cooperative learning	an instructional approach in which students work together in groups to accomplish a common task or learning goal, and are accountable for their individual effort and learning

"I'LL NEED THE S.A.T.'s, G.E.D.'s AND A.C.T.'s, A.S.A.P."

Criterion-referenced	tests and grading systems based on achievement in subject matter (the opposite of norm-referenced); for example, scores and grades (89%; B+) that are made on tests that include only information taught in a given class
Critical thinking	thought processes requiring higher levels of thought, such as analysis, synthesis, and evaluation
Curriculum mapping	a process of identifying redundancies and gaps within a total curriculum program
Differentiated instruction	modified content, instructional process, and product designed to accommodate all children
Distance education	use of technology to connect students and teachers or speakers who are separated by location
District office	the head offices of a school district where the top administrators are located

Divergent thinking	a type of thinking that expands outward in seeking multiple correct responses, answers, or solutions (the opposite of convergent thinking)
EL	English (language) learner
Engaged learning time	time during which students are engaged actively in learning, as opposed to involvement in numerous other kinds of activities (or nonactivities) that compromise the school day.
ESL	English as a second language
ESOL	English for speakers of other languages
Gifted and talented education (GATE)	children who show evidence of high achievement or potential in academic, creative, artistic, or leadership areas
Home schooling	a growing trend (although a longtime practice) of parents educating their children at home for religious or philosophical reasons
Individualized Education Plan (IEP)	plan approved by parents or guardians that clarifies and organizes the educational program and related services to meet a student's individual needs
Inclusion	commitment to educate every child to the maximum extent possible in the regular school and classroom
Individuals with Disabilities Education Act of 1990 (IDEA)	federal legislation requiring that all students with disabilities be accommodated in regular education classrooms to the extent possible
In-service	a class, workshop, program, or the like provided for the professional growth of employed teachers
Interstate New Teacher Assessment and Support Consortium (INTASC)	a consortium that has developed standards and an assessment process for initial teacher certification
Limited English proficient/ non-English proficient (LEP/NEP)	used for students and/or programs or materials

Limited English speaking/ non-English speaking (LES/NES)	used for students and/or programs or materials
Looping	an educational practice in which teacher and students remain together for two or more years
Magnet school	an alternative school that offers specialized programs in science, performing arts, and other areas, so constituted as to attract students from diverse ethnic and racial groups
Master teachers	teachers, perceived to be highly skilled in their instruction and management, who have student teachers in their classroom; may be called master, cooperating, or lead teachers
Mentor teachers	teachers designated because of their unusual expertise or involvement in a special project to assist other teachers in developing proficiency (e.g., reading, math, or technology mentor)
Mind map	any graphic, easy-to-read diagram that combines the information of a word outline with the clarity of a picture to show how to organize an idea, solve a problem, or perform a series of steps
Minimum day	an instructional day shortened for various reasons, most commonly so teachers can participate in grade-level planning activities and in-services during the afternoon
Mission statement	a statement that spells out the goals of a school or district, together with the plans for achieving them
Multi-age classes	heterogeneous classes with all ability and discipline levels in which students are grouped and work at levels according to their progress over time and their developmental growth rather than their chronological ages
Multicultural curriculum	practice of including and honoring cultural diversity to promote appreciation and understanding of diversity by making differences and similarities, respect and affirmation explicit parts of the curriculum

Multiple intelligences	a theory that identifies eight intellectual capacities that people use to approach projects and problems and create products
National Education Goals	U.S. education goals that were intended to be reached by the year 2000; legislated by Congress after they were established by the president and the fifty state governors
National Board for Professional Teaching Standards (NBPTS)	a nonprofit agency that has developed five core propositions regarding what experienced teachers should know and be able to do, and that issues professional certificates for this ability
National Council for Accreditation of Teacher Education (NCATE)	an accrediting agency that has identified six criteria for prospective teacher performance in a context of professional and liberal arts studies
No Child Left Behind Act	President George W. Bush's 2001 reauthorization of The Elementary and Secondary Act (ESEA of 1965); emphasizes standards and annual testing of all children to document progress toward meeting standards, district report cards of student achievement, and the goals that all schools provide quality and competent education and that newly hired teachers be NCLB qualified
Norm-referenced	tests and grading systems that compare a student's performance against the performance of many other students (the opposite of criterion-referenced); for example, grading on the curve and reporting achievement test scores in terms of percentiles or grade-level equivalencies
On task	an expression used to indicate that students are working at assigned learning activities rather than daydreaming or goofing off
Open house	a function usually held toward the end of a school year, when parents and other interested persons are invited to visit the school and classrooms
Opportunity class	self-contained classroom for students who have shown problems of behavior and/or attendance

Outcomes-based education (OBE)	educational plans that focus and organize the school's programs and instructional efforts around very specifically defined learning outcomes that all students are expected to achieve, rather than topics to be covered
Public Law 94-142	Education of All Handicapped Children Act of 1975; intended to ensure that all children receive a free and appropriate public education in the least restrictive environment (the regular classroom, when and to the extent possible); incorporated into the Individuals with Disabilities Education Act in 1990 (IDEA)
Praxis Series	a series of tests to assess skills and knowledge of beginning teachers, from entry into the profession to actual classroom performance
Prep period	time during the school day for teachers to plan lessons, prepare materials, and handle administrative tasks; elementary teachers rarely have prep periods, middle and high school teachers usually do
Reflective teaching	thinking that is focused on a prior act or occurrence to understand better what did and did not occur, and why, and to identify changes that could lead to future improvement
Resource specialist	a teacher highly qualified in one or more subject areas, such as reading, language, or mathematics, who provides assistance to other teachers or works with students who qualify for extra assistance
Scope and sequence	characteristics of the overall school curriculum; scope refers to the subject matter and activities, sequence refers to the order in which topics and activities receive attention
Specially Designed Academic Instruction in English (SDAIE)	teaching approaches and strategies used to help students with limited English proficiency
Service learning	opportunities for students to learn helping skills and provide service to others

Sheltered

students who, because of language limitations or other traits, require specialized instruction (frequently used for students with limited English proficiency); now referred to as SDAIE, Specially Designed Academic Instruction in English

Special Day class (SDC)

a class for students who are handicapped and unable to profit from attendance in the regular classroom

Standards

generally, what students need to know or be able to do, as related to content, performance, and opportunity-to-learn

Student Study Team (SST)

a team of interested adults, initiated by the regular education teacher, to review the student's apparent needs and develop a plan of action to further investigate and then best meet the needs

Team teaching

an arrangement where two teachers collaborate and teach the same students

Title I

a section of the 1965 Elementary and Secondary Education Act; a federally funded program established to address special learning needs of disadvantaged children by, among other things, providing monies to improve student performance in reading and math

Title VII

a federally funded program to assist limited English proficient (LEP) students

Vouchers

an educational plan option that gives parents a receipt or written statement that they can exchange for the school (public or private) they feel is most desirable for their child

APPENDIX B

Professional Organizations

If the only tool you have is a hammer, you tend to see every problem as a nail.
—Abraham Maslow

Teachers have available to them membership in many professional organizations. Organizations such as the National Council for Teachers of English (NCTE) focus on specific content areas. These organizations, especially the larger ones, have national, state, and local chapters. Membership can be of value to teachers for several reasons. Such organizations usually publish journals that investigate current issues and trends and supply information on the latest materials and techniques. They offer members reduced rates for materials available for sale. They inform members of national and area conferences and extend reduced attendance rates. Organizations such as the American Federation of Teachers (AFT) and the National Education Association (NEA) deal with education in general. Other organizations such as the Association for Supervision and Curriculum Development (ASCD) and Phi Delta Kappa give broader coverage to curriculum, instruction, technology, assessment, and other topics of interests to educators.

Addresses and information regarding state and local organizations follow.

Content-Specific Organizations

Art

National Art Education Association (NAEA)
1916 Association Drive
Reston, VA 20191-1590
703-860-8000
naea@dgs.dgsys.com, www.naea-reston.org

English

National Council of Teachers of English (NCTE)
1111 Kenyon Road
Urbana, IL 61801-1091
800-369-6283
public_info@ncte.org, www.ncte.org

Foreign Language

American Council on the Teaching of Foreign Languages
700 S. Washington St., Suite 210
Alexandria, VA 22314
703-894-2900 (telephone)
703-894-2905 (fax)
actfl.org

Health and Physical Education

American Alliance for Health, Physical Education, Recreation, and Dance
1900 Association Drive
Reston, VA 20191-1598
800-213-7193
www.aahperd.org

Mathematics

National Council of Teachers of Mathematics (NCTM)
1906 Association Drive
Reston, VA 20191-1502
http://nctm@nctm.org

Music

Music Educators National Conference (MENC)
1806 Robert Fulton Drive
Reston, VA 20091-20191
800-336-3768 (general inquiries)
800-828-0229 (membership services)
www.menc.org/index2.html

Reading

International Reading Association (IRA)
800 Barksdale Road
P.O. Box 8139
Newark, DE 19714-8139
www.read.org

Science

National Science Teachers Association
1840 Wilson Blvd.
Arlington, VA 22201-3000
www.nsta.org

GRADE 5
ASSEMBLY
REQUIRED

Social Studies

National Council for the Social Studies (NCSS)
8555 Sixteenth Street, Suite 500
Silver Springs, MD 20910
301-588-1800
www.socialstudies.org

Other Organizations of Interest

American Federation of Teachers (AFT)

Affiliated with the American Federation of Labor and Congress of Industrial Organizations (AFL-CIO), AFT's mission is to "[represent] teachers, school support staff, higher education faculty and staff, health care professionals, and state and municipal employees."

555 New Jersey Avenue NW
Washington, DC 20001
202-879-4400
www.aft.org

National Education Association (NEA)

NEA's mission is to "represent elementary, secondary, and higher education teachers; [offer] news on education, school administration, and legislative action."

1201 16th Street NW
Washington, DC 20036-3290
202-833-4000
www.nea.org

American Educational Research Association (AERA)

AERA's mission is "concerned with improving the educational process by encouraging scholarly inquiry related to education and by promoting dissemination and practical application of research results."

1230 17th Street NW
Washington, DC 20036
202-223-9485

Association for Supervision and Curriculum Development (ASCD)

ASCD is an international organization of educators that "addresses all aspects of effective teaching and learning—such as professional development, educational leadership, and capacity building."

1703 N. Beauregard Street
Alexandria, VA 22311
800-933-2723; 703-578-9600
www.ascd.org

Phi Delta Kappa International (PDK)

PDK is an international association of professional educators whose mission is to "promote quality education as essential to development and maintenance of a democratic way of life by providing innovating programs, relevant research, visionary leadership, and dedicated service."

Eighth and Union
P.O. Box 789

Bloomington, IN 47402
812-339-1156
www.pdkintl.org

Childhood Education

National Association for the Education of Young Children
1509 16th Street NW
Washington, DC 20036
800-424-2460
www.naeyc.org

Gifted Children

National Association for Gifted Children (NAGC)
1707 L Street NW, Suite 550
Washington, DC 20036
www.nagc.org

Educational Technology

International Society for Technology in Education (ISTE)
1710 Rhode Island Ave. NW, Suite 900
Washington, DC 20036
800-366-5191
iste@iste.org

National PTA

330 N. Wabash Avenue, Suite 2100
Chicago, IL 60611
800-307-4PTA
312-670-6783
www.pta.org

APPENDIX C

Professional Journals

Learning is like rowing against the stream: if one does not advance, one falls right back.

—Vietnamese proverb

Professional journals are intended to keep members of the profession current about new research, discoveries, studies, ideas, and materials related to their field of expertise. Educational publications range from highly theoretical, esoteric research journals to practical resources written for and by classroom teachers. Some educational journals focus on single content areas; some are aimed specifically at elementary, middle, or high school teachers; others publish articles and thematic issues for the broader educational community. The following are some of the most widely read journals and teacher magazines in education.

Journals of General Interest to All Educators

Educational Leadership. Association for Supervision and Curriculum Development (ASCD), 1250 North Pitt Street, Alexandria, VA 22314
Intended primarily for leaders in elementary, middle, and secondary education but is also for anyone interested in curriculum instruction, supervision, and leadership in schools. Published monthly September through May, except bimonthly December/January.

Phi Delta Kappan. Phi Delta Kappa, Eighth and Union, P.O. Box 789, Bloomington, IN 47402-0789
Articles concerned with educational research, service, and leadership; issues, trends, and policies are emphasized. Published monthly, except July and August.

Journals and Magazines of General Interest to Elementary Teachers

Highlights for Children. 1800 Watermark Drive, P.O. Box 269, Columbus, OH 43216-0269; 614-486-0631
Monthly (index issue, December). "Wholesome fun dedicated to helping children grow in basic skills and knowledge, in creativity, in ability to think and reason, in sensitivity to others, in high ideals and worthwhile ways of living."

Instructor. Scholastic, 2931 E. McCarty St., P.O. Box 3710, Jefferson City, MO 65102-3710
New ideas and teaching devices for language arts, reading, science, social studies, math, computers, and other subjects, and recent research and innovation related to child development. Nine issues annually.

The Mailbox Teacher. P.O. Box 54293, Boulder, CO 80322-4293; 800-334-0298
Magazine of ideas and activities for kindergarten and elementary teachers. Four issues a year.

National Geographic Kids. National Geographic Society, 1145 17th Street N. W., Washington, DC 20036-4688.

Published monthly. Combines learning with fun with puzzles, games, and stories about wildlife, adventure, other kids, sports, science, places around the world, and more.

Teaching preK–8. 40 Richards Avenue, Norwalk, CT 06854; 800-249-9363

Magazine (formerly *Early Years*) published monthly except June, July, August, and December with feature articles, ideas, and reproducibles for teachers of young children.

Journals and Magazines of Topical Interest to Elementary Teachers

Arithmetic Teacher. National Council of Teachers of Mathematics, 1906 Association Drive, Reston, VA 20191-1502; 703-620-9840

A forum where ideas and techniques for teaching kindergarten through eighth-grade math are exchanged. Nine issues per year.

Arts and Activities. Publishers' Development Corporation, 591 Camino de la Reina, Suite 200, San Diego, CA 92108

Stimulating material on photography, children's art, and art ideas for teachers who have not had extensive art training.

Gifted Child Quarterly. National Association for Gifted Children, 4175 Lovell Road, Suite 140, Circle Pines, MN 55014

Scholarly articles dealing with theory and research related to psychology and the education of gifted children.

The Horn Book Magazine. Horn Book, 56 Roland Street, Suite 200, Boston, MA 02129; 800-325-1170

Bimonthly reviews of the newest children's literature, articles, editorials, and columns related to aspects of children's books.

Language Arts. National Council of Teachers of English, 1111 Kenyon Road, Urbana, IL 61801-1096; 800-369-6283

Deals with topics related to teaching of English at the elementary school level. Eight issues per year.

Primary Voices K–6. National Council of Teachers of English, 1111 Kenyon Road, Urbana, IL 61801-1096; 800-369-6283 Quarterly.

The Reading Teacher. International Reading Association, 800 Barksdale Road, P.O. Box 8139, Newark, DE 19714-8139; 302-731-1600

Articles dealing with the teaching of reading at the preschool and elementary school levels. Eight issues per year, with an annual index included in the May issue.

Science and Children. National Science Teachers Association, 1840 Wilson Blvd., Arlington, VA 22201-3000; 703-243-7100

Practical emphasis for kindergarten through ninth-grade science teachers; includes projects, experiments, book reviews, and audiovisual and software information.

Social Studies and the Young Learner. National Council of Social Studies, 8555 Sixteenth Street, Suite 500, Silver Springs, MD 20910; 800-683-0812 (pub orders). Articles on teaching social studies in the elementary grades. Published quarterly.

Zoobooks. Wildlife Education, Ltd. 3590 Kettner Blvd., San Diego, CA 92101; 800-477-5034

Monthly themed issues feature an animal or wildlife family.

APPENDIX D

Websites, Music, and Resource Books of Interest

Don't be apprehensive if some of your attempts seem risky. This is appropriate, since so much of life involves taking risks—for you as well as the children. That's how we grow.

—Anonymous

Honestly, resources abound. In fact, it is quite easy to get lost in the jungle of potential websites, music, and resource books. It is our intent to offer a few select resources that teachers have found helpful. You will find links to other websites, and if you visit teacher stores and general bookstores, you will probably discover many other wonderful resources. Best advice: Be open to possibilities, but remember the reality of time and practicality. In other words, investigate and then carefully select what best suits your needs at the moment, but also what will help with the larger picture of your teaching experience.

Websites of Interest

www.bluewebn.com
> Web resources and pages across grades and curricula that you can bookmark and access from anywhere.

www.backflip.com
> A place on the Web where you can bookmark web pages to access from anywhere. Especially handy when you search at home and don't want to write the sites down before you go to school.

www.brainpop.com
> Offers informative animated short movie clips and quizzes across subject areas

www.cooltext.com
> Free online graphics generator for web pages and other things. Create web banners, fun fonts.

www.discoveryschool.com
> Links to puzzle maker and study starters, lesson plans, teacher tools, curriculum center, homework helpers, and others.

www.education-world.com
> Designed as a resource for educators, with the goal of making it easy for educators to integrate the Internet into the classroom. Includes lesson planning, professional development, technology integration, school issues, and more.

www.funbrain.com
> Fun for kids. Teachers can post quizzes for their class.

www.geosense.net

A geography game that students can play with other students around the world, plus links to numerous other related sites.

www.gsn.org

The Global School House. Online collaborative learning, collaborative projects, communication tools, and professional development.

www.inspiration.com and www.kidspiration.com

Inspiration. Helps learners to organize and rearrange information in varied formats (outline, narrative text, and concept map with pictures or symbols).

Kidspiration. Helps kindergarten through fifth-grade learners develop strong thinking skills through brainstorming, planning, organizing, and creating.

Through Our Eyes. Site provides opportunities for collaborative writing projects.

www.KidPix

Premier art and graphics program. Small cost.

www.kn.sbc.com

Filmentality, a public tool on the Internet.

www.nationalgeographic.com/xpeditions

National Geographic Xpeditions. Activities and resources to learn geographic concepts and issues. Blue-Ribbon Links to other resources for teaching online and learning geography.

www.scholastic.com

Links to free tools and resources, including online activities, lesson plans, and strategies.

www.school.discovery.com/schrockguide

Discovery School. Kathy Schrock's guide for educators, sponsored by the Discovery Channel.

www.songsforteaching.com

A host of educational experts bring you tested ideas for using the magic of music in your lesson plans. Educational songs from popular artists are presented by subject.

www.teachingideas.co.uk

Teaching ideas for primary teachers. Literacy, science, music, history, geography, art, PE, and more

www.thinkquest.org

Student team research topics/contest

www.themoonlitroad.com

Member of the Storytelling Ring, a group of websites dedicated to the art of storytelling. Ghost stories and folk tales from the American South.

http://tryscience.org

Virtual field trips (video camera clips and narration) to international science centers and museums

Music for Elementary Classrooms

Music can set a tempo for transitions, but as we said in an earlier chapter, teachers also can select the right type of music for the desired objective—thinking, productivity, relaxing, learning, de-stressing, concentration, and inspiration. Enjoy!

Don Campbell. *The Mozart Effect: Music for Children.* [CD]

Mozart's music stimulates the intellectual and creative development of students, increasing verbal, emotional, and spatial intelligence along the way. Appropriate for all grades.

Clint Klose and Larry Wolfe. *Lyrical Lessons.* [CDs and lyrics and cassettes]
> Curriculum songs integrate music across curriculum. Appropriate for primary grades K–3 and intermediate grades 3–6.

Clint Klose and Larry Wolfe. *Monthly Melodies.* [CD and lyrics]
> Fun teachable moments out of calendar events for grades K–3.

Mark Krantz. *Story Songs.* [CD]
> Words directly from classic children's stories, including *Where the Wild Things Are, The Polar Express,* and *Goodnight Moon.* Appropriate for early grades.

Gary Lamp. *Music for the Classrooms: Sixty Beats per minute.* [CD]
> Piano music to increase concentration, productivity, and higher-level thinking for all grades.

Gary Lamp. *Music for the Classrooms.* [CD]
> Piano-based instrumental recordings with original music at sixty beats per minute. Appropriate for all grades.
> - *Watching the Night Fall*
> - *A Walk in the Garden*
> - *Distant Fields*
> - *Language of Love*
> - *Love Themes*

Greg Scelsa and Steve Millang. *We all live together* (Vols. 2, 4) [CD]
> Singable lyrics and catchy melodies. Volume 2 teaches children basic concepts. Volume 4 includes songs "It's a Beautiful Day," "Hand Jive," and "The Ugly Duckling."

The Sound Health Series [CDs]
> Music based on clinical research of the effect of music and sound on the human nervous system. Performed by the Arcangelos Chamber Ensemble.
> - *Music for Thinking*
> - *Music for Productivity*
> - *Music to Relax*
> - *Music for Learning*
> - *Music to De-Stress*
> - *Music for Concentration*
> - *Music for Inspiration*

Teacher Resource Books

An astonishing number and variety of resource books exist that can help teachers strengthen their curriculum and generally make their classrooms more lively and enjoyable for themselves and their students. It is well worth several visits to teacher supply and general bookstores to see the types and varieties of such materials. The following titles have been selected as a few examples of the many excellent resources available.

Barbour, A., & Desjean-Perrotta, B. (2002) *Prop box play: 50 themes to inspire dramatic play.* Beltsville, MD: Gryphon House.
> This book makes it easy for children to be creative and have fun, with its fifty different themes, lists of props, easy extensions, related vocabulary, and associated children's literature.

Bernstein, S. (1994). *Hand clap! "Miss Mary Mack" and 42 other hand clapping games for kids.* Avon, MA: Adams Media Corporation.
> Hand clapping and rhythms, including "Miss Mary Mack," by twelve-year-old Sara Bernstein.

Brougher, K. (2000). *Thinklers! A collection of brain ticklers.* Auburn, WA: Missing Piece Press.
 Based on developing cultural literacy and on thinking, these riddles and puzzles provide activities that involve thinking in a fun way.

Burke, K. (1999). *The mindful school: How to assess authentic learning* (3rd ed.). Arlington Heights, IL: Skylight.
 Repertoire of evaluation tools related to learning standards, standardized tests and multiple intelligences, performance tables and rubrics, portfolios, learning logs and journals, observation checklists and graphic organizers, interviews and conferences.

Cassidy, J. (1992). *Kids' shenanigans: Great things to do that mom and dad will just barely approve of.* Palo Alto, CA: Klutz Press.
 Tricks and shenanigans that, selected judiciously, can be used to mystify children and enliven the classroom. Kids like reading this book, too.

Cassidy, J., & Stroud, M. (1992). *The Klutz book of magic.* Palo Alto, CA: Klutz Press.
 Helps teachers and students perform feats of magic.

Collins, H. (1992). *Signing at school: Beginning sign language series.* Eugene, OR: Garlic Press.

Croft, D. J., & Hess, R. (2000). *An activities handbook for teachers of young children.* Boston: Houghton Mifflin.
 This classic just gets better and better. Includes instructions and the lists of materials you'll need for the activities.

Culham, R. (2003). *6+1 traits of writing: The complete guide.* New York: Scholastic.
 Including both theory and teaching activities and scoring guides, this book lives up to the claim that it gives you "everything you need to teach and assess writing."

Daley, P., & Dahlie, M. S. (2001). *50 debate prompts for kids.* New York: Scholastic Professional Books.
 "Get them reading, writing, and thinking with 50 thought-provoking topics that let students see both sides of an issue, then debate the pros and cons."

Feldman, J. (2000). *Transitions: Tips and tricks.* Beltsville, MD: Gryphon House.
 Transitions become fun learning experiences with creative activities that "reflect current brain research and reinforce early literacy."

Fry, E. (2001). *Dr. Fry's instant word practice book, primary.* Westminster, CA.: Teacher Created Materials. www.teachercreated.com
 Tons of puzzles and activities to build and reinforce vocabulary and reading ability.

Gilbert, L. (2002). *Daily jump-start learning: Multi-subject, motivating, mini-exercises.* Indianapolis, IN: D. V. Stanton Publications.
 One great exercise after another by subject, including math, language arts, geography/social studies, and analogies, for each day of the year.

Gore, M. C., & Dowd, J. F. (1999). *Taming the time stealers: Tricks of the trade from organized teachers.* Thousand Oaks, CA: Corwin Press.
 Organizing administrative paperwork, handling and storing materials, and ways to help students to become better organized to maximize performance of teacher and students.

Gruber, B., and Gruber, S. (2003). *Super simple science lessons.* Cathedral City, CA: Practice and LearnRight Publications.
 These lessons and reproducible pages are "instant ideas for elementary teachers." Includes biology, earth sciences, and physical science subjects.

Herr, J., & Libby-Larsen, Y. (2003). *Teacher made materials that really teach.* Florence, KY: Delmar.
 Contains ideas, instructions, and photographs of teacher-made instructional materials that really help students, primarily kindergartners, to learn.

Jurenka, N. A. (2001). *Hobbies through children's books and activities.* Libraries Unlimited.
 A compendium of ideas and suggestions for using hobby activities to enhance reading and reasoning skills. For classroom teachers for grades 3 through 6.

Karges-Bone, L. (2000). *Lesson planning: Long-range and short-range models for grades K–6.* Boston: Allyn & Bacon.

Step-by-step guidance for writing plans, tables, sample plans, and schedules; glossary of common planning terms.

Leimback, J., & Eckert, S. (2001). *Detective club mysteries for young thinkers.* San Luis Obispo, CA: Dandy Lion. www.dandylionbooks.com

Six interesting mysteries help students develop critical thinking, problem-solving, and logic skills.

Lunsford, S. (2001). *100 skill-building lessons using 10 favorite books: A teacher's treasury of irresistible lessons and activities that help children meet important learning goals in reading, writing, math and more.* New York: Scholastic Books.

"Use favorite books to create skill-building lessons in every subject area."

Lyons, S. (Ed.) (2002). *Ready-to-go lessons: The essential resource of complete lessons for your curriculum. Grades 1–5.* Greensboro, NC: The Education Center. www.themailbox.com

Curriculum-based lessons include step-by-step instructions, pages to reproduce, materials lists, and more. One book for each grade.

Miller, D. (2002). *Reading with meaning: Teaching comprehension in the primary grades.* Portland, ME: Stenhouse Publishers.

A "workshop" on how to teach your students to read for meaning.

Salvert, E. K. (1998). *Computer fun for everyone: Things to do and make with any computer.* New York: John Wiley.

Draw pictures, create graphs, design books and newspapers, exchange secret codes, and write stories without buying special computer programs.

Sheldon, K. (n.d.). *Sing along and learn around the year, pre K–2.* New York: Scholastic Professional Books.

"Twenty month by month learning songs with instant activities that teach and delight."

Skills-based reading: A teaching resource. (2002). Scottsdale, AZ: Remedia Publications. www.rempub.com

Stories and activities that interest students as they build essential vocabulary, comprehension, and thinking skills.

Sugar, S., & Sugar, K. K. (2002). *Primary games: Experiential learning activities for teaching children K–8.* San Francisco: Jossey-Bass.

Twenty-five curriculum-based games that will "engage and stimulate students, as well as promote teamwork, skill building, and interactive problem solving."

Sweeney, J. (1998). *Prompt a day! Grades 3–6.* New York: Scholastic Professional Books.

"625 thought-provoking writing prompts linked to each day of the school year."

Walters, C. (1995). *Multicultural music lyrics to familiar melodies and native songs.* Minneapolis, MN: T. S. Denison.

Facts, lyrics, and projects about eight places (Africa, Australia, Canada, France, Japan, Mexico, Netherlands, and Poland).

Series

Brain Quest. New York: Workman Publishing. 800-722-7202 www.brainquest.com

Question packs across grades and subjects.

Klutz. Scholastic. www.klutz.com

Question decks across primary grades for math, reading, multiplication, and general knowledge.

Teacher Created Materials. www.teachercreated.com CD-ROM.

Activities, with user's guide and software for Windows and MacIntosh.

APPENDIX E

U.S. State and Territory Departments of Education

The journey of a thousand miles begins with one step.

—Chinese Proverb

All states, the District of Columbia, and the territories of American Samoa, Guam, the Northern Mariana Islands, Puerto Rico, and the Virgin Islands maintain their own departments of education. Most are listed here.

Alabama

Superintendent of Education
State Department of Education
50 North Ripley Street
P.O. Box 302101
Gordon Persons Building
Montgomery, AL 36104
Phone 334-242-9700
www.alsde.edu

Alaska

Commissioner of Education
State Department of Education
801 West 10th Street #200
Juneau, AK 99801-1878
Phone 907-465-2800
www.educ.state.ak.us

Arizona

Superintendent of Public Instruction
State Department of Education
1535 West Jefferson
Phoenix, AZ 85007
Phone 800-352-4558
www.ade.state.az.us

Arkansas

Director of the Department of Education
#4 Capitol Mall
Little Rock, AR 72201
Phone 501-682-4475
arkedu.state.ar.us

California

State Superintendent of Public Instruction
California Department of Education
1430 N Street
P.O. Box 944272-2720
Sacramento, CA 94244
Phone 916-319-0791
www.cde.ca.gov

Colorado

Commissioner of Education
State Department of Education
201 East Colfax
Denver, CO 80203-1799
Phone 303-866-6600
www.cde.state.co.us

Connecticut

Commissioner of Education
State Department of Education
P.O. Box 2219
Hartford, CT 06145-2219
Phone 860-713-6548
www.state.ct.us/sde

Delaware

Department of Education
P.O. Box 14002—Townsend Building
Dover, DE 19903-1402
Phone 302-739-4601
www.doe.state.de.us

District of Columbia

Superintendent of Public School
District of Columbia Public Schools
825 North Capitol Street NE, 9th floor
Washington, DC 20002
Phone 202-724-4222
www.k12.dc.us

Florida

Commissioner of Education
State Department of Education
Turlington Building, Suite 1514
325 West Gaines Street
Tallahassee, FL 32399-0400
Phone 850-245-0505
http:www.fldoe.org

Georgia

Superintendent of Public Instruction
State Department of Education
2066 Twin Towers East
Atlanta, GA 30334
Phone 404-656-2800
www.doe.k12.ga.us

Hawaii

Superintendent of Public Instruction
P.O. Box 2360
Honolulu, HI 96804
Phone 800-305-5104
www.k12.hi.us

Idaho

Superintendent of Public Instruction
State Department of Education
P.O. Box 83720
Boise, ID 83720-0027
Phone 208-332-6800
www.sde.state.id.us/certification

Illinois

Superintendent of Public Instruction
State Board of Education
100 North First Street
Springfield, IL 62777
Phone 866-262-6663
www.isbe.state.il.us

Indiana

Superintendent of Public Instruction
State Department of Education
State House, Room 229
Indianapolis, IN 46204-2798
Phone 317-232-6665
www.doe.state.in.us

Iowa

Director of Education
State Department of Education
Grimes State Office Building
Des Moines, IA 50319-0146
Phone 515-281-5294
www.state.ia.us

Kansas

Commissioner of Education
State Department of Education
120 SE 10th Avenue
Topeka, KS 66612-1182
Phone 785-296-3201
www.ksbe.state.ks.us

Kentucky

Superintendent of Public Instruction
State Department of Education
500 Mero Street, 18th floor
Frankfort, KY 40601
Phone 502-564-4770
www.kde.state.ky.us

Louisiana

Superintendent of Public Instruction
State Department of Education
P.O. Box 94064
Baton Rouge, LA 70804-9064
Phone 225-342-3774
www.doe.state.la.us

Maine

Commissioner of Education
Department of Educational and Cultural Services
23 State House Station
Augusta, ME 04333-0023
Phone 207-287-5800
www.state.me.us

Maryland

State Superintendent of Schools
State Department of Education
200 West Baltimore Street
Baltimore, MD 21201
Phone 410-767-0412
www.mse.state.md.us

Massachusetts

Commissioner of Education
State Department of Education
350 Main Street
Malden, MA 02148-5023
Phone 781-338-3000
www.doe.mass.edu

Michigan

Superintendent of Public Instruction
State Department of Education
P.O.Box 30008
608 West Allegan Street
Lansing, MI 48933
Phone 517-373-3354
www.michigan.gov/mde

Minnesota

Commissioner of Education
State Department of Education
1500 Highway 36 West
Roseville, Minnesota 55113-4266
Phone 651-582-8200
www.education.state.mn.us

Mississippi

Superintendent of Public Instruction
State Department of Education
359 North West Street
P.O. Box 771
Jackson, MS 39205
Phone 601-359-3513
www.mde.k12.ms.us+

Missouri

Commissioner of Education
Department of Elementary and Secondary
    Education
205 Jefferson Street
P.O. Box 480
Jefferson State Office Building
Jefferson City, MO 65101
Phone 573-751-4212
www.dese.state.mo.us

Montana

Office of Public Instruction
Certification Division
P.O. Box 202501
Helena, MT 59620-2501
Phone 406-444-3059
www.metnet.state.mt.us

Nebraska

Commissioner of Education
State Department of Education
P.O. Box 94987
301 Centennial Mall, South
Lincoln, NE 68509
Phone 402-471-2295
www.nde.state.ne.us

Nevada

Superintendent of Public Instruction
State Department of Education
700 East 5th Street
Carson City, NV 89701
Phone 775-687-9200
www.nsn.k12.nv.us\nvdoe

New Hampshire

Commissioner of Education
State Department of Education
101 Pleasant Street
State Office Park South
Concord, NH 03301-3860
Phone 603-271-3494
www.state.nh.us

New Jersey

Commissioner of Education
State Department of Education
100 Riverview Plaza
P.O. Box 500
Trenton, NJ 08625-0500
Phone 609-292-4041

New Mexico

Superintendent of Public Instruction
State Department of Education
300 Don Gaspar
Santa Fe, NM 87501-2786
Phone 505-827-5800
www.sde.state.nm.us

New York

Commissioner of Education
State Department of Education
Education Building
Albany, NY 12234
Phone 518-474-5844
www.nysed.gov

North Carolina

Superintendent of Public Instruction
State Department of Public Instruction
301 N. Wilmington Street
Raleigh, NC 27601
Phone 919-807-3300
www.dpi.state.nc.us

North Dakota

Superintendent of Public Instruction
State Department of Public Instruction
600 East Boulevard Ave., Dept 202
Bismark, ND 58505-0080
Phone 701-328-2264
www.state.nd.us/espb

Ohio

Superintendent of Public Instruction
State Department of Education
25 S. Front Street
Columbus, OH 43215-4183
Phone 877-644-6338
www.ode.state.oh.us

Oklahoma

Superintendent of Public Instruction
State Department of Education
2500 North Lincoln Blvd.
Oklahoma City, OK 73105-4599
Phone 405-521-3301
sde.state.ok.us

Oregon

Superintendent of Public Instruction
State Department of Education
255 Capitol Street N.E.
Salem, OR 97310-0203
Phone 503-378-3569
www.ode.state.or.us

Pennsylvania

Secretary of Education
State Department of Education
333 Market Street
Harrisburg, PA 17126-0333
Phone 717-783-6788
www.pde.psu.edu

Rhode Island

Commissioner of Education
State Department of Education
255 Westminster Street
Providence, RI 02903
Phone 401-222-4600
www.ridoe.net

South Carolina

Superintendent of Public Instruction
State Department of Public Instruction
Division of Teacher Quality
Landmark II Office Building
3700 Forest Drive, Suite 500
Columbia, SC 29204
Phone 803-734-8466
www.scteachers.org

South Dakota

Secretary of Education
Department of Education
Division of Elementary and Secondary Education
700 Governors Dr.
Pierre, SD 57501-2291
www.state.sd.us/

Tennessee

Commissioner of Education
State Department of Education
Andrew Johnson Tower, 6th Floor
Nashville, TN 37243-0375
Phone 615-741-2731
www.state.tn.us/education/

Texas

Commissioner of Education
Texas Education Agency
William B. Travis Building
1701 North Congress Ave.
Austin, TX 78701
Phone 512-463-9734
www.tea.state.tx.us

Utah

State Department of Education
State Office of Education
250 East 500 South
P O Box 144200
Salt Lake City, UT 84114-4200
Phone 801-538-7740
www.usoe.k12.ut.us/cert

Vermont

Commissioner of Education
State Department of Education
120 State Street
Montpelier, VT 05620-2501
Phone 802-828-3135
www.state.vt.us/educ

Virginia

Superintendent of Public Instruction
State Department of Public Instruction
P.O. Box 2120
Richmond, VA 23218
Phone 800-292-3820
www.pen.k12.va.us

Washington

Superintendent of Public Instruction
State Department of Public Instruction
P.O. Box 47200
Olympia, WA 98504-7200
Phone 360-725-6000
www.k12.wa.us

West Virginia

State Superintendent of Schools
State Department of Education
1900 Kanawha Blvd. East
Charleston, WV 25305
Phone 304-558-7842
www.wvde.state.wv.us

Wisconsin

Superintendent of Public Instruction
State Department of Public Education
125 South Webster Street
P.O. Box 7841
Madison, WI 53707-7841
Phone 800-441-4563
www.dpi.state.wi.us

Wyoming

Superintendent of Public Instruction
State Department of Education
2300 Capitol Ave.
Hathaway Building, 2nd floor
Cheyenne, WY 82002-0050
Phone 307-777-7673
www.k12.wy.us

Virgin Islands

St. Thomas/St. John District
Commissioner of Education
Department of Education
44-46 Kongens Gade
St. Thomas, VI 00802
Phone 340-774-0100

APPENDIX F

Overseas Teaching Opportunities

Overseas teaching positions in English-speaking schools are available in many parts of the world and have considerable appeal for those who would like to live and work in a foreign country. Included among the numerous programs are the following. You can link to program information through the websites below.

European Council of International Schools (ECIS)
www.ecis.org

Fulbright Teacher and Administrator Exchange Program
Sponsored by the Bureau of Educational and Cultural Affairs, United States Department of State
www.fulbrightexchanges.org

International Schools Services
Annually publishes *The ISS Directory of Overseas Schools*
www.iss.edu

Japan Exchange and Teaching Programme (JET)
www.embjapan.org

Search Associates
www.search-associates.com

United States Department of Defense Dependent Schools
www.odedodea.edu

Parting Thought

The Essence of Teaching

What nobler profession than to touch the next generation—
to see children hold your understanding in their eyes,
your hope in their lives,
your world in their hands.
In their success you find your own
And so to them you give your all.

—Author Unknown

APPENDIX G

Comprehensive List of References and Recommended Readings

Albert, L. (1996). *Cooperative discipline.* Circle Pines, MN: American Guidance Service.

Allard, H. (1977). *Miss Nelson is missing!* Boston: Houghton Mifflin.

Alphonso, C. (2003, August 8). A poor student's worst nightmare. *The Globe and Mail.* Retrieved August 2003 from www.globetechnology.com/servlet/ArticleNews/TPStory/LAC/20030808/USTUDNO

Ames, C. (1992). Achievement goals and the classroom motivational climate. In D. J. Schunk & J. L. Meece (Eds.). *Student perceptions in the classroom.* Hillsdale, NJ: Erlbaum.

Annie E. Casey Foundation. (2002). *Kids count data book, 2002.* Baltimore: Author.

Arends, R. (1997). *Classroom instruction and management.* New York: McGraw-Hill.

Armstrong, T. (1994). *Multiple intelligences in the classroom.* Alexandria, VA: Association for Supervision and Curriculum Development.

Bandura, A. (1977). *Social learning theory.* Englewood Cliffs, NJ: Prentice-Hall.

Berman, S., Diener, S., Dieringer, L., & Lantieri, L. (2003, March). *Talking with children about war and violence in the world.* Cambridge, MA: Educators for Social Responsibility. Retrieved August 2003 from www.esrnational.org

Berne, E. (1964). *Games people play.* New York: Grove Press.

Brimijoin, K., Marquissee, E., & Tomlinson, C. (2003, February). Using data to differentiate instruction. *Educational Leadership, 60,* 70–73.

Bloom, B. S. (Ed.). (1956). *Taxonomy of education objectives: The classification of educational goals: Handbook I, cognitive domain.* New York: Longmans, Green.

Brophy, J. (1987). Synthesis on strategies for motivating students to learn. *Educational Leadership, 45,* 40–48.

Brophy, J. (1998). *Motivating students to learn.* Boston: McGraw-Hill.

Bruner, J. (1960). *The process of education.* New York: Vintage.

Bureau of Education. (1918). *Cardinal principles of secondary education.* (Bulletin #35). Washington, DC: Department of the Interior, Bureau of Education.

California Department of Education. (1997). *Reducing exceptional stress and trauma: Facilitator's guide.* Sacramento, CA: Author.

Campbell, D. G. (1992). *Introduction to the musical brain.* St. Louis: MMB Music.

Campbell, D. G. (1997). *The Mozart Effect: Tapping the power of music to heal the body, strengthen the mind, and unlock the creative spirit.* New York: Avon Books.

Campbell, D. G. (2000). *The Mozart Effect for children: Awakening your child's mind, health, and creativity with music.* New York: William Morrow.

Canter, L., & Canter, M. (1992). *Assertive discipline: Positive behavior management for today's classroom.* Santa Monica, CA: Canter & Associates.

Canter, L., & Canter, M. (1993). *Lee Canter's succeeding with difficult students: New strategies for reaching your most challenging students.* Santa Monica, CA: Canter & Associates.

Canter, L., & Canter, M. (2001). *Assertive discipline: Positive behavior management for today's classroom* (3rd ed.). Los Angeles: Lee Canter & Associates.

Carr, J., & Harris, D. (2001). *Succeeding with standards: Linking curriculum, assessment, and action planning.* Alexandria, VA: Association for Supervision and Curriculum Development.

Cartwright, G., Cartwright, C., & Ward, M. (1984). *Educating special learners* (2nd ed.). Belmont, CA: Wadsworth.

Cary, S. (1997). *Second language learners.* Los Angeles: Galef Institute.

Center for the Study of Social Policy. (1992). *What the 1990 census tells us about children.* Washington, DC: Author.

Chamot, A., & O'Malley, J. (1994). *The CALLA handbook: Implementing the Cognitive Academic Language Learning Approach.* New York: Addison-Wesley.

The changing lives of children [Special issue]. (1997, April). *Educational Leadership.* Alexandria, VA: Association for Supervision and Curriculum Development.

Charles, C. (2000). *The synergetic classroom: Joyful teaching and gentle discipline.* New York: Addison Wesley Longman.

Charles, C. (2005). *Building classroom discipline* (8th ed.). Boston: Allyn & Bacon.

Children's Defense Fund. (1994). *Child poverty data from the 1990 census.* Washington, DC: Author.

Children's reaction to trauma: Suggestions for parents. (n.d). National Mental Health and Education Center. Retrieved December 2003 from www.naspcenter.org/safe_school/trauma.html

Childs, G. (2002). *Workshop and critical response team guidebook: Critical incident stress management training.* Poway, CA: Poway Unified School District.

Christopher, C. (1996). *Building parent–teacher communication: An educator's guide.* Lancaster, PA: Technomic Publishing.

Churma, M. (1999). *A guide to integrating technology standards into the curriculum.* Upper Saddle River, NJ: Merrill.

Cole, R. (Ed.). (1995). *Educating everybody's children: Diverse teaching strategies for diverse learners.* Alexandria, VA: Association for Supervision and Curriculum Development.

Collins, M., & Tamarkin, C. (1990). *Marva Collins' way.* New York: G. P. Putnam's Sons.

Coloroso, B. (1990). *Winning at teaching . . . without beating your kids.* [Videotape from the series *Kids Are Worth It!*]. Littleton, CO: Kids Are Worth It!

Coloroso, B. (1994). *Kids are worth it! Giving your child the gift of inner discipline.* New York: Avon Books.

Coloroso, B. (1999). *Parenting with wit and wisdom in times of chaos and loss.* Toronto, Ontario, Canada: Viking.

Coloroso, B. (2002). *The bully, the bullied, and the bystander.* Toronto, Ontario, Canada: HarperCollins.

Creating caring schools [Special issue]. (2003, March). *Educational Leadership.* Alexandria, VA: Association for Supervision and Curriculum Development.

Creating a climate for learning [Special issue]. (1996, September). *Educational Leadership.* Alexandria, VA: Association for Supervision and Curriculum Development.

Cruickshank, D., Bainer, D., & Metcalf, K. (1999). *The act of teaching* (2nd ed.). Boston: McGraw-Hill.

Cruickshank, D., & Callahan, R. (1983). The other side of the desk: Stages and problems of teacher development. *Elementary School Journal, 83,* 251–258.

Culp, K., Hawkins, J., & Honey, M. (1999). *Review paper on educational technology research and development.* New York: Education Development Center, Center for Children and Technology.

Curtiss, K., & English, S. (2003). *Choice theory certification.* Retrieved August 2003 from www.kathycurtissco.com/what_we_do.htm

Curwin, R., & Mendler, A. (1997). *As tough as necessary: Countering violence, aggression, and hostility in our schools.* Alexandria, VA: Association for Supervision and Curriculum Development.

Da Costa Nunez, R., & Collignon, K. (1997, October). Creating a community of learning for homeless children. *Educational Leadership, 55*(2), 56–60.

Dembo, M. (1994). *Applying educational psychology* (5th ed.). White Plains, NY: Longman.

Divorce Rates in Families with Children. (n.d.). Retrieved December 18, 2003, from www.divorcereform.org/chilrate.html

Doll, R. (1992). *Curriculum improvement: Decision making and process* (8th ed.). Boston: Allyn & Bacon.

Dreikurs, R., & Cassel, P. (1972). *Discipline without tears.* New York: Hawthorn.

Dreikurs, R., Grunwald, B., & Pepper, F. (1982). *Maintaining sanity in the classroom.* New York: Harper & Row.

Duebber, D. (2000, May). Substitute teaching: Sink or swim. *Educational Leadership, 57*(8), 73–74.

Dwyer, K., Richardson, J., Danley, K., Hansen, W., Sussman, S., Brannon, B., et al. (1990, September). Characteristics of eighth grade students who initiate self-care in elementary and junior high school. *Pediatrics, 86*(3), 448–454.

Education of All Handicapped Children Act, PL 94-142, S.6. (1975, November 29).

Education of All Handicapped Children Act Amendment of 1986.

Eisner, E. (1985). *The educational imagination: On the design and evaluation of school programs* (2nd ed.). New York: Macmillan.

Elam, S., Rose, L., & Gallup, A. (2003). 35th annual Phi Delta Kappan/Gallup poll. *Phi Delta Kappan, 75*(2), 137–152.

Engaging parents and the community in schools [Special issue]. (1998, May). *Educational Leadership.* Alexandria, VA: Association for Supervision and Curriculum Development.

English, F. (1983). Contemporary Curriculum Circumstances. In F. W. English (Ed.), *Fundamental curriculum decisions.* Alexandria, VA: Association for Supervision and Curriculum Development.

Equity and opportunity [Special issue]. (2002–2003, December–January). *Educational Leadership.* Alexandria, VA: Association for Supervision and Curriculum Development.

Evertson, C., Emmer, E., Clements, B., Sanford, J., & Worsham, M. (2003). *Classroom management for elementary teachers* (6th ed.). Boston: Allyn & Bacon.

Falvey, M., Givner, C., & Kimm, C. (1995). What is an inclusive school? In R. Villa & J. Thousand (Eds.), *Creating an inclusive school* (pp. 1–12). Alexandria, VA: Association for Supervision and Curriculum Development.

Federal Register. (1977, August 23). Washington, DC: U.S. Government Printing Office.

Fleming, D., & Kilcher, A. (1991, November). Presentation at Organizing and Managing School Change Workshop, NEA National Center for Innovation National Conference, Colorado Springs, CO.

Ford, M. (1992). *Motivating humans.* Newbury Park, CA: Sage.

Foster, E. (1992). *Tutoring: Learning by helping: A student handbook for training peer and cross-age tutors* (Rev. ed.). Minneapolis, MN: Educational Media Corporation.

Fraser, B., & O'Brien, P. (1985). Student and teacher perceptions of the environment of elementary school classrooms. *Elementary School Journal, 85*(5), 567–580.

Freiberg, H. (1996, September). From tourists to citizens in the classroom. *Education Leadership, 54*(1), 32–36.

Fuery, C. (1996). *Winning year one: A survival guide for first year teachers.* Captiva, FL: Sanibel Sanddollar Publications.

Gardner, H. (1991). *The unschooled mind: How children think and how schools should teach.* New York: Basic Books.

Gardner, H. (1993). *Frames of mind* (10th ed.). New York: Basic Books.

Gardner, H. (1993). *Multiple intelligences: The theory in practice.* New York: Basic Books.

Gardner, H. (1997). Reflections on multiple intelligences: Myths and messages. *Phi Delta Kappan, 77*(3), 200–209.

Gardner, H. (1999). *Intelligence Reframed: Multiple intelligences.* New York: Basic Books.

Gardner, H. (2000). *Disciplined minds.* New York: Penguin.

Gardner, H. (n.d.) *Eye on San Diego* [Interview on television broadcast].

Ginott, H. (1972). *Teacher and child.* New York: Macmillan.

Glasser, W. (1969). *Schools without failure.* New York: Harper & Row.

Glasser, W. (1988). On students' needs and team learning: A conversation with William Glasser. *Educational Leadership, 45,* 38–41.

Glasser, W. (1998). *Choice theory in the classroom* (Rev. ed.). New York: HarperCollins.

Glasser, W. (1998). *Control theory in the classroom* (Rev. ed.). New York: Harper & Row.

Glasser, W. (1998). *The quality school: Managing students without coercion* (Rev. ed.). New York: HarperCollins.

Glasser, W. (1998). *The quality school teacher* (Rev. ed.). New York: HarperCollins.

Glasser, W. (2000). *Every student can succeed.* Chatsworth, CA: Author.

Glick, P., & Lin, S. (1986). Recent changes in divorce and remarriage. *Journal of Marriage and the Family, 48,* 737–741.

Goldsborough, R. (1997, August/September). Let the reader beware. *Reading Today, 15*(1), 8.

Good, T., & Brophy, J. (2002). *Looking into classrooms* (8th ed.). New York: Longman.

Goodlad, J. (1984). *A place called school: Prospectives for the future.* New York: McGraw-Hill.

Gordon, T. (1970). *Parent effectiveness training: A tested new way to raise responsible children.* New York: New American Library.

Gordon, T. (1974). *T.E.T.: Teacher effectiveness training.* New York: David McKay.

Gordon, T. (1976). *P.E.T. in action.* New York: Bantam Books.

Gordon, T. (1989). *Discipline that works: Promoting self-discipline in children.* New York: Random House.

Gusky, T. (2003, February). How classroom assessments improve learning. *Educational Leadership, 60,* 6–11.

Hadley, M., & Sheingold, K. (1993, May). Commonalities and distinctive patterns in teachers' integration of computers. *American Journal of Education, 101,* 261–315.

Harvey, S., & Goudvis, A. (2000). *Strategies that work: Teaching comprehension to enhance understanding.* New York: Stenhouse Publishers.

Hathaway, W., et al. (1992). *A study into the effects of light on children of elementary school age—a case of light robbery.* (Unpublished manuscript, Planning and Information Services, Alberta Department of Education, Edmonton, Alberta, Canada.)

Hebert, E. (1998, September). Designing matters: How school environment affects children. *Educational Leadership, 56*(1), 69–70.

Hunter, M. (1982). *Mastery learning.* El Segundo, CA: TIP Publications.

Individuals with Disabilities Act (IDEA) of 1990, PL 101-476. (1990).

Integrating technology into the curriculum [Special issue]. (1999, February). *Educational Leadership.* Alexandria, VA: Association for Supervision and Curriculum Development.

Interstate New Teacher Assessment and Support Consortium (2003). *INTASC Projects.* Retrieved August 2003 from www.ccsso.org/projects/Interstate_New_Teacher_Assessment_and_Support_Consortium/Projects

Jacobs, H. (1989). *Interdisciplinary curriculum: Design and implementation.* Alexandria, VA: Association for Supervision and Curriculum Development.

Jacobs, H. (1997). *Mapping the big picture: Integrating curriculum and assessment K–12.* Alexandria, VA: Association for Supervision and Curriculum Development.

Jensen, R. (1998). *Teaching with the brain in mind.* Alexandria, VA: Association for Supervision and Curriculum Development.

Johnson, D., & Johnson, R. (1998). *Learning together and alone* (5th ed.). Boston: Allyn & Bacon.

Johnson, S., & Johnson, C. (1986). *The one minute teacher: How to teach others to teach themselves.* New York: William Morrow.

Jones, F. (1987). *Positive classroom instruction.* New York: McGraw-Hill.

Jones, F. (1992). *Positive classroom discipline.* New York: McGraw-Hill.

Jones, F. (2000). *Tools for teaching: Discipline instruction motivation.* Santa Cruz, CA: Fredric H. Jones & Associates.

Jones, F. (n.d.). *A weekly planner with Fredisms.* Santa Cruz, CA: Fredric H. Jones & Associates.

Jones, V., & Jones, L. (2001). *Comprehensive classroom management: Creating communities of support and solving problems* (6th ed.). Boston: Allyn & Bacon.

Joyce, B., Weil, M. (with Calhoun, E.). (2000). *Models of teaching* (6th ed.). Boston: Allyn & Bacon.

Kabat, J. (1990). *Full catastrophe living: Using the wisdom of your body and mind to face stress, pain, and illness.* New York: Bantam Doubleday Dell.

Kagan, L. (2003). *The successful dynamic trainer: Engaging all learners: Course workbook.* San Clemente, CA: Kagan Publishing.

Kagan, L., Kagan, M., & Kagan, S. (1997). *Cooperative learning structures for teambuilding.* San Clemente, CA: Kagan Cooperative Learning.

Kagan, M., Robertson, L., & Kagan, S. (1995). *Cooperative learning structures for classbuilding.* San Clemente, CA: Kagan Cooperative Learning.

Kagan, S. (1994). *Cooperative learning.* San Clemente, CA: Resources for Teachers.

Kagan, S. (2000). *Silly sports and goofy games.* San Clemente, CA: Kagan Publishing.

Kagan, S., & Kagan, M. (1998). *Multiple intelligences: The complete MI book.* San Clemente, CA: Kagan Cooperative Learning.

Kagan, S., Kyle, P., and Scott, S. (2004). *Win-win discipline.* San Clemente, CA: Kagan Cooperative Learning.

Kagan, S., & Minor, J. (2002). *Boost achievement through brain-based instruction Course workbook.* San Clemente, CA: Kagan Publishing.

Kaufman, J., & Burbach, H. (1997). On creating a climate of classroom civility. *Phi Delta Kappan, 79,* 320–325.

Keene, E., & Zimmermann, S. (1997). *Mosaic of thought: Teaching comprehension in a reader's workshop.* Portsmouth, NH: Heinemann.

Kirk, S., & Gallagher, J. (1996). *Educating exceptional children* (8th ed.). Boston: Houghton Mifflin.

Kounin, J. (1970). *Discipline and group management in classrooms.* New York: Holt, Rinehart & Winston.

Krashen, S. (1985). *Inquiries and insights.* Hayward, CA: Alemany Press.

Krashen, S., & Terrell, T. (1996). *The natural approach: Language acquisition in the classroom.* Oxford: Pergamon.

Lantieri, L., Diener, S., Jones, S., & Berman, S. (1999). Talking to children about violence and other sensitive and complex issues in the world. Cambridge, MA: Educators for Social Responsibility. Retrieved August 2003 from www.esrnational.org/guide.htm

Levin, D. (2003, April). When the world is a dangerous place. *Educational Leadership, 60,* 72–75.

Lewis, C., Schaps, E., & Watson, M. (1996). The caring classroom's academic edge. *Educational Leadership, 54,* 16–21.

Lieberman, A., & Miller, L. (1999). *Teachers—Transforming their world and their work.* New York: Teachers College.

Long, L., & Long, T. (1989). Latchkey adolescents: How administrators can respond to their needs. *NASSP Bulletin, 73,* 02–108.

Lucent Technologies. (1999). *Reinventing today's classrooms with wireless technology.* Retrieved August 2003 from www.wavelan.com/educational

Marshall, M. (2002). *Discipline without stress, punishments, or rewards: How teachers and parents promote responsibility and learning.* Los Alamitos, CA: Piper Press.

Marzano, R. (1998, December). Advances in grading. *Education Update, 40*(8), 4.

Marzano, R. (2000). *Transforming classroom grading.* Alexandria, VA: Association for Supervision and Curriculum Development.

Maslow, A. (1943). A theory of human motivation. *Psychological Review, 50,* 370–396.

McClelland, D. (1965). Toward a theory of motive acquisition. *American Psychologist, 20,* 321–333.

McTighe, J., & Thomas, R. (2003, February). Toward better report cards. *Educational Leadership, 60,* 52–55.

McWilliams, J., & McWilliams, P. (1995). *The portable life 101.* Los Angeles: Prelude Press.

Morrison, G. (2002). *Teaching in America* (3rd ed.). Boston: Allyn & Bacon.

National Board for Professional Teaching Standards. (2003). *What teachers should know and be able to do.* Retrieved August 2003 from www.nbpts.org/about/coreprops.com

National Center for Education Statistics. (2003). *Digest of Education Statistics, 2002* (NCES 2003–060). Washington, DC.

National Center for Education Statistics. (2003). *Overview of Public Elementary and Secondary Schools and Districts School Year 2001–02.* Retrieved December 18, 2003, from http://nces.ed. gov/pubs2003/overview03/table_10.asp.

National Clearinghouse for English Language Acquisition. (2002). *Survey of the states' limited English proficient students and available educational programs and services.* Washington, DC: George Washington University, National Clearinghouse for English Language Acquisition.

National Coalition for the Homeless. (1999). *Education of homeless children and youth* (NCH Fact Sheet #10). Retrieved December 15, 2003, from http://nch.ari.net/edchild.html

National Coalition for the Homeless. (2001, June). *Homeless families with children* (NCH Fact Sheet #7). Retrieved December 15, 2003, from http://www.nationalhomeless.org

National Council for Accreditation of Teacher Education. (2002). *Standards.* Retrieved August 2003 from www.ncate.org/standards/m_stds.htm

National Council of Teachers of English. (1989). *Substitute teachers' lesson plans: Classroom-tested activities from the National Council of Teachers of English.* Urbana, IL: Author.

Nelsen, J., Lott, L., & Glenn, H. (2000). *Positive discipline in the classroom* (3rd ed.). Rocklin, CA: Prima Publishing.

Newmann, D. (1997). *The compleat teacher's almanack: A daily guide to all 12 months of the year.* New York: Fine Communications.

Olweus, D. (1999). *Core program against bullying and antisocial behavior: A teacher handbook.* Bergen, Norway: Research Center for Health Promotion, University of Bergen.

Orlich, D., Harder, R., Callahan, R., & Gibson, H. (2001). *Teaching strategies: A guide to better instruction* (6th ed.). Boston: Houghton Mifflin.

Paulson, F., Paulson, P., & Meyer, C. (1991). What makes a portfolio a portfolio? *Educational Leadership, 48*(5), 60–63.

Pearpoint, J., & Forest, M. (1992). Foreword. In S. Stainback & W. Stainback (Eds.), *Curriculum considerations in inclusive classrooms: Facilitating learning for all students* (pp. xv–xviii). Baltimore: Paul H. Brookes.

Perrone, V. (Ed.). (1991). *Expanding student assessment.* Alexandria, VA: Association for Supervision and Curriculum Development.

Personalized learning [Special issue]. (1999, September). *Educational Leadership.* Alexandria, VA: Association for Supervision and Curriculum Development.

Picciotto, L. (1999, August). Let your students take the lead. *Scholastic Instructor, 109*(1), 33–35.

Pintrich, P., & DeGroot, E. (1990). Motivational and self-regulated learning components of classroom academic performance. *Journal of Educational Psychology, 82,* 33–40.

Poplin, M. (1992). Educating in diversity. *Executive Educator, 14*(3), A18–A24.

Power, B. (1999, October). Strengthen your parent connection. *Instructor, 109*(3), 30–31.

Pullis, M. (1992). An analysis of the occupational stress of teachers of the behaviorally disordered: Sources, effects, and strategies for coping. *Behavioral Disorders, 17*(3), 191–201.

Putnam, J. (1993). Make every minute count. *Instructor, 103*(1), 38–40.

Quiroz, B., Greenfield, P., & Altchech, M. (1999, April). Bridging cultures with a parent–teacher conference. *Educational Leadership, 56*(7), 68–70.

Race class and culture [Special issue]. (1999, April). *Educational Leadership.* Alexandria, VA: Association for Supervision and Curriculum Development.

Rauscher, R., Shaw, G., Levine, L., Ky, K., & Wright, E. (1993). Music and spatial task performance. *Nature, 365,* 611.

Reauthorization of IDEA of 1997. (1997).

Reeves, T. (1998). *The impact of media and technology in schools: A research report prepared for the Bertelsmann Foundation.* Retrieved August 2003 from www.athensacademy.org/instruct/media_tech/reves0.html

Ribas, W. (1998). Tips for reaching parents. *Educational Leadership, 56*(1), 83–85.

Rief, S., & Heimburge, J. (1996). *How to reach & teach all students in the inclusive classroom.* West Nyack, NY: The Center for Applied Research in Education.

Ringstaff, C., & Kelley, L. (2002). *The learning return on our educational technology investment.* San Francisco: WestEd RTEC.

Rogers, C. (1969). *Freedom to learn.* Columbus, OH: Merrill.

Rosales-Dordelly, C., & Short, E. (1985). *Curriculum professors' specialized knowledge.* Lanham, MD: University Press of America.

Ryan, K., & Cooper, J. (2000). *Those who can, teach* (9th ed.). Boston: Houghton Mifflin.

Salt Lake City School District. (1992). *SMILES (Senior Motivators in Learning and Educational Services)* [Senior volunteer program]. Salt Lake City, UT: Author.

Scelsa, G., & Millang, S. (1978). *We all live together* (Vol. 2, 4). [CD]. Los Angeles: Little House Music.

Schifini, A. (1988). *Sheltered English: Content area instruction for limited English Proficient Students.* Downey, CA: Los Angeles County Office of Education.

Schools as safe havens [Special issue]. (1997, October). *Educational Leadership.* Alexandria, VA: Association for Supervision and Curriculum Development.

Schuster, S. (1992). *Classroom connections: A sourcebook for teaching stress management and fostering self-esteem.* Spring Valley, CA: Innerchoice.

Schwartz, F. (1981). Supporting or subverting learning: Peer group patterns in four tracked schools. *Anthropology and Education Quarterly, 12*(2), 99–120.

Sesame Workshop Education and Research Division. (2001). *Tragic times, healing words: Helping children cope.* Retrieved December 2003 from www.sesameworkshop.org/parents/advice/article.php?contentID=49560

Simkins, M., Cole, K., Tavalin, F., & Means, B. (2002). *Increasing student learning through multimedia projects.* Alexandria, VA: Association for Supervision and Curriculum Development.

Skinner, B. (1968). *The technology of teaching.* New York: Appleton-Century-Crofts.

Slavin, R. (Ed.). (1989). *School and classroom organization.* Hillsdale, NJ: Erlbaum.

Smith, D. (2004). *Introduction to special education: Teaching in an age of opportunity* (5th ed.). Boston: Pearson/Allyn & Bacon.

Sollman, C., Emmons, B., & Paolini, J. (1994). *Through the cracks.* Worcester, MA: Davis Publications.

Sprenger, M. (1999). *Learning and memory: The brain in action.* Alexandria, VA: Association for Supervision and Curriculum Development.

Stanley, S. (1991). Substitute teachers can manage their classrooms effectively. *NASSP Bulletin, 75*(532), 84–88.

Stuart, J. (1949). *The thread that runs so true.* New York: Simon & Schuster.

Stull, A. (1998). *Education on the Internet: A student's guide.* Upper Saddle River, NJ: Merrill.

Supporting new teachers [Special issue]. (1999, May). *Educational Leadership.* Alexandria, VA: Association for Supervision and Curriculum Development.

Talking with kids about war and violence: Learn how to answer children's questions by seeing the world through their eyes. (n.d.). PBS Parents. Retrieved December 2003 from www.pbs.org/parents/issuesadvice/talkingwithkids/war

Tannenbaum, M. (2000, May). No substitute for quality. *Educational Leadership, 57*(8), 70–72.

Thaler, M. (1989). *The teacher from the Black Lagoon.* New York: Scholastic.

There's no substitute for a great sub! A collection of creative tips and lifesavers from substitute teachers. (1998). [Back to school issue]. *The Mailbox Teacher, 27*(1) 32–35.

Thousand, J., Villa, R., & Nevin, A. (2002). *Creativity and collaborative learning The practical guide to empowering students, teachers, and families.* Baltimore: Paul H. Brookes.

Tomlinson, C. (1999). *The differentiated classroom: Responding to the needs of all learners.* Alexandria, VA: Association for Supervision and Curriculum Development.

Tomlinson, C. (2002, September). Do students care about learning? *Educational Leadership. 60*(1), 6–10.

Tomlinson, C. (2002, September). Invitations to learn. *Educational Leadership, 60*(1), 6–10.

Traver, R. (1998). What is a good guiding question? *Educational Leadership, 55*(6), 70–73.

Tyler, R. (1949). *Basic principles of curriculum and instruction.* Chicago: University of Chicago Press.

Udavari-Solner, A. (1995). A process for adapting curriculum in inclusive classrooms. In R. Villa & J. Thousand (Eds.), *Creating an inclusive school* (pp. 110–124). Alexandria, VA: Association for Supervision and Curriculum Development.

U.S. Census Bureau. (2003). *Language use and English-speaking ability: 2000.* Retrieved December 18, 2003, from www.census.gov/prod/2003pubs/c2kbr-29.pdfs

U.S. Census Bureau Public Information Office. (2003, October 18). News release. Retrieved December 13, 2003, from www.census.gov/Press-Release/www/releases

U.S. Conference of Mayors. (1994). *Status report on hunger and homelessness in America's cities.* Washington, DC: Author.

U.S. Conference of Mayors. (2000). *Status report on hunger and homelessness in America's cities.* Washington, DC: Author.

U.S. Department of Health and Human Services. (2002). *HHS programs and initiatives to combat homelessness.* Retrieved December 18, 2003, from www.hhs.gov/news/press/2002pres/homeless.html

Using standards & assessment [Special Issue]. (1999, March). *Educational Leadership.* Alexandria, VA: Association for Supervision and Curriculum Development.

Van Ripper, C. (1978). *Speech correction: Principles and methods* (6th ed.). Englewood Cliffs, NJ: Prentice-Hall.

Villa, R., & Thousand, J. (Eds.). (1995). *Creating an inclusive school.* Alexandria, VA: Association for Supervision and Curriculum Development.

Waddell, D., & Thomas, A. (1998). *Helping children cope: A handout for parents.* National Mental Health and Education Center. Retrieved December 2003 from www.naspcenter.org/safe_schools/coping.html

Wallerstein, J., & Kelly, J. (1980). *Surviving the breakup.* New York: Basic Books.

Wallis, C. (1994, July 18), Life in overdrive. *Time, 144*(3), 50.

Weiner, B. (1990). History of motivational research in education. *Journal of Educational Psychology, 82,* 616–622.

Whalen, S., & Csikszentmihalyi, M. (1991). *Putting flow theory into educational practice: The key school's flow activities room.* Report to the Benton Center for Curriculum and Instruction. Chicago: University of Chicago.

What do we mean by results? [Special issue]. (2000, February). *Educational Leadership.* Alexandria, VA: Association for Supervision and Curriculum Development.

Whelan, R., & Gallagher, P. (1972). Effective teaching of children with behavior disorders. In N. G. Haring & A. H. Hayden (Eds.), *The improvement of instruction.* Seattle: Special Child Publications.

Wiggins, G. (1994, November). Toward better report cards. *Educational Leadership, 52,* 28–37.

Wiggins, G., & McTighe, J. (1998). *Understanding by design.* Alexandria, VA: Association for Supervision and Curriculum Development.

Winning the tattle battle. (1998). [Back to school issue]. *The Mailbox Teacher, 27*(1), 52–55.

Wolfe, P. (2001). *Brain matters: Translating research into classroom practice.* Alexandria, VA: Association for Supervision and Curriculum Development.

Woolfolk, A. (2004). *Educational psychology* (9th ed.). Boston: Allyn & Bacon.

Wong, H., & Wong, R. (2001). *The first days of school: How to be an effective teacher.* Mountain View, CA: Harry K. Wong Publications.

Woods, C. (1996, November). Hope for homeless students. *Educational Leadership, 54*(3), 58–60.

Yancy, K. (Ed.). (1992). *Portfolios in the writing classroom.* Urbana, IL: National Council of Teachers of English.

Youngerman, S. (1998). The power of cross-level partnerships. *Educational Leadership, 56*(1), 58–61.

Ysseldyke, J., & Algozzine, B. (1995). *Special education: A practical approach for teachers* (3rd ed.). Boston: Houghton Mifflin.

Zabel, R., & Zabel, M. (1996). *Classroom management in context: Orchestrating positive learning environments.* Boston: Houghton Mifflin.

Parting Thought

When you reach for the stars you may not quite get one, but you won't come up with a handful of mud, either.

—Leo Burnett

NAME INDEX

SUBJECT INDEX